Helping Families and Communities Recover From Disaster

Helping Families and Communities Recover From Disaster

Lessons Learned From Hurricane Katrina and Its Aftermath | Disaster

Edited by
Ryan P. Kilmer
Virginia Gil-Rivas
Richard G. Tedeschi
Lawrence G. Calhoun

American Psychological Association
Washington, DC

Published by
American Psychological Association
750 First Street, NE
Washington, DC 20002
www.apa.org

To order
APA Order Department
P.O. Box 92984
Washington, DC 20090-2984
Tel: (800) 374-2721; Direct: (202) 336-5510
Fax: (202) 336-5502; TDD/TTY: (202) 336-6123
Online: www.apa.org/books/
E-mail: order@apa.org

In the U.K., Europe, Africa, and the Middle East, copies may be ordered from
American Psychological Association
3 Henrietta Street
Covent Garden, London
WC2E 8LU England

Typeset in Goudy by Circle Graphics, Inc., Columbia, MD

Printer: Courier, Westford, MA
Cover Designer: Naylor Design, Washington, DC
Technical/Production Editor: Harriet Kaplan

The opinions and statements published are the responsibility of the authors, and such opinions and statements do not necessarily represent the policies of the American Psychological Association.

Library of Congress Cataloging-in-Publication Data

Helping families and communities recover from disaster : lessons learned from Hurricane Katrina and its aftermath / edited by Ryan P. Kilmer . . . [et al.]. — 1st ed.
   p. cm.
 Includes bibliographical references and index.
 ISBN-13: 978-1-4338-0544-8
 ISBN-10: 1-4338-0544-8
 1. Hurricane Katrina, 2005. 2. Emergency management—Louisiana—New Orleans.
3. Emergency management—Gulf Coast (U.S.) 4. Disaster relief—Louisiana—
New Orleans. 5. Disaster relief—Gulf Coast (U.S.) 6. Intergovernmental cooperation—
United States. I. Kilmer, Ryan P.

 HV551.4.G85H45 2009
 363.34'8—dc22

                                                        2009012586

British Library Cataloguing-in-Publication Data

A CIP record is available from the British Library.

Printed in the United States of America
First Edition

To the children, families, and communities affected by
Hurricane Katrina and its aftermath

CONTENTS

CONTRIBUTORS

Andrea Allen, Barry University, Miami Shores, FL

Jennifer J. Baumgartner, Louisiana State University, Baton Rouge

Teresa K. Buchanan, Louisiana State University, Baton Rouge

Renée M. Casbergue, Louisiana State University, Baton Rouge

Karen L. Davidson, Louisiana State University, Baton Rouge

M. Whitney Fry, Public Health Consultant to the Middle East, Amman, Jordan

M. E. Betsy Garrison, Louisiana State University Agricultural Center, Baton Rouge

Virginia Gil-Rivas, University of North Carolina at Charlotte

Tonya Cross Hansel, Louisiana State University Health Sciences Center, New Orleans

Lauren Hensley-Maloney, Tulane University, New Orleans, LA

Yael Hoffman, University of Chicago and University of Illinois at Chicago, Chicago, IL

Annada W. Hypes, University of North Carolina at Charlotte

Pamela Jenkins, University of New Orleans, New Orleans, LA

Mary Lou Kelley, Louisiana State University, Baton Rouge

Ryan P. Kilmer, University of North Carolina at Charlotte

Robin Knowles, Louisiana State University, Baton Rouge

Mindy Kronenberg, Louisiana State University Health Sciences Center, New Orleans

Megan Littrell, Tulane University, New Orleans, LA

Jacqueline MacDonald, East Baton Rouge Parish School System, Baton Rouge, LA

Fran H. Norris, Dartmouth Medical School, Hanover, NH

Claudio D. Ortiz, Florida International University, Miami

Howard J. Osofsky, Louisiana State University Health Sciences Center, New Orleans

Joy D. Osofsky, Louisiana State University Health Sciences Center, New Orleans

Jennette L. Palcic, Louisiana State University, Baton Rouge

Angie Pellegrin, Louisiana State University, Baton Rouge

Betty Pfefferbaum, University of Oklahoma Health Sciences Center, Oklahoma City

Rose L. Pfefferbaum, Phoenix College, Phoenix, AZ

Brenda Phillips, Oklahoma State University, Stillwater

Katherine A. Roof, University of North Carolina at Charlotte

Kenneth J. Ruggiero, Medical University of South Carolina, Charleston

Diane D. Sasser, Louisiana State University Agricultural Center, Baton Rouge

Shannon Self-Brown, Georgia State University, Atlanta

Ariana Shahinfar, University of North Carolina at Charlotte

Wendy K. Silverman, Florida International University, Miami

Leslie Snider, War Trauma Foundation, Amsterdam, the Netherlands, and Tulane University, New Orleans, LA

Annie W. Spell, Louisiana State University, Baton Rouge

Mya Thornburgh, New Orleans Veterans Affairs Hospital, New Orleans, LA

R. Enrique Varela, Tulane University, New Orleans, LA

Eric M. Vernberg, University of Kansas, Lawrence

Julia F. Vigna, Louisiana State University, Baton Rouge

Tanya Vishnevsky, University of North Carolina at Charlotte

Jing Wang, Louisiana State University, Baton Rouge

ACKNOWLEDGMENTS

We extend our sincere thanks to the children, families, service providers, educators, and administrators whose participation and assistance made this work possible. Work on this volume was supported by National Institute of Mental Health Award R03 MH078197-01 to Virginia Gil-Rivas and Ryan P. Kilmer, for which the editors express their gratitude. We also wish to thank the scholars who contributed chapters to this volume and offered their insights about how to meet the needs of children, families, and communities following a disaster.

Several individuals have contributed significantly to our Hurricane Katrina Parent–Child Relationship Project and the preparation of this volume. Among them, we offer special thanks to Katherine A. Roof, for her ongoing work as project coordinator and for her substantial assistance in preparing the final manuscript; to Justin L. Williams, for her time as project coordinator, her multiple trips to the Gulf Coast, and her efforts in facilitating data collection and management; and to Annada W. Hypes, for her assistance with multiple facets of the project from the initial stages. Our appreciation also goes to Judith Cloutier-Chenier, Michelle Resor, Kelli Triplett, and Tanya Vishnevsky, for their assistance in collecting data in Louisiana and Mississippi, and to Jennifer Mott, Brittnie Simms, and Melissa Smith, who helped with data entry and coding. We also thank our Baton Rouge–based research assistants, Louisiana State University students Amanda Reulet and Rachel Schoen.

Our thanks also go to Superintendent Charlotte Placide and Assistant Superintendent for Accountability and Assessment Jennifer Baird of the East Baton Rouge Parish School System—we are grateful for their support of this work and of our partnership with Jacqueline MacDonald. It was our pleasure to help tell Mayfair's story.

Special thanks to Teresa Buchanan, who contributed meaningfully to our study's evolution. We appreciated gaining both a collaborator and a friend. We also thank our colleagues, Arnie Cann and Kanako Taku, who offered their expertise and insight as we developed our Katrina project, its methodology and measures, and the conceptualization of this volume. Additional thanks to the chairs of our department during this effort, Brian Cutler and David Gilmore, for their ongoing support of our work.

On a final, personal note, Ryan P. Kilmer acknowledges the support, encouragement, and love of his wife, Sarah, and his children, Alex and Amelia. Virginia Gil-Rivas acknowledges the support of her lifetime partner in this endeavor.

Helping Families and
Communities Recover From
Disaster

INTRODUCTION: ATTENDING TO ECOLOGY

RYAN P. KILMER AND VIRGINIA GIL-RIVAS

On August 29, 2005, Hurricane Katrina made landfall along the central Gulf Coast region of the United States, and the hurricane and its aftermath would constitute the most severe, damaging, and costly natural disaster in the nation's history, reflected in the size of the region affected, the loss of life, the extensive destruction of property, and the thousands displaced. Roughly 90,000 square miles were declared a federal disaster area, including 60% of Mississippi (Select Bipartisan Committee to Investigate the Preparation for and Response to Hurricane Katrina [Select Bipartisan Committee], 2006; Weisler, Barbee, & Townsend, 2006), and the human cost was staggering—more than 1,700 verified deaths, with 1,464 recorded in Louisiana alone, and many persons still missing (Louisiana Recovery Authority [LRA], 2007). The scope of the disaster's damage was astounding; the infrastructure of entire neighborhoods and cities was destroyed. This disruption was potentiated by Hurricane Rita, which arrived 3 weeks later.

Property losses have been estimated at more than $100 billion in Louisiana alone, and estimates of the cost to recover from the storm and

Preparation of this chapter was supported by National Institute of Mental Health Award R03 MH078197-01 to Virginia Gil-Rivas and Ryan P. Kilmer.

rebuild the areas affected have exceeded $200 billion. The storms and their aftermath, including the flooding in New Orleans, destroyed more than 200,000 homes, as well as thousands of businesses, numerous hospitals and public buildings, and key transportation infrastructure (LRA, 2007; Select Bipartisan Committee, 2006). Moreover, Katrina initially displaced between 1.0 and 1.3 million Gulf Coast residents (LRA, 2007; Select Bipartisan Committee, 2006).

In light of its magnitude, Katrina yields an opportunity for work to help mental health and social service professionals, as well as policymakers, better understand child, family, and community needs following a disaster and the psychological and physical consequences of the storm and its aftermath. Many suffered multiple losses and experienced extreme deprivation, unsafe living conditions, and violence, and many face a range of persistent challenges as they try to reestablish their lives. More than 2 years after Katrina, as the work on this volume was well underway, many children and families still lived in temporary housing and struggled to gain access to necessary services and meet basic needs.

In addition, reports had begun to highlight the mental health sequelae for those affected by Katrina (Abramson & Garfield, 2006; Hurricane Katrina Community Advisory Group [HKCAG], 2006; Kessler, Galea, Jones, & Parker, 2006; Sastry & VanLandingham, 2008) and their unmet needs; investigators found that significant proportions of those with mental health concerns were receiving no, minimal, or inadequate care (e.g., Wang et al., 2007). For instance, one study found that 19.0% of those surveyed reported developing a mental disorder following Katrina, but only 18.5% of respondents with new disorders were receiving treatment (Wang et al., 2008). Another large-scale effort reported that rates of both serious mental illness and mild to moderate mental health concerns had doubled in the area, relative to prevalence estimates found in the years before Katrina (HKCAG, 2006; Kessler et al., 2006), and one report found that less than half of those with serious disorders were receiving treatment (Wang et al., 2007). Because of issues with accessing and sampling a population that had become widely dispersed, many of whom were facing ongoing adversity, these reports likely underestimate the mental health consequences of the disaster. It is clear that in addition to the extreme economic costs related directly to the devastation, Katrina exacted profound human costs as well.

Because its impact was exacerbated by a multitude of human failures and shortcomings in predisaster planning, response, and postdisaster resource delivery, Hurricane Katrina has been described as both a natural and human-made disaster (e.g., Grunwald, 2007; Select Bipartisan Committee, 2006). Indeed, given the issues surrounding system, community, and governmental responses, numerous authors have documented these failures and analyzed critically the processes that played out both before Katrina and in the disaster's aftermath (e.g., Gheytanchi et al., 2007; Grunwald, 2007; Select Bipartisan Committee, 2006; U.S. Senate Committee on Homeland Security and Governmental Affairs, 2006). Such examinations reveal lessons learned and elucidate steps necessary to better meet the needs of children, families, and communities in the wake of future disasters, including well-timed and targeted response and intervention.

The latter notion drives this volume. As some contextual backdrop, the idea for the book grew out of our own work after Katrina. We met with children and caregivers evacuated as a result of the hurricane and its aftermath in an effort to better understand the complex array of factors that influence children's adjustment following an event of this magnitude. Our experiences in Louisiana and Mississippi and, critically, our discussions with caregivers, children, educators, and practitioners led us to want to provide an outlet for empirical and conceptual Katrina work, one with an emphasis on application. The chapters of this volume review the relevant knowledge base for each topic of focus; consider the issues raised by this unique disaster; present Katrina-related research, where available; and emphasize actionable recommendations for future work, intervention, and preparedness and other practical implications.

This volume builds on the work of La Greca, Silverman, Vernberg, and Roberts (2002b), which detailed the short- and longer term effects of trauma on children and youths who have experienced a diverse array of natural, human-made, and technological disasters as well as acts of violence. Their work described factors that may increase or reduce risk of severe trauma responses, strategies for coping in the context of the events experienced, and approaches to intervention and treatment. La Greca et al.'s book, comprehensive in its breadth of content coverage, presented state-of-the-art information for practitioners and researchers and has been the standard for texts in the area since its publication. The present volume incorporates updated findings from the still-emerging disaster research area, emphasizes children and families, and engages the topic of Katrina in depth, applying what has been learned from this disaster (and its far-reaching repercussions), as well as the past 5 years of disaster research, to provide guidance for responding to future disasters.

Indeed, there has been burgeoning interest in the area of disaster research in recent years (e.g., Allen, Saltzman, Brymer, Oshri, & Silverman, 2006; Pfefferbaum, Stuber, Galea, & Fairbrother, 2006; see also Weems & Overstreet, 2008b), extending the base established by earlier studies examining the impact of disasters on children (e.g., Earls, Smith, Reich, & Jung, 1988; Lonigan, Shannon, Finch, Daugherty, & Taylor, 1991; Saylor, Swenson, & Powell, 1992). This work has identified a range of possible outcomes, with some children and youths evidencing pronounced problems in adjustment and others demonstrating resilience (i.e., effective coping and adaptation in the face of adversity). However, notwithstanding the increased focus on disaster research, the bulk of the extant literature has focused on problems and pathology (particularly posttraumatic stress symptoms and posttraumatic stress disorder [PTSD]) related to disaster exposure and factors that appear to influence the impact of disaster on children (see, e.g., Davis & Siegel, 2000; Silverman & La Greca, 2002; Vogel & Vernberg, 1993).

It is crucial to understand the potential negative sequelae of disaster, to be sure, so that caregivers, providers, and policymakers can take steps (e.g., mental health screenings, resource allocation) to meet the needs of children and youths following a disaster. Beyond this work on the consequences of disaster, several models of children's postdisaster (or posttrauma) response have been posited (see, e.g., Cicchetti & Lynch, 1993; Green et al., 1991; Kilmer, 2006; La Greca, Silverman, Vernberg, & Prinstein, 1996; Pynoos, Steinberg, & Piacentini, 1999; Pynoos, Steinberg, & Wraith, 1995), and they have meaningfully informed research and intervention work in the area. Within disaster-specific work, those frameworks have largely highlighted pathways to problems in adjustment, such as posttraumatic stress symptomatology (e.g., Green et al., 1991; Pynoos et al., 1995), or focused on relatively circumscribed elements of functioning, such as coping approaches (e.g., La Greca et al., 1996). Those foci have been necessary and have yielded key, generative findings (Cowen, 1980) that have helped inform subsequent projects, programs, and policies in the early stages of the field's development and evolution. However, as La Greca and colleagues (La Greca, Silverman, Vernberg, & Roberts, 2002a; Silverman & La Greca, 2002) asserted, research needs to move beyond main effects–focused models and consider the ways that factors interact in influencing child adjustment outcomes. As the field continues to grow and mature, it will prove fruitful to expand and extend current models to incorporate a more broadly based developmental theoretical approach to better understand the interplay of factors that influence children's adjustment following major disasters. Indeed, a well-integrated approach is necessary to study adaptation and, in the longer term, to use that knowledge profitably to inform optimally targeted efforts to promote the well-being of children and families.

UNDERSTANDING CONTEXTS: ATTENDING TO ECOLOGY

Ecological systems theory (Bronfenbrenner, 1979, 2005), recently revised as the *bioecological model* (Bronfenbrenner & Morris, 2006), is particularly well suited to considering the diverse factors and processes that may influence a youngster's adjustment trajectory following a disaster. This approach accounts for intraindividual factors (e.g., cognitive development, biological maturation), as well as a range of environmental and sociocultural forces (e.g., caregiver–child relationships, family environment, socioeconomic factors, cultural values and beliefs), and views the individual as embedded within mutually interacting systems and levels of context, including family, neighborhood, school, community, and the broader society. It builds on transactional notions of development (Sameroff & Chandler, 1975), which posit that a child's development (as well as the caregiver–child relationship and relationships with important others) is influenced bidirectionally, such that, for example, influence flows both from parent to child and from child to parent. Thus, the ecological approach describes development as occurring within the context of multiple nested levels (typically depicted as concentric circles, with the child at the center of the model), including the child's unique characteristics and the contextual influences that transact with him or her.

Consequently, according to Bronfenbrenner (1979, 2005; Bronfenbrenner & Morris, 2006), individual behavior, development, and adaptation can be viewed as a process involving the interaction of person and environment that necessarily must account for the growth of the individual, the changing nature of the settings in which he or she functions, the individual's subjective experience of these settings, the larger contexts in which these settings are embedded, and the interrelationships between and among settings. This process is influenced by both proximal factors (i.e., factors that that more directly influence the child himself or herself, such as the family milieu, teachers, and peers) and distal factors (i.e., factors or conditions that influence the child through an impact on his or her larger ecology—including proximal factors—such as societal-level cultural values and beliefs and neighborhood qualities). The factors within these levels, and the levels themselves, are viewed as being interrelated and in dynamic interaction (see Bronfenbrenner, 2005).

We recommend this approach as a framework within which researchers and professionals can function in working to understand child and family responses after a disaster and to develop strategies for meeting the needs of those within their communities. The bioecological model can readily incorporate findings to date as well as existing conceptual models for understanding children's reactions to disasters. For instance, this framework can guide efforts to understand the direct and interactive effects of variables shown to influence children's adjustment following a disaster, such as degree of trauma exposure, perceived threat, child characteristics and resources, and aspects of the postdisaster environment (see, e.g., Silverman & La Greca, 2002).

This position is not unique—others (e.g., Edwards, 1998; Murray, 2006; Trickett, 1995; see also Weems & Overstreet, 2008a) have advocated for the promise and applicability of the bioecological approach. However, although this perspective seemingly provides a useful springboard for elucidating the interactions of elements of children's worlds that influence the trajectories they follow after a disaster, including factors, conditions, and processes contributing to the erosion or enhancement of their adjustment over time, ecological models have largely gone underutilized in both disaster research and applied endeavors (e.g., practice, preventive interventions). In fact, at issue for disaster research and its implications is the fact that most work has been conducted at the individual level; it has largely focused on the child, often without viewing the youngster in relationships or assessing broader aspects of context. Such work does not take into account the mutual influences at play in a child's world, including the sets of "correlated constraints," or related factors that can serve to support positive developmental paths or problematic trajectories (Farmer & Farmer, 2001). Such factors work together to affect children and families, with multiple elements of a child's context interacting and influencing adaptation (Farmer & Farmer, 2001). Unless researchers and practitioners build on such notions and use them as a guide, the applicability of research and the reach of interventions will be limited.

In turn, consistent with the core tenets of the ecological framework, the critical importance of attending to context is a recurrent theme of this volume. In some instances, attending to context involves examining efforts at the level of the school or classroom; in others, it involves considering the unique experiences of each family system. More broadly, in considering the multiple and varied lessons learned on the basis of the preparation and response to Hurricane Katrina, one key notion struck a chord that serves as an undercurrent to the descriptions, views, findings, and recommendations put forth in this volume: *one size does not fit all.* Whether planning for disaster or intervening in a disaster's wake, efforts need to be grounded in context. Culture, socioeconomic status (SES), faith, family history—each carries weight and may contribute to a person's reactions, responses, risks, and recovery following disaster. The effects of contextual factors are pervasive (see Norris & Alegria, 2006), and disaster response must be similarly comprehensive.

Katrina brought issues of race, poverty, and their intersection to the fore (e.g., Bobo, 2006; Cutter, 2006; Dass-Brailsford, 2008; Elliott & Pais, 2006; Huddy & Feldman, 2006), as historically underserved and disenfranchised populations were disproportionately affected and had many needs that went unmet. Poverty bleeds into all aspects of families' lives, increasing their vulnerability to a wide range of additional, often chronic, adverse conditions and, in turn, psychological consequences (e.g., Luthar, 1999; Wadsworth & Santiago, 2008). In addition, the majority of disaster studies have found that minority ethnic groups evidence more pronounced negative consequences than those who belong to the majority (Norris & Alegria, 2006). Although these findings may reflect the impact of low SES, ongoing adversity, differential event exposure or property damage, and the like (Norris & Alegria, 2006; Sastry & VanLandingham, 2008), evidence exists that both race and social class contribute independently to aspects of postdisaster reaction and response (Elliott & Pais, 2006).

In the case of Katrina, long-standing issues of poverty and race—including discrimination, disempowerment, neighborhood disadvantage, and disparities in resources and access to support—placed many families at greater risk. Moreover, the problems in planning and response at all levels of government and reports of disparities in recovery left many survivors feeling marginalized and disconnected and reinforced historically grounded mistrust of institutions, systems, and government (e.g., Dass-Brailsford, 2008). The obstacles and adversities many families faced did not begin with Katrina, and this fact underlines a stark reality of postdisaster work: Practitioners, providers, and policymakers have to acknowledge the need to address issues with roots that extend well beyond the disaster itself. Indeed, predisaster characteristics of children and families, as well as of their communities, will influence their needs and risks and, optimally, should influence the nature of the intervention and supports they receive.

Cultural competence, being responsive and sensitive to the unique backgrounds—whether reflecting cultural, racial, ethnic, socioeconomic, linguistic, historical, sexual orientation, or religious or faith-based differences—and the special needs of those being served, is a key value in many service delivery models (e.g., Stroul & Friedman, 1986; see also Dass-Brailsford, 2008; Norris & Alegria, 2006; U.S. Department of Health and Human Services, 2003, for relevant discussions of cultural competence) and is necessary following a disaster to ensure that the needs of children and families are met within their specific contexts. Cultural competence and appropriate attention to ecology, as well as an awareness of historical, political, and social factors that may affect the well-being and orientation of diverse groups, are not only necessary for those providing posttrauma support and intervention. Rather, the struggles after Katrina should serve as a clarion call to researchers, providers, and policymakers alike: Our understanding and our interventions must reflect the populations affected and the settings in which they function.

Within the context of disaster research, it may not always be possible to study the diverse array of factors that may have an influence within children's environments, but in light of the degree to which disasters may affect multiple contexts or settings in which a child (and family) functions, the likelihood of accurate understanding will be increased by efforts to assess pre- and postevent characteristics of the child and his or her environment. Indeed, many sources have discussed the "new normal" youngsters face after a disaster. It behooves researchers to explore the true nature of the impact of this new reality; doing so is consistent with Bronfenbrenner's (2005) attention to individuals' perceptions and subjective experiences of the environment and will likely yield the most "profit" in knowledge.

Figure 1 displays several variable clusters hypothesized to be relevant following a disaster, reflecting child characteristics as well as proximal and distal factors. Because a comprehensive discussion of the diverse factors and conditions that warrant attention is not possible in this short space, we briefly highlight selected variables and constructs—specifically, child resources and variables related to postdisaster caregiver–child interactions. We focus on these variables because they are among those most accessible for assessment and, perhaps, more amenable to intervention. In addition, existing findings from disaster work or parallel literatures (e.g., resilience) point to the salient role of the caregiver, the function of the caregiver–child relationship, and a range of child resources as key influences in youngsters' responses to adversity.

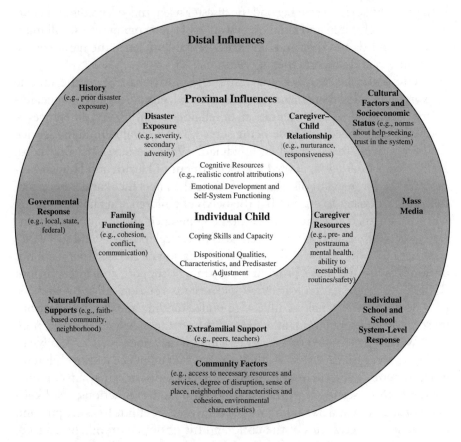

Figure 1. Examples of proximal and distal ecological influences on children's post-disaster adjustment.

Among child characteristics, most studies in the disaster literature have focused on age, gender, coping approaches, and, on occasion, predisaster functioning (e.g., anxiety symptoms). Although these are of interest, a far wider range of child variables warrants investigation. It is possible, for example, to draw from the broader trauma literature as well as work in child resilience to identify other variables that may be active. For example, research has identified a range of child variables and competencies that appear associated with positive adaptation despite exposure to major life stress. Variables reflecting children's self-system functioning, including perceived competencies, self-esteem, sense of efficacy, and future expectations (Cowen et al., 1991; Luthar, 2003; Luthar, Cicchetti, & Becker, 2000; Masten & Coatsworth, 1998; Wyman, Sandler, Wolchik, & Nelson, 2000), have consistently been meaningful predictors of child adjustment in the face of adversity. It appears that a child's positive beliefs about his or her competencies or future may influence his or her perceptions of and response to an event and, of importance, the effort he or she sustains in coping actively with the trauma (Wyman, Cowen, Work, & Kerley, 1993; see Kilmer, 2006, for more on the hypothesized role of the self-system following trauma).

In addition, numerous authors have noted that the child's developmental level and maturity are of great relevance (Pynoos et al., 1995; Salmon & Bryant, 2002; Silverman & La Greca, 2002). This notion is particularly salient when considering cognitive capacity and the resources a child might have at his or her disposal for processing and making meaning of an event (Cryder, Kilmer, Tedeschi, & Calhoun, 2006). That is, the variation in youngsters' cognitive capabilities across different developmental stages may very well influence their encoding and appraisal of the trauma, the attributions they make about their situation, their approach to coping, their ability to marshal resources effectively, and their capacity to attend to and report their internal experiences (Cryder et al., 2006; Hasan & Power, 2004; Salmon & Bryant, 2002). Developmental level also affects the accuracy of a youngster's expectations and attributions about the events, problems, or outcomes they can and cannot control in their lives, known as *realistic control* (Wannon, 1990). Prior work with high-risk samples has suggested that accurate control expectations differentiated those exhibiting resilient adaptation from peers evidencing problems in adjustment (Cowen et al., 1992; Wyman, 2003). In the face of uncontrollable events, such as disasters, the accuracy of one's attributions (and the degree to which events are viewed as controllable or not) may be of great salience to subsequent adaptation, because they may influence problem-solving approaches, emotion regulation, and self-system functioning (Hasan & Power, 2004; Kilmer, 2006; Pynoos et al., 1995).

Children's predisaster characteristics and adjustment are also relevant. For instance, a child's temperamental or dispositional style directly relates to emotional regulation and, in turn, may influence the nature of his or her response to the event as well as to others in the environment (Lieberman & Van Horn, 2004; Pynoos et al., 1995, 1999). Moreover, consideration of a child's predisaster assumptive world or representational system, including his or her basic assumptions about and models of self, others, and the world (often described as an *internal working model*; see, e.g., Bretherton, 1985; Lynch & Cicchetti, 1998), may also yield useful insights. These working models are thought to shape elements of how a child reacts to, and is affected by, trauma, for example, by informing how the child engages with or responds to others and the environment and how he or she appraises and reacts to new situations (Kilmer, 2006). Of note, these models are thought to be influenced by a child's emotional and cognitive development and are influenced substantially by his or her attachment relationships.

In that vein, the caregiving system (including pre- and postdisaster characteristics) is of prime importance. Studies of risk and adaptation have consistently identified emotionally responsive, competent caregiving as a key variable that can mediate the impact of adverse events or circumstances (Luthar, 2003; Luthar et al., 2000; Wyman et al., 2000), with a substantial research base (e.g., Masten & Coatsworth, 1998), suggesting that positive caregiver–child relationships can serve a protective function for children, reducing the likelihood of maladjustment and increasing the likelihood of positive adjustment outcomes despite major stress exposure. Warm, responsive caregiving is also thought to foster the development of adaptive self-system characteristics (e.g., positive self-regard, competency beliefs), sound problem-solving skills, and other child qualities associated with positive adjustment under adverse conditions (Yates, Egeland, & Sroufe, 2003).

Similarly, there is wide recognition of parents' important role in their children's postdisaster adaptation. For instance, studies have examined the response and functioning of parents during and after trauma, as affected by caregiver resources, past and current mental health, and caregiver responses to the trauma (e.g., Green et al., 1991; Koplewicz et al., 2002; Laor, Wolmer, & Cohen, 2001; Scheeringa & Zeanah, 2001; Smith, Perrin, Yule, & Rabe-Hesketh, 2000). In particular, researchers have highlighted the degree to which caregivers can influence their child's appraisal and coping efforts by assisting with interpreting and understanding what has taken place, reestablishing routines in their daily lives, providing emotional support and sharing their perspective, and guiding or modeling coping behaviors (Gil-Rivas, Holman, & Silver, 2004; Israelashvili, 1999; Kliewer, Sandler, & Wolchik, 1994; Prinstein, La Greca, Vernberg, & Silverman, 1996; Pynoos et al., 1995; see also chaps. 2 and 3, this volume). Parenting under "normal" circumstances is complex (Osofsky, 2004). In the aftermath of disaster, parenting may become even more difficult, particularly in situations in which both parent and child have been exposed to the same trauma. For example, the trauma experience may affect parenting behaviors and the quality of care and support parents are able to provide (Masten, Best, & Garmezy, 1990), and it bears underscoring that these reactions, interactions, and behaviors (i.e., parenting) occur in a social context, one influenced by the family milieu (Scheeringa & Zeanah, 2001), cultural values and beliefs, SES, issues of trust in the government, perception of voice and power, one's sources of support, and the like (Goenjian et al., 2001; Laor et al., 2001).

The preceding paragraphs point to the importance and value of considering the caregiver–child dyad as a system and, in turn, the numerous mutually influential factors that contribute to adaptation within that system. However, although there are exceptions (e.g., Gil-Rivas, Silver, Holman, McIntosh, & Poulin, 2007; Kiliç, Özgüven, & Sayil, 2003; Koplewicz et al., 2002; Laor et al., 2001; Smith et al., 2001), much work in the existing disaster literature has focused on one individual or a select characteristic of that system. When dealing with dyads, it limits the accuracy of the picture that emerges to rely on just one reporter, assess indicators of adjustment for only child or parent, or fail to inquire about the other party or the nature of the relationship from each respondent. This notion is reinforced by the findings documenting parental underreporting of their children's internalizing symptoms (e.g., Earls et al., 1988; Pullins, McCammon, Lamson, Wuensch, & Mega, 2005; Smith et al., 2001) as well as issues regarding the accuracy of child self-reports (e.g., underreporting anxiety; Gurwitch, Sitterle, Young, & Pfefferbaum, 2002). Our research and programming cannot do full justice to the complexity of the processes and relationships at play without fully accounting for the caregiver–child system and the larger context in which it functions.

THE PRESENT VOLUME

Because we hope the volume will serve as a useful reference for (a) professionals, scholars, and graduate students across fields, including mental health and social services (e.g., psychologists, social workers, school psychologists, counselors), particularly those providing services to children and families and helping them cope and meet their needs or those in training programs preparing professionals in disaster mental health, preparedness, emergency management, or community response postdisaster, and (b) policymakers at local, state, and national levels, we have assembled contributors representing diverse backgrounds, including psychology, public health, sociology, education, and psychiatry.

The volume is guided broadly by the framework of ecological theory. Two chapters introduce and provide context for the volume, highlighting key issues in postdisaster work. In addition to this Introduction, Snider, Hoffman, Littrell, Fry, and Thornburgh set the stage in chapter 1 by framing the background and setting on the Gulf Coast and underscoring issues of context in this unique disaster. They discuss cogently the challenges to recovery for children and caregivers following Katrina and highlight key elements in work to support and facilitate positive adjustment for children following a disaster, emphasizing the significance of children's environment and the well-being of important adults in their lives.

The remaining chapters are organized into three parts. The first considers a range of risks, resources, and factors that may influence the multiple pathways and processes involved in adaptation for children and families influenced by Katrina, with a focus on proximal influences such as a child's family milieu or teachers. In chapter 2, using child and caregiver reports, Gil-Rivas, Kilmer, Hypes, and Roof examine the contribution of selected child characteristics, caregiver symptomatology, and the quality of the caregiver–child relationship to children's posttraumatic stress symptoms following Hurricane Katrina. The authors report very high symptom levels 1 year after Katrina (roughly one fifth of children obtained scores suggesting probable PTSD), and their findings suggest that caregivers play an important role in their children's adjustment in the aftermath of disaster, highlighting the salience of addressing caregivers' needs in efforts aimed at promoting children's postdisaster adaptation and well-being.

In chapter 3, Kelley and colleagues describe their work with caregiver–child dyads, examining differences between a displaced, Katrina-affected sample from New Orleans and a nondisplaced comparison sample from Baton Rouge. They describe child symptom levels and explore hypothesized relationships between multiple proximal variables (including hurricane exposure, parenting behaviors, and family routines) and child adjustment.

In chapter 4, Knowles, Sasser, and Garrison draw on quantitative and qualitative data to study family resilience processes and outcomes. They assess needs, detail the patterns of adaptation evidenced by families affected by Katrina, and underscore the importance of studying family processes and supporting family systems following a disaster.

In chapter 5, Buchanan, Casbergue, and Baumgartner describe their multi-method approach to assessing teachers' developmentally appropriate classroom activities following the hurricane, the relationship between teachers' experiences and posttraumatic stress symptom levels and curricular response, and the influence of those activities on students' knowledge about hurricanes. The authors discuss implications of their work for educators and for teacher preparation and training, including the need for additional empirically based information about ways teachers can help children cope and adapt after a disaster.

The volume's second part emphasizes a range of distal factors that reflect the large-scale system- or community-level responses to assessing need and mobilizing resources, services, and supports. This part's focus includes an emphasis on community-level indicators regarding the hurricane's impact (e.g., mental health needs, service utilization) and community responses to those in need. In chapter 6, Shahinfar, Vishnevsky, Kilmer, and Gil-Rivas draw on interviews with caregivers and service providers to assess the degree to which families were able to meet their needs following Katrina. They describe arenas of success and weakness and explore themes that can inform how service delivery for children and families may be improved to better meet the needs of those affected by future disasters.

In chapter 7, Kilmer, Gil-Rivas, and MacDonald consider the consequences of disaster for educators and school-based mental health staff more globally, then frame recommendations following a detailed discussion of Mayfair Elementary, a school in East Baton Rouge Parish, Louisiana, opened exclusively for children displaced by Katrina. The example of Mayfair conveys the key role schools can play in restoring children's sense of normalcy and aiding caregivers' efforts to recover by providing support to children and families and facilitating access to needed resources and services.

In chapter 8, Varela, Hensley, and Vernberg discuss the role of social and community responses in meeting child and family needs across different chronological "phases" from planning to impact and from short-term to long-term adaptation. Such responses include supports and services provided in a broad and systematic fashion by organizations at the local, state, or national level, as well as informal assistance provided by others.

In chapter 9, Phillips and Jenkins analyze the roles of faith-based organizations following Hurricane Katrina, with an emphasis on their disaster response (e.g., sheltering, family reunification) and recovery (e.g., rebuilding, community organizing) activities in New Orleans. The efforts of these organizations have garnered less attention in the formal literature; however, they may play important roles in the postdisaster social contexts of children and families, and the authors identify recommendations for policy, practice, and future research that may guide efforts to respond to their needs and recovery.

The volume's third part focuses on the applications of the preceding material, summarized into analysis, lessons learned, and recommendations regarding necessary efforts to better meet the needs of those affected by disasters. In chapter 10, Osofsky, Osofsky, Kronenberg, and Hansel discuss their work "on the ground," screening children, providing services, and working with first responders and their families. They present data regarding the needs, experiences, and functioning of children and adolescents after Katrina and outline a range of lessons learned and recommendations for well-targeted and appropriately focused response following disaster.

Next, in chapter 11, Pfefferbaum, Pfefferbaum, and Norris explore the application of wellness approaches to disaster work and examine the construct of community resilience following Katrina, considering a range of child-supporting strategies for disaster readiness and response. Their discussion and recommendations fit well with an ecological framework and underscore the community's integral role in strategies for promoting healthy adaptation in children and families following disasters.

In chapter 12, Silverman, Allen, and Ortiz summarize current knowledge regarding preparedness, response, and intervention. They describe a range of intervention approaches, many empirically informed in their development, and underscore those that have research support. Of critical importance, they also highlight several cultural and ethical issues in postdisaster work.

Finally, in the volume's Epilogue, Kilmer and Gil-Rivas consider opportunities for future investigation and action on the basis of the work presented here. They suggest a framework for predisaster preparedness and postdisaster response that is consistent with the System of Care approach (e.g., Stroul & Friedman, 1986) and urge that efforts following disaster not simply focus on rebuilding infrastructure and reducing symptomatology and distress; rather, they advocate for steps aiming to promote wellness in the nation's children, families, and communities.

CONCLUSION

These chapters reflect several crucial elements of children's ecologies, ones thought to play a salient role following a disaster. However, the current contributions largely consider a select set of variables and their influence on the child and/or family, and in many cases, they address potential influences on youngsters in a more circumscribed manner. As the field moves forward, a more integrated approach is needed. Nonetheless, the present collection of chapters points to a range of contextual issues in disaster work and to many diverse possible sources of impact and settings through which efforts may be directed, such as the schools (e.g., chap. 7). Moreover, some of these contributions (chaps. 2 and 3) reflect the growing interest in caregiver–child dyads, a system that warrants further study.

Using longitudinal methodologies, future studies can explore the changing ways in which children's ecologies influence them over time and developmental levels, assessing shifts in the weight of influence for certain factors or settings. For example, caregivers will play a far larger role early on in supporting children, facilitating coping, and helping them attempt to make meaning of their disaster experience; however, over time, as the child matures and develops, his or her peers will demonstrate a greater influence on the pathway he or she follows. What is the specific nature of this impact, and how might that be relevant for intervention approaches? Additional research is necessary to address such issues.

Furthermore, although the emphasis on PTSD in the existing literature has furthered an understanding of children's postdisaster responses and reactions, the reliance on the disorder or its symptoms as the gold standard in outcome research may overshadow other child and family processes, problematic or otherwise. Indeed, the field needs to expand its foci to include outcomes that go beyond the negative consequences of disaster exposure—further work is needed to increase understanding of factors that may mitigate the impact of disaster and the factors, conditions, and processes that contribute to resilience as well as posttraumatic growth (see, e.g., Alisic, van der Schoot, van Ginkel, & Kleber, 2008; Cryder et al., 2006; Kilmer, 2006).

We well recognize that the realities of research, program development, and funding mechanisms preclude the inclusion of all elements of interest within the ecological framework and that many aspects of relevance to a given child's context might be difficult to assess at best (and impossible, given current methodologies, at worst). However, it is necessary to take steps toward a more integrative approach that reflects the realities and mutual influences (i.e., transactions) at play that may affect both the pathways children follow and their environments. Over time, such work can facilitate understanding of the processes or mechanisms that might contribute to continuity and discontinuity (i.e., change) in adaptation (Egeland, Carlson, & Sroufe, 1993) for youngsters affected by disasters. Moreover, increasing evidence for context-specific processes—that is, evidence that particular factors or conditions (a) may be salutary in some contexts but associated with negative consequences in others or (b) may vary in their effectiveness, depending on contextual factors, issues of setting, and the child's individual resources and characteristics (see Wyman, 2003, for a discussion of this issue)—underscores the salience of accounting for children's larger developmental contexts in disaster research and its applications. A focus on the multitude of variables that may influence the caregiver–child dyad (including proximal influences such as the family milieu and the child's relationship with his or her teacher), as well as the complex processes that may play out within that system, would appear to be a fruitful next step, laying critical groundwork for subsequent studies to ascertain the nature of the transactions among children, the caregiver–child dyad, and their larger environments.

REFERENCES

Abramson, D., & Garfield, R. (2006). *On the edge: Children and families displaced by Hurricanes Katrina and Rita face a looming medical and mental health crisis.* New York: Columbia University Mailman School of Public Health. Retrieved December 30, 2008, from http://www.ncdp.mailman.columbia.edu/files/On%20 the%20Edge%20L-CAFH%20Final%20Report_Columbia%20University.pdf

Alisic, E., van der Schoot, T. A. W., van Ginkel, J. R., & Kleber, R. J. (2008). Looking beyond posttraumatic stress disorder in children: Posttraumatic stress reactions, posttraumatic growth, and quality of life in a general population sample. *Journal of Clinical Psychiatry, 29,* 1455–1461.

Allen, A., Saltzman, W. R., Brymer, M. J., Oshri, A., & Silverman, W. K. (2006). An empirically informed intervention for children following exposure to severe hurricanes. *Behavior Therapist, 29,* 118–124.

Bobo, L. D. (2006). Katrina: Unmasking race, poverty, and politics in the 21st century. *Du Bois Review, 3,* 1–6.

Bretherton, I. (1985). Attachment theory: Retrospect and prospect. In I. Bretherton & E. Waters (Eds.), *Growing points of attachment theory and research: Monographs of the Society for Research in Child Development, 50*(Serial No. 209), 3–35.

Bronfenbrenner, U. (1979). *The ecology of human development: Experiments by nature and design.* Cambridge, MA: Harvard University Press.

Bronfenbrenner, U. (Ed.). (2005). *Making human beings human: Bioecological perspectives on human development.* Thousand Oaks, CA: Sage.

Bronfenbrenner, U., & Morris, P. A. (2006). The bioecological model of human development. In R. M. Lerner & W. R. Damon (Eds.), *Handbook of child psychology: Vol. 1. Theoretical models of human development* (6th ed., pp. 793–828). Hoboken, NJ: Wiley.

Cicchetti, D., & Lynch, M. (1993). Toward an ecological/transactional model of community violence and child maltreatment: Consequences for children's development. *Psychiatry, 56,* 96–118.

Cowen, E. L. (1980). The wooing of primary prevention. *American Journal of Community Psychology, 8,* 258–284.

Cowen, E. L., Work, W. C., Hightower, A. D., Wyman, P. A., Parker, G. R., & Lotyczewski, B. S. (1991). Toward the development of a measure of perceived self-efficacy in children. *Journal of Clinical Child Psychology, 20,* 169–178.

Cowen, E. L., Work, W. C., Wyman, P. A., Parker, G. R., Wannon, M., & Gribble, P. A. (1992). Test comparisons among stress-affected, stress-resilient and non-classified fourth through sixth grade urban children. *Journal of Community Psychology, 20,* 200–214.

Cryder, C. H., Kilmer, R. P., Tedeschi, R. G., & Calhoun, L. G. (2006). An exploratory study of posttraumatic growth in children following a natural disaster. *American Journal of Orthopsychiatry, 76,* 65–69.

Cutter, S. (2006). The geography of social vulnerability: Race, class, and catastrophe. In *Understanding Katrina: Perspectives from the social sciences*. Retrieved December 31, 2008, from http://understandingkatrina.ssrc.org/Cutter

Dass-Brailsford, P. (2008). After the storm: Recognition, recovery, and reconstruction. *Professional Psychology: Research and Practice, 39*, 24–30.

Davis, L., & Siegel, L. J. (2000). Posttraumatic stress disorder in children and adolescents: A review and analysis. *Clinical Child and Family Psychology Review, 3*, 135–154.

Earls, F., Smith, E., Reich, W., & Jung, K. G. (1988). Investigating psychopathological consequences of a disaster in children: A pilot study incorporating a structured diagnostic interview. *Journal of the American Academy of Child & Adolescent Psychiatry, 27*, 90–95.

Edwards, M. L. K. (1998). An interdisciplinary perspective on disasters and stress: The promise of an ecological framework. *Sociological Forum, 13*, 115–132.

Egeland, B., Carlson, E., & Sroufe, L. A. (1993). Resilience as process. *Development and Psychopathology, 5*, 517–528.

Elliott, J. R., & Pais, J. (2006). Race, class, and Hurricane Katrina: Social differences in human responses to disaster. *Social Science Research, 35*, 295–321.

Farmer, T. W., & Farmer, E. M. Z. (2001). Developmental science, systems of care, and prevention of emotional and behavioral problems in youth. *American Journal of Orthopsychiatry, 71*, 171–181.

Gheytanchi, A., Joseph, L., Gierlach, E., Kimpara, S., Housley, J., Franco, Z., & Beutler, L. E. (2007). The dirty dozen: Twelve failures of the Hurricane Katrina response and how psychology can help. *American Psychologist, 62*, 118–136.

Gil-Rivas, V., Holman, E. A., & Silver, R. C. (2004). Adolescent vulnerability following the September 11th terrorist attacks: A study of parents and their children. *Applied Developmental Science, 8*, 130–142.

Gil-Rivas, V., Silver, R. C., Holman, E. A., McIntosh, D. N., & Poulin, M. (2007). Parental response and adolescent adjustment to the September 11th terrorist attacks. *Journal of Traumatic Stress, 20*, 1063–1068.

Goenjian, A. K., Molina, L., Steinberg, A. M., Fairbanks, L. A., Alvarez, M. L., Goenjian, H. A., et al. (2001). Posttraumatic stress and depressive reactions among Nicaraguan adolescents after Hurricane Mitch. *American Journal of Psychiatry, 158*, 788–794.

Green, B. L., Korol, M., Grace, M. C., Vary, M. G., Leonard, A. C., Gleser, G. C., & Smitson-Cohen, S. (1991). Children and disaster: Age, gender, and parental effects on PTSD symptoms. *Journal of the American Academy of Child & Adolescent Psychiatry, 30*, 945–951.

Grunwald, M. (2007). Katrina anniversary: The threatening storm. *Time*. Retrieved November 23, 2007, from http://www.time.com/time/specials/2007/article/0,28804,1646611_1646683_1648904-1,00.html

Gurwitch, R. H., Sitterle, K. A., Young, B. H., & Pfefferbaum, B. (2002). The aftermath of terrorism. In A. M. La Greca, W. K. Silverman, E. M. Vernberg, & M. C. Roberts (Eds.), *Helping children cope with disasters and terrorism* (pp. 327–357). Washington, DC: American Psychological Association.

Hasan, N., & Power, T. G. (2004). Children's appraisal of major life events. *American Journal of Orthopsychiatry, 74*, 26–32.

Huddy, L., & Feldman, S. (2006). Worlds apart: Blacks and Whites react to Hurricane Katrina. *Du Bois Review, 3*, 97–113.

Hurricane Katrina Community Advisory Group. (2006). *Overview of baseline survey results.* Retrieved November 22, 2007, from http://hurricanekatrina.med.harvard.edu/pdf/baseline_report%208-25-06.pdf

Israelashvili, M. (1999). Adolescents' help-seeking behaviour in times of community crisis. *International Journal for the Advancement of Counselling, 21*, 87–96.

Kessler, R. C., Galea, S., Jones, R. T., & Parker, H. A. (2006). Mental illness and suicidality after Hurricane Katrina. *Bulletin of the World Health Organization* (Article No. 06-33019). Retrieved December 30, 2008, from http://www.who.int/bulletin/volumes/84/10/06-033019.pdf

Kiliç, E. Z., Özgüven, H. D., & Sayil, I. (2003). The psychological effects of parental mental health on children experiencing a disaster: The experience of Bolu earthquake in Turkey. *Family Process, 42*, 485–495.

Kilmer, R. P. (2006). Resilience and posttraumatic growth in children. In L. G. Calhoun & R. G. Tedeschi (Eds.), *Handbook of posttraumatic growth: Research and practice* (pp. 264–288). Mahwah, NJ: Erlbaum.

Kliewer, W., Sandler, I., & Wolchik, S. (1994). Family socialization of threat appraisal and coping: Coaching, modeling, and family context. In F. Nestmann & K. Hurrelmann (Eds.), *Social networks and social support in childhood and adolescence* (pp. 271–291). New York: de Gruyter.

Koplewicz, H. S., Vogel, J. M., Solanto, M. V., Morrissey, R. F., Alonso, C. M., Abikoff, H., et al. (2002). Child and parent response to the 1993 World Trade Center bombing. *Journal of Traumatic Stress, 15*, 77–85.

La Greca, A. M., Silverman, W. K., Vernberg, E. M., & Prinstein, M. J. (1996). Symptoms of posttraumatic stress in children after Hurricane Andrew: A prospective study. *Journal of Consulting and Clinical Psychology, 64*, 712–723.

La Greca, A. M., Silverman, W. K., Vernberg, E. M., & Roberts, M. C. (2002a). Children and disasters: Future directions for research and public policy. In A. M. La Greca, W. K. Silverman, E. M. Vernberg, & M. C. Roberts (Eds.), *Helping children cope with disasters and terrorism* (pp. 405–423). Washington, DC: American Psychological Association.

La Greca, A. M., Silverman, W. K., Vernberg, E. M., & Roberts, M. C. (Eds.). (2002b). *Helping children cope with disasters and terrorism.* Washington, DC: American Psychological Association.

Laor, N., Wolmer, L., & Cohen, D. J. (2001). Mother's functioning and children's symptoms 5 years after a SCUD missile attack. *American Journal of Psychiatry, 158*, 1020–1026.

Lieberman, A. F., & Van Horn, P. (2004). Assessment and treatment of young children exposed to traumatic events. In J. D. Osofsky (Ed.), *Young children and trauma: Intervention and treatment* (pp. 111–138). New York: Guilford Press.

Lonigan, C. J., Shannon, M. P., Finch, A. J., Daugherty, T. K., & Taylor, C. M. (1991). Children's reactions to a natural disaster: Symptom severity and degree of exposure. *Advances in Behaviour Research and Therapy, 13*, 135–154.

Louisiana Recovery Authority. (2007). *Moving beyond Katrina and Rita: Recovery data indicators for Louisiana.* Retrieved November 18, 2007, from http://www.lra.louisiana.gov/assets/twoyear/Indicators082107.pdf

Luthar, S. (1999). *Children in poverty: Risk and protective factors in adjustment.* Thousand Oaks, CA: Sage.

Luthar, S. S. (Ed.). (2003). *Resilience and vulnerability: Adaptation in the context of childhood adversities.* New York: Cambridge University Press.

Luthar, S. S., Cicchetti, D., & Becker, B. (2000). The construct of resilience: A critical evaluation and guidelines for future work. *Child Development, 71*, 543–562.

Lynch, M., & Cicchetti, D. (1998). Trauma, mental representation, and the organization of memory for mother-referent material. *Development and Psychopathology, 10*, 739–759.

Masten, A. S., Best, K. M., & Garmezy, N. (1990). Resilience and development: Contributions from the study of children who overcome adversity. *Development and Psychopathology, 2*, 425–444.

Masten, A. S., & Coatsworth, J. D. (1998). The development of competence in favorable and unfavorable environments. *American Psychologist, 53*, 205–220.

Murray, J. S. (2006). Understanding the effects of disaster on children: A developmental–ecological approach to scientific inquiry. *Journal for Specialists in Pediatric Nursing, 11*, 199–202.

Norris, F. H., & Alegria, M. (2006). Promoting disaster recovery in ethnic-minority individuals and communities. In E. C. Ritchie, P. J. Watson, & M. J. Friedman (Eds.), *Interventions following mass violence and disasters: Strategies for mental health practice* (pp. 319–342). New York: Guilford Press.

Osofsky, J. D. (2004). Different ways of understanding young children and trauma. In J. D. Osofsky (Ed.), *Young children and trauma: Intervention and treatment* (pp. 3–9). New York: Guilford Press.

Pfefferbaum, B., Stuber, J., Galea, S., & Fairbrother, G. (2006). Panic reactions to terrorist attacks and probable posttraumatic stress disorder in adolescents. *Journal of Traumatic Stress, 19*, 217–228.

Prinstein, M. J., La Greca, A. M., Vernberg, E. M., & Silverman, W. K. (1996). Children's coping assistance: How parents, teachers and friends help children cope after a natural disaster. *Journal of Clinical Child Psychology, 25*, 463–475.

Pullins, L. G., McCammon, S. L., Lamson, A. S., Wuensch, K. L., & Mega, L. (2005). School-based post-flood screening and evaluation: Findings and challenges in one community. *Stress, Trauma, and Crisis, 8,* 229–249.

Pynoos, R. S., Steinberg, A. M., & Piacentini, J. C. (1999). A developmental psychopathology model of childhood traumatic stress and intersection with anxiety disorders. *Biological Psychiatry, 46,* 1542–1554.

Pynoos, R. S., Steinberg, A. M., & Wraith, R. (1995). A developmental model of childhood traumatic stress. In D. J. Cohen & D. Cicchetti (Eds.), *Developmental psychopathology: Vol. 2. Risk, disorder, and adaptation* (pp. 72–95). Oxford, England: Wiley.

Salmon, K., & Bryant, R. A. (2002). Posttraumatic stress disorder in children: The influence of developmental factors. *Clinical Psychology Review, 22,* 163–188.

Sameroff, A. J., & Chandler, M. J. (1975). Reproductive risk and the continuum of caretaking casualty. In F. D. Horowitz, M. Hetherington, S. Scarr-Salapatek, & G. Siegel (Eds.), *Review of child development research* (pp. 187–244). Chicago: University of Chicago Press.

Sastry, N., & VanLandingham, M. (2008). *Prevalence and disparity in mental illness among pre-Katrina residents of New Orleans one year after the Hurricane Katrina.* Retrieved December 31, 2008, from http://paa2008.princeton.edu/download.aspx?submissionId=81457

Saylor, C. F., Swenson, C. C., & Powell, P. (1992). Hurricane Hugo blows down the broccoli: Preschoolers' post-disaster play and adjustment. *Child Psychiatry and Human Development, 22,* 139–149.

Scheeringa, M. S., & Zeanah, C. H. (2001). A relational perspective on PTSD in early childhood. *Journal of Traumatic Stress, 14,* 799–815.

Select Bipartisan Committee to Investigate the Preparation for and Response to Hurricane Katrina. (2006). A *failure of initiative: Final report of the Select Bipartisan Committee to Investigate the Preparation for and Response to Hurricane Katrina.* U.S. House of Representatives. Retrieved November 22, 2007, from http://www.gpoaccess.gov/katrinareport/mainreport.pdf

Silverman, W. K., & La Greca, A. M. (2002). Children experiencing disasters: Definitions, reactions, and predictors of outcomes. In A. M. La Greca, W. K. Silverman, E. M. Vernberg, & M. C. Roberts (Eds.), *Helping children cope with disasters and terrorism* (pp. 11–33). Washington, DC: American Psychological Association.

Smith, P., Perrin, S., Yule, W., & Rabe-Hesketh, S. (2001). War exposure and maternal reactions in the psychological adjustment of children from Bosnia-Hercegovina. *Journal of Child Psychology and Psychiatry and Allied Disciplines, 42,* 395–404.

Stroul, B. A., & Friedman, R. M. (1986). A *system of care for children and youth with severe emotional disturbances* (Rev. ed.). Washington, DC: Georgetown University Child Development Center, CASSP Technical Assistance Center.

Trickett, E. J. (1995). The community context of disaster and traumatic stress: An ecological perspective from community psychology. In S. E. Hobfoll & M. W. deVries (Eds.), *Extreme stress and communities: Impact and intervention* (pp. 11–25). New York: Kluwer Academic/Plenum Publishers.

U.S. Department of Health and Human Services. (2003). *Developing cultural competence in disaster mental health programs: Guiding principles and recommendations* (DHHS Publication No. SMA 3828). Rockville, MD: Center for Mental Health Services, Substance Abuse and Mental Health Services Administration.

U.S. Senate Committee on Homeland Security and Governmental Affairs. (2006, May). *Hurricane Katrina: A nation still unprepared.* Retrieved October 24, 2008, from http://www.gpoaccess.gov/serialset/creports/katrinanation.html

Vogel, J. M., & Vernberg, E. M. (1993). Task force report: Part I. Children's psychological responses to disasters. *Journal of Clinical Child Psychology, 22,* 464–484.

Wadsworth, M. E., & Santiago, C. D. (2008). Risk and resiliency processes in ethnically diverse families in poverty. *Journal of Family Psychology, 22,* 399–410.

Wang, P. A., Gruber, M. J., Powers, R. E., Schoenbaum, M., Speier, A. H., Wells, K. B., et al. (2007). Mental health service use among Hurricane Katrina survivors in the eight months after the disaster. *Psychiatric Services, 58,* 1403–1411.

Wang, P. A., Gruber, M. J., Powers, R. E., Schoenbaum, M., Speier, A. H., Wells, K. B., et al. (2008). Disruption of existing mental health treatments and failure to initiate new treatments after Hurricane Katrina. *American Journal of Psychiatry, 165,* 34–41.

Wannon, M. (1990). *Children's control beliefs about controllable and uncontrollable events: Their relationship to stress resilience and psychosocial adjustment.* Unpublished doctoral dissertation, University of Rochester, Rochester, NY.

Weems, C. F., & Overstreet, S. (2008a). Child and adolescent mental health research in the context of Hurricane Katrina: An ecological needs-based perspective and introduction to the Special Section. *Journal of Clinical Child and Adolescent Psychology, 37,* 487–494.

Weems, C. F., & Overstreet, S. (Eds.). (2008b). Special Section: Child and adolescent mental health research in the context of Hurricane Katrina. *Journal of Clinical Child and Adolescent Psychology, 37,* 487–587.

Weisler, R. H., Barbee, J. G., & Townsend, M. H. (2006). Mental health and recovery in the Gulf Coast after Hurricanes Katrina and Rita. *JAMA, 296,* 585–588.

Wyman, P. A. (2003). Emerging perspectives on context specificity of children's adaptation and resilience: Evidence from a decade of research with urban children in adversity. In S. S. Luthar (Ed.), *Resilience and vulnerability: Adaptation in the context of childhood adversities* (pp. 293–317). New York: Cambridge University Press.

Wyman, P. A., Cowen, E. L., Work, W. C., & Kerley, J. H. (1993). The role of children's future expectations in self-system functioning and adjustment to life stress:

A prospective study of urban at-risk children. *Development and Psychopathology*, 5, 649–661.

Wyman, P. A., Sandler, I., Wolchik, S. A., & Nelson, K. (2000). Resilience as cumulative competence promotion and stress protection: Theory and intervention. In D. Cicchetti, J. Rappaport, I. Sandler, & R. P. Weissberg (Eds.), *The promotion of wellness in children and adolescents* (pp. 133–184). Thousand Oaks, CA: Sage.

Yates, T. M., Egeland, B., & Sroufe, L. A. (2003). Rethinking resilience: A developmental process perspective. In S. S. Luthar (Ed.), *Resilience and vulnerability: Adaptation in the context of childhood adversities* (pp. 243–266). New York: Cambridge University Press.

1

SUPPORTING CHILDREN AFTER HURRICANE KATRINA: REFLECTIONS ON PSYCHOSOCIAL PRINCIPLES IN PRACTICE

LESLIE SNIDER, YAEL HOFFMAN, MEGAN LITTRELL,
M. WHITNEY FRY, AND MYA THORNBURGH

Arriving in Baton Rouge with the international aid agency I had just joined for Katrina relief work, I saw for the first time a familiar face from beloved New Orleans. My friend looked rough—dirty T-shirt and overalls, haggard face—as if she had trekked all the way to Baton Rouge through the swamp. She had been cutting out sections of drywall from the flooded homes of friends to prevent the creeping mold from rising up and taking over the rest of their houses. She looked at me seriously when I said I hoped to get to the city soon. "Brace yourself," she warned, "I mean it. It looks like a war zone."

As aid workers and returnees after Katrina, we were faced with a complex challenge—a "complex emergency" in our own backyard. The scope and severity of the destruction were unprecedented, and indeed, my friend was right. It looked just like the war zones I had seen overseas. A huge swath of devastation stretched from the Mississippi Gulf Coast to New Orleans and beyond—you could drive for 3 hours and not get beyond the damage. There were almost no basic services—few if any functioning gas stations, restaurants, pharmacies, or grocery stores—let alone movie theaters, churches, parks, or stretches of beach free enough of dangerous debris to allow a child to play. There were large numbers of displaced persons, a sudden diaspora of New Orleanians and Mississippians crowding into Baton Rouge and Jackson and scattering to all states in the Union. Our "camps" were astrodomes, gymnasiums, tent cities, and eventually trailer parks. Suddenly, after the storm, there were rampant violence, looters, men with guns (legally and illegally), humvees carrying National Guard troops, soldiers posted as guards in front of hospitals to protect their drug supplies, and then an influx of the familiar white vehicles of government and nongovernmental relief organizations carrying busy people with smart phones. The streetlights didn't work, phone and electricity lines were down, and we were told not to bathe in (and certainly not to drink!) the water. And, as in many developing countries where a disaster or human-made emergency sweeps through, the veneer was gone from our city, revealing the dark underbelly of preexisting poverty and lack of social services and structures. As a popular bumper sticker used to advertise on the back of New Orleans cars, "Third World and Proud of It." But now we weren't so proud; we were shattered.

—Leslie Snider

"PRE-K": THIRD WORLD AT THE MOUTH OF THE MISSISSIPPI

Louisiana and Mississippi are home to diverse cultures and rich traditions. A strong sense of identity, history, place, and belonging among people in both states forms the foundation for family and community bonds. The states also share a history of poverty, with serious impacts on child and family well-being. Before Katrina, Mississippi and Louisiana had the highest percentages in the nation of children living in poverty (31% and 28%, respectively, vs. a national average of 19%); living in single-parent homes (47% and 42%); living in homes in which no parent had full-time, year-round employment (43% and 42%); and with the lowest family median incomes ($37,000 and $42,000, vs. the national average of $53,000). A composite measure, based on Kids Count 2005 indicators, ranked Mississippi 50th and Louisiana 49th nationally on child and family well-being (Annie E. Casey Foundation, 2005).

Measures of educational attainment in these states have been equally poor, and most children affected by Katrina were already struggling academically. More than half (51%) of 4th graders in Louisiana could not read at a basic level, only 1 in 5 possessed the literacy skills necessary to pass to the next grade, and roughly 30% of children could read at grade level in both states, far below national standards (Save the Children, 2006). Indeed, before Katrina, the New Orleans public school system was widely considered to be among the nation's worst, with only half of its students—96% of whom were African American—graduating from high school (Abramson & Garfield, 2006).

Widespread destruction and dislocation caused by Hurricane Katrina added further risk to child and family well-being. Thousands of families and children lost everything, including homes, personal possessions, pets, livelihoods, friends, and family members. Individual and family losses were compounded by the disruption of whole communities and the very fabric of life. Historical landmarks were laid to waste; places of business, worship, education, and recreation were damaged beyond repair; and feelings of safety, familiarity, and normalcy were gone for all who remained as well as for those displaced.

In assessing resources on which to ground recovery and rebuilding efforts, the strong local value placed on community was a key asset. Although a lack of housing and services and the absence of many friends and family members provided challenges to "community," those who remained had a passion to rebuild and found strength in their shared experience and vision. A more difficult constraint, however, was that many of these communities had already long struggled to meet their children's needs. Interventions for children after the storm therefore sought not just to restore preexisting systems but also to bring indicators of child well-being and protection up to a higher standard; this need made the Katrina context similar to emergencies in developing countries.

We were on the Gulf Coast as psychosocial support personnel, our mission to implement programs to promote the recovery of children. Reflecting on this disaster and the role of psychosocial support personnel in the response, the following questions merit consideration:

- How is psychosocial programming for children who are affected by disasters to be understood?
- What specifically were the impacts of this hurricane on children and caregivers, and how did the context influence support personnel's understanding of their needs?
- Were principles of best practice as learned from previous emergencies followed?
- How well was the wisdom of best practices balanced with organizational pressures to scale up and demonstrate results quickly? Was quality sacrificed for quantity?
- Whose priorities were truly served—those of beneficiaries, or those of outside agencies?

In this chapter, we describe elements key to children's recovery, placing their well-being in the context of individual factors, their environment, and the well-being of important adults in their lives. Using a bioecological framework (Bronfenbrenner, 2000), we examine challenges to psychosocial recovery for children and caregivers in the Katrina context, in which the compromised safety and stability of home, school, and family environments were implicated in negative outcomes (Abramson & Garfield, 2006). The ways in which a large-scale disaster destroys the sustaining fabric of social and cultural life and formal and informal safety nets—particularly for already vulnerable children and families—deserves focus in our discussion of Katrina's impact and the design of our responses (Abramson & Garfield, 2006; Salloum

& Overstreet, 2008; Salmon & Bryant, 2002). The bioecological model is a useful approach for examining the interrelated contextual factors surrounding children at various levels (proximally, such as family, and distally, such as political factors and access to services) and reminds us of guideposts for our work in chaotic environs (Weems & Overstreet, 2008; see also Introduction, this volume).

We also share personal reflections as aid workers. Each unique disaster affords the opportunity for an honest accounting of successes, challenges, failures, and, most importantly, lessons learned so we can do a better job the next time around. As a test of best practices, Katrina offers fertile ground for examining real-life pitfalls in implementing psychosocial programs and underscores the importance of maintaining the standards and principles that keep us from doing harm.

COLLECTIVE WISDOM

Psychosocial assistance in emergency settings has received growing attention from aid agencies over the past 2 decades, resulting in an evolving evidence base to guide interventions. The collective experience and literature include work with children and families affected by armed conflict (e.g., Apfel & Bennett, 1996; Dawes & Cairns, 1998) and by natural disasters (e.g., Belter & Shannon, 1993; Pynoos, Goenjian, & Steinberg, 1995; Vernberg, 1999), including large-scale devastation such as that wrought by the 2004 Indian Ocean tsunami (e.g., Kostelny & Wessells, 2005).

In this chapter, we wish to add our collective wisdom to the knowledge base and to measure our approach against knowledge gained by our predecessors from years of work with children in emergencies. We first examine the determinants of psychosocial risk and resilience in emergency contexts, then explore the evolution of psychosocial assistance in these settings and reminders for appropriate intervention.

Emergency Preparedness and the Katrina Experience

By all accounts, Hurricane Katrina constituted the largest natural disaster in U.S. history. Although warning systems tracked the storm's path and strength as it moved toward the southern United States, Katrina overwhelmed both the imagination and experience of Gulf Coast residents and emergency preparedness plans (to the extent that they existed) for evacuation and coping. The lack of readiness at all levels of government to provide rapid and safe evacuation before the storm, to rescue victims, and to coordinate critical survival and emergency medical care—as well as the absence of a recovery plan for the population—is considered the real, human-made disaster (Cooper & Block, 2006).

Poverty and Vulnerability

In accordance with the bioecological model, the well-being of persons and communities is threatened not only by the immediate risk of injury and fatality in a disaster but also by profound changes to the landscape in which they attempt to recover their former lives. Hurricane Katrina destroyed infrastructure, halted services, and severely damaged the economic bases of Mississippi and Louisiana (Time, 2005). Furthermore, the ability of families to cope with threat and recover is related to their socioeconomic, cultural, and political status, in terms of both their available resources and access to emergency services (Berkman & Kawachi, 2000; Krieger, 1994). Poor families have fewer options for evacuation and resettlement, experience greater risk during the event, and encounter extended hardship in rebuilding their lives (Masozera, Bailey, & Kerchner, 2006). These observations are consistent with our experience in the aftermath of Hurricane Katrina.

The Personal Meaning of Disaster

The bioecological model frames children's and families' exposure to traumatic events in the context of personal circumstance and the social, economic, and political environment (Abramson & Garfield, 2006). Consistent with the model, these same forces influenced the meaning children and families placed on the Katrina experience by affecting their perceptions of harm exposure. As Weems and Overstreet (2008) noted, "Prejudice, discrimination, and lack of social support represent factors . . . that pose a powerful threat to one's sense of physical safety, self-worth, self-efficacy, and social relatedness" (p. 489) For example, local persons were aware of the difference in experiences of residents of the Mississippi Gulf Coast and of those from urban New Orleans, with its history of violence, inner-city poverty, and racial tensions. Accusations that the failed government response for the largely African American victims in the city was rooted in racial discrimination were further fueled by rumors that evacuees at the convention center ran in fear when helicopters finally arrived to drop food and water. According to the documentary *When the Levees Broke: A Requiem in Four Acts* (Lee, 2006), many believed the government was trying to rid New Orleans of its Black population. Whether true or false or manipulated for political purposes, the meaning of the experience for inner-city families—perhaps perceiving themselves abandoned by their government—may profoundly affect their course of recovery.

In contrast, although also severely affected, Mississippi Gulf Coast residents neither expressed the same distrust of government motives nor faced or perceived the problems with looting and violence seen in New Orleans (Weems et al., 2007). Although the impact of perceived discrimination on recovery from trauma remains unclear, one study found that high levels of extrafamilial support among Black participants may have mitigated the negative effects of societal prejudices (Pina et al., 2008). This finding lends emphasis to the importance of the social aspect of psychosocial interventions in promoting healing and buffering risks to recovery, described further in the next section.

Context and Recovery: Protective Factors

Emergencies clearly affect individuals, families, and communities differently depending on the nature of the emergency and the resources available to cope. Viewed through the lens of the bioecological model, the Katrina experience dramatically highlights the role of contextual factors as risk determinants in psychosocial outcomes. However, contextual factors such as available natural supports and community resources can also mitigate negative outcomes (Weems & Overstreet, 2008; see also Introduction, this volume). To maximize impact, recovery interventions must consider the influence of these factors on distress and resilience and must recognize and foster inherent strengths. Although some within the population will have specific vulnerabilities, psychosocial aid workers must remember that those affected are not merely helpless, passive victims. Rather, they have individual and collective strengths rooted in local cultural, religious, and family traditions that can promote recovery in the face of adversity (Shultz, Espinel, Flynn, Cohen, & Hoffman, 2007).

Evolution of Psychosocial Assistance in Emergencies

Ensuring basic survival and population safety is of primary concern following an emergency. Attention to psychosocial interventions within crisis response evolved from a growing recognition of the socioemotional effects of trauma (Barron, 1999). The ability of those affected by extreme events to recover, reorganize internally and socially, and adapt and survive in a very changed environment depends on their psychosocial functioning in real ways. In 1946, the World Health Organization (1948) defined *health* as "a state of complete physical, mental and social well-being and not merely the absence of disease or infirmity" (p. 2). This holistic definition underscored the significance of psychosocial aspects of health (in addition to physical aspects) and the dynamic interplay of these elements in a person's functioning and well-being (UNICEF, 2002). Psychosocial assessments in emergencies aim to describe the impacts of events on the thoughts, feelings, behaviors, relationships, and functioning of affected persons—critical elements of their stabilization and recovery (Duncan & Arntson, 2004).

Psychosocial interventions emerged from an understanding of humans as multidimensional beings, whose response and recovery go beyond physical and security concerns. Psychosocial approaches, however, have not been clearly defined and may include broad-based community support as well as specific, trauma-focused, individual therapies. The recently released Inter-Agency Standing Committee (IASC; 2007) guidelines use the composite term *mental health and psychosocial support* to encompass the range of complementary interventions in emergencies and define this support as "any type of local or outside support that aims to protect or promote psychosocial well-being and/or prevent or treat mental disorder" (p. 1).

As the field matures, debates persist regarding the appropriateness and usefulness—or harm—of some types of "local or outside support" (Becker, 1995; Summerfield, 1996). Some debates center on psychopathology-focused interventions with "traumatized persons" that ignore the coping strategies and inherent resilience of those affected (Loughry & Eyber, 2003; Van Ommeren, Saxena, & Saraceno, 2005). Many interventions are further criticized for focusing on individuals to the exclusion of communities (Ager, 2002; Eyber, 2002; Summerfield, 1996; Wessells & Monteiro, 2003). Indeed, beyond individual pain, disasters bring a shared sense of loss—for community, traditions, ways of life, and identity. Although mental health professionals come from a field traditionally focused on the internal lives of persons, many realize the importance of understanding how community members perceive traumatic events and how they communally grieve and recover (Snider et al., 2004; Summerfield, 1996; Wessells & Monteiro, 2003). Inherent in this debate is the importance of cultural competence—appreciating the values, beliefs, and history of persons affected by emergencies—in the design of interventions (e.g., Dougherty, 1999; Duncan & Arntson, 2004).

The societal dimension of psychological wounds is reflected in the following excerpt from a Save the Children Alliance (1996) publication, *Promoting Psychosocial Well-Being Among Children Affected by Armed Conflict and Displacement: Principles and Approaches:*

> Knowledge in child development and psychology . . . is not a sufficient basis for psychosocial programs. It needs to be combined with knowledge about culture, history, traditions and political realities where the program is to take place, as well as consequences of different aid methods and techniques. No individual discipline can claim to have expertise in all these areas; the point is that all are relevant and inter-related. (p. 5)

Specialized mental health care for the small proportion of seriously affected individuals is one aspect of mental health and psychosocial support in emergencies (IASC, 2007). The "specialist approach" described by Richman (1996) focuses on treating trauma and symptoms through technical knowledge and support, usually by foreign mental health experts. However, generalist aid agencies, rooted in public health models and the humanitarian imperative for stabilization of large populations, most often implement psychosocial support programs geared toward restoration of social and emotional functioning for the majority of the affected population (Loughry & Eyber, 2003; Psychosocial Working Group, 2003). Mental health treatment for those with severe reactions or disorders may be beyond their technical capacity and mandate. However, it is our experience that such organizations inevitably interface with individuals requiring specialized mental health care and may be challenged by a lack of clinical expertise within their staff. Damaged or nonexistent mental health infrastructure in disaster-affected areas further stymies their ability to refer individuals to local professional support services. Thus, aid agencies must take care that their initiatives do not overreach the capacities of their staff and volunteers—who are themselves often affected, local persons (Richman, 1996)—and that they have adequate clinical backup and support.

Guiding Principles for Psychosocial Interventions for Children and Families

On the basis of the extant literature and aid agencies' experience from different emergencies, certain principles and approaches have emerged as psychosocial good practice. The following basic tenets are practical, tested strategies that can help agencies implementing psychosocial programs minimize their risk of doing harm, ensure relevant and appropriate programs, and maximize effectiveness (Shultz et al., 2007; U.S. Department of Health and Human Services, 2004):

- No one who experiences a disaster is unaffected, and disaster impacts can be defined at the level of both individuals and the community.
- Individual and community resilience, normal recovery, and positive adaptation in the face of adversity are the rule, not the exception.
- Psychosocial services must be tailored to communities and must tap into a wide range of supports for survivors to cope with loss of, and change in, family, friends, and community.
- Psychosocial interventions must recognize survivors' strengths and resilience, assume they are competent, and help them to master the disaster experience.

Other publications support these guidelines; for example, the Save the Children Alliance (1996) underscored the "need for community-based solutions to problems; for genuine participation of affected groups in decision-making and implementation; [and for] understanding of and drawing upon local culture, tradition and resources." (p. 11). These reflections highlight the potential creativity and strength of emergency-affected families and communities in adapting to very changed circumstances.

Caregivers can promote the personal and social attributes that help children cope, recover, and reclaim the joys of childhood after a disaster. They can also reduce the unpredictability and chaos related to disasters and post-disaster life. The following sections detail some essential components in promoting the care, protection, and healthy development of children following extreme events (Arntson & Knudsen, 2004; Duncan & Arntson, 2004; Loughry & Eyber, 2003; Save the Children Alliance, 1996; UNICEF, 2002), including stable and secure attachments to caregivers; physical and economic security; opportunity for intellectual, physical, and spiritual development; meaningful peer relationships and social connection; sense of belonging; sense of agency, trust, and control; self-esteem; and hope.

Stable and Secure Attachments to Caregivers

A close connection to a primary caregiver—one who provides consistent and competent care—is essential to children's physical, emotional, and social development (e.g., Masten & Coatsworth, 1998). For children exposed to traumatic events, the presence of a stable caregiver to provide comfort and protection is a key factor in mitigating stress responses and ensuring longer term positive outcomes. Best practices in emergencies include reunifying children with primary caregivers (or with other stable, caring adults when primary caregivers are unavailable), supporting caregivers in their own recovery and increasing their capacity to cope with their own reactions, and transferring skills and knowledge to caregivers to support their own children after the disaster (Arntson & Knudsen, 2004; Duncan & Arntson, 2004; Loughry & Eyber, 2003; UNICEF, 2002; see also chaps. 2 and 3, this volume).

Physical and Economic Security

The first priority following a disaster is ensuring that people's safety and basic survival needs are met. As recovery progresses, empowering families to meet their own needs is key to their sustainable restoration (Arntson & Knudsen, 2004; UNICEF, 2002). Families unable to regain control and stability face the potential for further displacement, stress, and rupture. At the community level, recovery is fostered by the existence of social and economic safety nets for vulnerable families and by the re-creation of livelihood opportunities. These efforts include practical interventions: providing emergency relief funds, helping families through insurance claims and disaster assistance applications, and reestablishing assets and gainful employment. Practical interventions can have a substantial impact on family and child well-being and the restoration of viable communities (Shultz et al., 2007).

Families and communities recovering from a disaster must also address new physical insecurities and threats to children's safety (Weems & Overstreet, 2008). The changed landscape may present new hazards and a lack of safe play spaces. Further, rebuilding efforts introduce new people to communities, and housing shortages often dictate that different groups are housed together, thereby increasing potential risks for children. One aspect of psychosocial intervention is raising awareness of new threats and helping caregivers minimize children's risk exposure (Save the Children, 2008).

Temporary housing and school facilities must maximize child-safe areas. Schools in Mississippi and Louisiana had to develop new procedures for screening and monitoring those coming in and out of their schools as they were rebuilding. Temporary housing areas also contained potential threats to children. For example, cruise ships presented challenges to supervision of children moving about the many corridors. Some trailer communities were remote and lacked recreational facilities and access to services; several became breeding grounds for boredom, drugs, and violence. Thus, when creating temporary facilities, the Katrina experience points to the need for including "child-friendly" green spaces, well-lit playgrounds, places of worship, and community centers to facilitate child safety and recovery.

In addition to outside threats, the increased risk of discord, domestic violence, and substance abuse within families following disasters further threatens children's safe recovery (Norris, Friedman, & Watson, 2002). Many families lived in overcrowded temporary housing after Katrina, increasing the potential for stress and conflict. Practical strategies (e.g., helping families obtain adequate temporary housing and access to services) are critical in reducing family stressors and supporting family members in achieving a mutual understanding of their grief and anger and finding positive ways of coping and supporting one another.

Opportunity for Intellectual, Physical, and Spiritual Development

In addition to essential services to ensure their health and welfare, children require intellectual, physical, and spiritual nurturing from their family, schools, and, in some cultures and traditions, from faith communities. Education, recreation, and socialization form the elements of structured life and routine that help children reconstitute, regain a sense of normalcy, and recover (IASC, 2007; Save the Children Alliance, 1996). Families displaced by Katrina often developed new routines; creative alternatives (e.g., church services held in makeshift tents); and new family traditions, particularly around holidays. The initiative of families and communities in creating alternatives demonstrates the importance of these structures to reconstructing life and all that binds it in a cohesive way.

Meaningful Peer Relationships and Social Connection

Both adults and children suffer from the separation from members of their social network following a disaster. The nature and impact of separations may differ depending on the age of the child (Shultz et al., 2007). A colleague from our partner organization, Health Care Centers in Schools, noted that for teenagers, especially incoming high school seniors, loss of their school community and separation from graduating classmates were particularly painful (S. Catchings, personal communication, November 19, 2005). Because the opportunity to relate to peers facing similar difficulties is an important part of social support and recovery, helping children connect with old and new friends, extended family, and other social networks is a key psychosocial intervention (Richman, 1996). Moreover, the ability to form and maintain relationships is a developmental skill and component of resilience for children (Arntson & Knudsen, 2004; UNICEF, 2002). Rebuilding social networks for caregivers is also salient as they work to recover and to support their children adequately (Loughry & Eyber, 2003).

A Sense of Belonging

Children form a sense of identity and learn norms for behaviors and values through their relationships with others. A drastically changed physical and social landscape—both for those remaining in the disaster area and those who are displaced—can destabilize feelings of community and belonging for children and adults. The sudden loss of a secure sense of place can contribute to fear, anxiety, and disorganized behavior in children and may add to the adverse impacts on their recovery, irrespective of caregiver attachment (Salloum & Overstreet, 2008; Substance Abuse and Mental Health Services Administration [SAMHSA], 2008). Active efforts to reestablish a sense of community in directly affected areas and to bring displaced children and families into the local community fold help restore a sense of belonging and place as members of a system larger than themselves (Arntson & Knudsen, 2004; UNICEF, 2002).

A Sense of Agency, Trust, and Control

One of the most devastating aspects of a major disaster is the attendant feelings of powerlessness and helplessness for children and adults. Disruptions to every aspect of daily life in the aftermath of disasters may leave children frightened and impede their ability to reorganize and regain a sense of competence and agency (SAMHSA, 2008; Weems & Overstreet, 2008). After Katrina, parents found that even small ways of reestablishing routines for children, such as a regular mealtime and bedtime, lent needed predictability to a child's day. Engaging children, particularly adolescents, safely in rebuilding homes and neighborhoods seemed to help restore their sense of control and mastery. Playing a role in community recovery draws on children's resourcefulness and can bolster self- and collective efficacy and a sense of public responsibility—important factors in adjustment following adversity more broadly and in recovery from disasters specifically (Apfel & Simon, 1995; Garmezy & Masten, 1990; Hobfoll et al., 2007).

Shattered Assumptions

Helplessness, impotence, and guilt in the face of a disaster can harm adults' and children's self-esteem. Caregivers may feel powerless to fully protect their children during the disaster or incapable of "fixing" everything or "making it right" (Janoff-Bulman, 1992). Adults and children may feel guilty about their own survival or may believe they should have or could have done something differently about circumstances over which they likely had no control. Depending on their age and developmental stage, children may blame themselves for bad things that happened during the disaster (Lubit & Eth, 2003). Caregivers can provide necessary reassurance, correct distortions, and help children focus on their strengths—namely, those things over which they *do* have control and that help them feel loved and valued. It is important to address symptoms and cognitive distortions in caregivers before addressing those in children because of the powerful role that the caregiver–child relationship plays in children's coping and recovery (Scheeringa & Zeanah, 2001; see also chaps. 2 and 3, this volume).

Hope

The devastation brought by disasters can reverberate through families and communities for months and years. Physical, emotional, spiritual, and economic healing is often slow and arduous, challenging the ability of people to maintain a vision of and hope for a better future. In Mississippi, we witnessed the experience of many families living in Federal Emergency Management Agency (FEMA) trailers set up next to their ruined homes in destroyed communities devoid of neighbors and usual services. Every day, they told us, they looked out on the ruin of their former lives.

Hope is both a necessary means and an end to recovery (Arntson & Knudsen, 2004; Wyman, Cowen, Work, & Kerley, 1993). Just as cues from caregivers give children a sense of safety, adults can also foster their feelings of hope (Madrid & Grant, 2008). They can encourage and value children's dreams and contributions to recovery and can model adaptability, flexibility, and belief in a positive future (Apfel & Simon, 1995). Parents can involve children (age appropriately) in recovery efforts, foster their creativity in developing new games or family traditions, encourage future planning, and create cheerful spaces (Snider & Littrell, 2006). In turn, children's creativity and imagination have the power to inspire adults.

Many caregivers after Katrina found the strength to persevere in the desire to re-create a stable and positive life for their children, but they also needed a way to see beyond the devastation surrounding them. In our experience, encouraging a longer term perspective on the process of recovery and rebuilding helped them have realistic expectations of themselves and envision life beyond their present circumstances. Helping adults accept change and realize that, despite difficult circumstances, they can establish goals and make progress toward them can be important in strengthening coping in parents (Madrid & Grant, 2008).

THE CHALLENGE OF KATRINA

Katrina disrupted the start of school for many children in the region. Affected families focused on getting children back in school as quickly as possible to minimize the disruption to their education. Psychosocial interventions also naturally focused on restoring schools, both as points of access to children and their caregivers and as critical institutions for restoring normalcy and a sense of community (Abramson & Garfield, 2006). Relative to other community institutions, schools reopened quickly and served as community centers and sources of assistance for children and families in need (see chaps. 5 and 7, this volume; Dean et al., 2008).

Impacts on Children and Families

Katrina had a devastating impact on children and families. Many were exposed to serious traumatic events, such as separation from caregivers while fleeing to safety, death or injury of friends and family members, and damage to or loss of homes and treasured personal possessions (Osofsky & Osofsky, 2006; see also chaps. 2 and 10, this volume). Given these experiences, it is not surprising that a study by Abramson and Garfield (2006) of 665 households in trailer communities and hotels throughout Louisiana found that nearly half of parents reported that their children had developed new emotional or behavioral problems since the storm. These families relocated an average of 3.5 times following Katrina, and some as many as 9 times, wreaking havoc on their ability to access and maintain health care, education, employment, and routines.

Parents and other caregivers faced many new challenges in daily life and caring for their families. The lack of basic services and closure of businesses in devastated areas made securing basic necessities labor intensive. Many caregivers lost jobs, and their future livelihoods were tenuous. Economically sustaining their families became an all-consuming effort, leaving considerably fewer resources for emotional support to children, spouses, and other family members. The ability of parents to cope effectively with the stress of postdisaster daily living influences the availability and quality of parental support for children (Belter & Shannon, 1993; see also chaps. 2 and 3, this volume). Children are also affected by increased family tension and conflict, which is exacerbated by irritability and stress in adults (Lubit & Eth, 2003).

Impacts on Schools and Teachers

With the massive physical destruction of schools and surrounding communities, thousands of teachers were displaced and confronted unique challenges (Abramson & Garfield, 2006; see also chaps. 5 and 7, this volume). We found that many schools had combined with others because of ruined facilities and reduced student populations, particularly along the devastated Mississippi Coast. In addition, high teacher-to-student ratios meant that many teachers were sharing classrooms and team teaching, which restricted their sense of professional autonomy. Family relocations and flows of displaced populations made it difficult to locate staff and students and estimate enrollment. Teachers further coped with the loss of books, supplies, and years of accumulated teaching material.

While charged with helping students cope, teachers themselves were traumatized by loss of homes, personal possessions, and loved ones. Of teachers working in Mississippi schools that reopened after the storm, about 80% had lost their own homes (Madrid & Grant, 2008). As we worked with these teachers, they shared with us their daily struggles with insurance and disaster assistance assessments, the search for housing, adjustment to new and often cramped living conditions, and constant witnessing of the devastated landscape. As parents and caregivers, they focused on securing basic family needs with little time to process their own feelings or emotional support needs. The constant, daily-life stress for teachers in postdisaster settings has been noted elsewhere by others engaged in school-based programs following Katrina (Dean et al., 2008).

In addition to the pressures of clearing the devastation and creating a safe school environment, school administrators and teachers shared with us the pressure they felt to demonstrate to state educational boards that they had sufficiently recovered and could remain viable educational institutions. State testing deadlines remained in effect, and although informed that the scores would not count, some school administrators reduced or eliminated holiday and vacation time for students and teachers in order to recoup curricular time lost. Some school staff noted that given the impacts of grief, loss, and adjustment on the ability of students and teachers to concentrate and perform, these academic pressures were particularly taxing. Allowing space for emotional stabilization and recovery might have done more for students' academic performance in the long term (see chaps. 5 and 7, this volume). However, the pressures on schools to reopen, operate as usual, and meet testing standards meant some were hesitant to allow outside mental health providers and programs into the school setting (Dean et al., 2008). Aid agencies potentially play an important advocacy role in encouraging state educational boards to prioritize recovery and wellness—rather than academic outcomes—in the aftermath of disaster.

LESSONS FROM OUR INTERVENTIONS

Psychosocial support for children in postdisaster settings involves the re-creation of an enabling environment—a safe, predictable, protective, and caring world—in which they can recover and grow. No one roadmap exists for disaster relief organizations to support this restoration process. Tailoring responses to each setting is one of the key components and challenges of psychosocial recovery efforts (IASC, 2007). In the case of post-Katrina relief interventions, respect for local culture was important to beneficiaries, who were confronted with many outside aid agencies that were unfamiliar with their priorities and values (Dean et al., 2008).

Relief organizations are further challenged by their mandate to get "on the ground" quickly, respond to large numbers of affected people in a chaotic environment, and work with the distress, grief, and traumatic material of the affected population. The scale of the Katrina disaster tested the capacities of emergency response organizations. In light of the Gulf Coast context and Katrina's serious impact on children, families, and communities, in the next section we consider the success with which aid agencies provided useful and relevant psychosocial programs according to our collective wisdom and observations.

A Focus on Schools

Schools are tremendously important and valued institutions in children's ecologies around which children, caregivers, and communities can gather and reestablish a sense of order and normalcy after a disaster. Schools also provide a stabilizing framework in which to restore children's imaginations, social lives, and learning (Apfel & Simon, 1995; see also chaps. 5 and 7, this volume). In their effort to support existing institutions and ground interventions in community-based programming, many aid agencies responding to Katrina focused on assisting the reopening of schools and targeted psychosocial programming within schools. Schools provide a logical point of access for reaching children and their caregivers. They also potentially extend the reach of psychosocial interventions by engaging school staff to implement programs for many more children than agency core staff could do alone. Engaging school staff in program implementation may stimulate the imaginative capacity of adults in developing new coping strategies for themselves and creative avenues for supporting children (Apfel & Simon, 1995).

Struggling with a multitude of stressors and challenges in rebuilding and restarting, schools were grateful to outside organizations for practical support and tools to address the impact of Katrina on children. School administrators overwhelmingly seemed to recognize the importance of meeting the psychosocial recovery needs of their incoming students and staff and were eager for information, materials, and assistance. In many cases, administrators and teachers especially wanted to know what to do and say—or what *not* to do and say—to help children process their experience and "return to normal." They expressed a need for new knowledge and capacities to deal with an event so far beyond their usual realm of experience.

The outpouring of relief and assistance to Gulf Coast schools also presented challenges. In the midst of rebuilding, monitoring construction, resupplying, and tracking the student and teacher body, administrators further had to sift through the various psychosocial techniques and programs being offered. During the course of our work, we discovered that many agencies entered schools with free materials and programs ranging from coloring books on healing after disasters to complete class sessions using therapeutic techniques to address children's exposure to trauma. State education departments also offered information, advice, and counseling support. Although desperate for support and information, teachers and school administrators reflected that they did not always have the time and capacity to carefully assess the quality and relevance of the programs being offered.

Lack of coordination among aid agencies was just as much a problem in the post-Katrina landscape as it often is in overseas disasters. This lack of coordination is fueled not only by a desire to respond quickly to massive need but also by competition among agencies to be important players following an emergency. Agencies are ultimately responsible for initiating collaboration with government and other coordinating bodies for disaster relief, obtaining approval for their assessments and programs, and ensuring they are not duplicating services.

In the chaos of a disaster's aftermath, agencies also bear a key responsibility in ensuring that their approaches and messages are appropriate and effective. Often, however, they burdened schools with recommendations for specific psychosocial programming. While raising awareness of children's psychosocial health needs and promoting their programs, some inadvertently conveyed that schools were negligent if they did not implement particular strategies. This highlights how important it is for agencies to conduct careful assessments of needs and local capacities for school-based psychosocial programs and to tailor their interventions accordingly.

Higher level interventions to help children process grief and loss can have value and relevance in the wake of a major disaster. However, they require implementers with clinical skills, who may be difficult to identify among the local populace after a disaster. Before using school staff as implementers for post-Katrina programs, it was important to assess their ability to cope with the added demands of program implementation. Local school staff were themselves survivors, and many were grieving losses equal to or greater than those of their students (Dean et al., 2008). In general, agencies must be aware that local implementers may also be directly affected by the disaster; must screen and prepare them to manage possible exposure to the traumatic stories of children; and must provide close and regular monitoring, support, and supervision (IASC, 2007). Adequate and skilled supervision is essential to ensuring that programs are implemented safely and effectively, both for children and for implementers. Finally, if possible, referral resources for children requiring higher level mental health care should be in place before the start of the program (IASC, 2007). Fulfilling this need proved challenging following Katrina; community-based mental health resources had been viewed as inadequate before the storm, private practices had been destroyed, and many mental health professionals were still displaced (Madrid & Grant, 2008).

One post-Katrina psychosocial program illustrates the opportunities and challenges described above. In some cases, the program was readily embraced by schools that found innovative ways of scheduling and had access to staff with basic clinical skills (school counselors) to safely and effectively implement the program. Other schools reported that the program itself became a burden or left some implementers (often teachers) feeling overwhelmed by their own unaddressed emotional needs or the traumatic stories of children. Other schools modified, shortened, or abandoned the program because of time constraints and the intense focus on meeting academic requirements.

Organizations should consider gathering a toolbox of strategies and materials that offer a range of options for psychosocial care. Examples of useful tools include informational materials for teachers, school administrators, and parents; teaching strategies for affected children (e.g., games, creative arts, and therapeutic play); materials or programs that address specific reactions in children or teacher concerns; and basic self-care strategies. In this way, agencies can still offer pre-prepared models and materials but can better tailor support to local school needs and capacities. Engaging schools in creating or adapting materials and strategies increases cultural and contextual relevance, fosters local ownership, and empowers recovery. Some agencies were surprised to discover that Louisiana and Mississippi schools represented very different cultures!

Programs "for Children"

Some agencies have developed general psychosocial interventions that can be rapidly implemented and scaled up in postemergency settings. These interventions range from school-in-a-box educational programs (UNICEF, 2008) and child-centered spaces in postconflict areas for safely starting children's activities (Christian Children's Fund, 2008) to more structured grief and trauma interventions based on cognitive–behavioral and narrative exposure therapies (Jaycox, Morse, Tanielian, & Stein, 2003; Salloum & Overstreet, 2008). Prepackaged programs have advantages—they may have been tested in other settings, are ready to go, and provide a framework for schools struggling to restore order from chaos. However, their cultural and contextual relevance are not ensured for the new environment.

In addition, historical debates question whether—and how—psychosocial programs should engage children in processing their traumatic experiences (Save the Children Alliance, 1996). Allowing children to safely express their emotions and fears in developmentally appropriate ways may help children's recovery, and some feel that schools provide the supportive structure and caring adults to enable that expression to occur (Abramson & Garfield, 2006; Dean et al., 2008). Others argue that school should be a place where a child can temporarily find relief from distressing thoughts and experiences, focus on productive activities, and have time to just be a child (Apfel & Simon, 1995). Most important, encouraging the expression of traumatic experiences without providing appropriate safeguards for the child, his or her peers, and the adults hearing the stories is simply unethical. As stated by the Save the Children Alliance (1996),

> The process of healing in an emergency is not promoted by a premature, intensive focus on children's psychological wounds. Encouragement to recall traumatic worst moments, for example, may tear down needed defenses and undermine active coping. Helping . . . affected children to build on their strengths and resilience, in collaboration with trusted caregivers, is, we believe, a more effective and appropriate strategy. (p. 12)

In designing and targeting programs "for children," agencies must ask, "Who is the actual target audience for the intervention?" For reasons of impact, sustainability, scale, and safety, implementing specialized programs directly with children is less desirable than designing programs that strengthen the support system around children. Children live and grow within a layered system of people, institutions, culture, and society that provide for their care and protection (Bronfenbrenner, 2000). Closest to them are family, extended family, and friends, then teachers, health care workers, and others, all existing within a particular political, economic, and sociocultural environment. The disaster is one event in a child's life within this system that provides identity, belonging, memory, history, and future and that attributes meaning to the disaster. Strengthening the system of services around children; engaging the political, sociocultural, and economic context for their protection and care; and supporting the people who raise and teach them are the most appropriate and effective avenues for agencies to provide support (e.g., Madrid & Grant, 2008; Salloum & Overstreet, 2008; Weems & Overstreet, 2008).

The Critical Need to Support Caregivers

Two important questions in mapping a response to children's psychosocial needs are (a) who will play a key role in the long-term care, support, and protection of children and (b) what will they need to be successful? Caregivers, even if also directly affected by the storm, are the most important resource for children's long-term recovery (Abramson & Garfield, 2006). Supporting caregivers in their own recovery, equipping them to talk with their children, and helping them to heal are essential to the success of psychosocial programs (Madrid & Grant, 2008). Thus, programs addressing the well-being and recovery of adult caregivers will best benefit children.

Indeed, caregiver well-being directly influences the well-being of children (see, e.g., chap. 2, this volume). Children take behavioral and emotional cues from the adults in their lives (Shaw, Espinel, & Shulz, 2007). They often mirror the distress of parents and are especially sensitive to postdisaster distress and conflict within the family. A recent review found that the presence of a psychiatric disorder in a parent was the best predictor of child psychopathology; the authors concluded that parents who were healthier, less irritable, and more supportive had healthier children (Norris, Byrne, Diaz, & Kaniasty, 2007).

School-based psychosocial programs can target teachers, school administrators, and parents—the people who form the key protective systems in children's lives and are therefore most critical for fostering children's resilience (Duncan & Arntson, 2004). As role models, teachers can have a profound influence on children's self-concept and skills for coping and adapting. Their ability to create a sensitive and structured classroom environment can provide the safety and routine children need to recover. However, they also need support to maintain consistent and reliable care and a positive surround for children in the postdisaster environment (Apfel & Simon, 1995). Teachers we recruited as facilitators for our psychosocial program for schoolchildren after Katrina told us, "We need this too!"

Klingman (1993) and others have noted the importance of preparing teachers for myriad postdisaster challenges and sustaining them as they provide encouragement and emotional support to their students. Teachers can first be assisted with processing their own experiences and responses. Programs can also help prepare them for the demands of a disrupted school environment, loss of their teaching materials, changes in students' academic performance, possible emotional and behavioral problems of children, and parents' responses possibly marked by greater intensity and urgency than before the disaster (Pynoos et al., 1995).

We cannot overemphasize the value of creating space after Katrina for teachers to come together for their own support and healing. School administrators and teachers often needed help carving out time and space for self- and team care and permission to consider their own recovery needs. With the intense focus on children's needs, we found that most teachers had not received any supportive intervention, even 3 to 4 months after the storm. In taking care of everyone else, they were rapidly burning out their own finite personal resources, causing strain in their relationships at home and school. Providing space for teachers to understand the recovery process, to share practical strategies for new life challenges (e.g., finding a place to do laundry), and to offer mutual support created a profound positive shift for caregivers. An unexpected benefit of post-Katrina workshops for teachers was the team building and culture of caring that emerged among colleagues, even those with long-standing conflicts before the storm.

Given their immense responsibilities, school administrators can also benefit from psychosocial support following a disaster. However, providing that support may be challenging. Their presence in workshops for teachers may hamper open dialogue and sharing "when the boss is around." Personal support or forums that bring school administrators in the area together are other options.

Another critical focus area of support programs for children is strengthening the capacity of families to provide nurturing care (Duncan & Arntson, 2004; UNICEF, 2002). Although schools are generally a place where parents come together—for children's sporting and other events, parent–teacher conferences, and so on—parents proved difficult to reach after Katrina. Like teachers, parents were pressed for time, searching for new employment and racing to rebuild homes before the next hurricane season. Many lacked transportation, having lost vehicles to flood and wind damage. Parent–teacher organizations noted dramatic decreases in attendance following Katrina. One innovative program hosted parent "university" days, providing lunch, child care, and other special activities for children while parents were engaged in practical informational sessions about insurance, access to services, self-care, recovery, and caring for their children's needs. Creative solutions such as these are necessary to engage caregivers in postdisaster settings and to help them circumvent barriers to receiving support.

Caring for Our Own Staff

In the rush to respond following a disaster, agencies must quickly create a team and design an intervention plan. Staff may be pulled together at a moment's notice, given a brief orientation, and deployed to the field, often to an unfamiliar locale with little time to understand the landscape, people, and culture. Psychosocial support staff may have widely varying expertise and training. The post-Katrina network of psychosocial programs included both seasoned mental health professionals (some with previous emergency experience) and relatively young or inexperienced personnel who lacked clinical backgrounds.

Appropriate staffing for psychosocial programs depends on the scope and type of intervention planned. But all staff, whether seasoned or new recruits—particularly those interfacing directly with the traumatic stories of affected children and adults—require functioning agency systems and support. Agency systems further require emergency team leaders with knowledge of agency policies, procedures, and culture who can facilitate clear communication and logistical support for safe and efficient operations (Antares Foundation, 2006). Also key are adequate briefing and training of technical field staff, clear job descriptions, and regular communication and support from headquarters (Antares Foundation, 2006). Persons working together for the first time in emergency settings must quickly build team trust and cohesiveness. Working in conditions of deprivation and under intense pressure, the potential for burnout and conflict among field staff is high. Managers play an important role in creating healthy working environments, promoting good relationships, and encouraging self-care among team members.

In particular, psychosocial support personnel encounter survivors' stories of grief and loss up close. Agencies must anticipate this exposure and plan for support and supervision of staff on the front lines. Staff members' ability to provide effective programs for healing and recovery depends on their own wellness. If psychosocial support personnel are not well—as individuals and as a team—it is nearly impossible to produce an effective and successful program for others.

CONCLUSION: THE TALE OF THE FOUR SANTAS

Reflecting on psychosocial support services following Hurricane Katrina, we have tried to recall the road map of experience that guides our work and to evaluate our efforts to help children in light of the unique context of this hurricane. Key lessons we learned, though perhaps not new to the field, deserve emphasis and reiteration. They reflect the practical wisdom of supporting systems and persons who care for children and of vigilance to ensure that aid programs do no harm. The lessons we have learned include the importance of

- fully understanding the context in which we work, including the culture, conditions for children and families before and after the hurricane, the meaning of the disaster to those affected, and the resources and strengths we can foster in the natural recovery of persons;
- respecting local knowledge and empowering communities in their own recovery;
- focusing interventions to support existing structures and persons critical to children's safety, well-being, and development to have the most sustainable and relevant impact;
- caring first for children's caregivers as the primary focus of programs "for children";
- attending to the real needs and capacities of program beneficiaries, being flexible, and offering a range of tools adaptable to different contexts and needs;
- remaining cautious in our approach so as not to overburden child caregivers or do harm; and
- coordinating among ourselves as aid agencies and appropriately managing and supporting our own staff so that we can provide support to others from a place of wellness.

In the race to be the first on the ground with the most visible program, aid agencies run the risk of pushing their own agenda at the expense of the priorities of those they intend to help. Agencies must be aware of the tension between quantity and quality in programming while they are under pressure to demonstrate scale and impact. Taking time to conduct meaningful assessment, build trust, and maintain flexibility alongside program beneficiaries in the evolving postemergency environment will help to minimize some of the pitfalls.

In that vein, we recall a dilemma one Mississippi school encountered on the last day before the Christmas holidays in 2005. Four Santa Clauses from different states had shown up to give gifts to the children, all very well intentioned. The school faced a complicated coordination effort to ensure that each Santa could operate out of sight of the others and shuffled children on a carefully timed schedule to one or the other. The trick was ensuring that the children did not see more than one Santa, or else they might stop believing! We should be careful to avoid being like the four Santas: well-intentioned but uncoordinated, ultimately overburdening those we wish to help and potentially making a short-term impact that only we will remember in the end.

In contrast, mental health professionals at a local clinic recounted a helpful intervention provided to them by a small group of visiting mental health professionals. The visitors sat in the staff break rooms of the badly damaged center and were present and available when local staff needed to vent, share, or just cry. They were simply there, and they listened. When requests came to provide information to the community, they joined with local colleagues, stood by them, and offered support—practical information and simple, key messages.

Stepping back from the race to respond, relief workers can take the time to be thoughtful, truly assess community needs, and offer support relevant to their priorities. By taking time to be with communities and the caregivers of children as they recover and rebuild, and by considering community-specific answers to recovery challenges for children, we as aid workers can better understand our roles and responsibilities. In this way, we can best honor the resourcefulness and bravery of the children and adults in disasters who teach us so much about life and hope.

REFERENCES

Abramson, D., & Garfield, R. (2006, April 17). *On the edge: Children and families displaced by Hurricanes Katrina and Rita face a looming medical and mental health crisis*. New York: National Center for Disaster Preparedness & Operation Assist, Columbia University Mailman School of Public Health. Retrieved November 8, 2008, from http://www.ncdp.mailman.columbia.edu/files/On%20the%20Edge%20 L-CAFH%20Final%20Report_Columbia%20University.pdf

Ager, A. (2002). Psychosocial needs in complex emergencies. *The Lancet, 360,* S43–S44.

Annie E. Casey Foundation. (2005). *2005 Kids Count data book*. Baltimore: Author.

Antares Foundation. (2006, July). *Managing stress in humanitarian workers: Guidelines for good practice* (2nd ed.). Amsterdam: Author. Retrieved November 8, 2008, from http://www.antaresfoundation.org/Guidelines.htm

Apfel, R., & Bennett, S. (1996). *Minefields in their hearts: The mental health of children in war and communal violence*. New Haven, CT: Yale University Press.

Apfel, R., & Simon, B. (1995). *On psychosocial interventions for children: Some minders and reminders*. New York: UNICEF.

Arntson, L., & Knudsen, C. (2004). *Field guide to psychosocial programs: Care and protection of children in emergencies*. Westport, CT: Save the Children Federation. Retrieved November 8, 2008, from http://www.savethechildren.org/ publications/technical-resources/emergencies-protection/PSYCHOSOCIAL_ CONTENTS_1.pdf

Barron, R. (1999). Psychological trauma and relief workers. In J. Leaning, S. Briggs, & L. C. Chen (Eds.), *Humanitarian crises: The medical and public health response* (pp. 143–178). Cambridge, MA: Harvard University Press.

Becker, D. (1995). The deficiency of the concept of posttraumatic stress disorder when dealing with victims of human rights violations. In R. J. Kleber, C. R. Figley, & B. P. R. Gersons (Eds.), *Beyond trauma: Cultural and social dynamics* (pp. 99–110). New York: Plenum Press.

Belter, R. W., & Shannon, M. P. (1993). Impact of natural disasters on children and families. In C. F. Saylor (Ed.), *Children and disasters* (pp. 85–103). New York: Plenum Press.

Berkman, L. F., & Kawachi, I. (Eds.). (2000). *Social epidemiology*. New York: Oxford University Press.

Bronfenbrenner, U. (2000). Ecological systems theory. In A. E. Kazdin (Ed.), *Encyclopedia of psychology* (Vol. 3, pp. 129–133). Washington, DC: American Psychological Association.

Christian Children's Fund. (2008). *Child-centered spaces*. Retrieved November 15, 2008, from http://christianchildrendsfund.org/content.aspx?id=171

Cooper, C., & Block, R. (2006). *Disaster: Hurricane Katrina and the failure of homeland security*. New York: Time Books.

Dawes, A., & Cairns, D. (1998). The Machel report: Dilemmas of cultural sensitivity & universal rights of children. *Peace & Conflict: Journal of Peace Psychology, 4,* 335–348.

Dean, K. L., Langley, A. K., Kataoka, S. H., Jaycox, L. H., Wong, M., & Stein, B. D. (2008). School-based disaster mental health services: Clinical, policy and community challenges. *Professional Psychology: Research and Practice, 39,* 52–57.

Dougherty, G. (1999). Cross-cultural counseling in disaster settings. *Australian Journal of Disaster and Trauma Studies, 2.* Retrieved November 8, 2008, from http://www.massey.ac.nz/~trauma/issues/1999-2/doherty.htm

Duncan, J., & Arntson, L. (2004). *Children in crisis: Good practices in evaluating psychosocial programming.* Retrieved November 8, 2008, from http://www.savethe children.org/publications/technical-resources/emergencies-protection/Good_ Practices_in_Evaluating_Psychosocial_Programming.pdf

Eyber, C. (2002, October). *Forced Migration Online thematic guide: Psychosocial issues.* Retrieved November 8, 2008, from http://www.forcedmigration.org/guides/ fmo004/

Garmezy, N., & Masten, A. (1990). The adaptation of children to a stressful world: Mastery of fear. In L. E. Arnold (Ed.), *Childhood stress* (pp. 459–473). New York: Wiley.

Hobfoll, S. E., Watson, P., Bell, C. C., Bryant, R. A., Brymer, M. J., Friedman, M. J., et al. (2007). Five essential elements of immediate and mid-term mass trauma intervention: Empirical evidence. *Psychiatry, 70,* 283–315.

Inter-Agency Standing Committee. (2007). *Guidelines on mental health and psychosocial support in emergency settings.* Geneva, Switzerland: Author.

Janoff-Bulman, R. (1992). *Shattered assumptions*. New York: Free Press.

Jaycox, L. H., Morse, L. K., Tanielian, T., & Stein, B. D. (2003). *How schools can help children recover from traumatic experiences: A tool-kit for supporting long-term recovery* (Tech. Rep. TR-413). Santa Monica, CA: Rand Corporation.

Klingman, A. (1993). School-based intervention following a disaster. In C. F. Saylor (Ed.), *Children and disasters* (pp. 187–210). New York: Plenum Press.

Kostelny, K., & Wessells, M. (2005). Psychosocial aid to children after the Dec 26 tsunami. *The Lancet, 366*, 2066–2067.

Krieger, N. (1994). Epidemiology and the web of causation: Has anyone seen the spider? *Social Science and Medicine, 39*, 887–903.

Lee, S. (Producer/Director). (2006). *When the levees broke: A requiem in four acts* [Motion picture]. New York: HBO Documentary Films.

Loughry, M., & Eyber, C. (2003). *Psychosocial concepts in humanitarian work with children: A review of the concepts and related literature*. Washington, DC: National Academies Press.

Lubit, R., & Eth, S. (2003). Children, disasters, and the September 11th World Trade Center attacks. In R. J. Ursano & A. E. Norwood (Eds.), *Trauma and disaster responses and management* (pp. 63–96). Washington, DC: American Psychiatric Publishing.

Madrid, P. A., & Grant, R. (2008). Meeting mental health needs following a natural disaster: Lessons from hurricane Katrina. *Professional Psychology: Research and Practice, 39*, 86–92.

Masozera, M., Bailey, M., & Kerchner, C. (2006). Distribution of impact of natural disasters across income groups: A case study of New Orleans. *Ecological Economics, 63*, 299–306.

Masten, A. S., & Coatsworth, J. D. (1998). The development of competence in favorable and unfavorable environments: Lessons from research on successful children. *American Psychologist, 53*, 205–220.

Norris, F. H., Byrne, C. M., Diaz, E., & Kaniasty, K. (2007, May 22). *Risk factors for adverse outcomes in natural and human-caused disasters: A review of the empirical literature*. Retrieved November 8, 2008, from http://www.ncptsd.va.gov/ncmain/ncdocs/fact_shts/fs_riskfactors.html

Norris, F. H., Friedman, M. J., & Watson, P. J. (2002). 60,000 disaster victims speak: Part II. Summary and implication of the disaster mental health research. *Psychiatry, 65*, 240–260.

Osofsky, J., & Osofsky, H. J. (2006, November). *Children and adolescents displaced by Katrina: In the eye of the storm—Resilience in Katrina's wake*. Program and abstracts from the 19th U.S. Psychiatric and Mental Health Congress, Session 25-8, New Orleans, LA.

Pina, A. A., Villalta, I. K., Ortiz, C. D., Gottschall, A. C., Costa, N. M., & Weems, C. F. (2008). Social support, perceived discrimination, and coping as predictors of posttraumatic stress reactions in youth survivors of Hurricane Katrina. *Journal of Clinical Child & Adolescent Psychology, 37*, 564–574.

Psychosocial Working Group. (2003). *Psychosocial intervention in complex emergencies: A conceptual framework*. Retrieved November 11, 2008, from http://forced migration.org/psychosocial/papers/pwgpapers.htm

Pynoos, R. S., Goenjian, A., & Steinberg, A. M. (1995). Strategies of disaster intervention for children and adolescents. In S. E. Hobfoll & M. W. de Vries (Eds.), *Extreme stress and communities: Impact and intervention* (pp. 445–471). New York: Kluwer Academic/Plenum Publishers.

Richman, N. (1996). *Principles of help for children involved in organized violence*. Westport, CT: Save the Children.

Salloum, A., & Overstreet, S. (2008). Evaluation of individual and group grief and trauma interventions for children post disaster. *Journal of Clinical Child & Adolescent Psychology, 37*, 495–507.

Salmon, K., & Bryant, R. A. (2002). Posttraumatic stress disorder in children: The influence of developmental factors. *Clinical Psychology Review, 22*, 163–188

Save the Children. (2006). *Facts of life for Gulf Coast children*. Retrieved November 11, 2008, from http://www.savethechildren.org/emergencies/us-gulf-coast-hurricanes/facts-of-life-for-gulf-coast-children.html

Save the Children. (2008). *Helping Katrina-affected children recover*. Retrieved November 11, 2008, from http://www.savethechildren.org/countries/usa/us-emergency-programs/hurricane-katrina-recovery/katrina-programs.html

Save the Children Alliance. (1996). *Promoting psychosocial well-being among children affected by armed conflict and displacement: Principles and approaches*. Retrieved November 8, 2008, from http://www.savethechildren.org/publications/technical-resources/emergencies-protection/psychsocwellbeing2.pdf

Scheeringa, M. S., & Zeanah, C. H. (2001). A relational perspective on PTSD in early childhood. *Journal of Traumatic Stress, 14*, 799–815.

Shaw, J. A., Espinel, Z., & Shultz, J. M. (2007). *Children, stress, trauma and disaster*. Tampa, FL: Disaster Life Support.

Shultz, J. M., Espinel, Z., Flynn, B., Cohen, R., & Hoffman, Y. (2007). *DEEP PREP: All-hazards behavioral health training*. Tampa, FL: Disaster Life Support.

Snider, L., Cabrejos, C., Huayllasco-Marquina, E., Trujillo, J. J., Avery, A., & Aguilar, H. A. (2004). Psychosocial assessment for victims of violence in Peru: The importance of local participation. *Journal of Biosocial Science, 36*, 389–400.

Snider, L., & Littrell, M. (2006). *Journey of hope: Tips for child caregivers in the aftermath of Katrina* [Handouts developed for Save the Children]. (Available from the author at lmsnider@gmail.com.)

Substance Abuse and Mental Health Services Administration, National Mental Health Information Center. (2008). *Disaster relief and crisis counseling: Psychosocial issues for children and adolescents in disasters*. Retrieved November 14, 2008, from http://mentalhealth.samhsa.gov/publications/allpubs/adm86-1070/chapter1.asp

Summerfield, D. (1996, April). *The impact of war and atrocity on civilian populations: Basic principles for NGO interventions and a critique of psychosocial trauma projects*.

London: Relief and Rehabilitation Network, Overseas Development Institute. Retrieved November 8, 2008, from http://www.reliefweb.int/rw/lib.nsf/db900sid/LGEL-5RRBDV/$file/hpn-atrocity-96.pdf?openelement

Time. (2005). *Hurricane Katrina: The storm that changed America.* New York: Author.

UNICEF. (2002). *Working with children in unstable situations: A guiding manual for psychosocial interventions.* New York: United Nations Children's Fund.

UNICEF. (2008). *School in a box.* Retrieved November 16, 2008, from http://www.unicef.org/supply/kits_flash/schoolinabox/

U.S. Department of Health and Human Services. (2004). *Mental health response to mass violence and terrorism: A training manual* (DHHS Publication No. SMA 3959). Rockville, MD: Center for Mental Health Services, Substance Abuse and Mental Health Services Administration.

Van Ommeren, M., Saxena, S., & Saraceno, B. (2005). Mental and social health during and after acute emergencies: Emerging consensus? *Bulletin of the World Health Organization, 83,* 71–76.

Vernberg, E. (1999). Children's responses to disaster: Family and systemic approaches. In R. Gist & B. Lubin (Eds.), *Response to disaster: Psychological, community, and ecological approaches* (pp. 193–210). Philadelphia: Taylor & Francis.

Weems, C., & Overstreet, S. (2008). Child and adolescent mental health research in the context of Hurricane Katrina: An ecological needs-based perspective and introduction to the special section. *Journal of Clinical Child & Adolescent Psychology, 37,* 487–494.

Weems, C., Watts, S., Marsee, M., Taylor, L., Costa, N., Cannon, M., et al. (2007). The psychosocial impact of Hurricane Katrina: Contextual differences in psychological symptoms, social support, and discrimination. *Behavior Research and Therapy, 45,* 2295–2306.

Wessells, M., & Monteiro, C. (2003). Healing, social integration and community mobilization for war-affected children: A view from Angola. In S. Krippner & T. M. McIntyre (Eds.), *The psychosocial impact of war trauma on civilians* (pp. 179–191). Westport, CT: Praeger.

World Health Organization. (1948). *Constitution of the World Health Organization, Geneva.* Retrieved January 30, 2008, from http://www.who.int/governance/eb/who_constitution_en.pdf

Wyman, P. A., Cowen, E. L., Work, W. C., & Kerley, J. H. (1993). The role of children's future expectations in self-esteem functioning and adjustment to life stress: A prospective study of urban at-risk children. *Development and Psychopathology, 5,* 649–661.

I

POSTDISASTER ADJUSTMENT OF FAMILIES AFFECTED BY HURRICANE KATRINA: RISKS, RESOURCES, AND FACTORS INFLUENCING ADAPTATION

1

2

THE CAREGIVER–CHILD RELATIONSHIP AND CHILDREN'S ADJUSTMENT FOLLOWING HURRICANE KATRINA

VIRGINIA GIL-RIVAS, RYAN P. KILMER, ANNADA W. HYPES, AND KATHERINE A. ROOF

During and following Hurricane Katrina, families and children in the central Gulf Coast experienced multiple losses, forced relocation, unsafe living conditions, violence, and deprivation (see Introduction and chaps. 1 and 10, this volume). Indeed, in the days and weeks following the floods, many children and their families were exposed to violence, did not know the whereabouts of their loved ones, and were unable to meet their basic needs (Osofsky, Osofsky, & Harris, 2007). Entire communities and social networks were severely damaged; fragmented by forced relocation; or, in some cases, even disappeared, limiting families' ability to rely on these sources to help them cope with Katrina's aftermath.

The process of reconstruction and recovery from the hurricane has been slow and plagued with difficulties. One year after the hurricane, about 100,000 survivors, many of them children, remained in trailers provided by the Federal Emergency Management Agency (FEMA) or other types of temporary housing (Save the Children, 2006). Families continued to face financial

Support for this research was provided by National Institute of Mental Health Grant 5R03MH78197 to Virginia Gil-Rivas and Ryan P. Kilmer.

difficulties, had difficulty meeting basic needs, and struggled to obtain needed government assistance (Save the Children, 2006; Ydstie, 2006).

Exposure to major stressful events frequently elicits posttraumatic stress symptoms (PTSS; Davis & Siegel, 2000; Dyregrov & Yule, 2006; Pfefferbaum, 1997), anxiety, depression (Goenjian et al., 1995; Pine & Cohen, 2002), and behavioral and academic difficulties (La Greca, Silverman, & Wasserstein, 1998) among children. After natural disasters, the prevalence rates of posttraumatic stress disorder (PTSD) in children range from 0% to 5%, and rates of PTSD following exposure to violence range from 27% to 33% (Salmon & Bryant, 2002).

Disasters and other major stressful events may not always lead to symptoms of clinical significance or contribute to long-lasting social and behavioral difficulties in children. Rather, as suggested by conceptual models of the impact of disasters on children (Silverman & La Greca, 2002), their impact is contingent on factors such as degree of event exposure, child characteristics (e.g., age, gender, mental health history), event-related secondary adversity (e.g., housing instability, access to resources), and postevent social context (e.g., support, sociocultural factors; Pine & Cohen, 2002; Silverman & La Greca, 2002).

The caregiving context, such as the quality of the caregiver–child relationship (e.g., perceived warmth, conflict) and parental symptomatology and functioning, carries great significance for children's development and adjustment. As such, pre- and postdisaster characteristics of the caregiving context may be of particular relevance for understanding children's adaptation following a disaster (see Introduction, this volume). This notion is congruent with the bioecological model (Bronfenbrenner, 1979, 2005), which considers adaptation to be the result of interactions between the individual and his or her environment. The next sections briefly summarize findings regarding the role of caregiver factors and individual characteristics on children's postdisaster adjustment.

ROLE OF CAREGIVERS IN CHILDREN'S ADJUSTMENT

In the aftermath of disasters, caregivers can provide a supportive, responsive environment in which children can process, understand, and attempt to incorporate traumatic experiences into their view of the world. Caregivers can guide interpretations, reframe, and perhaps even transform their child's sense of the event (Janoff-Bulman, 1992; Pynoos, Steinberg, & Wraith, 1995; Salmon & Bryant, 2002). Moreover, warm and supportive caregiving has been shown to foster positive adaptation in the face of stress (Klingman, 2001; Masten & Coatsworth, 1998). In the aftermath of disasters, caregivers are frequently encouraged to provide support, be respon-sive to their children's needs, talk and listen to them, and aid them in the processing of traumatic experiences (American Academy of Child and Adolescent Psychiatry, 2004; American Psychological Association, 2005; National Institute of Mental Health, 2006). However, despite the widely held belief that caregivers play a key role in children's adjustment, relatively few studies have examined the processes by which caregivers exert their influence.

Caregivers' ability to monitor their children, accurately interpret their behavior and emotions, and respond appropriately to their needs for care and support may be negatively influenced by their own trauma-related symptoms and psychological distress (Gil-Rivas, Silver, Holman, McIntosh, & Poulin, 2007; Kiliç, Özgüven, & Sayil, 2003; Masten, Best, & Garmezy, 1990; Scheeringa & Zeanah, 2001). This risk may be particularly high when both children and their caregivers were exposed to trauma, as both are attempting to manage their emotional response to the event. In addition, children's per-ceptions of their caregivers' distress in the aftermath of trauma and concerns about not upsetting them may further contribute to higher levels of child symptomatology (Dyregrov & Yule, 2006).

Prior findings regarding the relationship between caregivers' symptoms and children's adjustment following trauma exposure are mixed. Some studies have found that caregivers' PTSS, psychological distress, and depressive symp-toms are associated with higher levels of PTSS (Gil-Rivas et al., 2007; Korol, Green, & Gleser, 1999; McFarlane, 1987; Meiser-Steadman, Yule, Dalgleish, Smith, & Glucksman, 2006), internalizing (e.g., depressed mood, somati-zation), and externalizing (e.g., hyperactivity, aggression) symptoms among children exposed to trauma (Laor, Wolmer, & Cohen, 2001; P. Smith, Perrin, Yule, & Rabe-Hesketh, 2001), with caregivers' reexperiencing and avoidance symptoms appearing to have the most deleterious impact on child adjustment (Laor et al., 2001). In contrast, other studies have found that after account-ing for degree of trauma exposure, caregivers' symptoms are not significantly associated with children's PTSS (Koplewicz et al., 2002). In sum, it appears that caregivers' symptoms may negatively affect their parenting and elicit sim-ilar behaviors and emotional states in children (Kliewer, Fearnow, & Miller, 1996; Pfefferbaum, 1997).

Hurricane Katrina affected both children and their primary caregivers significantly and substantially altered their postevent contexts. As such, chil-dren's ability to successfully manage these events and caregivers' ability to maintain a warm and caring relationship and aid their children in this effort may have been severely compromised. Characteristics of the child, degree of event exposure, and postdisaster adversity are also important factors to con-sider in understanding children's adjustment following this disaster.

FACTORS THAT INFLUENCE THE IMPACT OF DISASTERS

A substantial body of work has documented that aspects of the trauma experience, such as degree of event exposure, physical harm, material loss, and the amount of violence involved are significant predictors of the severity of PTSS and psychological distress among youths (Pfefferbaum, 1997; Silverman & La Greca, 2002). For example, in a study of elementary school children exposed to Hurricane Andrew (which made landfall in South Florida in 1992), higher levels of injury to self or others, damage to one's home, and disruption of daily activities explained about 35% of the variance in children's PTSS 3 months after the hurricane (Vernberg, La Greca, Silverman, & Prinstein, 1996). Similarly, a study of children exposed to Hurricane Floyd (which occurred on the East Coast of the United States in 1999) found that children whose homes were flooded had significantly higher PTSS 6 months later compared with those whose homes were not flooded (Russoniello et al., 2002). Children's subjective appraisal also relates to their symptomatology, such that higher event-related perceived threat to self and others is predictive of greater PTSS and depressive symptomatology (Goenjian et al., 2001; Roussos et al., 2005; Thienkrua et al., 2006). Moreover, exposure to multiple and ongoing risk conditions (e.g., unstable housing, financial difficulties) in the aftermath of disasters may increase the probability of long-term negative effects associated with trauma exposure (Laor et al., 2001).

Several demographic characteristics, such as age, gender, and ethnic background, as well as predisaster mental health and trauma exposure, have been shown to be associated with child adjustment following a disaster. Children's cognitive, emotional, and social development influences their appraisal of the event, their emotional response, and their efforts to cope with these experiences (Salmon & Bryant, 2002). For example, compared with older children, younger children typically report fewer PTSS (Copeland, Keeler, Angold, & Costello, 2007). The evidence regarding the role of gender in postdisaster adjustment is mixed. Some studies suggest that girls are more vulnerable to trauma than boys (Goenjian et al., 1995; Green et al., 1991; Weems et al., 2007), whereas others have not found gender differences in symptom severity (La Greca, Silverman, Vernberg, & Prinstein, 1996; Laor et al., 2001; Silva et al., 2000). Few studies have examined ethnic differences in child adjustment after a disaster. Preliminary findings suggest that Hispanic and African American children report significantly higher levels of PTSS than White children (La Greca et al., 1996; March, Amaya-Jackson, Terry, & Constanzo, 1997). In addition to children's demographic characteristics, predisaster factors such as a history of trauma exposure, adverse family conditions (Copeland et al., 2007), mental health difficulties (e.g., PTSD, anxiety, depression), anxiety and negative affect (Weems et al., 2007), learning disabilities (La Greca et al., 1998), and academic problems (Yule, 1994) are associated with higher symptom levels and functional impairment in the aftermath of disasters (see, e.g., Asarnow et al., 1999; La Greca et al., 1998).

THE PRESENT STUDY

We sought to examine the contribution of child characteristics, caregiver symptomatology, and the quality of the caregiver–child relationship to children's PTSS following Hurricane Katrina. Specifically, we expected that

1. greater hurricane exposure, exposure to violence, and secondary adversity would be associated with higher levels of children's PTSS;
2. children with a history of prior trauma exposure and mental and behavioral difficulties would report higher levels of PTSS;
3. caregivers' psychological distress (i.e., depression and anxiety) and trauma-related symptoms, particularly reexperiencing and avoidance symptoms, would be associated with higher levels of PTSS, even after accounting for child exposure to hurricane and prior trauma; and
4. higher levels of perceived parental warmth and acceptance would be associated with lower levels of PTSS, even after accounting for child exposure to hurricane and prior trauma. In contrast, we hypothesized that greater caregiver–child conflict would be associated with higher PTSS.

METHOD

Study Design

Face-to-face interviews were conducted in Louisiana (i.e., Baton Rouge and New Orleans) and Mississippi with 68 children ages 7 to 10 years and their primary caregiver. The interviews were conducted approximately 1 year following Hurricane Katrina ($M = 12.4$ months, $SD = 3.4$). Participants were recruited via flyers that were distributed at elementary schools in the East Baton Rouge Parish and Baker School Systems, FEMA-operated trailer parks, community-based organizations (i.e., churches, boys and girls clubs), and service providers and via participant referral. Trained research assistants conducted the interviews at participants' homes or at a location convenient to caregivers. Participants were compensated with gift cards for their participation and that of their child. This study was approved by the institutional review boards of the University of North Carolina at Charlotte and the Louisiana State University.

Measures

Descriptions of the measures administered in this study are provided in the following sections.

Caregiver-Completed Measures

Demographic Characteristics. Caregivers provided information regarding their age, gender, ethnic background, marital status, employment, annual income, and housing status. In addition, caregivers provided information regarding their child's age, grade, and ethnicity.

Caregiver Hurricane Exposure. Caregivers completed a 12-item check-list adapted from previous disaster research (Silver, Holman, McIntosh, Poulin, & Gil-Rivas, 2002) assessing the number of hurricane-related events they experienced. A summary score of number of hurricane-related events experienced was computed.

Caregiver Hurricane-Related Violence and Secondary Adversity. A three-item scale was used to assess caregivers' violence exposure in the aftermath of Hurricane Katrina. In addition, caregivers completed a three-item scale assessing the degree to which they experienced adversity (e.g., lost job, discrimination) following the hurricane. Summary scores of total number of violence and secondary adversity items endorsed were created.

Caregiver Posttraumatic Stress Symptoms. Caregivers completed the 17-item PTSD Checklist—Civilian (PCL; Weathers, Litz, Herman, Huska, & Keane, 1993) indicating how bothered they were by symptoms related to Hurricane Katrina during the previous 7 days. Participants reported their reexperiencing, avoidance, and arousal using a scale ranging from $0 = not\ at\ all$ to $3 = extremely$. A total score was computed ($\alpha = .93$). Following scoring recommendations by M. Y. Smith, Redd, DuHamel, Vickberg, and Ricketts (1999), scores of 50 and above were considered to indicate the presence of probable PTSD. In addition, we assessed the number of clinically significant PTSS following scoring recommendations by Blanchard, Jones-Alexander, Buckley, and Forneris (1996). Specifically, item responses of 3 (*quite a bit*) to 5 (*extremely*) were coded as indicating the presence of that symptom. Variables representing the total number of positive reexperiencing, arousal, and avoidance symptoms and the overall number of symptoms were created to examine their contribution to children's PTSS.

Caregiver Distress. The Hopkins Symptom Checklist—25 (Derogatis, Lipman, Rickels, Uhlenhuth, & Covi, 1974) was used to assess symptoms of depression, anxiety, and somatization. Caregivers indicated how frequently they had experienced symptoms during the past week using a scale ranging from 0 (*not at all*) to 3 (*extremely*). A mean score was computed ($\alpha = .96$).

Child Lifetime Trauma Exposure. The parent version of the University of California at Los Angeles (UCLA) Posttraumatic Stress Disorder Reaction Index Revised—1 (UCLA–PTSD RI–1; Pynoos, Rodriguez, Steinberg, Stuber, & Frederick, 1998) assessed criteria of the *Diagnostic and Statistical Manual of Mental Disorders* (4th ed., *DSM–IV*; American Psychiatric Association [APA], 1994) for objective lifetime exposure to multiple traumatic events (e.g., disasters, serious accidents, violence, violent death of a loved one, physical abuse). A summary score of reported lifetime events was created.

Lifetime History of Mental and Behavioral Difficulties. Caregivers indicated if their child had ever been diagnosed by a health or mental health professional with any of a number of learning, social–emotional, or behavioral concerns, such as anxiety disorders, depression, PTSD, and attention-deficit/hyperactivity disorder/attention-deficit disorder (ADHD/ADD). A dichotomous variable indicating a lifetime history of any of the diagnoses was created. In addition, caregivers completed five items assessing children's behavioral problems in school (e.g., detention, expulsion) during the year prior to Katrina, indicating if their child had engaged in the listed behavior more than three times during the past year. A summary score was created.

Child-Completed Measures

Hurricane-Related Exposure. Part I of the child version of the UCLA–PTSD RI–1 (Pynoos et al., 1998) assessed *DSM–IV* PTSD criteria (APA, 1994) for trauma exposure. Specifically, children responded to seven items assessing objective exposure (criterion A1, "the person experienced, witnessed, or was confronted with an event or events that involve actual or threatened death or serious injury; or threat to the physical integrity of himself or herself or others"; APA, 1994, p. 427), five items assessing subjective response (criterion A2, a response to the event that involves "intense fear, helplessness, or horror"; APA, 1994, p. 428), and one item assessing peritraumatic dissociation (i.e., felt like what was happening was not real). A summary score of items endorsed was created. In addition, children completed an eight-item checklist that parallels in content the Hurricane-Related Traumatic Experiences scale (La Greca et al., 1996; Vernberg et al., 1996) to assess children's exposure to Katrina. A total score of events reported was computed.

Exposure to Violence and Secondary Adversity. Children completed a checklist assessing hurricane-related violence exposure (three items) and secondary adversity (e.g., not having enough food or water; five items). A total score of events reported was computed.

Child Posttraumatic Stress Symptoms. The UCLA–PTSD RI–1 (Pynoos et al., 1998) was used to assess PTSS related to Hurricane Katrina. This instrument assesses the following *DSM–IV* symptoms: reexperiencing (e.g., intrusive memories, nightmares; five items), arousal (e.g., irritability, sleep difficulties, concentration problems; five items), and avoidance (e.g., avoiding people, activities, or feelings, detachment; seven items). In addition, the scale includes two items assessing other symptoms of clinical significance (i.e., fears of recurrence and trauma-related guilt). Children reported how much of the time they had experienced these symptoms during the past month using a scale ranging from 0 (*none*) to 4 (*most of the time*). Possible scores in this scale range from 0 to 68; following the authors' suggestions (Steinberg, Brymer, Decker, & Pynoos, 2004), a total score of 38 or greater on the scale was considered to indicate the presence of probable PTSD. The UCLA–PTSD RI–1 has demonstrated good internal consistency and test–retest reliability (Roussos et al., 2005); Cronbach's alpha for this sample was .88. Children's total score on the UCLA–PTSD RI–1 was the primary outcome examined in this study.

To gain a better understanding of children's PTSS, variables reflecting positive symptoms for each subscale were created in accord with recommendations by the measure's developers (Rodriguez, Steinberg, Saltzman, & Pynoos, 2001). Specifically, item responses of "much of the time" and "most of the time" were coded as 1 (*present*), and all others were coded as 0 (*not present*). Variables reflecting total number of positive symptoms endorsed from each subscale were created.

Caregiver Warmth and Acceptance. Children completed a 10-item version of a scale used in previous research to assess children's perceptions of caregiver warmth and acceptance (e.g., "My caregiver really understands me," "My caregiver enjoys spending time with me"; Greenberger & Chen, 1996; Greenberger, Chen, & Beam, 1998). Children responded using a scale ranging from 1 (*not at all true*) to 4 (*very true*), and a mean score was created; Cronbach's alpha was .68.

Caregiver–Child Conflict. The frequency of caregiver–child disagreements during the past month was assessed with a nine-item scale used in previous research (Greenberger & Chen, 1996). The scale was modified to assess age-appropriate disagreements regarding schoolwork, friends, family relationships, chores, routines, physical appearance, and obedience. Children responded regarding the frequency of disagreements using a scale ranging from 1 (*never*) to 4 (*almost every day*); the scale demonstrated adequate reliability ($\alpha = .71$). A mean score was created.

Perceived Caregiver Distress and Unavailability. Children responded to three questions used in previous research (Gil-Rivas, Holman, & Silver, 2004) to assess their perceptions of their caregiver's hurricane-related distress, willingness to talk about the hurricane and what happened, and the extent to which their caregiver had been too upset to talk about the hurricane in the past month. Children responded using a scale ranging from 0 (*never*) to 3 (*almost every day*). Correlations among these items ranged from .33 to .46.

Plan of Analysis

Variables were screened for deviations from normality. Correlation analyses were conducted to examine associations among study variables. Hierarchical multiple regression analyses examined the contribution of child and caregiver variables to children's PTSS. Variables were entered into the model in the following order: (1) child demographic characteristics; (2) child prehurricane functioning (i.e., lifetime mental health diagnosis, behavioral problems in school) and lifetime trauma exposure; (3) child hurricane exposure, hurricane-related violence exposure, and secondary adversity; (4) caregiver distress, PTSS (intrusion, arousal, and avoidance), and physical and emotional functioning; and (5) perceived caregiver warmth and acceptance, caregiver–child conflict, and perceived caregiver distress and availability. Steps 4 and 5 emphasize the caregiving context. Variables were screened for their association with children's PTSS using regression analyses, adjusting for children's hurricane exposure; nonsignificant variables ($p > .05$) were not included in the final model.

RESULTS

The children's average age was 8.3 years ($SD = 1.1$), and about half were female (54.4%). In terms of race or ethnicity, 78.0% were African American, 14.7% were White, and 7.3% were from other backgrounds. The majority of caregivers were female (86.8%), and their average age was 38.1 years ($SD = 9.5$); 80.9% of the caregivers were biological parents of the participating child, 10.3% were grandparents, 5.9% were step- or adopted parents, and 2.9% were other family members. Regarding education level, 25.0% of the caregivers had less than a high school education, 38.2% had a high school or equivalency diploma, 5.9% had some vocational or technical training, 16.2% had some college, 8.8% had a college degree, and 5.9% held a graduate degree. A little over one third (36.7%) of the caregivers were married or living as married, 27.9% were divorced or separated, and 35.4% were single. The vast majority (95.6%) of the families had to evacuate, and 89.7% became homeless as a result of the hurricane. On average, the families had moved 3.1 times ($SD = 2.1$, range = 0–11) in the year following Katrina. At the time of the interviews, 38.2% of the participants were living in FEMA trailers, 16.2% in their own house or apartment, 36.8% in a rented apartment or house, 5.9% with relatives, and 3.0% in other living arrangements. More than two thirds

(67.6%) of the caregivers were unemployed; 57.4% reported an annual household income of less than $9,999, 16.2% had an income of $10,000 to $19,999, 8.8% reported an income of $20,000 to $29,999, and 17.6% had an income of $30,000 or more (range ≤ $9,999 to ≥ $80,000).

Children's Lifetime Trauma Exposure and Prehurricane Adjustment

Nearly three quarters (73.5%) of the caregivers reported that their child had experienced at least one potentially traumatic event prior to Hurricane Katrina ($M = 1.9$, $SD = 1.8$). The events most frequently reported were community violence (39.7%), violent death of a loved one (33.3%), domestic violence (23.5%), and painful medical treatment (23.5%). At the time of the interviews, about one third (33.8%) of the children had been diagnosed with a psychiatric or behavioral disorder. The most commonly reported diagnoses were ADHD/ADD (14.7%), learning disability (13.2%), depression (8.8%), and behavioral disorders (8.8%). In the year before the hurricane, 18.6% of the children exhibited problem behaviors in school (e.g., given detention, talked to seriously by school personnel) three or more times.

Children's Hurricane-Related Exposure and Symptoms

A substantial number of children endorsed experiencing at least one hurricane-related traumatic event (86.8%), and 83.8% endorsed at least one item indicating subjective distress associated with the hurricane on the UCLA–PTSD RI–1. More than half (61.8%) reported that at the time of the hurricane, they were scared that they would die, and 58.8% were scared that they would be hurt badly. For 63.2% of the children, Hurricane Katrina was one of the "most scary" events they had ever experienced. About half (57.4%) indicated that they felt confused during the hurricane, and 43.3% reported peritraumatic dissociation (i.e., felt like what was happening was not real). On average, the children reported that they experienced 3.6 ($SD = 4.0$) hurricane-related events; 32.4% were exposed to violence, and 89.7% reported hurricane-related secondary adversity. Table 2.1 summarizes children's self-reported hurricane-related experiences.

The average UCLA–PTSD RI–1 total score for children's PTSS was 26.5 ($SD = 15.0$, range $= 0$–64), and 21.0% obtained a score of 38 or greater, suggesting a probable PTSD diagnosis. Boys and girls did not significantly differ in the severity of PTSS; the mean total score on the UCLA–PTSD RI–1 was 24.6 ($SD = 14.4$) for boys and 28.0 ($SD = 15.5$) for girls. However, African American children, on average, obtained higher total PTSS scores than those from other backgrounds (28.4 vs. 19.7); $F(1, 65) = 4.14$, $p < .05$. With regard

TABLE 2.1
Child-Reported Hurricane Exposure and Secondary Adversity (*N* = 68)

Experience	%
Hurricane exposure	
Was in a home badly damaged by the hurricane	70.6
Was injured or hurt	7.4
Witnessed a family member getting hurt	11.8
Saw a dead body	11.8
A pet was hurt or died	22.4
Lost favorite toys or things	76.5
Lost friends	67.6
Hurricane-related violence exposure	
Was hit, punched, or kicked very hard	4.4
Witnessed a family member getting hit, punched, or kicked	14.7
Witnessed someone being beaten up, shot, or threatened	27.9
Secondary adversity	
Family did not have enough food or water	50.0
Was separated from family	39.7
Had to live away from parents for a week or more	14.7
Attended a new school because of hurricane	85.3

to responses to each of the items suggesting the presence of potentially clinically significant symptoms, nearly all (94.0%) children reported experiencing at least one positive PTSS (item responses of "much" to "most of the time") in the past month. Specifically, 92.5% of the children reported at least one positive symptom, with 91.0% reporting at least one arousal symptom, 83.3% at least one avoidance symptom, and 74.6% at least one reexperiencing symptom; 76.5% reported positive symptoms in all of these categories. Table 2.2 presents descriptive statistics for children's total and subscale positive PTSS.

Caregivers' Hurricane-Related Exposure and Symptoms

Caregivers were exposed to an average of 6.7 hurricane-related events (*SD* = 1.9), and 67.6% reported that they felt their life or the life of a loved one was threatened quite a bit or a great deal by Hurricane Katrina. About one fourth (26.5%) of the caregivers reported hurricane-related violence exposure, and 97.1% reported experiencing secondary adversity (e.g., caregiver or other family member lost his or her job) in the aftermath of Katrina. A summary of caregivers' hurricane-related experiences is presented in Table 2.3.

TABLE 2.2
Child and Caregiver Positive Posttraumatic Stress Symptoms

Positive posttraumatic stress symptom	Child[a]		Caregiver[b]	
	M (SD)	Range	M (SD)	< Range
Reexperiencing	1.7 (1.5)	0–5	2.2 (1.8)	0–5
Arousal	1.6 (1.3)	0–4	2.3 (1.9)	0–7
Avoidance	2.0 (1.9)	0–6	2.6 (2.0)	0–5
Total	5.3 (4.1)	0–15	7.0 (5.2)	0–17

[a]Child-reported scores on the child version of the University of California at Los Angeles Posttraumatic Stress Disorder Reaction Index Revised (Pynoos et al., 1998); item responses of "much of the time" to "most of the time" indicate the presence of a symptom. [b]Caregiver-reported scores on the PTSD Checklist (Weathers, Litz, Herman, Huska, & Keane, 1993); item responses of "quite a bit" to "extremely" indicate the presence of a symptom.

TABLE 2.3
Caregiver-Reported Hurricane Exposure and Secondary Adversity (N = 68)

Experience	%
Hurricane exposure	
Was in a community hit by Hurricane Katrina	98.5
Was in a community hit by Hurricane Rita	48.5
Was in a community that was flooded	83.8
Had to evacuate home or neighborhood	95.6
Was injured during one of the hurricanes	14.7
Someone close was injured during one of the hurricanes	30.9
Someone close died or is missing and presumed dead	36.8
Was exposed to chemicals or contaminated water	36.8
A pet was lost or killed	25.4
Lost property because of the hurricanes	92.6
Someone close lost property because of the hurricanes	91.0
Witnessed someone being injured or killed	20.6
Hurricane-related violence exposure	
Was robbed or assaulted	8.8
Someone close was robbed or assaulted	7.4
Witnessed someone being robbed or assaulted	11.8
Secondary adversity	
Lost job as a result of the hurricanes	58.8
Was discriminated against by those providing help	36.4
Experienced discrimination in community or neighborhood	27.3

Caregiver Posttraumatic Stress Symptoms and Psychological Distress

The majority (96.0%) of caregivers reported at least one positive hurricane-related PTSS (item response of "quite a bit" to "extremely"). The average caregiver total PTSS score was 44.5 ($SD = 18.0$), and 42.6% of caregivers had a score $\geq$ 50, suggesting a probable PTSD diagnosis. Table 2.2 presents descriptive statistics for caregivers' total and subscale positive PTSS. In addition, at the time of the interview, caregivers reported low levels of distress ($M = 1.1, SD = 0.8$).

Caregiver–Child Relationship

Overall, children perceived their caregivers as warm and accepting ($M = 3.3, SD = 0.5$) and reported experiencing conflict with their caregiver once or twice per month ($M = 2.0, SD = 0.6$). On average, children perceived their caregiver as having been moderately upset about the hurricane in the past month ($M = 1.8, SD = 1.2$), with more than half of the children (61.3%) indicating that their caregiver had been somewhat upset or very upset. Thirty percent of the children reported that they thought their caregiver had been too upset to talk about the hurricane several times or almost every day ($M = 1.0$, $SD = 1.2$) during the past month. In addition, 29.0% of youngsters indicated that several times or almost every day in the past month they felt that their caregiver did not want to talk to them about the hurricane ($M = 0.9, SD = 1.2$).

Associations Among Key Variables

Contrary to expectations, children's prehurricane trauma exposure, behavioral difficulties in school, and history of a mental health diagnosis by a professional were not significantly associated with their PTSS. As expected, children's self-reported hurricane exposure, hurricane-related violence, and secondary adversity were positively associated with their PTSS. Consistent with expectations, caregivers' self-reported psychological distress and hurricane-related reexperiencing and avoidance symptoms were associated with higher levels of PTSS among children. In contrast, caregivers' arousal symptoms were not significantly associated with children's symptomatology. Several aspects of the caregiver–child relationship assessed in this study were significantly associated with children's PTSS. Specifically, higher levels of caregiver–child conflict, children's perceptions of caregivers' hurricane-related distress, caregiver unavailability to talk about the hurricane, and the extent to which children perceived their caregivers as too upset to talk were associated with higher levels of symptoms. In contrast, children's perception of caregiver warmth and acceptance was not significantly associated with their PTSS. Table 2.4 summarizes the associations among key variables of interest.

TABLE 2.4
Associations Among Key Variables

Variable	1	2	3	4	5	6	7	8	9	10	11	12	13
1. Child PTSS	—												
2. Child hurricane exposure	.51***	—											
3. Child hurricane-related violence	.37**	.36**	—										
4. Child secondary adversity	.27*	.53***	.35**	—									
5. Caregiver distress[a]	.25*	.24*	.16	.14	—								
6. Caregiver reexperiencing symptoms[a]	.42***	.32**	.29*	.27*	.66***	—							
7. Caregiver arousal symptoms[a]	.20	.25*	.25*	.20	.80***	.70***	—						
8. Caregiver avoidance symptoms[a]	.35**	.32**	.17	.21†	.80***	.70***	.78***	—					
9. Perceived caregiver warmth and acceptance	.01	-.08	-.11	-.11	-.08	.03	-.06	-.05	—				
10. Caregiver–child conflict	.30*	.19	.12	.35**	.22†	.18	.29*	.25*	-.30*	—			
11. Perceived caregiver hurricane-related distress	.41**	.55***	-.01	.09	.16	.19	.05	.16	-.06	.26*	—		
12. Caregiver did not want to talk about hurricane	.38**	.25*	.01	-.01	-.02	.03	-.03	.13	-.05	.03	.35**	—	
13. Caregiver was too upset to talk about hurricane	.53***	.44**	.22†	.14	.14	.23†	.14	.15	.04	.12	.46***	.33**	—

Note. Ns range from 61 to 68. PTSS = posttraumatic stress symptoms.
[a]Caregiver reported.
†$p < .10$. *$p < .05$. **$p < .01$. ***$p < .001$.

Regression Model Predicting Children's Posttraumatic Stress Symptoms

To develop the most parsimonious regression model, we conducted preliminary analyses adjusting for hurricane exposure. Variables that did not significantly ($p > .05$) contribute to explaining the variability in children's PTSS were not included in the final model (see Table 2.5). Higher levels of hurricane exposure were associated with greater PTSS; in contrast, exposure to hurricane-related violence and secondary adversity did not significantly contribute to children's symptomatology. Consistent with expectations, self-reported caregiver reexperiencing symptoms and children's perceptions of their caregiver's distress and unavailability to talk about the hurricane were associated with higher levels of PTSS. Contrary to expectations, the frequency of caregiver–child conflict was not significantly associated with children's symptom levels. It is important to note that the inclusion of the variables reflecting caregiver symptoms and caregiver–child interactions reduced the size of the regression coefficient for hurricane exposure in half, highlighting the importance of caregivers in predicting children's PTSS following Hurricane Katrina.

DISCUSSION

This study examined the contribution of caregiver symptoms and aspects of the caregiver–child relationship to children's PTSS nearly 1 year after Hurricane Katrina. The results suggest that caregivers play an important role in their children's adjustment in the aftermath of disasters and highlight

TABLE 2.5
Summary of Hierarchical Regression Analyses Predicting
Children's Posttraumatic Stress Symptoms

Variable	Model 1			Model 2		
	B	SE B	β	B	SE B	β
Hurricane exposure	4.3	0.94	0.51***	2.0	0.94	0.24*
Caregiver reexperiencing symptoms	—	—	—	1.9	0.86	0.23*
Caregiver did not want to talk about hurricane[a]	—	—	—	2.8	1.33	0.22*
Caregiver was too upset to talk about hurricane[a]	—	—	—	3.5	1.41	0.28*
Caregiver–child conflict[a]	—	—	—	3.8	2.45	0.13

Note. Nonsignificant variables ($p > .05$) were not included in this final model. Model 1 adjusted $R^2 = .25$, $p < .001$; Model 2 adjusted $R^2 = .44$, $p < .001$. Dashes indicate that the variable was not included in the model.
[a]Child reported.
*$p < .05$. ***$p < .001$.

the importance of addressing caregivers' needs in efforts aimed at promoting children's well-being following a disaster.

The majority of the caregivers and children in this sample felt that their life or the lives of others were in danger as a result of the hurricane. In fact, for many children, this was one of the scariest experiences in their lives. Children reported exposure to multiple hurricane-related events, with nearly one quarter reporting hurricane-related violence exposure, and the majority of them became homeless in the aftermath of Katrina. Consistent with the findings on the impact of other hurricanes (Russoniello et al., 2002; Vernberg et al., 1996), the degree of exposure was the strongest predictor of children's PTSS.

One year after Hurricane Katrina, 21.0% of the children obtained PTSS scores suggesting the presence of a probable PTSD diagnosis, and nearly all reported experiencing at least one posttraumatic stress symptom "much" or "most" of the time during the previous month. Though higher in an absolute sense, these findings are similar to those reported 10 months following Hurricane Andrew (La Greca et al., 1996); in that earlier study, 12.5% of participants reported severe to very severe levels of PTSS, and 18.0% reported significant levels of all three major PTSD symptom clusters (i.e., reexperiencing, avoidance–numbing, and arousal). Furthermore, in the present sample, more than one third of caregivers reported PTSS of clinical significance. The slow reconstruction efforts, the ongoing difficulties these families faced, the loss of social networks, and the lack of clarity regarding the resolution of many of their experienced difficulties (see, e.g., Dewan, 2006) may have contributed to the long-term negative impact of the hurricane on children and families. Moreover, many hurricane survivors felt betrayed and abandoned by local, state, and federal agencies in the days and weeks following the hurricane (Varney, 2006). These findings suggest that children and families may benefit from psychosocial interventions even months following exposure to major traumatic events.

Caregiver-related variables accounted for 19.0% of the variance in children's PTSS, over and above children's hurricane-related exposure. For instance, caregivers' hurricane-related reexperiencing symptoms were associated with higher levels of PTSS among children. It is possible that the negative emotions associated with these symptoms may interfere with caregivers' ability to identify and accurately interpret their children's behaviors and emotions and respond to their needs. Moreover, children may perceive their caregivers' struggles, and these symptoms may foster a family environment characterized by a sense of ongoing fear and threat that may serve to maintain children's posttraumatic stress symptomatology. In addition, we found that children's perceptions that their caregiver did not want to talk about the hurricane and that their caregiver was too upset to talk were associated with greater PTSS levels. Contrary to expectations, caregivers' psychological distress, hurricane-related avoidance and arousal symptoms, and caregiver–child conflict were not significantly associated with children's PTSS. Future studies may benefit from longitudinal designs and the development of multi-item measures that may further elucidate the role of these factors in predicting children's adjustment following a disaster.

This study expands our understanding of caregiver influences on children's adjustment following a major disaster. Nonetheless, it is important to note several limitations. The cross-sectional nature of the data and our reliance on retrospective reports of hurricane exposure, hurricane-related violence, and secondary adversity limit our ability to make causal inferences about the contribution of these factors to children's adjustment. In addition, the characteristics of this sample (i.e., evacuees and residents of FEMA-provided housing) and its small size limit our ability to generalize these findings to all children affected by Hurricane Katrina. Despite these limitations, ours is one of the few studies to assess children–caregiver dyads in the aftermath of a disaster, and it represents an important step toward understanding caregivers' contributions to children's adjustment.

LESSONS LEARNED AND ACTIONABLE RECOMMENDATIONS

Our study suggests that caregivers play a key role in children's post-disaster adjustment. As one case in point, caregivers' PTSS may interfere with their parenting abilities and their efforts to help their children successfully adjust in the aftermath of disasters. These findings suggest that services aimed at promoting children's well-being must include interventions targeting the needs of caregivers. Indeed, Norris (n.d.) suggested that addressing the needs of caregivers after a disaster may be among the most successful approaches to providing necessary care and support to their children.

The present findings, which underscore the importance of interactions between caregiver and child, also suggest potential strategies for well-targeted intervention. That is, beyond the child- or caregiver-specific interventions typically employed, it may be of great benefit to implement dyadic models. Such parent–child approaches have been used successfully with other populations (e.g., Lieberman, 1992; Toth, Rogosch, Manly, & Cicchetti, 2006), including those who have experienced trauma (e.g., Toth, Maughan, Manly, Spagnola, & Cicchetti, 2002). In that vein, Salmon and Bryant (2002) recommended parental involvement in some cases, noting that treatment goals can include helping caregivers provide appropriate support for their children and aiding them in fostering adaptive coping strategies (e.g., Gil-Rivas et al., 2004; Kliewer et al., 1996). Whatever the specific approach used, the available data suggest that outreach, prevention, and clinical approaches focusing on caregivers and caregiver–child dyads may be particularly fruitful in both reducing PTSS following trauma and facilitating positive postdisaster adjustment.

REFERENCES

American Academy of Child and Adolescent Psychiatry. (2004). *Helping children after a disaster* [Fact sheet]. Retrieved November 23, 2007, from http://aacap.org/page.ww?name=Helping+Children+After+a+Disaster&section=Facts+for+Families

American Psychiatric Association. (1994). *Diagnostic and statistical manual of mental disorders* (4th ed.). Washington, DC: Author.

American Psychological Association. (2005). *Tornadoes, hurricanes and children*. Retrieved November 23, 2007, from http://www.apahelpcenter.org/articles/article.php?id=109

Asarnow, J., Glynn, S., Pynoos, R. S., Nahum, J., Guthrie, D., Cantwell, D. P., et al. (1999). When the earth stops shaking: Earthquake sequelae among children diagnosed for pre-earthquake psychopathology. *Journal of the American Academy of Child & Adolescent Psychiatry, 38,* 1016–1023.

Blanchard, E. B., Jones-Alexander, J., Buckley, T. C., & Forneris, C. A. (1996). Psychometric properties of the PTSD Checklist (PCL). *Behaviour Research and Therapy, 34,* 669–673.

Bronfenbrenner, U. (1979). *The ecology of human development: Experiments by nature and design*. Cambridge, MA: Harvard University Press.

Bronfenbrenner, U. (Ed.). (2005). *Making human beings human: Bioecological perspectives on human development*. Thousand Oaks, CA: Sage.

Copeland, W. E., Keeler, G., Angold, A., & Costello, E. J. (2007). Traumatic events and posttraumatic stress in childhood. *Archives of General Psychiatry, 64,* 577–584.

Davis, L., & Siegel, L. J. (2000). Posttraumatic stress disorder in children and adolescents: A review and analysis. *Clinical Child and Family Psychology Review, 3,* 135–154.

Derogatis, L. R., Lipman, R. S., Rickels, K., Uhlenhuth, E. H., & Covi, L. (1974). The Hopkins Symptom Checklist: A self-report symptom inventory. *Behavioral Science, 19,* 1–15.

Dewan, S. (2006, April 18). Evacuee study finds declining health. *New York Times*. Retrieved November 30, 2007, from http://www.nytimes.com/2006/04/18/us/nationalspecial/18health.html

Dyregrov, A., & Yule, W. (2006). A review of PTSD in children. *Child and Adolescent Mental Health, 11,* 176–184.

Gil-Rivas, V., Holman, E. A., & Silver, R. C. (2004). Adolescent vulnerability following the September 11th terrorist attacks: A study of parents and their children. *Applied Developmental Science, 8,* 130–142.

Gil-Rivas, V., Silver, R. C., Holman, E. A., McIntosh, D. N., & Poulin, M. (2007). Parental response and adolescent adjustment to the September 11th terrorist attacks. *Journal of Traumatic Stress, 20,* 1063–1068.

Goenjian, A. K., Molina, L., Steinberg, A. M., Fairbanks, L. A., Alvarez, M. L., Goenjian, H. A., et al. (2001). Posttraumatic stress and depressive reactions among Nicaraguan adolescents after Hurricane Mitch. *American Journal of Psychiatry, 158,* 788–794.

Goenjian, A. K., Pynoos, R. S., Steinberg, A. M., Najarian, L. M., Asarnow, J. R., Karayan, I., et al. (1995). Psychiatric comorbidity in children after the 1998 earthquake in Armenia. *Journal of the American Academy of Child & Adolescent Psychiatry, 34,* 1174–1184.

Green, B. L., Korol, M., Grace, M. C., Vary, M. G., Leonard, A. C., Gleser, G. C., & Smitson-Cohen, S. (1991). Children and disaster: Age, gender, and parental effects on PTSD symptoms. *Journal of the American Academy of Child & Adolescent Psychiatry, 30,* 945–951.

Greenberger, E., & Chen, C. (1996). Perceived family relationships and depressed mood in early and late adolescence: A comparison of European and Asian Americans. *Developmental Psychology, 32,* 707–716.

Greenberger, E., Chen, C., & Beam, M. R. (1998). The role of "very important" nonparental adults in adolescent development. *Journal of Youth and Adolescence, 27,* 321–343.

Janoff-Bulman, R. (1992). *Shattered assumptions.* New York: Free Press.

Kiliç, E. Z., Özgüven, H. D., & Sayil, I. (2003). The psychological effects of parental mental health on children experiencing a disaster: The experience of Bolu earthquake in Turkey. *Family Process, 42,* 485–495.

Kliewer, W., Fearnow, M. D., & Miller, P. A. (1996). Coping socialization in middle childhood: Test of maternal and paternal influences. *Child Development, 67,* 2339–2357.

Klingman, A. (2001). Stress responses and adaptation of Israeli school-age children evacuated from homes during massive missile attacks. *Anxiety, Stress, and Coping, 14,* 149–172.

Koplewicz, H. S., Vogel, J. M., Solanto, M. V., Morrissey, R. F., Alonso, C. M., Abikoff, H., et al. (2002). Child and parent response to the 1993 World Trade Center bombing. *Journal of Traumatic Stress, 15,* 77–85.

Korol, M., Green, B. L., & Gleser, G. C. (1999). Children's response to a nuclear waste disaster: PTSD symptoms and outcome prediction. *Journal of the American Academy of Child & Adolescent Psychiatry, 38,* 368–375.

La Greca, A. M., Silverman, W. K., Vernberg, E. M., & Prinstein, M. J. (1996). Symptoms of posttraumatic stress in children following Hurricane Andrew: A prospective study. *Journal of Consulting and Clinical Psychology, 64,* 712–723.

La Greca, A. M., Silverman, W. K., & Wasserstein, S. B. (1998). Children's predisaster functioning as a predictor of posttraumatic stress following Hurricane Andrew. *Journal of Consulting and Clinical Psychology, 66,* 883–892.

Laor, N., Wolmer, L., & Cohen, D. J. (2001). Mother's functioning and children's symptoms 5 years after a SCUD missile attack. *American Journal of Psychiatry, 158*, 1020–1026.

Lieberman, A. F. (1992). Infant–parent psychotherapy with toddlers. *Development and Psychopathology, 4*, 559–574.

March, J. S., Amaya-Jackson, L., Terry, R., & Constanzo, P. (1997). Posttraumatic symptomatology in children and adolescents after an industrial fire. *Journal of the American Academy of Child & Adolescent Psychiatry, 36*, 1080–1088.

Masten, A. S., Best, K. M., & Garmezy, N. (1990). Resilience and development: Contributions from the study of children who overcome adversity. *Development and Psychopathology, 2*, 425–444.

Masten, A. S., & Coatsworth, J. D. (1998). The development of competence in favorable and unfavorable environments. *American Psychologist, 53*, 205–220.

McFarlane, A. C. (1987). Posttraumatic phenomena in a longitudinal study of children following a natural disaster. *Journal of the American Academy of Child & Adolescent Psychiatry, 26*, 764–769.

Meiser-Steadman, R., Yule, W., Dalgleish, T., Smith, P., & Glucksman, E. (2006). The role of the family in child and adolescent posttraumatic stress following attendance at an emergency department. *Journal of Pediatric Psychology, 31*, 397–402.

National Institute of Mental Health. (2006). *Helping children and adolescents cope with violence and disasters.* Washington DC: U.S. Department of Health and Human Services. Retrieved November 23, 2007, from http://www.nimh.nih.gov/health/publications/helping-children-and-adolescents-cope-with-violence-and-disasters-what-parents-can-do.pdf

Norris, F. H. (n.d.). *Psychosocial consequences of major hurricanes and floods: Range, duration, and magnitude of effects and risk factors for adverse outcomes* (Research and Education in Disaster Mental Health, National Center for PTSD fact sheet). Retrieved December 3, 2007, from http://www.redmh.org/research/specialized/hurricanes_floods.html

Osofsky, J. D., Osofsky, H. J., & Harris, W. W. (2007). Katrina's children: Social policy considerations for children in disasters. *Social Policy Report, 21*, 3–18.

Pfefferbaum, B. (1997). Posttraumatic stress disorder in children: A review of the past 10 years. *Journal of the American Academy of Child & Adolescent Psychiatry, 36*, 1503–1511.

Pine, D. S., & Cohen, J. A. (2002). Trauma in children and adolescents: Risk and treatment of psychiatric sequelae. *Biological Psychiatry, 51*, 519–531.

Pynoos, R., Rodriguez, N., Steinberg, A., Stuber, M., & Frederick, C. (1998). *The University of California at Los Angeles Posttraumatic Stress Disorder Reaction Index for DSM–IV (Revision 1).* Los Angeles: UCLA Trauma Psychiatry Program.

Pynoos, R. S., Steinberg, A. M., & Wraith, R. (1995). A developmental model of childhood traumatic stress. In D. Cicchetti & D. J. Cohen (Eds.), *Developmental psychopathology: Vol. 2. Risk, disorder, and adaptation* (pp. 72–95). New York: Wiley.

Rodriguez, N., Steinberg, A. S., Saltzman, W. S., & Pynoos, R. S. (2001). *PTSD Index: Preliminary psychometric analyses of child and parent versions*. Symposium conducted at the Annual Meeting of the International Society for Traumatic Stress Studies, New Orleans, LA.

Roussos, A., Goenjian, A. K., Steinberg, A. M., Sotiropoulou, C., Kakaki, M., Kabakos, C., et al. (2005). Posttraumatic stress and depressive reactions among children and adolescents after the 1999 earthquake in Ano Liosia, Greece. *American Journal of Psychiatry, 162*, 530–537.

Russoniello, C. V., Skalko, T. K., O'Brien, K., McGhee, S. A., Bingham-Alexander, B. S., & Beatley, J. (2002). Childhood posttraumatic stress disorder and efforts to cope after Hurricane Floyd. *Behavioral Medicine, 28*, 61–71.

Salmon, K., & Bryant, R. A. (2002). Posttraumatic stress disorder in children: The influence of developmental factors. *Clinical Psychology Review, 22*, 163–188.

Save the Children. (2006, September). *Katrina response: Protecting the children of the storm*. Retrieved November 7, 2007, from http://www.savethechildren.org/publications/reports/katrina-issue-brief.pdf

Scheeringa, M. S., & Zeanah, C. H. (2001). A relational perspective on PTSD in early childhood. *Journal of Traumatic Stress, 14*, 799–815.

Silva, R. R., Alpert, M., Munoz, D. M., Singh, S., Matzner, F., & Dummit, S. (2000). Stress and vulnerability to posttraumatic stress disorder in children and adolescents. *American Journal of Psychiatry, 157*, 1229–1235.

Silver, R. C., Holman, E. A., McIntosh, D. N., Poulin, M., & Gil-Rivas, V. (2002). Nationwide longitudinal study of psychological responses to September 11. *JAMA, 288*, 1235–1244.

Silverman, W. K., & La Greca, A. M. (2002). Children experiencing disasters: Definitions, reactions, and predictors of outcomes. In A. La Greca, W. Silverman, E. Vernberg, & M. Roberts (Eds.), *Helping children cope with disasters and terrorism* (pp. 11–33). Washington, DC: American Psychological Association.

Smith, M. Y., Redd, W. H., DuHamel, K. N., Vickberg, J., & Ricketts, P. (1999). Validation of the PTSD Checklist—Civilian version in survivors of bone marrow transplantation. *Journal of Traumatic Stress, 12*, 485–499.

Smith, P., Perrin, S., Yule, W., & Rabe-Hesketh, S. (2001). War exposure and maternal reactions in the psychological adjustment of children from Bosnia-Hercegovina. *Journal of Child Psychology and Psychiatry and Allied Disciplines, 42*, 395–404.

Steinberg, A. M., Brymer, M. J., Decker, K. B., & Pynoos, R. S. (2004). The University of California at Los Angeles Post-Traumatic Stress Disorder Reaction Index. *Current Psychiatry Reports, 6*, 96–100.

Thienkrua, W., Cardozo, B. L., Chakkraband, M. L. S., Guadamuz, T. E., Pengjuntr, W., Tantipiwatanaskul, P., et al. (2006). Symptoms of posttraumatic stress disorder and depression among children in tsunami-affected areas in southern Thailand. *JAMA, 296*, 594–559.

Toth, S. L., Maughan, A., Manly, J. T., Spagnola, M., & Cicchetti, D. (2002). The relative efficacy of two interventions in altering maltreated preschool children's representational models: Implications for attachment theory. *Development and Psychopathology, 14,* 877–908.

Toth, S. L., Rogosch, F. A., Manly, J. T., & Cicchetti, D. (2006). The efficacy of toddler–parent psychotherapy to reorganize attachment in the young offspring of mothers with major depressive disorder: A randomized preventive trial. *Journal of Consulting and Clinical Psychology, 74,* 1006–1016.

Varney, J. (2006, August 29). They came seeking refuge, then suffered days in anguish. *Times–Picayune.* Retrieved November 7, 2007, from http://www.nola.com/news/t-p/frontpage/index.ssf?/base/news-6/11568293918830.xml&coll=1

Vernberg, E. M., La Greca, A. M., Silverman, W. K., & Prinstein, M. J. (1996). Prediction of posttraumatic stress symptoms in children after Hurricane Andrew. *Journal of Abnormal Psychology, 105,* 237–248.

Weathers, F. W., Litz, B. T., Herman, D. S., Huska, J. A., & Keane, T. M. (1993, October). *The PTSD Checklist: Reliability, validity, and diagnostic utility.* Paper presented at the Annual Meeting of the International Society for Traumatic Stress Studies, San Antonio, TX.

Weems, C. F., Pina, A. A., Costa, N. M., Watts, S. E., Taylor, L. K., & Cannon, M. F. (2007). Predisaster trait anxiety and negative affect predict posttraumatic stress in youths after Hurricane Katrina. *Journal of Consulting and Clinical Psychology, 75,* 154–159.

Ydstie, J. (2006, August 27). Katrina victims still struggle to find way home. *All Things Considered* [Radio broadcast]. Washington, DC: National Public Radio. Retrieved November 7, 2007, from http://www.npr.org/news/specials/katrina/oneyearlater/

Yule, W. (1994). Posttraumatic stress disorder. In T. H. Ollendick, N. J. King, & W. Yule (Eds.), *International handbook of phobic and anxiety disorders in children and adolescents* (pp. 223–240). New York: Springer-Verlag.

3

THE EFFECTS OF PARENTING BEHAVIOR ON CHILDREN'S MENTAL HEALTH AFTER HURRICANE KATRINA: PRELIMINARY FINDINGS

MARY LOU KELLEY, JENNETTE L. PALCIC, JULIA F. VIGNA,
JING WANG, ANNIE W. SPELL, ANGIE PELLEGRIN,
KAREN L. DAVIDSON, SHANNON SELF-BROWN,
AND KENNETH J. RUGGIERO

In the aftermath of Hurricane Katrina, many adults and children experienced a high level of secondary stressors and mental health problems associated with their hurricane exposure (see Introduction and chap. 10, this volume; Brewin et al., 2006; Kessler, Galea, Jones, & Parker, 2006). The full impact of the disaster's effect on these children and families has yet to be elucidated. In general, research on children and families affected by disasters is limited; in fact, only 16% of disaster studies have targeted youth samples (Norris & Elrod, 2006). However, some studies have provided a general understanding of key outcomes and common trajectories of disaster-affected youth. Most children return to their premorbid level of functioning following exposure to natural disasters, although a sizeable minority continue to evidence symptoms of posttraumatic stress disorder (PTSD) months after the traumatic experience (La Greca, Silverman, Vernberg, & Prinstein, 1996). Although PTSD is the most common psychological outcome studied in individuals who experience trauma, children may present with a variety of difficulties, including anxiety, depression, or behavior problems (Goenjian et al., 2001; Shaw et al., 1995).

Completion of this chapter was supported in part by National Institute of Mental Health Grant
RMH-078148A.

Research has documented a host of significant correlates of postdisaster mental health in children. The prevalence of PTSD symptoms following a disaster generally is higher in girls than in boys (Goenjian et al., 2001) and in minority youths (Garrison et al., 1995). Amount of perceived personal threat and loss of resources due to hurricane exposure consistently account for significant variance in children's mental health (Asarnow et al., 1999; La Greca, Silverman, & Wasserstein, 1998; Lonigan, Shannon, Finch, Daugherty, & Taylor, 1991; Vernberg, La Greca, Silverman, & Prinstein, 1996). Additionally, predisaster psychological adjustment (Asarnow et al., 1999; Earls, Smith, Reich, & Jung, 1988) and past exposure to traumatic events have been associated with negative outcomes. It is likely that families affected by Katrina, the majority of whom were low-income African Americans living in adverse conditions, are at increased risk of multiple trauma exposure in their lifetime (Dempsey, Overstreet, & Moely, 2000; Hausman, Spivak, & Prothrow-Stith, 1994; Osofsky, Wewers, Hann, & Fick, 1993). In fact, recent research found that maternal financial strain and violence exposure were negatively related to toddlers' adjustment after Katrina in a very impoverished sample (Scaramella, Sohr-Preston, Callahan, & Mirabile, 2008). Further, some studies suggest that Katrina-affected ethnic minority families perceived more discrimination than nonminority families (Weems & Overstreet, 2008; Weems et al., 2007). Thus, the child victims of Hurricane Katrina may be at heightened risk of experiencing PTSD symptoms.

Research on adult disaster survivors has documented that a wide range of mental health and physical health risk reactions emerge. These include PTSD, depression, generalized anxiety, and increased substance use (e.g., Acierno et al., 2007; Galea et al., 2002, 2003; Kessler et al., 2006; Vlahov, Galea, Ahern, Resnick, & Kilpatrick, 2004; see also Norris et al., 2002). Although parental mental health has been linked with child postdisaster functioning (Jones, Ribbe, Cunningham, Weddle, & Langley, 2002; Koplewicz et al., 2002), few studies have extended this line of research to parenting behavior. Because major disasters and displacement may affect parenting, children's routines, and family relationships, the influence of these factors on child outcomes is an important public health concern. Limited research has addressed the role of parenting in children's adjustment after exposure to a disaster. Within the community violence literature, parent involvement and support, parental monitoring, and positive discipline have been found to serve as protective variables against maladjustment (e.g., Kliewer et al., 2004, 2006; Lanclos, 2002; Overstreet, Dempsey, Graham, & Moely, 1999; Sullivan, Kung, & Farrell, 2004). Whether this relationship holds following a disaster is less well established.

As the aforementioned review illustrates, factors contributing to children's adjustment after a disaster occur at multiple levels. As discussed in Weems and Overstreet (2008) and the Introduction to this volume, Bronfenbrenner's ecological systems theory (Bronfenbrenner & Morris, 2006) states that an individual's functioning is influenced by multiple layers of "ecologies" that interact and influence one another and children's development. The multiple layers of influence range from distal ecologies, including cultural values; to proximal ecologies, including the environments in which children interact; as well as the ontogenic level, or individual characteristics associated with adjustment. This study evaluates the contribution of variables at various ecological levels to youths' adjustment following Katrina, with emphasis on the effects of parenting behavior.

The purposes of the current study were twofold. First, the study examined group differences between a displaced, Hurricane Katrina–affected sample from New Orleans and a nondisplaced comparison sample from Baton Rouge. Baton Rouge, approximately 90 miles from New Orleans, suffered negligible direct physical damage from Katrina. However, many Baton Rouge families were inundated with relatives and friends staying in their homes, and their family roles, routines, and environments often were disrupted. It was hypothesized that compared with the nondisplaced sample, the displaced sample would report greater hurricane exposure and psychological symptoms (i.e., internalizing, externalizing, and PTSD), as well as greater exposure to hurricane-related events.

Second, the study examined whether parenting behaviors predicted PTSD and other psychological symptoms in children who experienced Hurricane Katrina beyond the variance accounted for by hurricane exposure and demographic variables. It was hypothesized that negative parenting practices, such as inconsistent discipline and corporal punishment, would be associated with relatively poor adjustment in children, including increased PTSD and internalizing and externalizing symptoms. Conversely, positive parenting practices, such as family routines and parent involvement, were hypothesized to serve as protective factors associated with more positive adjustment.

METHOD

Participants

Participants were 279 displaced mother–child dyads from New Orleans and surrounding parishes directly affected by Hurricane Katrina and 96 non-displaced mother–child dyads from Baton Rouge who served as a comparison sample. Children were recruited from regular education classrooms approximately 3 to 7 months after Katrina.

Measures

Mothers completed the measures discussed in the following sections.

Demographic Questionnaire

Mothers were queried for information regarding child age, grade, and gender and family characteristics such as income, parent education, and employment.

Externalizing Symptoms

Mothers completed one of two versions of the Behavior Assessment System for Children, Second Edition—Parent Report Scale (BASC–2 PRS; Reynolds & Kamphaus, 2004) depending on their child's age. The BASC–2 PRS has demonstrated adequate psychometric characteristics (Reynolds & Kamphaus, 2004; Waggoner, 2006). The Externalizing Problems composite scale scores were used as indicators of mother-reported behavior problems in their children. Cronbach's alphas for the Externalizing Problems composite were .92 for the child version and .93 for the adolescent version of the measure for the current sample.

Parenting Behaviors

The Alabama Parenting Questionnaire (APQ; Shelton, Frick, & Wootton, 1996) is a six-factor scale and consists of 42 total items. Items are rated on a 5-point scale (1 = *never*, 5 = *always*) and reflect the following factors: Parent Involvement, Positive Parenting, Poor Monitoring/Supervision, Inconsistent Discipline, Corporal Punishment, and Other Discipline Techniques. Items on the first two subscales represent positive parenting practices, and those on the latter four represent negative parenting practices. The APQ has adequate psychometric support (Essau, Sasagawa, & Frick, 2006). Cronbach's alphas for the current sample were as follows: Parent Involvement, .83; Positive Parenting, .77; Poor Monitoring/Supervision, .81; Inconsistent Discipline, .71; Corporal Punishment, .74; and Other Discipline Techniques, .59.

Household Routines

The Child Routines Questionnaire (Sytsma, Kelley, & Wymer, 2001) is a 36-item questionnaire that consists of four subscales: Daily Living Routines, Household Responsibilities, Discipline Routines, and Homework Routines. Items are rated on a 5-point scale ranging from 0 to 4. The questionnaire has adequate psychometric support (Sytsma et al., 2001). Cronbach's alpha for the total score was .96 in the current sample.

Children's Self-Report Questionnaires

Children completed three self-report questionnaires. The first was Hurricane-Related Traumatic Experiences (HURTE; Vernberg et al., 1996). On the basis of the sum of child responses of either yes or no to a series of questions assessing traumatic exposure, two factors are derived: Threat and Loss/Disruption. The HURTE has demonstrated sufficient test–retest and predictive validity (La Greca et al., 1996; Vernberg et al., 1996).

Internalizing symptoms were assessed using the BASC–2 Self Report of Personality, which is analogous to the BASC–2 PRS. Children completed one of two versions depending on their age. The Internalizing Problems composite scale was used as an indicator of internalizing symptoms. Cronbach's alpha in the current sample was .95 for both the child and adolescent versions.

PTSD symptoms were assessed using the University of California at Los Angeles PTSD Reaction Index Revised (UCLA PTSD–RI; Pynoos, Rodriguez, Steinberg, Stuber, & Frederick, 1998), which is a revised version of the Child PTSD Reaction Index (Nader, Pynoos, Fairbanks, & Frederick, 1990). This 22-item scale screens for PTSD in children and adolescents and corresponds to criteria of the *Diagnostic and Statistical Manual of Mental Disorders* (4th ed.; American Psychiatric Association, 1994). The revised measure has demonstrated very good psychometric properties (Pynoos, Goenjian, & Steinberg, 1998; Steinberg, Brymer, Decker, & Pynoos, 2004). Children completed the scale by rating the degree to which they experienced symptoms during the past month without identifying a specific traumatic event. A summary score was used as an index of child-reported PTSD symptoms. Cronbach's alpha was .91 in this sample.

Procedure

Following institutional review board approval and school consent, mothers and students in Grades 4 through 8 were recruited via flyers. Data collection occurred 3 to 7 months after Hurricane Katrina; New Orleans participants were recruited from the first several schools to open up after the storm. Baton Rouge schools with student bodies similar demographically to the New Orleans sample were selected for sampling. Interested mothers completed consent forms and questionnaires. Approximately 36% of contacted mothers participated in the study. Following the return of completed questionnaires and parent consent forms, a researcher described the study to the child and solicited his or her assent to participate. Children completed questionnaires in small groups under the supervision of the researchers. Questionnaires were read to younger children and children with reading difficulties. All measures were completed according to standard directions. Depending on school personnel preference, various forms of compensation were used. For child participants, compensation included $5 or participation in a pizza party. Mother participants were entered into a cash prize drawing or were individually paid $20.

RESULTS

Comparisons of the displaced and nondisplaced families indicated that the samples were equivalent on all demographic variables except gender, with the displaced sample including more girls than the nondisplaced sample. Children ranged in age from 8 to 16, with an average age of 11.6 years ($SD = 1.59$). The majority of participants were African American, and the mean total yearly family income was roughly $17,000. Approximately half of the total sample (50.5%)—47.9% of the displaced sample and 58.5% of the nondisplaced sample—consisted of single-parent homes. No group differences in household composition emerged.

Missing data were identified and replaced using multiple imputation methods recommended by Schafer and Graham (2002). Group differences between the displaced and nondisplaced samples were tested using the general linear model. Because significant group differences in gender were obtained, group mean differences were tested with gender as a covariate. These findings are discussed next.

Hurricane-Related Exposure

The displaced and nondisplaced groups differed on hurricane-related life-threatening experiences, $F(2, 369) = 5.18, p < .01$, and hurricane-related loss/disruption, $F(2, 369) = 61.73, p < .001$, such that displaced children experienced more life threat ($M = 0.80, SD = 1.03$) and loss ($M = 3.84, SD = 1.95$) than the nondisplaced children (life threat $M = 0.44, SD = 0.85$; loss $M = 1.23, 2.98$). In addition, 51% of displaced children reported at least one life-threatening event, and 98% of this group reported at least one loss/disruption incident, compared with 30% and 44%, respectively, of their nondisplaced counterparts.

Parenting Behavior

We examined frequencies of family routines according to the Child Routines Questionnaire and each of the parenting behaviors assessed on the APQ. For each of the subscales, a higher score indicates a higher level of frequency for that particular factor. The two groups did not differ significantly on any of the parenting variables. Generally, parents endorsed higher levels of positive parenting behaviors on the APQ (Parent Involvement, Positive Parenting,

Positive Discipline) versus negative behaviors (Poor Monitoring/Supervision, Inconsistent Discipline, Corporal Punishment), with the highest mean scores for both groups on Parent Involvement and the lowest for both on Corporal Punishment.

Children's Adjustment

The groups did not differ significantly on self-reported PTSD symptoms and prevalence of meeting PTSD symptom criteria (using a cut score of 38 to indicate severe PTSD symptoms on the UCLA PTSD–RI; see Steinberg et al., 2004); 12% of displaced children met criteria for severe PTSD symptomatology, compared with 8% of nondisplaced children. Clinically significant levels of self-reported internalizing symptoms were endorsed by 13% of displaced children and 10% percent of nondisplaced children. With regard to externalizing problems, 12% of displaced and 17% of nondisplaced children scored in the clinical range. Neither of these differences was statistically significant.

Intercorrelations among variables are listed in Table 3.1. Child internalizing and externalizing symptoms were significantly correlated with most of the parenting variables, whereas child PTSD symptom severity was significantly correlated with hurricane-related life-threatening experiences and loss/disruption.

Regression Analyses

We conducted hierarchical regression analyses to investigate the effects of family environment on child mental health in the aftermath of Katrina. Three mental health outcomes were examined separately: child self-reported internalizing problems, PTSD symptoms, and parent-reported child externalizing problems. Hurricane variables were entered on the first step (child report of hurricane life threat and loss/disruption). On Step 2, demographic variables were entered (gender and age). Family environment factors (child routines, parent involvement, positive parenting, poor monitoring, inconsistent discipline, corporal punishment, and other/positive discipline) were entered on Step 3. Tables 3.2, 3.3, and 3.4 present the results of these analyses, conducted separately for displaced and nondisplaced samples.

Child-Rated Posttraumatic Stress Disorder

The final model for PTSD symptom severity in the displaced sample (see Table 3.2) accounted for 20% of the variance, which was significant. Examination of the individual variables in the final model revealed that children who reported more life-threatening experiences and more loss/disruption had significantly higher levels of PTSD symptoms. The final model for the nondisplaced sample also was significant, with 27% of the variance explained by

TABLE 3.1

Bivariate Intercorrelations Among Variables of Interest

Variable	1	2	3	4	5	6	7	8	9	10
1. UCLA PTSD–RI index score	—									
2. HURTE child loss/disruption	.31**	—								
3. HURTE child life threat	.36**	.38**	—							
4. CRQ total	.08	-.02	-.01	—						
5. APQ parent involvement	.05	-.11*	-.05	.45**	—					
6. APQ positive parenting	.05	-.10	-.10	.47**	.74**	—				
7. APQ poor monitoring/supervision	.06	.04	.07	.35**	-.31**	-.26**	—			
8. APQ inconsistent discipline	.06	.05	.07	-.24**	-.17**	-.11*	.64**	—		
9. APQ corporal punishment	.15**	.10	.12*	-.16**	-.07	-.10	.47**	.44**	—	
10. APQ other discipline	.11*	-.03	.10	.12**	.27**	.25**	.23**	.26**	.48**	—
11. Child-reported BASC internalizing	.59**	.13*	.21**	-.03	-.02	-.01	.11*	.13*	.11*	.10
12. Mother-reported BASC externalizing	.14*	.01	.08	-.27**	-.24**	-.13*	.37**	.37**	.32**	.21**

Note. APQ = Alabama Parenting Questionnaire (Shelton, Frick, & Wootten, 1996); BASC = Behavior Assessment System for Children (Reynolds & Kamphaus, 2004); CRQ = Child Routines Questionnaire (Sytsma, Kelley, & Wymer, 2001); HURTE = Hurricane-Related Traumatic Experiences (Vernberg et al., 1996); UCLA PTSD–RI = University of California at Los Angeles Posttraumatic Stress Disorder Reaction Index—Revised (Pynoos, Rodriguez, Steinberg, Stuber, & Frederick, 1998).
*p < .05, two-tailed. **p < .01, two-tailed.

TABLE 3.2

Hierarchical Regression Analyses Predicting Posttraumatic Stress Disorder in the Displaced and Nondisplaced Samples

Step	Nondisplaced sample			Displaced sample		
	B	β	F model	B	β	F model
1			$F_{(2, 92)} = 7.28^{**}$			$F_{(2, 269)} = 31.76^{**}$
Child loss/disruption	-0.17	-0.03		2.13	0.27	
Child life threat	6.29	0.38		3.86	0.26	
2			$F_{(4, 90)} = 4.18^{**}$			$F_{(4, 267)} = 18.37^{**}$
Child age	1.01	0.12		-1.41	-0.14	
Child gender	2.31	0.08		2.37	0.08	
3			$F_{(11, 83)} = 2.83^{**}$			$F_{(11, 260)} = 7.08^{**}$
APQ parent involvement	-0.16	0.06		0.05	0.02	
APQ positive parenting	1.32	0.33		0.02	0.01	
APQ poor monitoring/supervision	-0.14	-0.08		0.21	0.11	
APQ inconsistent discipline	-0.10	-0.03		-0.08	-0.03	
APQ corporal punishment	1.69	0.33		0.04	0.01	
APQ other discipline techniques	-0.16	-0.04		0.05	0.02	
CRQ total	0.02	0.04		0.05	0.08	

Note. APQ = Alabama Parenting Questionnaire (Shelton, Frick, & Wootten, 1996); CRQ = Child Routines Questionnaire (Systsma, Kelley, & Wymer, 2001). Nondisplaced sample: Step 1 $R^2 = .14$, Step 2 $R^2 = .27$, $\Delta R^2 = .02$; Step 3 $R^2 = .16$, $\Delta R^2 = .02$. Displaced sample: Step 1 $R^2 = .19$, Step 2 $R^2 = .20$, $\Delta R^2 = .01$; Step 3 $R^2 = .20$, $\Delta R^2 = .00$.
$^{**}p < .01$.

TABLE 3.3
Regression Analyses Predicting Internalizing Problems
in the Displaced Sample

Step	R^2	ΔR^2	B	β	F model
1	.08	.00			$F(2, 251) = 10.19^{**}$
Child loss/disruption			0.82	0.15	
Child life threat			1.99	0.19	
2	.08	.00			$F(4, 249) = 5.54^{**}$
Child age			−0.25	−0.04	
Child gender			−1.57	−0.07	
3	.10	.02			$F(11, 242) = 2.36^{**}$
APQ					
Parent involvement			−0.02	−0.02	
Positive parenting			0.08	0.03	
Poor supervision/monitoring			0.07	0.06	
Inconsistent discipline			0.12	0.06	
Corporal punishment			−0.01	0.30	
Other discipline techniques			0.09	0.04	
CRQ total			−0.01	0.04	

Note. APQ = Alabama Parenting Questionnaire (Shelton, Frick, & Wootten, 1996); CRQ = Child Routines Questionnaire (Sytsma, Kelley, & Wymer, 2001).
$^*p < .05.$ $^{**}p < .01.$

these variables (see Table 3.2). Results indicate that hurricane-related life-threatening experiences, positive parenting, and corporal punishment were positively related to PTSD symptoms.

Child-Rated Internalizing Problems

Ten percent of the variance in child internalizing problems in the displaced sample was accounted for by the variables in the model (Table 3.3). Children who experienced more life-threatening experiences and more loss/disruption endorsed more internalizing symptoms. In the nondisplaced sample, the model for child internalizing problems was not significant.

Parent-Reported Externalizing Problems

Results indicate that 33% of the variance in child externalizing problems in the displaced sample was accounted for by these variables (see Table 3.4). Child sex was significantly associated with mothers' reports of child externalizing problems, such that mothers of boys rated their children as having more externalizing problems than did mothers of girls. Additionally, parents who reported higher use of corporal punishment and other discipline practices rated their children as exhibiting higher levels of externalizing problems. Parents who reported higher parent involvement and more family routines reported that their children exhibited fewer externalizing problems.

TABLE 3.4
Regression Analyses Predicting Externalizing Problems in the Nondisplaced and Displaced Samples

Step	Nondisplaced sample			Displaced sample		
	B	β	F model	B	β	F model
1			$F(2, 75) = .30$			$F(2, 222) = 1.88$
Child loss/disruption	−0.59	−0.10		0.29	0.05	
Child life threat	0.40	2.14		1.22	0.11	
2			$F(4, 73) = 4.40^{**}$			$F(2, 220) = 2.63^{*}$
Child age	3.51	0.43		1.05	0.13	
Child gender	1.88	0.07		−2.92	−0.12	
3			$F(11, 66) = 3.30^{**}$			$F(11, 213) = 9.30^{**}$
APQ parent involvement	−0.91	−0.44		−0.31	−0.19	
APQ positive parenting	0.99	0.27		0.45	0.16	
APQ poor supervision/monitoring	−0.05	−0.03		0.21	0.12	
APQ inconsistent discipline	0.64	0.23		0.30	0.12	
APQ Corporal punishment	0.39	0.08		0.61	0.15	
APQ Other discipline techniques	−0.45	−0.13		0.47	0.18	
CRQ total	−0.01	−0.02		−0.13	−0.21	

Note. APQ = Alabama Parenting Questionnaire (Shelton, Frick, & Wootten, 1996); CRI = Child Routines Questionnaire (Sytsma, Kelley, & Wymer, 2001). Nondisplaced sample: Step 1 $R^2 = .01$, Step 2 $R^2 = .19$, $\Delta R^2 = .18$; Step 3 $R^2 = .36$, $\Delta R^2 = .17$. Displaced sample: Step 1 $R^2 = .02$, Step 2 $R^2 = .05$, $\Delta R^2 = .03$; Step 3 $R^2 = .33$, $\Delta R^2 = .28$.
$^{*}p < .05.$ $^{**}p < .01.$

The final model predicting child externalizing problems for the non-displaced sample was also significant. As seen in Table 3.4, mothers of older children reported more externalizing symptoms than mothers of younger children. In addition, mothers who reported greater parental involvement endorsed fewer externalizing symptoms in their children than their counterparts with less parental involvement.

DISCUSSION

This study examined whether severity of hurricane exposure (loss/disruption, and perception of life threat) and parenting practices were associated with child PTSD, internalizing, and externalizing symptoms. A unique feature of the study was the inclusion of mother–child dyads displaced by Hurricane Katrina and a nondisplaced comparison sample. As expected, the two samples differed in their hurricane exposure, with the New Orleans sample reporting greater exposure than the nondisplaced comparison sample. The hypothesis that the displaced sample would endorse greater PTSD, internalizing, and externalizing symptoms was not supported. In fact, there were no significant differences between the two samples, with both reporting fewer symptoms of PTSD compared with children in Grades 3 to 5 who were studied 3 months (Vernberg et al., 1996) and 7 months (La Greca et al., 1996) after Hurricane Andrew (South Florida, 1992). Our sample was considerably older than the sample in the two Hurricane Andrew studies, and evidence suggests that younger children report more symptoms than adolescents after trauma exposure (Shannon, Lonigan, Finch, & Taylor, 1994). Compared with other postdisaster studies with children of similar age, our findings were more consistent. Specifically, symptom rates in children following the 2004 Indian Ocean tsunami (11%–13%; Thienkrua et al., 2006) and in another sample of Katrina-exposed youths (12.6%; Hensley & Varela, 2008) were very similar to the rates in our sample. Thus, it is likely that differences found between the two samples are due to differences in trauma exposure or the ages of the children. It also may be that cultural, socioeconomic, or racial differences between our sample and those of other researchers contributed to the lower rates of PTSD symptoms seen here. Finally, it also may be that more of the families in the current sample evacuated during the hurricane than did those in the La Greca et al. (1996) sample.

The high prevalence of PTSD symptoms in the nondisplaced Baton Rouge sample was unexpected and considerably higher than those reported in large scale epidemiological studies (see Fairbanks, Putnam, & Harris, 2007; Kilpatrick et al., 2003). There are several potential explanations for this finding. First, although the Baton Rouge sample was not directly affected by Hurricane Katrina, the community was affected indirectly. For instance, many families housed relatives and friends from New Orleans. Second, the population of Baton Rouge doubled following Hurricane Katrina, and the swelling of the city with displaced families caused considerable inconvenience (e.g., grocery stores were depleted, stores were more crowded, and traffic was heavier). Third, the effects of media exposure should not be ruled out as a potential correlate or risk factor, as a significant relationship between disaster-related television viewing and mental health outcomes has been documented (Ahern, Galea, Resnick, & Vlahov, 2004), and these effects are likely enhanced when what is presented on the news is tragic and involves a neighboring city. Fourth, past research suggests that higher rates of PTSD symptoms are commonly reported in samples exposed to considerable community violence and other stressors (Kilpatrick et al., 2003). Given that the Baton Rouge sample was of low socioeconomic status and primarily African American, it is likely that these children had encountered prior traumatic events, including violence exposure (Hastings & Kelley, 1997). Finally, questionnaires with clinical cutoff scores may have a tendency to produce higher prevalence estimates relative to structured clinical interviews (e.g., Engelhard et al., 2007; Ruggiero, Rheingold, Resnick, Kilpatrick, & Galea, 2006). Specifically, some research indicates that scores obtained from rating scales, in contrast with structured interviews, produce higher rates of children "diagnosed" with PTSD.

Likewise, the two groups did not differ significantly on the frequency of internalizing or externalizing symptoms or on the percentage of respondents who scored in the clinical range on the BASC scales (scores at or above the 98th percentile; T scores of 70 or above). Specifically, clinically significant levels of self-reported internalizing symptoms were endorsed by 13% of displaced children and 10% percent of nondisplaced children. With regard to externalizing problems, 12% of displaced and 17% of nondisplaced children scored in the clinical range. The relatively higher rates of externalizing symptoms in the comparison sample is similar to the results of Shaw and colleagues (1995) following Hurricane Andrew; teachers reported that low-impact students displayed more externalizing behavior problems than a high-impact group. Also, our sample was more psychologically distressed than would be expected on the basis of BASC standardization data. This finding is consistent with the higher rates of clinical symptoms frequently seen in impoverished minority samples (Mash & Dozois, 2003). It is possible that lifetime exposure to multiple traumatic events may have diluted the effects of Hurricane Katrina.

Consistent with the literature, hurricane exposure predicted severity of PTSD symptoms in the displaced sample (La Greca et al., 1996). Studies on children's adjustment to disasters consistently report that exposure accounts for the most variance in PTSD symptoms. Contrary to our hypotheses, however, parenting behaviors did not add to the variance accounted for above and beyond hurricane exposure in the displaced sample. It is likely that hurricane exposure was such a salient trauma that other variables assessed did not significantly contribute to the model. Conversely, it may be that variables such as parental responsivity or other variables not assessed in this study would more substantially contribute to the model.

Hurricane exposure, corporal punishment, and positive parenting were all significant correlates of PTSD symptoms in the nondisplaced sample. The relation between hurricane exposure and PTSD symptoms in this sample may be due to the fact that the data were collected within a few months after Hurricane Katrina, and the community perceived the New Orleans evacuees as causing increased crime (Johnson, 2007). Thus, the life threat and PTSD noted may have had more to do with the aftermath of the disaster than with the hurricane itself. It is possible, and perhaps likely, that this possibility will not be a contributing factor over time. Examination of longitudinal data will help delineate this relation. Corporal punishment was also significantly correlated with PTSD symptoms in the nondisplaced sample. Although abusive parenting behavior was not measured, the Corporal Punishment factor consists of three items that refer to spanking, hitting, or slapping one's child when he or she has done something wrong. It may be that these forms of parenting behavior contributed to the development of PTSD symptoms in a manner similar to that reported in physically abused children. The role of positive parenting in predicting PTSD symptoms is less clear and seems counterintuitive. It may be that the mothers who tend to use corporal punishment also perceive themselves as providing more guidance, praise, and structure. Another possible explanation is that parents who observe PTSD symptoms in their children may make an increased effort to parent positively in response. Clearly, further research is warranted.

The hurricane exposure variables were the only factors significantly associated with internalizing symptoms in the displaced sample. None of the other variables predicted internalizing symptoms for the displaced or nondisplaced samples. Furthermore, only 10% of the variance was accounted for by exposure variables in predicting internalizing symptoms in the displaced group. It is likely that other variables not measured in this study, such as coping skills and social support, would aid in the prediction of internalizing symptoms (Vernberg et al., 1996).

Consistent with our hypotheses, parenting behavior contributed significantly to externalizing behavior in children in the displaced sample and, to a lesser degree, the nondisplaced sample. For the displaced children, being a boy and having parents who used more corporal punishment and other discipline practices (such as time-out and withdrawal of privileges) but who were less involved and provided fewer routines accounted for 35% of the variance in child externalizing problems. For such problems, hurricane exposure did not add to the model. The presence of negative parenting practices and the absence of positive ones, such as routines and parent involvement, consistently are associated with conduct problems (Hinshaw & Lee, 2003; Patterson, 1982).

It is less clear why many of these parenting variables did not add to the model for externalizing problems in the nondisplaced sample. Specifically, in this sample, only child age and corporal punishment significantly contributed to externalizing problems, and much less of the variance was accounted for than with the displaced sample. The lack of significant findings may be due to the sample size, which may have had reduced power to detect significant associations.

STRENGTHS AND LIMITATIONS

The current study has several strengths. It is one of very few to evaluate the role of parenting behavior and family routines in children's adjustment following a natural disaster. The study also is one of few postdisaster studies to include a comparison sample. The comparison sample allowed us to compare the prevalence of child psychopathology and parenting behaviors in two samples and to more thoroughly understand the unique contribution of effects directly related to Hurricane Katrina displacement compared with the effects of nondisplaced postdisaster environments. Finally, this is one of the first studies conducted with a large subset of African American children and their mothers after a disaster. Thus, the current study contributes to knowledge of postdisaster recovery in a predominantly African American sample that lacked many resources that may aid in recovery.

The study evaluated variables related to youth adjustment within multiple contexts or ecologies. For example, at a distal level of effects, the study examined community violence exposure and its relation to children's adjustment. Within more proximal contexts, the study examined the effects of parenting behavior on adjustment. Finally, the use of a primarily impoverished ethnic minority sample highlighted relationships and PTSD severity levels that may be unique to this population.

This study is limited methodologically in a number of ways. First, we relied on rating scale data only and did not conduct structured diagnostic interviews. Thus, whether the participants met diagnostic criteria for PTSD or other psychological problems cannot be determined. Also, we did not assess participants' predisaster functioning. Consequently, causal effects of the hurricane cannot be determined. Third, because of the nature of sample recruitment, it is unclear whether the data are representative of the full populations of Baton Rouge families and displaced New Orleans families.

The current study reflects the first wave of data collection with families being followed over a 2-year period. It will be interesting to examine whether the prevalence of symptomatology changes across time and whether the independent variables observed are predictive over time. Generally, children and adults report a decrease in psychological symptoms across time after experiencing a traumatic event such as a natural disaster (Norris et al., 2002). We plan to examine whether a similar decrease will be observed in this sample.

LESSONS LEARNED AND ACTIONABLE RECOMMENDATIONS

Findings from this study advance our knowledge relative to the post-disaster recovery of displaced youths. However, several major gaps in the evidence base persist. First, very little is known about the postdisaster mental health trajectories of children and adolescents. Much more research is needed across different types of disasters to provide a clearer picture of the ways in which youths are affected. Second, whereas 40 adult samples were identified in the disaster literature, only 3 youth samples were identified. Longitudinal research that recruits youth participants via random sampling is needed to maximize the generalizability of findings. Sampling is especially complicated in research with displaced samples and limited budgets; these factors precluded the use of random sampling in the present study. Third, interventions and educational resources are very limited for children and families affected by disaster. Gibson (2006) reviewed intervention studies published from 1967 to 2005 and identified only 10 postdisaster intervention studies conducted with youth samples. Six of these studies examined formal, multisession interventions that were delivered between 6 months and several years after the disaster, and only two were randomized controlled studies. The remaining four studies were of brief interventions conducted within 6 months following a disaster; three were of debriefing (a contraindicated intervention), and one was of back massage therapy. Although ongoing and recently completed research in the aftermath of the terrorist attacks of September 11, 2001, and Hurricane Katrina likely will advance our knowledge in this area, much more work is needed. Clearly, there is a significant unmet need for evidence-informed resources for disaster-affected youths and families.

REFERENCES

Acierno, R., Ruggiero, K. J., Galea, S., Resnick, H. S., Koenen, K., Roitzsch, J., et al. (2007). Psychological sequelae resulting from the 2004 Florida hurricanes: Implications for post-disaster intervention. *American Journal of Public Health, 97,* S103–S108.

Ahern, J., Galea, S., Resnick, H., & Vlahov, D. (2004). Television images and probable posttraumatic stress disorder after September 11: The role of background characteristics, event exposures, and perievent panic. *Journal of Nervous and Mental Disease, 192,* 217–226.

American Psychiatric Association. (1994). *Diagnostic and statistical manual of mental disorders* (4th ed.). Washington, DC: Author.

Asarnow, J., Glynn, S., Pynoos, R. S., Nahum, J., Guthrie, D., Cantwell, D. P., et al. (1999). When the earth stops shaking: Earthquake sequelae among children diagnosed for pre-earthquake psychopathology. *Journal of the American Academy of Child and Adolescent Psychiatry, 38,* 1016–1023.

Brewin, C., Galea, S., Jones, R., Kendrick, D., Kessler, R., King, D., et al. (2006, August 29). *Overview of baseline survey results: Hurricane Katrina Community Advisory Group.* Cambridge, MA: Harvard Medical School, Hurricane Katrina Community Advisory Group. Retrieved September 1, 2006, from http://www.hurricane katrina.med.harvard.edu/reports.php

Bronfenbrenner, U., & Morris, P. A. (2006). The bioecological model of human development. In R. M. Lerner & W. R. Damon (Eds.), *Handbook of child psychology: Vol. 1. Theoretical models of human development* (6th ed., pp. 793–828). Hoboken, NJ: Wiley.

Dempsey, M., Overstreet, S., & Moely, B. (2000). "Approach" and "avoidance" coping and PTSD symptoms in inner-city youth. *Current Psychology: Developmental, Learning, Personality, Social, 19,* 28–45.

Earls, F., Smith, E., Reich, W., & Jung, K. G. (1988). Investigating psychological consequences of a disaster in children: A pilot study incorporating a structured diagnostic interview. *Journal of the American Academy of Child and Adolescent Psychiatry, 27,* 90–95.

Engelhard, I. M., van den Hout, M. A., Weerts, J., Arntz, A., Hox, J. J. C. M., & McNally, R. J. (2007). Deployment-related stress and trauma in Dutch soldiers returning from Iraq. *British Journal of Psychiatry, 191,* 140–145.

Essau, C. A., Sasagawa, S., & Frick, P. J. (2006). Psychometric properties of the Alabama Parenting Questionnaire. *Journal of Child and Family Studies, 15,* 597–616.

Fairbanks, J. A., Putnam, F. W., & Harris, W. W. (2007). The prevalence and impact of child traumatic stress. In M. J. Friedman, T. M. Keane, & P. A. Resick (Eds.), *Handbook of PTSD: Science and practice* (pp. 229–251). New York: Guilford Press.

Galea, S., Ahern, J., Resnick, H., Kilpatrick, D., Bucuvalas, M., & Gold, J., et al. (2002). Psychological sequelae of the September 11 terrorist attacks in New York City. *New England Journal of Medicine, 346,* 982–987.

Galea, S., Vlahov, D., Resnick, H., Ahern, J., Susser, E., & Gold, J. (2003). Trends of probable post-traumatic stress disorder in New York City after the September 11 terrorist attacks. *American Journal of Epidemiology, 158,* 514–524.

Garrison, C. Z., Bryant, E. S., Addy, C. L., Spurrier, P. G., Freedy, J. R., & Kilpatrick, D. G. (1995). Posttraumatic stress disorder in adolescents after Hurricane Andrew. *Journal of the American Academy of Child and Adolescent Psychiatry, 34,* 1193–1201.

Gibson, L. E. (2006). *A review of the published empirical literature regarding early- and later-stage interventions for individuals exposed to traumatic stress.* Hanover, NH: Dartmouth College, Research Education in Disaster Mental Health.

Goenjian, A. K., Molina, L., Steinberg, A. M., Fairbanks, L. A., Alvarez, M. L., & Goenjian, H. A. (2001). Posttraumatic stress and depressive reactions among Nicaraguan adolescents after Hurricane Mitch. *American Journal of Psychiatry, 158,* 788–794.

Hastings, T. L., & Kelley, M. L. (1997). Development and validation of the Screen for Adolescent Violence Exposure (SAVE). *Journal of Abnormal Child Psychology, 25,* 511–520.

Hausman, A. J., Spivak, H., & Prothrow-Stith, D. (1994). Adolescents' knowledge and attitudes about experience with violence. *Journal of Adolescent Health, 15,* 400–406.

Hensley, L., & Varela, E. (2008). PTSD symptoms and somatic complaints following Hurricane Katrina: The roles of trait anxiety and anxiety sensitivity. *Journal of Clinical Child and Adolescent Psychology, 37,* 542–552.

Hinshaw, S. P., & Lee, S. S. (2003). Conduct and oppositional defiant disorders. In E. J. Mash & R. A. Barkley (Eds.), *Child psychopathology* (2nd ed., pp. 144–198). New York: Guilford Press.

Johnson, K. (2007, February 22). Post-Katrina Baton Rouge struggles with its identity. *USA Today.* Retrieved March 31, 2009, from http://www.usatoday.com/news/nation/2007-02-21-baton-rouge-cover_x.htm

Jones, R. T., Ribbe, D. P., Cunningham, P. B., Weddle, J. D., & Langley, A. K. (2002). Psychological impact of fire disaster on children and their parents. *Behavior Modification, 26,* 163–186.

Kessler, R. C., Galea, S., Jones, R. T., & Parker, H. A. (2006). Mental illness and suicidality after Hurricane Katrina. *Bulletin of the World Health Organization, 84,* 930–939.

Kilpatrick, D. G., Ruggiero, K. J., Acierno, R. E., Saunders, B. E., Resnick, H. S., & Best, C. L. (2003). Violence and risk of PTSD, major depression, substance abuse/dependence, and comorbidity: Results from the National Survey of Adolescents. *Journal of Consulting and Clinical Psychology, 71,* 692–700.

Kliewer, W., Cunningham, J. N., Diehl, R., Parrish, K. A., Walker, J. A., Atiyeh, C., et al. (2004). Violence exposure and adjustment in inner-city youth: Child and caregiver emotion regulation skill, caregiver–child relationship quality, and neighborhood cohesion as protective factors. *Journal of Clinical Child and Adolescent Psychology, 33,* 477–487.

Kliewer, W., Parrish, K. A., Taylor, K. W., Jackson, K., Walker, J. M., & Shivy, V. A. (2006). Socialization of coping with community violence: Influences of caregiver coaching, modeling, and family context. *Child Development, 77,* 605–623.

Koplewicz, H. S., Vogel, J. M., Solanto, M. V., Morrissey, R. F., Alonso, C. M., Abikoff, H., et al. (2002). Child and parent response to the 1993 World Trade Center bombing. *Journal of Traumatic Stress, 15,* 77–85.

La Greca, A. M., Silverman, W. K., Vernberg, E. M., & Prinstein, M. J. (1996). Symptoms of posttraumatic stress in children after Hurricane Andrew: A prospective study. *Journal of Consulting and Clinical Psychology, 64,* 712–723.

La Greca, A. M., Silverman, W. K., & Wasserstein, S. B. (1998). Children's predisaster functioning as a predictor of posttraumatic stress following Hurricane Andrew. *Journal of Consulting and Clinical Psychology, 66,* 883–892.

Lanclos, N. F. (2002). Parenting practices as a moderator of exposure to community violence. *Dissertations Abstracts International, 63,* 1035.

Lonigan, C. J., Shannon, M. P., Finch, A. J., Daugherty, T. K., & Taylor, C. M. (1991). Children's reactions to a natural disaster: Symptom severity and degree of exposure. *Behaviour Research and Therapy, 13,* 135–154.

Mash, E. J., & Dozois, D. J. (2003). Child psychology: A developmental-systems perspective. In E. J. Mash & R. A. Barkley (Eds.), *Child psychopathology* (2nd ed., pp. 3–71). New York: Guilford Press.

Nader, K. O., Pynoos, R., Fairbanks, L., & Frederick, C. (1990). Children's PTSD reactions one year after a sniper attack at their school. *American Journal of Psychiatry, 147,* 1526–1530.

Norris, F. H., & Elrod, C. L. (2006). Psychosocial consequences of disaster: A review of past research. In F. H. Norris, S. Galea, M. J. Friedman, & P. J. Watson (Eds.), *Methods for disaster mental health research* (pp. 20–42). New York: Guilford Press.

Norris, F. H., Friedman, M. J., Watson, P. J., Byrne, C. M., Diaz, E., & Kaniasty, K. (2002). 60,000 disaster victims speak: Part I. An empirical review of the empirical literature, 1981–2001. *Psychiatry: Interpersonal and Biological Processes, 65,* 207–239.

Osofsky, J. D., Wewers, S., Hann, D. M., & Fick, A. C. (1993). Chronic community violence: What is happening to our children? *Psychiatry: Interpersonal and Biological Processes, 56,* 36–45.

Overstreet, S., Dempsey, M., Graham, D., & Moely, B. (1999). Availability of family support as a moderator of exposure to community violence. *Journal of Clinical Child Psychology, 28,* 151–159.

Patterson, G. R. (1982). *Coercive family process.* Eugene, OR: Castalia.

Pynoos, R. S., Goenjian, A. K., & Steinberg, A. M. (1998). A public mental health approach to the post-disaster treatment of children and adolescents. *Child and Adolescent Psychiatric Clinics of North America, 7,* 195–210.

Pynoos, R., Rodriguez, N., Steinberg, A., Stuber, M., & Frederick, C. (1998). *The UCLA PTSD Reaction Index for DSM–IV (Revision 1).* Los Angeles: University of California at Los Angeles Trauma Psychiatry Program.

Reynolds, C. R., & Kamphaus, R. W. (2004). *Behavior assessment system for children, second edition manual.* Circle Pines, MN: American Guidance Service.

Ruggiero, K. J., Rheingold, A. A., Resnick, H. S., Kilpatrick, D. G., & Galea, S. (2006). Comparison of two widely used PTSD-screening instruments: Implications for public mental health planning. *Journal of Traumatic Stress, 19,* 699–707.

Scaramella, L. V., Sohr-Preston, S. L., Callahan, K. L., & Mirabile, S. P. (2008). A test of the family stress model on toddler-aged children's adjustment among Hurricane Katrina impacted and nonimpacted low income families. *Journal of Clinical Child and Adolescent Psychology, 37,* 530–541.

Schafer, J. L., & Graham, J. W. (2002). Missing data: Our view of the state of the art. *Psychological Methods, 7,* 147–177.

Shannon, M. P., Lonigan, C. J., Finch, A. J., & Taylor, C. M. (1994). Children exposed to disaster: I. Epidemiology of posttraumatic symptoms and symptom profile. *Journal of the American Academy of Child and Adolescent Psychiatry, 33,* 80–93.

Shaw, J. A., Applegate, B., Tanner, S., Perez, D., Rothe, E., Campo-Bowen, A. E., et al. (1995). Psychological effects of Hurricane Andrew on an elementary school population. *Journal of the American Academy of Child and Adolescent Psychiatry, 34*, 1185–1192.

Shelton, K. K., Frick, P. J., & Wootton, J. (1996). Assessment of parenting practices in families of elementary school-age children. *Journal of Clinical Child Psychology, 25*, 317–329.

Steinberg, A. M., Brymer, M. J., Decker, K. B., & Pynoos, R. S. (2004). The University of California at Los Angeles Posttraumatic Stress Disorder Reaction Index. *Current Psychiatry Reports, 6*, 96–100.

Sullivan, T. N., Kung, E. M., & Farrell, A. D. (2004). Relation between witnessing violence and drug use initiation among rural adolescents: Parental monitoring and family support as protective factors. *Journal of Clinical Child and Adolescent Psychology, 33*, 488–498.

Sytsma, S. E., Kelley, M. L., & Wymer, J. H. (2001). Development and initial validation of the Child Routines Questionnaire. *Journal of Psychopathology and Behavioral Assessment, 23*, 241–251.

Thienkrua, W., Cardozo, B. L., Chakkraband, M. L., Guadamuz, T. E., Tengjuntr, W., Tantipiwatanaskul, P., et al. (2006). Symptoms of posttraumatic stress disorder and depression among children in tsunami-affected areas in southern Thailand. *JAMA, 296*, 549–559.

Vernberg, E. M., La Greca, A. M., Silverman, W. K., & Prinstein, M. J. (1996). Prediction of posttraumatic stress symptoms in children after Hurricane Andrew. *Journal of Abnormal Psychology, 105*, 237–248.

Vlahov, D., Galea, S., Ahern, J., Resnick, H., & Kilpatrick, D. (2004). Sustained increased consumption of cigarettes, alcohol, and marijuana among Manhattan residents after September 11, 2001. *American Journal of Public Health, 94*, 253–254.

Waggoner, C. E. (2006). Comparison of the BASC–2 PRS to the BASC PRS in a population of children and adolescents classified as HFA, Asperger disorder or PDD NOS including convergent validity. *Dissertations Abstracts International, 66*, 6316.

Weems, C. F., & Overstreet, S. (2008). Child and adolescent mental health research in the context of Hurricane Katrina: An ecological needs-based perspective and introduction to the Special Section. *Journal of Clinical Child and Adolescent Psychology, 37*, 487–494.

Weems, C. F., Watts, S. E., Marsee, M. A., Taylor, K. K., Costa, N. M., Cannon, M. F., et al. (2007). The psychosocial impact of Hurricane Katrina: Contextual differences in psychological symptoms, social support, and discrimination. *Behavior Research and Therapy, 45*, 2295–2306.

4

FAMILY RESILIENCE AND RESILIENCY FOLLOWING HURRICANE KATRINA

ROBIN KNOWLES, DIANE D. SASSER, AND M. E. BETSY GARRISON

Families who "struggle well" and become resilient do so through processes that "can reduce stress and vulnerability in high-risk situations, foster healing and growth out of crisis, and empower families to overcome persistent adversity" (Walsh, 2003, p. 405). Although use of the term *resilience* has been the subject of some debate (e.g., Hawley & DeHaan, 1996; Luthar, Cicchetti, & Becker, 2000; Masten, 2001), it reflects the idea that a person (or, in our research, a family) has strengths or resources that have allowed him or her to overcome a challenging experience and to thrive following that experience (Cowan, Cowan, & Shultz, 1996; Patterson, 2002). As opposed to survival (Walsh, 1999), resilience is a dynamic process (Walsh, 2003). Because we share the view of some family scientists who differentiate *resilience*, a process, from *resiliency*, an outcome (e.g., Patterson, 2002), we designed our research project on the adaptation of families following Hurricane Katrina to investigate both resilience and resiliency. Considerable research has focused

This research was supported in part by the School of Human Ecology, the College of Agriculture, Louisiana State University, and the Louisiana State University Agricultural Center. We thank the participants in our research, as well as Vicky Tiller, research associate par excellence, without whom this project would not have been possible. This chapter was approved for publication by the director of the Louisiana Agricultural Experiment Station as Manuscript No. 07-36-0268.

on the experience and responses of individuals to disaster, yet the study of the family and the experiences of its members following disaster has been largely neglected. Using a mixed-method approach, the current work sought to investigate (a) family resiliency within and across time using quantitative methods and (b) family resilience using qualitative methods.

The roller coaster model, developed by Koos (1946) and further refined by Hill (1949), depicts a process in which a family experiencing a crisis goes through a plunge in functioning followed by an upsurge. The core premise underlying the model is that all families initially experience a postcrisis period of disorganization, characterized by lower and lower levels of functioning (Koos, 1946). Recovery is characterized by a pivot-type turnaround with improving levels of functioning, followed by a reorganized family. A review of the extant family literature shows that before Burr and Klein's study (1994), the assumption that families experienced a period of disorganization after a crisis had not been empirically tested, and no disaster studies had used this model.

Burr and Klein's (1994) work examined the functioning of 46 families that had experienced one of six different crises in their lifetime—bankruptcy, infertility, a problem teen, a family member with muscular dystrophy, a displaced homemaker, and a child who was handicapped and required institutionalization. They identified five distinct trajectories: a roller coaster model, an increased model, a mixed model, a no-change model, and a decrease model. The increased model characterized families that experienced increases in functioning without experiencing a decline after a crisis. The mixed model was characterized by an increase in functioning immediately following the crisis and a subsequent decline. The no-change model was characterized by family functioning that neither decreased nor increased after a crisis. The decrease model was characterized by a steady decline in family functioning and no increases. The models complemented Walsh's (2003) framework as they provided visual imagery regarding family functioning and the explicit passage of time.

On the basis of the bioecological model (Bronfenbrenner, 2005; see also Introduction, this volume), Walsh (2003) developed a family resilience framework that encompasses three domains of family functioning: belief systems, organizational patterns, and communication processes. Resilience is cultivated by a family's "shared facilitative beliefs" that help create meaning in times of crisis, promote optimism, and provide connectedness through transcendence and spirituality. For a family to make meaning out of adversity, it is necessary for family members to rely on each other to overcome challenges. A resilient family remains hopeful, focuses on how their strengths can help them through the situation, adopts a can-do attitude, and accepts the aspects of the situation that are out of their control. Through transcendence and spirituality, the family is able to find connectedness through their value system, faith beliefs and practices, and their own personal transformation that comes from experiencing and working through adversity (Walsh, 2003, p. 407).

Family organizational patterns include flexibility, connectedness, and resources used. Flexibility is vital if a family is to not just "bounce back," but also "bounce forward" (Walsh, 2003, pp. 410–411). Resilient families are able to balance change and stability when faced with challenge. Family connectedness is demonstrated through the "mutual support, collaboration, and commitment to weather troubled times together," even as members simultaneously respect the various reactions and needs of each other (Walsh, 2003, p. 411). The family's ability to grow from crisis situations depends partly on its ability to marshal its social and economic resources (Walsh, 2003).

Family communication processes include the family's ability to maintain clarity in crisis situations by communicating clear messages about the crisis and addressing any ambiguity that may arise. Open emotional expression is important when a family faces a crisis that can provoke a wide range of emotions among members, and such communication depends on their ability to share and empathize, to use humor, and to remain aware of and attuned to their own individual feelings. The family's collaborative problem solving involves all members working together to brainstorm and identify their resources, make decisions, work toward their goals, and prepare for future events (Walsh, 2003, pp. 413–414).

One way to conceptualize family resiliency is through the instrumental and expressive functions of family life. Instrumental functions of families typically include the adult roles of being in charge of tasks, taking care of the financial needs of the family, and other concrete assistance or capacities (Cochran & Niego, 2002). Examples of instrumental tasks are taking children to school, being the wage earner, and ensuring safety. Expressive functions include communication of caring, love, and emotional support, as well as tasks related to nurturing and comforting (Pierce, Sarason, & Sarason, 1996), including conflict resolution.

In the current work, we used both instrumental and expressive functions of family life to investigate the resiliency of families directly affected by Katrina. We used Walsh's (2003) framework, which is based on the bioecological perspective, to guide our work and the roller coaster model as the expected trajectory or pattern of recovery. Together, the roller coaster model and Walsh's framework provide a more complete and clearer picture of family life, including processes such as resilience.

CRISIS DESCRIPTION OF TARGETED STUDY SITE

Individual, family, and community functioning were put to the test with the destruction caused by Hurricane Katrina. One of the areas hit hard by the storm was the St. Tammany Parish area in Louisiana. The city of Slidell and its residents suffered major damage because of their proximity to Lake Pontchartrain. An estimated 4,000 of 10,300 homes in Slidell sustained serious damage from Katrina; 400 to 700 were complete losses. More than one of every seven businesses in the region was destroyed, and the estimated cost of the damage was $118,366,000 (*St. Tammany Parish Disaster Impact and Needs Assessment*, 2006). Every school was either damaged or destroyed, as were both universities in the parish. Twenty-five percent of the staff in local hospitals have yet to return, and the number of uninsured hospital patients has tripled (*St. Tammany Parish Disaster Impact and Needs Assessment*, 2006). Well after Katrina, the city's administrative center continued to bivouac in a series of temporary buildings, and the Slidell branch of the University of New Orleans was closed permanently (City of Slidell, 2007a, 2007b; Louisiana Speaks, 2006).

METHOD

Data for this study were collected in the first and second waves of a larger project on families and disasters, one that also includes families who were affected by Hurricane Rita. Before the study began, the institutional review board at Louisiana State University granted its approval. In early 2006, this project targeted families who had returned to a residential area in southern Louisiana following Hurricane Katrina. Geographic information systems technology was used to locate an area that had sustained wind damage or flooding. Respondents were recruited by door-to-door contact in the affected neighborhoods, and semistructured interviews were conducted between February and April 2006. Most interviews took place in the participant's home or in a Federal Emergency Management Agency (FEMA) trailer, though a few were conducted at an elementary school in Slidell. Some respondents provided names and phone numbers of friends and family members who also qualified for the study.

Before we began collecting data, we consulted disaster mental health professionals and conducted extensive interviewer training. Two trauma experts and two accomplished qualitative researchers reviewed the interview schedule. Participant packets included a list of local mental health professionals and agencies and informational bulletins about coping published by the Louisiana Cooperative Extension Service. The packet also included a copy of the description of the larger longitudinal study and a consent form. For the second wave of data collection, we updated the packet and again obtained informed consent.

The interviews ranged from 30 minutes to 2 hours, with an average length of 60 minutes; all interviews were voice recorded. During each interview, one of the interviewers logged notes and wrote down comments about the veracity of the information obtained. The narratives were transcribed verbatim, and the quantitative data were scored and entered.

For the second wave of interviews in spring 2007, the revised interview schedule included a protocol similar to that developed by Burr and Klein (1994); respondents were presented a chart (comparable to a sheet of graph paper) and were asked to draw a timeline depicting their functioning during "big events" that had occurred to their family. The chart was organized in a grid format (see Figure 4.1 for examples). The x-axis represented respondent-generated periods of time, and the y-axis represented a range from "low" to "high" family functioning. A dashed line drawn horizontally at the midpoint of the grid represented "normal" functioning. Respondents were asked to view the vertical lines as indicators of points in time before and after the hurricane, with respect to a vertical line that represented Hurricane Katrina's landfall. Events drawn to the left of the vertical "Katrina Landfall" line occurred before the storm, and events drawn to the right of the vertical line occurred after the storm. Respondents then rated their family's functioning when an event occurred by marking it on the chart. The respondent indicated periods of higher family functioning by marking events closer to the top of the chart and lower family functioning by marking events closer to the bottom. The resulting series of horizontal marks or points were then connected into a line to depict a family's recovery pattern. Participants were asked the following questions: "Thinking back to before the storm, what do you remember doing? How were you doing?" The following probes were also used: "Did you evacuate? What was going on in your family's life before the storm? Were you stressed out? Was there anything out of the ordinary?"

As in Wave 1, responses to the qualitative questions and conversations during the chart portions of the interview were voice recorded; these recordings supplemented the timeline of events before and after Hurricane Katrina. Also, data from the qualitative interviews framework in the first wave of the study and interviewer notes were used to construct more complete trajectories. Qualitative data from both waves were reviewed by separate members of the research team who had not conducted the interviews but who were immersed in the relevant literature, as recommended by Gilgun (1992). Open coding was conducted to generate themes, axial coding was then conducted to organize the themes, and finally selective coding was conducted to confirm interpretations and find quotes or cases that best illustrated the identified themes (Neuman, 2006).

The interview for the larger project contained several measures besides family resiliency. We developed the interview on the basis of our experiences in interviewing Katrina survivors at a local shelter in the storm's immediate aftermath. From those experiences, we realized the interview needed to be as

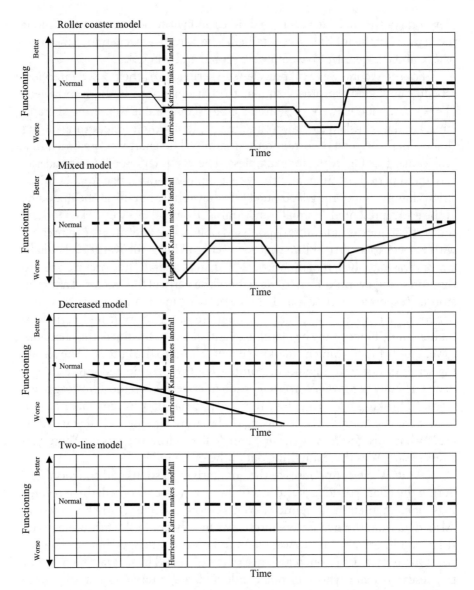

Figure 4.1. Sample roller coaster, mixed, decreased, and two-line models of family functioning. The *x*-axis represents respondent-generated periods of time. The *y*-axis represents a range from low to high family functioning; a dashed line drawn horizontally at midpoint represents "normal" functioning. A vertical line represents Hurricane Katrina's landfall.

simple and brief as possible, especially to allow sufficient time for open-ended questions. After several sessions, consultations with other disaster researchers (especially the Disaster Research Education and Mentoring Center at the University of Michigan School of Public Health, Ann Arbor), and pilot testing, we narrowed the quantitative measures to the following constructs: resource loss (Sattler, 2002), prior traumatic events and cumulative stress, family resiliency, and socioeconomic and demographic characteristics, including family structure and home ownership. We also developed a 17-item family resiliency assessment intended to capture the salient instrumental and expressive functions of family life (see Table 4.1).

RESULTS

The Wave 1 sample included 50 respondents living in St. Tammany Parish, Louisiana. They were primarily middle-aged ($M = 48.0$ years, $SD = 15.5$), married, employed, White women from middle-income families who owned or were paying a mortgage on their homes. Approximately one third of respondents reported that children were living in the household. One and a half years after Hurricane Katrina, 28 (56%) of the original respondents participated in the second wave of the study. Among those who did not take part in Wave 2, 10 had moved, 5 passively declined, 3 actively declined, and we were unable to contact 3. Fourteen (50%) of the Wave 2 respondents agreed to complete the chart portion of the interview. The other Wave 2 respondents did not complete the chart because they did not understand the procedure ($n = 6$), had medical problems or other challenges (e.g., hearing loss, lack of comprehension) so that the interviewer discreetly omitted the chart to preserve the respondents' dignity ($n = 5$), did not have time to complete the chart ($n = 2$), or otherwise declined to participate ($n = 1$). The socioeconomic and demographic profiles of the sample did not differ between Waves 1 and 2 or between the total sample from Wave 2 and the subsample of participants who completed charts.

Table 4.1 depicts participants' responses to family resiliency items for Waves 1 and 2. Notably, three of the seven expressive items demonstrated the most improvement after the storm. In Wave 2, all expressive aspects of family life, all but three instrumental items, and overall family life were reported as "better." These results suggest that the participants' families seem to have been resilient; they had been able to cope with their experiences and adapt to their current circumstances. The deterioration of physical health, in particular, warrants further attention. A more interesting question, however, might be, How did they become resilient? We explored this and other questions and processes through the data provided on the charts.

TABLE 4.1
Responses to Items in Family Resiliency Assessment by Dimension for Wave 1 ($n = 50$) and Wave 2 ($n = 28$)

Item	% Better		% Worse		% Same		Modal response	
	Wave 1	Wave 2	Wave 1	Wave 2	Wave 1	Wave 2	Wave 1	Wave 2
Instrumental items								
Financial situation	24	43	36	32	40	25	Same	Better
Safety	16	39	20	21	32	39	Same	Better/same
Decision making	28	46	20	25	32	29	Same	Better
Physical health	0	32	40	46	60	21	Same	Worse
Mental health	8	36	34	32	58	32	Same	Better
Ability to solve practical or daily problems	18	39	22	18	30	43	Same	Same
Ability to perform household responsibilities	6	39	32	32	62	28	Same	Better
Ability to set priorities	2	54	34	21	64	25	Same	Better
Expressive items								
Ability to respect each other	46	64	4	4	48	32	Same	Better
Ability to be supportive	58	71	6	7	34	21	Better	Better
Ability to resolve conflicts	38	57	10	7	52	36	Same	Better
Ability to communicate	52	57	10	7	38	36	Better	Better
Relationship between spouses (if applicable)	38	71	6	5	26	24	Better	Better
Relationship(s) between parent and child(ren)	42	64	2	8	40	28	Better	Better
Relationship between your family and extended family	28	50	18	8	54	42	Same	Better
Relationship between your family and your neighbors	38	52	12	11	50	37	Same	Better
Overall, my family's life since the hurricane is . . .	20	64	28	14	50	21	Same	Better

Note. Columns do not add up to 100% because of missing data.

The majority of family members ($n = 10$) who completed the chart indicated that their family experienced a roller coaster pattern after Katrina, characterized by a drop in family functioning after the crisis followed by a return to baseline functioning (see Figure 4.1). Three other patterns were identified: mixed ($n = 2$), decreased ($n = 1$), and two-line ($n = 1$). The roller coaster model of recovery was exhibited by one family in which the caregivers had divorced shortly before the storm, indicating that family functioning was very low. The storm hit the husband's property, destroying all the paperwork he had gathered during the property settlement for their divorce. "Hitting rock bottom" occurred after the storm, when the husband's mother died (no one was able to attend the funeral) and his ex-wife became engaged. The husband began his recovery with his engagement to a high school sweetheart, then reached a level of equal or higher functioning when his FEMA trailer arrived, enabling him to work on restoring his home. In Wave 2, the ex-wife had broken her engagement, the husband followed suit with his fiancée, and the two of them moved in together along with their daughter, establishing an even greater level of functioning for the entire family. In the husband's view during Wave 1,

> I don't know if it's 'cause of the hurricane, but my dad has stopped going to church since my mom died. I mean, that's the biggest thing, and I don't know if he's mad at God or whatever for my mom. . . . It was hard on him to lose her . . . 2005 was a big year for loss. Divorce, hurricane, death of my mother, just a lot.

His comments indicated the low level of functioning he was experiencing after the hurricane. However, during the Wave 2 interview, the same man reported,

> I looked toward my ex-wife for direction, and it was hard for me until she broke up with her boyfriend. . . . I told her in the note that I didn't want to be in the house by myself, and things were going bad in her relationships, so this was just a win–win situation. . . . We have talked about issues we had during the course of the divorce and explained things here and there. She is my one true love. . . . For me it was a rebirth.

The husband's spirituality, meaning making, open emotional expression, and collaborative problem solving with his ex-wife, all dimensions of Walsh's (2003) resilience framework, may have contributed to their success in recovery and higher levels of family functioning.

Another family exhibiting a roller coaster pattern had moved into a new home 4 months before the storm. They had experienced "normal" family functioning until that time. The hurricane flooded the first level of their home, the wife's parents' home, and the homes of other relatives. They cooked and ate in a FEMA trailer; however, the family spent their nights on the second floor of the damaged home. The husband maintained a job but was required to travel a great deal, leaving his wife alone to make the family decisions. She described her frustration:

> He's [her husband] been engulfed in his work and doesn't mind living in that room [the upstairs bedroom of the flooded home]. . . . I just want to get the house finished. . . . But he's out every day, and it [the housing situation] doesn't faze him the same way. . . . That's caused a lot of rift between us.

She maintained a positive attitude and reported,

> We're a very close, very close family. We still make time for family time. Sundays are still for crawfishing or doing something. We still maintain those things [family traditions] for the kids. . . . We get excited about new things we're putting in the house.

By Wave 2, the couple had a new baby, and the FEMA trailer had just been removed from in front of their home; priorities had changed for the family. Interviews with this respondent indicated a positive outlook along with economic and social resources, connectedness to her children, and open emotional expression with her family—all of which could account for their ability to bounce back and lend empirical support to Walsh's (2003) framework.

> My boys don't play with toys anymore. They go outside to play. For so long they didn't have any toys [because] we had to throw them away, and we didn't have room for toys in the trailer. . . . It has been quite peaceful. We had to learn to give each other space.

A family who reported a mixed pattern (see Figure 4.1) detailed some aspects of their lives that had become better, some worse, and some the same regarding their family functioning since the hurricane. The wife described their situation since the storm as follows: "[The storm] has affected everyone's lives and still affects them. . . . It's always pre-Katrina and post-Katrina talk; people haven't changed what they talk about."

The husband's business was just as busy as it had been before the storm, affording them the same financial resources. However, the wife reported that a loss of employees had created more work for her husband. Coupled with the husband's physical stress due to the increased workload, the wife experienced a few very stressful months at her work with a housing project providing homes for needy families; she viewed these challenges as almost as bad an experience as the storm. The wife's stress was due not only to a heavy caseload but also to having to turn people away because the housing project was no longer taking applications during a time when families were in desperate need of housing. She expressed her frustration by saying, "People still have problems. There was a young woman who came in and said, 'I need an application for a home.' And I said, 'We're not taking applications now.' She just walked out and cried . . . sometimes you don't sleep well."

This family's mixed level of functioning indicated the presence of spirituality and economic resources but showed a lack of positive outlook and social resources. Her husband's job showed promise, but he did not have all the help he needed. The respondent did not appear to have an opportunity for positive social interaction because of the nature of her job.

One family who experienced decreased functioning was living in close quarters in camper trailers and not seeing much progress on rebuilding their home (see Figure 4.1). Three daughters shared another FEMA trailer next to the parents' camper:

> All of my girls dropped their interests . . . and my oldest loved it [twirling baton], and she just dropped out; she said she had a lot of stress this year with school. . . . My kids' grades have gone down. . . . You have to find a place for the three of them to do homework all at the same time. . . . My girls are closer, but living here . . . I don't know if it's just so small that they tend to argue more often. They yell!

The lack of economic resources and physical crowding because of the living conditions could account for the family's reported decreased family functioning (see, e.g., Walsh, 2003).

The two-line pattern drawn by one of our respondents was unique in our study and was not present among Burr and Klein's (1994) models. With the exception of deaths in the family, the other families reported events that involved only members living under the same roof. However, the respondent who drew the two-line model indicated that the loss of her grandmother's home affected her family functioning, as did her grandmother's illnesses and the illnesses of two aunts, none of whom lived with her. The respondent lived in an apartment with her new husband, her mother, and her three younger siblings. Her extended kin all lived within walking distance from her home. The families were so closely networked and dependent on one another that a crisis was a shared event that was dealt with collectively. During the qualitative interview, when asked about the positive aspects of her family, she responded,

> I guess I could say that we kind of stick together, and when you need something from somebody, they will usually try to help you with it, try to. . . . I couldn't even deal with the heat [there was no electricity in the home] . . . so we would all take turns with the fan.

The two-line model indicated that the family was having both high and low functioning due to two separate events occurring simultaneously. Family functioning was high after the hurricane because she had just gotten married and had found out that she was pregnant. At the same time, two of her aunts found out that they had cancer, her grandmother had a stroke, and then her grandmother lost her house. She shared how her grandmother's loss in particular was a loss for the whole family, as the family's life centered on the grandmother:

> She [grandmother] got him [an insurance adjuster] to bring her to her house, and she was thinking that she was going there to stay, but he had to bring her back because they told her, "You can't live in this house. This house is not livable." . . . My grandpa and them built that house, and she raised all of her kids in that house. . . . We grew up in that house; my grandma would take care of anybody. . . . [Now there is a nursing staff to care for her] . . . [and she is] getting fed through a feeding tube. . . . I hate looking at her like that.

Because she considered her aunts and grandmother part of the immediate family, this participant included two lines on her chart. One conclusion that may be drawn from this example is that the family functioning line may depend on who is considered to be part of the immediate family and the degree to which a stressful event is shared among multiple households.

Although not an objective of the current work, a germane finding (from analysis of Wave 1 qualitative data for another project; $n = 17$) was that most parents were aware of their children's individual reactions and needs and took appropriate action, including obtaining counseling. In some cases, parents admitted they were experiencing a great deal of stress themselves and may have had trouble recognizing the symptoms in their children. Parents reported that their children displayed signs of grief or sadness, as indicated by crying; withdrawal from family, school, or other activities; regression in developmental stages; acting out; and/or school grade fluctuations. Children's reactions appeared to reflect their age and developmental level and to be exacerbated by loss (of a family member, close friend, or pet); the reaction of the parents, caregivers, and others to the disaster or to the child's distress; and whether or not the child had direct exposure to the disaster (Gaffney, 2006). Ongoing stress from the effects of disaster was due to being away from home, losing contact with friends and neighbors, and losing things that were important to them (e.g., a favorite toy, access to a playground). Their lives were disrupted, as in other disasters, when they no longer had a usual meeting place or their routines and living conditions changed. Parents' responses to their children's reactions were tied to their own stress reactions, their level of attendance to their children's needs, and their relationship with their spouses. Parents of infants, in particular, did not appear to be as attuned and responsive to their children's needs as parents of older children.

DISCUSSION

The current work's first objective was to investigate the resiliency of families. In Wave 1, respondents reported that all of the instrumental aspects and half of the expressive aspects of their families' functioning remained the same after Katrina. This finding suggests that families' instrumental functioning neither decreases nor improves in the immediate aftermath of a disaster, and their expressive functioning either stays the same or improves. More than a year postdisaster, in Wave 2, respondents reported that all expressive aspects and all but two of the instrumental aspects (ability to solve practical or daily problems and physical health) of their families had improved. This finding suggests that families affected by a disaster are resilient and that families' functioning may evolved more toward expressive than instrumental tasks.

As indicated previously, the notion that physical health was worse 1½ years after the disaster invites inquiry. A classic family disaster study found that individuals were more likely to rely on their families than their friends for social support (Drabek, Key, Erickson, & Crowe, 1975). More recent studies found that disasters often damage social support networks and that institutionalized support networks alone are not adequate for helping individuals manage their vulnerabilities (Bates & Perlanda, 1994; Myers, 1989).

Physical health may be affected by the quality of familial and social relationships, as Klinenberg (2002) described. One may hypothesize that the annihilation of communities following Katrina and Rita increased the vulnerabilities of those affected and, in turn, may have affected their susceptibility to disease. It may also be that study participants were more likely to admit to having physical rather than mental health problems. Future studies should address these issues and include comparison groups when possible. Although the basic needs of food, clothing, and shelter were provided by various groups or organizations, this assistance did not replace the social networks long established by many of these families. The family resilience framework focuses on the strengths of the family for recovery. Therefore, loss of the family's customary social network potentially removes a key family asset in rebuilding their lives (Walsh, 2003).

Based on the roller coaster model and Walsh's (2003) framework, the second objective of the current work was to investigate family resilience (a process). Participants indicated that their families experienced a period of decreased functioning following Katrina, thus supporting the theorized pattern of recovery. Models other than the roller coaster were also identified; some participants indicated that their families' recovery patterns were either mixed or decreased, and one family's pattern included two distinct trajectories. None of the families in our study drew patterns that were consistent with the increase or no-change models found by Burr and Klein (1994). Almost

1 out of 5 families in the Burr and Klein study experienced increases in family functioning, and 15% of their families experienced no changes in functioning. Several factors may account for these divergent findings. First, the current study had only 14 participants in 14 families, and the Burr and Klein study had 82 participants in 46 families. The inclusion of more participants allows for the greater possibility of finding more varied responses to crises. In addition, the Burr and Klein study had a variety of crises, and time since the crises ranged from several months to over 20 years.

Although they reported a range of experiences, the present participants experienced the same crisis, Hurricane Katrina, at the same time. The passage of time and the type of crisis may affect reports of family functioning. Specifically, decreases in family functioning may be more salient and easily remembered when less time has passed. A family that experienced a crisis 20 years before may not readily remember how badly they perceived family functioning less than 2 years after the crisis. Research has documented how time since a crisis affects individuals' views of their recovery, but less work has studied family systems and their collective views of their adaptive capacities (e.g., Briere & Elliott, 2000; Tedeschi & Calhoun, 1996; Wang et al., 2000).

We found the two-line model of family resilience surprising and intriguing and one that we wished we had anticipated. One explanation for not finding more frequent occurrences of the two-line model is that we did not ask about it. The chart setup implied that events were happening in a linear fashion, and listing several events at the same time that had varying effects on the family may have been too difficult a task. Interview fatigue may also have been an issue. If the chart had been completed in the beginning rather than at the end of the interview, respondents may have been more willing to report more stressful events that were occurring concurrently. The percentage of families that might have described several lines of family functioning would probably be higher than the number found in this study had we explicitly asked for them.

In the current work, many participants described multiple stressful events during the qualitative portion of the interview but, during the chart portion, generally included only two or three events, leaving out things that they had discussed in detail. Several reasons may have contributed to the omission of events that were seemingly relevant to family functioning. For many people, the directions for completing the chart were difficult, and it was easier to place two or three salient events on a line rather than eight or nine. Also, because different stressors may have affected their families in differing ways, it may have been confusing to place them on the same timeline with respect to "how their family was doing." Even within the broader category of qualitative methodology, different methods may provide different types of information and levels of detail and richness. The chart portion of the interview allowed respondents to illustrate how their family's functioning had changed. Because the interview itself did not capture such fluctuations, it may be that a picture is worth a thousand words. Such pictures may be of value to the families of the respondents as well as to practitioners and other researchers.

The present findings must be considered within the context of several limitations. Study participants were not randomly selected; a convenience sample of residents from a single community was used. The sample size was also small, especially for the subsample of Wave 2. In addition, a majority of participants were able to return to their homes. Because the participants had returned home, they likely had more options and resources and different levels of trauma and distress than those who were not able to return. Those who did not return may have been a more appropriate sample for understanding how loss and stress affect the family because they may have experienced more loss and greater stress. Although respondents were asked to provide a collective response that reflected the perceptions of their entire family, it must be acknowledged that the individual's experiences may have taken precedence over the family's collective experiences; we would expect some differences in responses between and among members of the same family, particularly under such trying circumstances. We hope that other researchers extend and improve on the work we have started here, including the use of multiple methods.

LESSONS LEARNED AND ACTIONABLE RECOMMENDATIONS

Since Hurricanes Katrina and Rita, our primary maxim as dual residents of the Gulf Coast and the family scholarship field has been, "One size doesn't fit all" (and that FEMA trailers fit no one). This statement takes into account the variations and contextual differences we found among children, families, neighborhoods, schools, and communities (see Introduction and chap. 1, this volume). Thus, we recommend that those involved with disaster response and recovery in any manner become knowledgeable about effective approaches and the populations that they are meant to serve and then determine, before disaster strikes, how well they may fit the target population. In many cases, families were taken out of their support systems and relocated, but their social resources were not also relocated. Although the families' immediate and basic needs were met, the disaster response seemed to assume that families lived in a social and cultural vacuum. As a result, families in crisis were unintentionally forced to reestablish or fashion new support systems while also struggling to recover physically and emotionally (Bronfenbrenner, 2005; Cook & Bickman, 1990; Kaniasty & Norris, 1995).

In considering approaches that may be effective and appropriate under almost all disastrous conditions and circumstances, one approach would be to ensure that basic needs are being met and then to start with where the particular person, family, neighborhood, and community are in the recovery process. What are their demands? What are their values? What are their resources? What are their proximal and distal influences (see Introduction, this volume)? We strongly recommend a thorough reading of Walsh's (2007) recent work on this topic and would advocate for a strengths-based approach, as well as the explicit inclusion of the bioecological model (Bronfenbrenner, 2005).

Related to this approach is to ensure cultural competence—it is essential that anyone involved in disaster response and recovery, especially those from outside of the affected area, be culturally competent. Each researcher or practitioner needs to approach survivors (whether research participant, patient, client, or student) with respect and appreciation for their distress and potential traumatization, as well as their values and lifestyles. To assume that each individual and family is the same would not only be untrue but discourteous. Race and ethnicity, as well as gender, influence the way disaster or other trauma is perceived and acted on (Enarson, 1998; Fordham, 1999; Fothergill, Maestas, & Darlington, 1999; Morrow, 1997; Perilla, Norris, & Lavizzo, 2002), and sensitivity to the historical, political, social, cultural, and economic environments in which families live is absolutely paramount. It is also essential to consider individual differences within families and their kin, as well as differences between similarly structured families and communities. To facilitate recovery and reduce concerns about opportunism, those from outside the affected area who may somehow benefit from a disaster (e.g., through grant support or publications) should make significant efforts to "give back" by, for example, volunteering time or services to a local agency in the area or delivering personally donated (and requested) items, even if research participants are being compensated in another manner. These donations need to be appropriate to the culture and environments of the beneficiaries.

Another one of our maxims is, "Life doesn't stop just because you've survived a disaster." In our research and the experiences of those we know from other areas of our lives, this maxim has been driven home over and over again. Daily life, with its ebb and flow of little and bigger stressors, goes on; new normative and nonnormative stressors, ones unrelated to the disaster, arise, and more chronic ones, such as illnesses or addictions, may rear their ugly heads. New family members are born; children start school or graduate; people marry, divorce, and retire; older family members develop age-related health problems; accidents happen; crime occurs; and mistakes are made. The construct of pileup from the family stress literature was never more salient to us than in the ongoing aftermath of Katrina.

Our last maxim is, "Do no harm." From a strengths-based perspective, our findings indicated that scientists and helping professionals may need to give parents more credit than they do for their parenting ability, even under disastrous conditions. Parents indicated that they were sensitive to and concerned about the reactions, responses, and coping strategies of their children. It would be a mistake for scholars and practitioners to assume that parents were unaware of the nonphysical needs of their children and that they would not ask for outside professional help. It appears that with some families, helping professionals should step aside after basic needs—food, clothing, and shelter—have been met.

In addition to what we have already discussed, there are a couple of lessons learned that are too important to leave out. One such lesson we and others in the region learned was that those who responded to the needs of families were often survivors themselves. Service providers in the St. Tammany Parish had also suffered losses. The many whose homes were flooded by the hurricane were trying simultaneously to deal with loss, insurance claims, and their own children while helping others in their roles as outreach professionals and service providers. Those of us conducting research in the affected areas were leading parallel lives, discovering that to some degree, we experienced distress by simply being in the affected area and working with colleagues who had lost their homes, were unsure where some of their family members had been evacuated, or had lost significant others, including pets.

Given the predicted increase in the frequency of natural disasters and an increased number of people susceptible to their impact (Cutter, 2003), it is critical to continue work to understand the effects of disaster on families. It is sometimes said that families are the bedrock of a society. In the event of a disaster, resources that keep families strong are often less readily available or diminished, rendering families vulnerable (Bates & Pelanda, 1994). When families are vulnerable, communities can become vulnerable. Therefore, the commitment to policies, resources, and practices that result in sustainable communities must also include the intentional and programmatic development of stronger, healthier, and resilient families.

REFERENCES

Bates, F. L., & Perlanda, C. (1994). An ecological approach to disasters. In R. R. Dynes & K. J. Tierney (Eds.), *Disasters, collective behavior, and social organization* (pp. 145–159). Newark: University of Delaware Press.

Briere, J., & Elliott, D. (2000). Prevalance, characteristics, and long-term sequelae of natural disaster exposure in the general population. *Journal of Traumatic Stress, 13*, 661–679.

Bronfenbrenner, U. (Ed.). (2005). *Making human beings human: Bioecological perspectives on human development*. Thousand Oaks, CA: Sage.

Burr, W. R., & Klein, S. R. (1994). *Reexamining family stress*. Thousand Oaks, CA: Sage.

City of Slidell. (2007a). *Annual report*. Retrieved October 15, 2007, from http://www.slidell.la.us/files/annualreportwebsite.pdf

City of Slidell. (2007b). Financial fuss over city rebuilding costs resolved. *Update: City of Slidell Newsletter*. Retrieved October 15, 2007, from http://www.slidell.la.us/files/CityofSlidell UpdateJulyAugustgSept2007web.pdf

Cochran, M., & Niego, S. (2002). Parenting and social networks. In M. H. Bornstein (Ed.), *Handbook of parenting: Vol. 4. Social conditions and applied parenting* (2nd ed., pp. 393–418). Mahwah, NJ: Erlbaum.

Cook, J. D., & Bickman, L. (1990). Social support and psychological symptomology following a natural disaster. *Journal of Traumatic Stress, 3*, 541–556.

Cowan, P. A., Cowan, C. P., & Shultz, M. S. (1996). Thinking about risk and resilience in families. In E. M. Hetherington & E. A. Blachman (Eds.), *Stress, coping and resiliency in children and families* (pp. 1–38). Mahwah, NJ: Erlbaum.

Cutter, S. (2003). The changing nature of risks and hazards. In S. Cutter (Ed.), *American hazardscapes: The regionalization of hazards and disasters* (pp. 1–12). Washington, DC: Joseph Henry Press.

Drabek, T., Key, W., Erickson, P., & Crowe, J. (1975). The impact of disaster on kin relationships. *Journal of Marriage and the Family, 37*, 481–494.

Enarson, E. (1998). Through women's eyes: A gendered research agenda for disaster social science. *Disasters, 22*, 157–173.

Fordham, M. (1999). The intersection of gender and social class in disaster: Balancing resilience and vulnerability. *International Journal of Mass Emergencies and Disasters, 17*, 15–37.

Fothergill, A., Maestas, E. M. G., & Darlington, J. D. (1999). Race, ethnicity and disasters in the United States: A review of the literature. *Disasters, 23*, 156–173.

Gaffney, D. (2006). The aftermath of disaster: Children in crisis. *Journal of Clinical Psychology: In Session, 62*, 1001–1016.

Gilgun, J. F. (1992). Definitions, methodologies, and methods in qualitative family research. In J. F. Gilgun, K. Daly, & G. Handel (Eds.), *Qualitative methods in family research* (pp. 22–39). Newbury Park, CA: Sage.

Hawley, D. R., & DeHaan, L. (1996). Toward a definition of family resilience: Integrating life-span and family perspectives. *Family Process, 35*, 283–298.

Hill, R. (1949). *Families under stress*. Westport, CT: Greenwood Press.

Kaniasty, K., & Norris, F. (1995). In search of altruistic community: Patterns of social support mobilization following Hurricane Hugo. *American Journal of Community Psychology, 23*, 447–477.

Klinenberg, E. (2002). *Heat wave: A social autopsy of disaster in Chicago*. Chicago: University of Chicago Press.

Koos, E. L. (1946). *Families in trouble*. New York: King's Crown.

Louisiana Speaks. (2006). *St. Tammany Parish goals: Long-term community recovery planning*. Retrieved January 27, 2007, from http://www.louisianaspeaks-parish-plans.org/IndParishHomepage_RecoveryGoals.cfm?EntID=16

Luthar, S. S., Cicchetti, D., & Becker, B. (2000). The construct of resilience: A critical evaluation and guidelines for future work. *Child Development, 71*, 543–562.

Masten, A. S. (2001). Ordinary magic: Resilience processes in development. *American Psychologist, 56*, 227–238.

Morrow, B. H. (1997). Stretching the bonds: The families of Andrew. In W. G. Peacock, B. H. Morrow, & H. Gladwin (Eds.), *Hurricane Andrew: Ethnicity, gender and the sociology of disasters* (pp. 141–170). London: Routledge.

Myers, D. (1989). Mental health and disaster. In R. Gist & B. Lubin (Eds.), *Psychosocial aspects of disaster* (pp. 190–228). New York: Wiley.

Neuman, W. L. (2006). *Social research methods: Qualitative and quantitative approaches* (6th ed.). Boston: Pearson Education.

Patterson, J. M. (2002). Integrating family resilience and family stress theory. *Journal of Marriage and the Family, 64*, 349–360.

Perilla, J. L., Norris, F. H., & Lavizzo, E. A. (2002). Ethnicity, culture and disaster response: Identifying and explaining ethnic differences in PTSD six months after hurricane Andrew. *Journal of Social and Clinical Psychology, 21*, 20–45.

Pierce, G. R., Sarason, B. R., & Sarason, I. G. (Eds.). (1996). *Handbook of social support and the family*. New York: Plenum Press.

Sattler, D. (2002). *El Salvador earthquakes: Resource loss, traumatic event exposure, and psychological functioning* (Quick Response Research Report No. 160). Boulder, CO: Natural Hazards Research and Applications Information Center, University of Colorado. Retrieved April 10, 2007, from http://www.colorado.edu/hazards/qr/qr160/qr160.html

St. Tammany Parish—Disaster impact and needs assessment. (2006). Retrieved June 7, 2007, from http://www.louisianaspeaks-parishplans.org/IndParishHomepage_BaselineNeeds Assessment.cfm?EntID=16

Tedeschi, R. G., & Calhoun, L. G. (1996). The Posttraumatic Growth Inventory: Measuring the positive legacy of trauma. *Journal of Traumatic Stress, 9*, 455–471.

Walsh, F. (1999). Religion and spirituality: Wellsprings for healing and resilience. In F. Walsh (Ed.), *Spiritual resources in family therapy* (pp. 3–27). New York: Guilford Press.

Walsh, F. (2003). Family resilience: Strengths forged through adversity. In F. Walsh (Ed.), *Normal family processes* (3rd ed., pp. 399–423). New York: Guilford Press.

Walsh, F. (2007). Traumatic loss and major disasters: Strengthening family and community resilience. *Family Process, 46*, 207–227.

Wang, X., Gao, L., Shinfuku, N., Zhang, H., Zhao, C., & Shen, Y. (2000). Longitudinal study of earthquake-related PTSD in a randomly selected community sample in north China. *American Journal of Psychiatry, 157*, 1260–1266.

5

CONSEQUENCES FOR CLASSROOM ENVIRONMENTS AND SCHOOL PERSONNEL: EVALUATING KATRINA'S EFFECT ON SCHOOLS AND SYSTEM RESPONSE

TERESA K. BUCHANAN, RENÉE M. CASBERGUE,
AND JENNIFER J. BAUMGARTNER

The impact of Hurricanes Katrina and Rita has been well documented (see Introduction and chap. 1, this volume), and few institutions fared worse than schools. Of 2,000 primary schools in Louisiana, 1,500 were within the parishes most affected by the storms (Kent, 2006). Hurricane Katrina directly affected 930 Louisiana schools with 480,000 students and teachers, whereas Rita affected 515 schools with 235,000 students and teachers. Some schools were closed for days and some for months, reopening when the initial cleanup

This chapter is based on work supported by National Science Foundation Grant 0555387 and the Louisiana Board of Regents, Teresa K. Buchanan, Principal Investigator. Any opinions, findings, conclusions, or recommendations expressed in this chapter are those of the authors and do not necessarily reflect the views of these organizations.

Diane C. Burts and Timothy Page were coinvestigators on this project. Diane Burts's work on the materials and protocol, as well as her work with Timothy Page to develop the stories for the interviews, was critically important to this project. Virginia Gil-Rivas provided the tools used to measure teachers' psychological well-being, training, and teachers' and children's hurricane-related personal experiences. Ana Morales provided invaluable assistance throughout the entire project. We are grateful to these wonderful colleagues. We also appreciate the hard work of research team members Rhonda Norwood, Susheel Brahmeshwarkar, Sharbari Dey, and Kyung-Ran Kim and the perceptive assistance of Deborah Conway on this manuscript. We are deeply indebted to project consultant David Klahr, who offered critically important support and insight.

of campuses and restoration of utilities were completed. In the most seriously affected areas, about 835 schools were significantly damaged in Louisiana, and 40 were completely destroyed. In Mississippi, 263 schools were damaged and 16 destroyed (Louisiana Recovery Authority, 2006).

In the three Louisiana parishes most affected by Hurricane Rita and the flooding that followed the failure of levees during Hurricane Katrina, the number of displaced students was staggering. In Cameron Parish, a community inundated by Rita's tidal surge, the student population dropped by 31% after the storm, and St. Bernard Parish lost 80% of its students. Schooling in Orleans Parish was equally disrupted. Although that system had more than 60,000 students enrolled in 128 schools before the storm, very few public schools reopened for the remainder of the 2005–2006 school year. For the 2006–2007 academic year, two newly constituted public school systems, a state-run Recovery School District with 21 schools and an Orleans Parish School Board District with 5 board-controlled schools and 12 charter schools, as well as 25 independent charter schools, could accommodate only 27,000 students (Rowley, 2007). As late as spring 2007, approximately 300 children were "wait listed" for enrollment in New Orleans public schools.

RESPONSE OF LOCAL SCHOOLS

The impact of the hurricanes extended beyond those schools that were damaged or destroyed. Even 20 months after the storms, significant numbers of displaced children remained enrolled in other school districts that struggled to make room for them. One such district was in Baton Rouge, Louisiana, located approximately halfway between the areas where the hurricanes made landfall. Baton Rouge schools reopened quickly once downed power lines and felled trees were cleared, and many families who evacuated to Baton Rouge, doubling that city's population immediately after the storms, scrambled to enroll their children in these schools.

As Baton Rouge area schools reopened with new children streaming in, we were intrigued by our informal observations of schools' responses to the hurricanes. Our university was an integral part of the relief efforts (Bacher, Devlin, Calongne, Duplechain, & Pertuit, 2005), and many faculty modified course requirements so our students could assist in the community response (Buchanan & Benedict, 2007; DiCarlo, Burts, Buchanan, Aghayan, & Benedict, 2007; Perlmutter, 2005). Other teachers also made changes to their curricula. For example, on reopening after Katrina, Louisiana State University (LSU) preschool teachers tried to continue teaching the transportation unit they began before the hurricanes (Aghayan et al., 2005), but the children seemed to relate everything to hurricanes and constantly engaged in hurricane-related play (Schellhaas, Burts, & Aghayan, 2007). In response to the children's obvious interest in hurricanes, the teachers guided the children in a study of hurricanes that lasted several weeks.

Similarly, Metairie Park Country Day, a private K–12 school in the New Orleans metropolitan area, reopened for an abbreviated semester in November 2005 with a schoolwide focus on defining and rebuilding a city. Children worked with teachers in multiage teams to study the culture and architecture of different neighborhoods before the storm and create their ideal vision of what the city could be after recovery. Through storytelling, reading, writing, science, math, social studies, and art activities related to understanding the hurricane and the recovery process, children shared their experiences and developed knowledge that empowered them to cope with the devastation around them.

We thought that many teachers in storm-affected areas would also follow this catastrophic event with emotional support and instruction (Damiani, 2006; Mack & Smith, 1991; Miller, 1996). We expected responses like those of the New York City school system following the terrorist attacks of September 11, 2001 (9/11; Pfefferbaum et al., 2004; Tucker, 2004), or the response of educators following the Red River flood of 1997, which affected cities in North Dakota, Minnesota, and Manitoba, Canada (Shreve, Danbom, & Hanhan, 2002; Silverman, 1999; Zevenbergen, Sigler, Duerre, & Howse, 2000). Of relevance, school systems in the Grand Forks, Minnesota, region and in New York made substantial changes to their administrative policies and curriculum guidelines that were designed to meet the changed educational, health, and safety needs of children and adults in their communities (Black, 2005; Tucker, 2004).

Contrary to our expectations, it appeared that many Baton Rouge area schools were going about "business as usual." During a visit to one elementary school, we asked a teacher about new children who we knew had enrolled in her class after being displaced by the storm. The teacher responded, "Well, I have four new children. They came a few weeks ago, but I'm not sure why they are here or where they are from." This apparent lack of awareness of the circumstances surrounding children's enrollment in new schools was reflected in responses we observed elsewhere. We could find no evidence that attempts were made to assess children's needs in the storms' immediate aftermath. It was not until January 2006 that the system implemented a process to screen elementary schoolchildren for posthurricane difficulties and advise teachers about referral options. In many schools during that fall, there were no assemblies, no counseling sessions, and apparently no instruction regarding the hurricanes. The response of two new schools that opened specifically to take in Katrina and Rita evacuees was an exception; those schools did a great deal to welcome the new families and children (Paulson, 2005).

WHAT IS AN APPROPRIATE RESPONSE FOR YOUNG CHILDREN?

Our beliefs about appropriate responses following catastrophes such as Katrina and Rita are rooted in Bronfenbrenner's (2005) ecological framework. Three main propositions from Bronfenbrenner influence our approach to working with young children. First, children have multiple developmental contexts, such as home, community, and school, and broader governance systems influence policies affecting them. Second, these contexts interact. So, for example, distal factors such as the No Child Left Behind Act of 2001 help determine teachers' qualifications and the curricula used in classrooms. These more proximal settings, in turn, directly influence much of what a child experiences every day. Third, continuity across contexts increases the likelihood of children's positive development. Thus, in the aftermath of the hurricanes, which disrupted all of the developmental contexts for so many children, we hoped to see recovery and relief efforts that placed children and their needs at the center of activities in the schools.

According to Damiani (2006), one role of educators following a crisis is to provide children with accurate information and knowledge about the event. Although some researchers have examined how schools can assist with children's emotional needs after disasters (e.g., Allen et al., 2002; Fairbrother, Stuber, Galea, Pfefferbaum, & Fleishman, 2004; Frost, 2005; Jimerson, Brock, & Pletcher, 2005; Mack & Smith, 1991; Miller, 1996; Pfefferbaum et al., 2004), and a number have presented recommendations for preparation for emergencies and disasters (Damiani, 2006; Jimerson et al., 2005; Klingman, 1978; Knox & Roberts, 2005), there is surprisingly little literature about educator curricular responses to disaster. We could find no research regarding general planning for curricula implemented in the wake of disaster.

The literature largely documents examples of specific school systems' activities in the aftermath of particular events or offers suggestions that do not appear to be empirically grounded. Literature related to three disasters—the Red River flood in 1997, the Wyoming Green Knoll fire of 2001, and the 9/11 terrorist attack in New York City—offer cogent examples of curricular adaptations. For instance, a survey of teachers in five elementary schools indicated that they had adjusted their curriculum following the 1997 Red River flood (Shreve et al., 2002; Zevenbergen et al., 2000). These teachers reported altering their reading, writing, and oral language instruction to incorporate stories, letters, and student-developed books about floods. Silverman (1999) documented funded efforts to create curricular activities designed to help children understand their experiences during the flood.

A study of the effects of those activities led to the conclusion that teachers "must listen carefully to what the children tell them through their words, actions, and drawings," then "build curriculum from children's responses, not from a predetermined plan" (Shreve et al., 2002, p. 106). The authors suggested that literature and play should be used to help children build an understanding about what happened. They emphasized, "Success of such a curriculum is dependent on how clearly children's voices are heard and respected, whether they are expressing their thoughts in art, writing, or conversation, and how closely the curriculum matches the concerns and questions being expressed" (p. 107).

As another case in point, following the 2001 Green Knoll fire, high school students in the Wilson, Wyoming, area conducted an investigation into the effects of fire on the soil's chemistry (McClennen, 2004). Their teachers developed this project and integrated it with the students' science curriculum. Their successful experiences support the idea that teachers can integrate curriculum requirements with events that occur in students' lives, including natural disasters.

Many authors offer intriguing suggestions about how to help children understand disasters while meeting learning objectives in the areas of physical education (Martinek, Hardiman, & Anderson-Butcher, 2006), science (Welch, 2006), and social studies (Hantula, 1984; Lintner, 2006). Hinde's (2005) review of integrated social studies curricula suggests that teachers should make sure such activities are educationally meaningful, do not distort the integrity of the content areas, include applications of skills from other content areas, and are appropriate for the particular children in the classroom.

When the New York City school system created curricula following 9/11, teams gathered resources and developed materials to help children understand what had happened while attempting to prevent violence toward people of Middle Eastern descent. Their curriculum provided information and activities organized around four goals: (a) advising teachers how to help students handle grief and anger, (b) presenting issues for discussion on terrorism and terrorists, (c) enhancing children's understanding and skills in conflict resolution, and (d) establishing common definitions and language about the issues (Degnan et al., 2004). These educators showed that curriculum can be a critical part of educational systems' response and recovery, especially when curricular adaptations reflect the unique nature of the school and support the learning community on issues related to tragedy or terrorism. Such adaptations reflect the concept of *context-appropriate practices*.

CONTEXT-APPROPRIATE PRACTICES

Early childhood educators implement effective teaching practices (or *developmentally appropriate practices*) and make decisions about curriculum (what to teach) and instruction (how to teach) based on three guiding notions. First, they create age-appropriate opportunities for learning. Second, they facilitate experiences that are appropriate for each individual child in the classroom. Third, they reflect the context and cultures of the children and classroom. Context-appropriate practices involve teaching decisions that are based on "knowledge of the social and cultural contexts in which children live to ensure that learning experiences are meaningful, relevant, and respectful for the participating children and their families" (Bredekamp & Copple, 1997, p. 9). Sometimes this principle is referred to as *culturally appropriate practices*.

One important aspect of culturally appropriate practices involves attending to the physical environment. Local plants, animals, weather, and geography are important determinants of how people live and what their culture "looks like." For example, in south Louisiana, where all types of wetlands abound, a large part of our cultural identity reflects our human relationship with this physical environment. Thus, a thematic exploration of wetlands is relevant to young children in our region but less appropriate for young children living in other areas.

Culturally appropriate teaching practices are most commonly used when a teacher designs his or her own *emergent curriculum*, one that emerges from student interest. For example, if a class of children becomes very interested in ants after an infestation in the classroom, the teacher might create a curriculum centered on ants that encompasses all content areas (see Klein, 1991, for an example). Science lessons might focus on comparisons of stinging and nonstinging species, the life cycle of ants, and the structure of ant colonies. Math content could include counting tunnels in an ant farm, measuring their length, or graphing their structure on graph paper. Literacy lessons would engage children in reading and writing nonfiction related to ants.

Effective early childhood educators bring aspects of the culture and context into their teaching (Damiani, 2006; Mack & Smith, 1991; Miller, 1996). We expected educators affected by Hurricanes Katrina and Rita to respond to the storms by teaching about hurricanes, weather, or the physical environment; loss or difficulties associated with changing schools; and evacuation or other effects that hurricanes and severe weather have on people and communities. We expected that students would dramatically re-create some of the experiences they had or had heard about in the news media and read books and write stories in class about their experiences.

OUR STUDY OF SCHOOLS IN THE WAKE OF KATRINA AND RITA

In light of the contrast between what we expected and what seemed to be occurring, we sought to systematically investigate what Louisiana and other southern schools and teachers were doing in the aftermath of the hurricanes and what children were learning about hurricanes. With funding from the National Science Foundation, we surveyed teachers in Louisiana and other geographically matched states to assess their response.

A primary study goal was to determine how teachers responded to the hurricanes in their classroom. Because of the national media attention on the hurricanes, we wondered if teachers in other areas of the country might respond by creating classroom activities to help students understand what they saw on television. To determine whether teachers in Louisiana did more hurricane-related activities than those in other states, we surveyed teachers in school districts that were matched geographically (i.e., southern, mostly rural with one suburban district). We compared responses of teachers in Louisiana with those of teachers in hurricane-prone areas and teachers in a state rarely affected by hurricanes. We also examined personal and professional teacher characteristics that might predict hurricane-related class activities.

A second goal was to investigate the effectiveness of teaching about hurricanes. Because children's demonstrated knowledge is a primary indicator of the effectiveness of instruction, we compared the knowledge of students who had teachers who incorporated many hurricane-related activities into lessons with that of students whose teachers reported fewer such activities. It has been posited that children may be empowered by knowledge so that they are more secure when faced with similar trauma in the future (Damiani, 2006; Shreve et al., 2002).

Teacher Survey

A teacher survey measured demographic characteristics of the sample, teachers' curricular responses to the hurricanes, and use of developmentally appropriate practices. We also incorporated measures of teacher self-reported posttraumatic stress, depressive symptoms, and personal and professional experiences related to the storms.

After approval from school districts and our university's institutional review board, we sent surveys to every principal of every elementary school in targeted districts. Principals distributed five surveys: one each to a preschool (PK), kindergarten (K), first grade (1st), second grade (2nd), and third grade (3rd) teacher. If there was more than one teacher for a given grade level, the principal was asked to identify the teacher with the earliest birthday month in an attempt to minimize systematic biases. Louisiana school districts that were most severely affected by the hurricanes were not included in this study because they had not yet reopened when we began recruitment activities in the fall of 2005.

The survey was sent the second week of November 2005 to a total of 2,010 teachers: 1,155 in Louisiana (school districts outside of the severely damaged area yet heavily affected by the hurricanes were oversampled because we anticipated a lower response rate in those areas), 560 to hurricane-prone school districts in costal South Carolina and Georgia, and 295 to southern landlocked districts in Tennessee. Teachers participated voluntarily with no compensation.

The final survey sample consisted of 592 teachers representing Louisiana ($n = 344$), Tennessee ($n = 93$), coastal South Carolina ($n = 77$), and coastal Georgia ($n = 78$). The overall response rate was 28%, with 30% of surveys returned from Louisiana and 27% from other states. Chi-square analysis showed that there were no grade-level differences by state (PK, 15%; K, 24%; 1st, 22%; 2nd, 19%; 3rd, 19%); $\chi^2(12, N = 587) = 12.37$, ns. A one-way analysis of variance (ANOVA) showed that, on average, Tennessee teachers reported fewer children ($M = 9.69$, $SD = 5.24$, $n = 77$) receiving free or reduced lunch per class than those in Louisiana ($M = 12.81$, $SD = 6.26$, $n = 269$); $F(3, 473) = 5.68$, $p < .01$. Teachers in all states reported having at least some classrooms with five or more evacuees (LA, 233; TN, 13; GA, 6; SC, 10).

Teachers' self-reported posttraumatic stress symptoms were measured with the Posttraumatic Stress Disorder Checklist (PCL; Weathers & Litz, 1994), a 17-item measure assessing the degree to which they had been bothered by symptoms (arousal, intrusion, avoidance) in the past month. Analyses identified differences in teachers' reports across states, $F(3, 580) = 18.78$, $p < .001$, and post hoc analysis (using Scheffé adjustments) showed that teachers from Louisiana reported more symptoms than other teachers (see Table 5.1), $F(3, 577) = 18.78$, $p < .001$.

Teachers reported their general psychological distress using the Hopkins Symptom Checklist—25 (Derogatis, Lipman, Rickels, Uhlenhuth, & Covi, 1974), indicating how much they had been bothered by symptoms of depression, anxiety, and somatization in the past week. ANOVA results showed that self-reported distress differed by state, $F(3, 578) = 7.24$, $p < .001$. Specifically, Louisiana teachers reported significantly more symptoms of distress than those in Tennessee and South Carolina but not Georgia (see Table 5.1).

Of the teachers in Louisiana, 24% had received training in children's reactions, and 15% had received training in how to help children and families following a disaster. Nearly half (45%) reported they would have liked to receive the latter training, including information about where to obtain resources, how to talk to children and answer questions, and how to help them cope, as well as literature to distribute to parents. Teachers also wanted information about offering emotional support to families and students, helping families and students adjust to changes, and helping them make transitions more easily.

Teachers described actions their schools had taken immediately after the hurricanes. The most frequently reported responses involved providing

TABLE 5.1
Selected Assessment Results by State

Variable	Louisiana			South Carolina			Georgia			Tennessee		
	M	SD	n	M	SD	n	M	SD	n	M	SD	n
Children with free or reduced lunch	12.81	6.26	269	12.31	7.21	64	11.14	5.45	64	9.69	5.24	77
Teacher PCL scores	23.01	8.25	340	18.58	3.26	92	18.62	3.10	77	19.17	3.28	92
Teacher distress	9.61	10.08	339	5.32	7.20	77	7.14	8.8	77	5.91	7.26	91
Child-initiated classroom activities	14.17	2.86	344	11.67	2.59	76	11.45	2.71	78	11.45	2.27	93
Teacher-planned classroom activities	19.67	4.18	340	20.12	5.34	74	19.69	4.44	44	20.37	4.27	90

Note. PCL = Posttraumatic Stress Disorder Checklist (Weathers & Litz, 1994).

materials to children (e.g., classroom supplies, 77%) and families (e.g., household supplies, 63%). Some teachers (24%) reported that their schools facilitated support groups or counseling sessions to address hurricane issues. Thirty-four teachers (6%) said an outside speaker had visited the school.

Teachers reported on the unplanned, spontaneous, or student-initiated activities that had occurred in their classrooms following the hurricanes. Those in Louisiana reported that their students initiated significantly more hurricane-related activities than those in other states, $F(3, 590) = 44.77$, $p < .001$ (see Table 5.1). The most common child-initiated activities were telling stories about Katrina or hurricanes (71%), discussing Katrina or hurricane-related events with the teacher (75%) and their peers (67%), and drawing pictures about hurricanes (48%).

Teachers reported on the classroom activities they planned for and implemented in the weeks immediately following the hurricanes on a 15-item scale that included items such as "read a story about death, loss, or sadness" and "taught a unit or theme or did a project about hurricanes." Contrary to expectations, there were no significant differences in teacher-planned classroom activities by state (see Table 5.1). The most common activities reported were reading a story about weather (54%), lecturing about hurricanes (46%), and doing planned learning activities about weather (43%).

We examined several hypotheses. The first hypothesis was that teachers who used model early childhood teaching practices would engage in more hurricane-related activities compared with those who did not use them. Use of model teaching strategies was assessed with a modified version of the Teacher Questionnaire (Buchanan, Burts, White, Bidner, & Charlesworth, 1998; Burts et al., 1992), which assesses developmentally appropriate early childhood teaching practices (30 items for preschool and kindergarten, 24 for Grades 1–3). On this scale, teachers indicated how often, on a scale of 1 = *almost never* or *less than monthly* to 5 = *very often* or *daily*, their students did things like "build with blocks" or "participate in musical activities."

As expected, teachers who reported typically doing more developmentally appropriate activities also reported doing more hurricane-related activities in their classrooms: PK and K, $F(1, 229) = 6.73$, $p < .05$; primary grade teachers, $F(1, 344) = 36.49$, $p < .001$. Given that curricula in preschool and kindergarten are typically more flexible than in primary grades, we were surprised that ANOVA, $F(1, 575) = 5.04$, $p = .02$, and post hoc analyses showed that preschool ($M = 19.22$, $SD = 3.73$, $n = 89$) and kindergarten ($M = 19.45$, $SD = 3.64$, $n = 139$) teachers reported doing fewer planned activities related to hurricanes than first-grade ($M = 19.91$, $SD = 5.31$, $n = 126$), second-grade ($M = 20.56$, $SD = 4.70$, $n = 109$), or third-grade ($M = 20.16$, $SD = 4.23$, $n = 113$) teachers.

Linear regression analyses were conducted to identify predictors of classroom activities. For these analyses, the measures of student-initiated and teacher-planned activities were combined into one 24-item, 3-point measure of total hurricane activities ($1 = $ *not at all* to $3 = $ *a lot*). Independent variables included in the analyses were those that correlated strongly with the measure of total hurricane classroom activities and those of theoretical interest. Among preschool and kindergarten teachers, developmentally appropriate practice significantly predicted total hurricane activities ($b = .17, p = .01$), accounting for 2.9% of the variance in teacher-planned and child-initiated activities, $F(1, 229) = 6.73, p = .01$. Among primary grade teachers, developmentally appropriate practice was a significant predictor of total hurricane activities ($b = .31, p < .001$), accounting for 9.6% of the variance in teacher-planned and child-initiated activities.

We also investigated the relationship between teachers' personal experiences with Katrina or Rita and total hurricane-related classroom activities. We measured direct hurricane-related experiences on a 6-item checklist (e.g., "I had to evacuate as a result of Katrina") and personal loss associated with the hurricanes on a 9-item checklist (e.g., "I lost property due to Katrina"). The measures accounted for 5.3% of the variance in total hurricane-related classroom activities, $F(2, 585) = 16.46, p < .001$.

Additional analyses found that reported direct hurricane-related personal experiences ($b = .12, p = .02$) and personal loss ($b = .14, p = .005$) demonstrated significant effects on classroom activities. Also, teachers' psychological well-being accounted for 7.7% of the variance in total classroom activities, $F(2, 575) = 23.82, p < .001$; although self-reported posttraumatic stress ($b = .23, p < .001$) was a significant predictor, general psychological distress was not ($b = .06, p = .15$).

Qualitative Survey Results

We analyzed the detailed descriptions of 25 teachers' posthurricane response. For this part of the study, we used constant comparative methodology (Glaser & Strauss, 1967) to create categories of responses across cases. We used an inductive analysis in which patterns and themes emerged from repeated examination of the data, rather than being imposed prior to data collection and analysis. The teachers' responses shed light on how they decided on a course of action following the storms. Three primary themes emerged: responding by helping, sticking to the curriculum, and offering emotional support.

Responding by Helping

In keeping with our observations of Baton Rouge area schools, some teachers reported that they did not directly teach anything related to the hurricanes in their classrooms but rather focused on helping children in some other way. One teacher reported that she did not have displaced children in her classroom, but many of her students had displaced or missing relatives. She related, "They were concerned and wanted to help and discuss everything. They filled and sent 100 tote bags to Ascension Elementary and Holy Rosary [school] and began a pen pal program." Another teacher described doing "a teddy bear donation project [through which] displaced students received a soft toy and/or a hand-held game to take home." These efforts engaged children in helping activities that grew from their interests and concerns.

A teacher in Louisiana reported efforts to offer community assistance: "Our school and community have been very generous. Many teachers worked at shelters while out of school. [Others] worked on weekends at shelters and distribution centers. Our school also held a blood drive and a penny drive." Another Louisiana teacher wrote poignantly about others' generosity:

> A school in North Carolina adopted us—donated supplies and wrote cards and e-mails. The [North Carolina] school is limited in resources. It was moving for [those] children and adults to give even some of their personal items. It moved us to tears as we opened the boxes.

Sticking to the Curriculum

The responses of those who reported conducting "business as usual" suggest that some teachers seemed to be concerned about affecting children's well-being negatively, others appeared to underestimate the impact of the storms on the children and did not see a need to address their emotional health, and still others believed that their primary role was to offer reassurance and support, even though they did not consider adapting their curriculum. Among teachers who expressed a desire to shield students from mention of the storms, most conveyed the belief that it could be harmful to engage children in activities or discussions that might recall painful experiences or elicit strong feelings. As one teacher wrote, "I found in many instances it was best not to discuss what happened during Katrina." Another said, "I listened to the children. . . . We did some talking, [but] the children seemed happiest when we stuck to the routine. As a result, we stayed pretty much on task with our planned curriculum." Still another noted,

> Although we had never experienced a catastrophe where so many had lost so much, we knew we had to provide some sense of security and normalcy to lives that had turned upside down. We had to reassure regular students who were overwhelmed by the changes.

These responses suggest that some teachers gave careful thought to curricular decisions they believed to be in the best interest of their students. They were clearly motivated by a desire to shield the children from a difficult subject. Others, however, may have underestimated the effects of the storms on the children. One teacher wrote, "I had only one student, and she stayed only 9 days," suggesting that she did not realize that even nonevacuee children might be affected by the catastrophe. Another expressed a relatively narrow view of the impact of traumatic events when she said, "The children I had did not lose anything. They were only displaced for about a month. Our counselor handled emotional issues through groups." Aside from her underestimation of this significant disruption to children's lives, this teacher evidently believed others might be better equipped to handle children's "emotional issues."

A commitment to the preeminence of academic concerns guided some teachers' lesson planning, as illustrated by one teacher who said, "We did not do much [related to the hurricanes] because we were already short on time because of missed school. So we did not have time for extra work." Evidently, this teacher believed that the preestablished, state-mandated curriculum had to be followed, regardless of the children's experiences. Other teachers echoed this belief when noting that they would have done more, but their administrators told them they had to follow the mandated curriculum. A teacher in a significantly affected district stated that teachers were informed that they were expected to "catch up," even though schools had been closed for over 6 weeks. In these instances, neither teachers nor administrators seemed to consider that following children's interests and teaching concepts related to hurricanes could have addressed the same goals and objectives as the existing curriculum while also offering relevant instruction.

Offering Emotional Support

Some teachers expressed a desire to support children emotionally. Numerous teachers prepared their students to welcome newly enrolled displaced students. One teacher wrote, "I talked to the kids . . . to prepare them for the children that were going to come and said that they might be depressed and sad." Another said, "I tried making displaced students feel at home in my classroom by making sure they had a peer buddy." These efforts may have helped children. "I had two evacuees join my class," one teacher said. "My other students really tried to reach out to them and befriend them. I never knew third graders could be as empathetic as mine were." Another reported, "Our school welcomed [them] with open arms, making them feel part of our school family. The students I have from the storm are happy and have adjusted very well. Their families have chosen to stay. They love the school."

Some teachers reported making sure to let children know that they were available to help. One teacher summed up the approach of others when she stated, "I explained to [the children and families] that they could come and talk to me at any time about anything." Others made time for children to talk about their experiences. As one teacher noted, "I gained a new student who was an evacuee; she really benefited from knowing we were there to help any way we could."

One teacher's response suggested that she limited her role to offering such emotional support because of a lack of knowledge about alternatives. She wrote, "We welcomed three new classmates—did not ask them about their homelessness. I asked students to be understanding about their needs [and] allowed time to talk about our experiences. But [we] did not have lessons due to a true lack of understanding." This teacher may have been willing to make curricular adaptations had she been aware of effective ways to do so.

Children's Knowledge About Hurricanes

Typically, educational research uses children's knowledge to evaluate the effectiveness of teaching practices. Thus, for the project's second goal, we evaluated children's knowledge about hurricanes to examine the effect of teacher-reported hurricane-related classroom experiences. We hypothesized that children in classrooms in which teachers reported more planned and child-initiated hurricane- or weather-related activities immediately following the hurricanes would know more than children in classrooms with less hurricane-related activity.

Formal testing is an ineffective way to evaluate young children's knowledge (Gullo, 2005). Because of developmental characteristics, young children demonstrate their knowledge best through what they say and do (Cohen, Stern, & Balaban, 1996). To assess very young children's knowledge of hurricanes quickly and accurately, we adapted the Narrative Story Stem Technique (NSST; Emde, Wolf, & Oppenheim, 2003; Page, 2001). The NSST was created to examine the narrative structures with which young children organize their experience (Bretherton & Oppenheim, 2003; Page, 2001). It uses a protocol of simple, semistructured story stems that the examiner introduces to the child using a set of family figures or dolls and simple play props. Each story stem provides a mildly stressful scenario with which most children are familiar (e.g., the parents go away for an overnight trip), and the child is asked to "show me and tell me what happens next." With the help of Timothy Page, a colleague and expert in the NSST, and other NSST experts, we modified this technique to observe and record children's knowledge about hurricanes in general and the 2005 Louisiana hurricanes in particular.

First, we developed story stems that would generate relevant stories from the children. We field tested the stories and materials with 15 children in preschool through 3rd grade to develop a set of stories and materials that would be just interesting enough for children to use to tell their own stories but would not distract or draw them off task. The entire procedure was piloted in a preschool classroom, a kindergarten classroom, and a second-grade classroom. A total of 31 children from classrooms in our laboratory schools participated in the pilot. A few changes to the protocol and script were made after the pilot.

The sample for the interviews came from classrooms of 15 Louisiana teachers selected in a stratified random sample of those who had returned the teacher survey. Using scores for total hurricane activities (teacher-planned and child-initiated), the teachers were randomly selected from the lower, middle, and upper thirds of the distributions for each grade level. Thus, three teachers from each grade (preschool; kindergarten; first, second, and third grades) represented teachers who did a lot, some, and very few hurricane-related activities in class. Teachers who agreed to participate were mailed packets (including a brief demographic survey, a study description, and consent forms) to distribute to their students' guardians. The survey included a section asking parents about the child's personal experiences with the hurricanes using the same measures used for the teachers. They included a 6-item checklist of hurricane-related experiences (e.g., "My child had to evacuate as a result of Katrina") and a 9-item checklist of personal loss associated with the hurricanes (e.g., "My child lost property due to Katrina").

The teachers were European American and averaged 12 years of teaching experience ($SD = 9.25$, range = 1–28 years). Two teachers were certified in early childhood education, one in elementary and early childhood education, and the other 12 in elementary education alone. Class sizes ranged from 17 to 23 children ($M = 20$, $SD = 1.59$). The percentage of African American children in the selected classrooms ranged from 0% to 99%, with an average of 27%. Most classes had children who had evacuated as a result of the hurricanes, and most of the represented schools had more than 10 evacuee children. According to state department of education data, the schools' average percentage of children on free or reduced lunch was 61% ($SD = 19.76$).

The final interview sample consisted of 84 children from six school districts. We sent a total of 280 family packets home, and of those, 164 (43%) were returned with parental consent, and 121 (43%) children were interviewed. Forty-five percent of the parents had a high school education. The majority of children were from families with two biological parents living in their homes, and their parents reported incomes from $20,000 to $75,000. Fifty-two percent of the children had evacuated during the hurricanes, 25% lived in temporary housing or shelters, 25% had evacuees living with them, and 31% lost property.

Child interviews took place over 2 consecutive days. Every child was first asked to give his or her signed assent (Helling & Buchanan, 1994; Helling & Hughes, 1992), then interviewers used the original NSST protocol to introduce the nature of story stem scenarios and prompts using familiar situations; the hurricane-story protocol was administered on the second day. The interviewer gave the child the story stem and asked a standard set of prompts. For example, one story stem began, "This is a family. They just found out that a big hurricane is coming. What are they going to do? Show me and tell me what the family will do now." The prompt for that story stem was, "What will they do?" If the child indicated that the family left their home, the child might have been asked the following: "Why did they leave?" "Where will they go?" If the child indicated the family left a pet at home, the following prompt was given: "What happened to the dog/cat then?" The story stems were designed to measure the children's knowledge about what happened to land and trees, animals, families, homes and property, and urban communities during and after hurricanes, as well as who helps people when hurricanes come.

After the six stories were completed, a seventh scenario more directly assessed children's knowledge (i.e., the child pretended to tell a friend all about hurricanes in general and what happened when Katrina or Rita came). Prompts for that scenario were asked only if the child had not already talked about or discussed those particular topics. The interviews were videotaped, and five trained coders achieved an interrater reliability of 81%. A reliability judge recoded 27% randomly sampled interviews ($n = 23$). The mean interrater reliability, calculated as percentage of agreement with number of identical codes divided by the total codes, was also .81.

The coding system scored each child's responses on a form with 69 statements about hurricanes, which were divided into categories including water/floods, property damage, effects on people, general scientific knowledge, and hurricane-related vocabulary. For example, under property damage, one statement read, "Some trees fell down/broke/were damaged/fell on power lines/houses/cars/buildings/streets." If a child's story mentioned the trees falling down or being damaged, that statement was coded with either a 1 (some demonstration of understanding) or a 2 (clear demonstration of understanding by actions, examples, or details). If the child never indicated with words or actions some understanding of the item, it was coded as a 0.

The analyses showed evidence that children understood that trees fell down or broke, people left their homes to evacuate, houses were damaged, and streets and houses flooded. Many children indicated they understood that hurricanes are weather systems that can be destructive, are accompanied by power outages, and often have heavy rain and strong winds. Very few stories indicated knowledge of other characteristics or causes of hurricanes.

Knowledge was moderately related to teachers' years of experience, $r(84) = -.25$, $p = .025$, and number of children in the classroom, $r(84) = -.30$, $p = .006$. Knowledge was also related to the age of the child, $r(74) = .56$, $p < .001$. Knowledge was not significantly correlated with parental education, family income, the child's experience with the hurricane, hurricane-related teacher-planned classroom activities, or child-initiated activities.

Summary of Findings

Many teachers reported doing something in their classrooms related to the storms; however, Louisiana teachers did not report doing more planned activities than teachers in other areas of the country. Those teachers personally affected by the hurricanes and those reporting higher levels of PTSD symptoms reported more storm-related activities than other teachers. There was a positive association between the use of developmentally appropriate classroom practices and teacher engagement in hurricane-related instructional activity.

One reason for the decision to "carry on as usual" was a desire to avoid upsetting children. Other teachers underestimated the impact of the storms on the children or did not recognize the possibility of addressing children's needs with curricular adaptations. Some teachers who wanted to assist children and families focused on helping, either by organizing and participating in volunteer efforts on behalf of other schools or shelters or by offering their emotional support to affected children. That support extended to initiating efforts to welcome children and help them adapt to their new surroundings. At least one teacher limited her role to offering emotional support rather than adapting the curriculum because of a lack of knowledge regarding the types of lessons that might have been beneficial to the children.

Young children's stories in response to narrative story stems revealed they did have knowledge of hurricanes in general and of Katrina and Rita in particular. Older children, children in smaller classes, and children in classes with teachers with fewer years of experience demonstrated more knowledge. Children's knowledge was not related to the classroom experiences reported by the teachers.

LESSONS LEARNED AND ACTIONABLE RECOMMENDATIONS

The results of this study are consistent with literature suggesting that in spite of information available to help with preparing for and managing the impact of disasters (e.g., Allen et al., 2002; Hurst, 2005; Jimerson et al., 2005; Klingman, 1978; Knox & Roberts, 2005; Poland, 1994), many teachers are unprepared to address the needs of traumatized children (Ashby, 2007; Graham, Shrim, Liggin, Aitken, & Dick, 2006; Kano, Ramirez, Ybarra, & Bourque, 2007; Watts, 2007). A striking finding from this study is that Louisiana teachers did not do more hurricane-related activities in their classrooms than those in other states, even though their children could be expected to have displayed significantly more interest in the storms. This lack of significant curricular response may reflect teachers' difficulties in developing relevant activities, a notion supported by some teachers' reports that they continued with the regular curriculum in part because they were unsure of alternatives. Teachers need to be able to develop an emergent curriculum, especially in response to disaster, and they need to feel empowered to pursue children's interests. Teacher educators need to show preservice teachers how to develop emergent curricula and context-appropriate teaching practices so they will be equipped to offer appropriate supportive instruction at all times, especially in the wake of disaster.

Although some teachers may have lacked knowledge about developing an emergent curriculum, others alluded to implied or explicit public policies that prevented them from designing curricula that followed children's interests, abilities, and needs after the storms. A mandated curriculum that placed specific content and skills above children's interests and needs apparently hindered teachers' response. Some school districts made local decisions that mandated flexibility, adjusting their standards for minimum hours of instruction for children to earn credit toward graduation and regulations about required courses versus electives. Despite these and other adjustments at the policy level, the teachers in our sample felt pressured to achieve as usual, probably as a result of teacher accountability systems. With high-stakes assessment driving much of what happens in schools, there is a tendency to adhere to state-imposed curricula that ostensibly lead to optimum achievement on mandated assessments.

Teacher educators and teachers can help policymakers and administrators recognize how relevant and emergent curricula can meet many of the same goals and objectives as preestablished curricula. Policymakers need to consider the wisdom of taking a flexible stance with regard to academic expectations for children and actively convey that flexibility to teachers. For example, the Louisiana Department of Education pragmatically suspended the usual consequences that accompany its high-stakes testing program in those parishes affected by the storms ("LEAP Change Seems Sensible," 2005).

A second implication of these findings is that teachers need research-based information about effective ways to help children after a disaster. Their concerns about "protecting" children from reliving painful episodes need to be addressed with specific constructive strategies for helping children safely discuss their experiences and express their feelings. Teachers specifically expressed a desire for information about how to talk to children and answer their questions and stated a need for strategies to help children cope with loss and the disruption of their lives, including methods for helping them adjust to changes and make smooth transitions as they moved from school to school. Finally, the teachers surveyed requested information for parents.

These needs should be addressed in teacher education and professional development programs through a focus on the nature of children's development, with major attention to their responses to traumatic events. Mental health professionals are especially well versed in issues related to children's social–emotional and cognitive development. They understand and can explain the effects of trauma on young children and thus help teachers recognize that adapting curricula and classroom routines to meet the needs of affected children is not a luxury, but an absolute necessity. Professionals can offer specific age-appropriate strategies that will enable teachers to support children and families and should assure teachers that the use of such strategies will not cause further trauma. With knowledge about children's cognitive, social, emotional, and physical growth and development, teachers are better able to make decisions regarding appropriate activities that are grounded in developmental theory and research rather than intuition or personal experience.

Another implication relates to the self-reported posttraumatic stress symptoms among teachers. Teachers must be made aware of the importance of addressing their own psychological health and well-being as they strive to support children. Those teachers with the most direct personal hurricane-related experiences were more likely to engage children in hurricane-related activities. They may have done so in an attempt to address their own needs (as suggested by teachers discussing these findings), or teachers who were directly affected by the hurricanes may have better understood the importance of talking and learning about what had happened. On the other hand, those teachers might have been doing hurricane-related activities at the expense of their own emotional well-being, as reported by the LSU preschool teachers (Aghayan et al., 2005). Teachers who suffered the loss of their homes or suddenly faced the stress of indefinitely hosting large numbers of extended family members, for example, had to forge ahead with their teaching responsibilities. Such teachers needed as much care as their students, but few seemed prepared to manage the dual challenge of self-care and care for children.

Mental health professionals can help teachers and teacher education students develop the skills necessary to locate relevant resources that can help them and children in their care. Mental health professionals can emphasize to teachers the importance of monitoring and preserving their own emotional well-being and help them recognize typical signs of posttraumatic stress. They can offer strategies for dealing with children's stress and, equally important, help teachers recognize when they should seek professional assistance in coping with their own trauma. Although teachers may be reluctant to ask for help, mental health professionals should stress the potential effects of their own emotional health on that of the children with whom they interact.

This study of educators' responses to Katrina offers a beginning understanding of teachers' curricular responses to disasters. An emergent curriculum that reflects both teachers' and young children's interests and needs following a disaster has the potential not only to allow rich academic experiences, but also to provide an opportunity for addressing stress and trauma. Additionally, teachers can benefit from more information about meeting the needs of young children following trauma, and such information must be grounded in empirical research and theory of children's social–emotional development. Finally, teachers who experience disaster personally need tools to be able to meet their own needs so they can thrive in their efforts to teach young children.

REFERENCES

Aghayan, C., Schellhaas, A., Wayne, A., Burts, D. C., Buchanan, T., & Benedict, J. (2005). Project Katrina. *Early Childhood Research and Practice, 7*. Retrieved September 15, 2007, from http://ecrp.uiuc.edu/v7n2/aghayan.html

Allen, M., Jerome, A., White, A., Marston, S., Lamb, S., Pope, D., et al. (2002). The preparation of school psychologists for crisis intervention. *Psychology in the Schools, 39*, 427–439.

Ashby, C. M. (2007). *Emergency management: Status of school districts' planning and preparedness* (Testimony before the Committee on Homeland Security, House of Representatives, released Thursday May 18, 2007). Washington, DC: U.S. Government Accountability Office.

Bacher, R., Devlin, T., Calongne, K., Duplechain, J., & Pertuit, S. (2005). *LSU in the eye of the storm: A university model for disaster response.* Baton Rouge: Louisiana State University Office of Public Affairs. Retrieved May 31, 2007, from http://www.lsu.edu/pa/book/

Black, S. (2005). From 9/11 to Katrina: Helping students grieve. *Education Digest, 71*, 8–13.

Bredekamp, S., & Copple, C. (Eds.). (1997). *Developmentally appropriate practice in early childhood programs.* Washington, DC: National Association for the Education of Young Children.

Bretherton, I., & Oppenheim, D. (2003). The MacArthur Story Stem Battery: Development, administration, reliability, validity and reflections about meaning. In R. N. Emde, D. P. Wolf, & D. Oppenheim (Eds.), *Revealing the inner worlds of young children: The MacArthur Story Stem Battery and parent–child narrative* (pp. 55–80). New York: Oxford University Press.

Bronfenbrenner, U. (2005). *Making human beings human: Bioecological perspectives on human development.* Thousand Oaks, CA: Sage.

Buchanan, T. K., & Benedict, J. (2007). Early childhood education students' reflections: Volunteering after Hurricanes Katrina and Rita. *Journal of Early Childhood Teacher Education, 28*, 83–88.

Buchanan, T., Burts, D. C., White, V. F., Bidner J., & Charlesworth, R. (1998). Predictors of the developmental appropriateness of the beliefs and practices of first, second, and third grade teachers. *Early Childhood Research Quarterly, 13,* 459–483.

Burts, D. C., Hart, C. H., Charlesworth, R., Fleege, P., Mosley, J., & Thomasson, R. H. (1992). Observed activities and stress behaviors of children in developmentally appropriate and inappropriate kindergarten classrooms. *Early Childhood Research Quarterly, 7,* 297–318.

Cohen, D., Stern, V., & Balaban, N. (1996). *Observing and recording the behavior of young children.* New York: Teachers College Press.

Damiani, V. B. (2006). *Crisis prevention and intervention in the classroom: What teachers should know.* Lanham, MD: Rowman & Littlefield.

Degnan, A., Thomas, G., Markenson, D., Song, Y., Fuller, E., & Redlener, I. (2004). *Uncommon senses, uncommon courage: How the New York City school system, its teachers, leadership, and students responded to the terror of September 11.* New York: Columbia University Mailman School of Public Health, National Center for Disaster Preparedness. Retrieved June 26, 2007, from http://www.ncdp.mailman.columbia.edu/files/9_11reportASSESSMENT.pdf

Derogatis, L. R., Lipman, R. S., Rickels, K., Uhlenhuth, E. H., & Covi, L. (1974). The Hopkins Symptom Checklist (HSCL): A self-report symptom inventory. *Behavioral Science, 19,* 1–15.

DiCarlo, C. F., Burts, D. C., Buchanan, T. K., Aghayan, C., & Benedict, J. (2007). Making lemonade out of lemons: Early childhood teacher educators' programmatic responses to hurricanes Katrina and Rita. *Journal of Early Childhood Teacher Education, 28,* 61–68.

Emde, R. N., Wolf, D. P., & Oppenheim, D. (Eds.). (2003). *Revealing the inner worlds of young children: The MacArthur Story Stem Battery and parent–child narratives.* New York: Oxford University Press.

Fairbrother, G., Stuber, J., Galea, S., Pfefferbaum, B., & Fleishman, A. R. (2004). Unmet need for counseling services by children in New York City after the September 11th attacks on the World Trade Center: Implications for pediatricians. *Pediatrics, 113,* 1367–1374.

Frost, J. L. (2005). Lessons from disasters: Play, work and the creative arts. *Childhood Education, 82,* 2–8.

Glaser, B., & Strauss, A. L. (1967). *The discovery of grounded theory: Strategies for qualitative research.* Chicago: Aldine.

Graham, J., Shrim, S., Liggin, R., Aitken, M. E., & Dick, R. (2006). Mass-casualty events at schools: A national preparedness survey. *Pediatrics, 117,* e8–e15. doi:10.1542/peds.2005-0927

Gullo, D. F. (2005). *Understanding assessment and evaluation in early childhood education* (2nd ed.). New York: Teachers College Press.

Hantula, J. (1984). Disasters and catastrophes: Springboards to discovery. *Social Studies, 24,* 88–91.

ensibile. (2005, October 3). *The Advocate*, p. 8-B.

138   BUCHANAN, CASBERGUE, AND BAUMGARTNER

Paulson, A. (2005, September 28). At school for storm evacuees, hugs before homework. *Christian Science Monitor*, p. 1.

Perlmutter, D. D. (2005). After Katrina: Teachers reaching out. *Education Digest, 71*, 4–7.

Pfefferbaum, R. L., Fairbrother, G., Brandt, E. N., Robertson, M. J., Gurwitch, R. H., Stuber, J., et al. (2004). Teachers in the aftermath of terrorism: A case study of one New York City school. *Community Health, 27*, 250–259.

Poland, S. (1994). The role of school crisis intervention teams to prevent and reduce school violence and trauma. *School Psychology Review, 23*, 175–190.

Rowley, K. (2007). *GulfGov reports: An examination of the impact of Hurricanes Katrina and Rita on the public school districts in 15 communities*. Baton Rouge, LA: Nelson A. Rockefeller Institute of Government and Public Affairs Research Council of Louisiana. Retrieved May 31, 2007, from http://www.la-par.org/studrep_date.cfm

Schellhaas, A., Burts, D. C., & Aghayan, C. (2007). Reflecting on "Project Katrina" and developmentally appropriate practices: A graduate student's perspective. *Journal of Early Childhood Teacher Education, 28*, 77–82.

Shreve, R., Danbom, K., & Hanhan, S. (2002). "Wen the flood km we had to lv": Children's understandings of disaster. *Language Arts, 80*, 100–108.

Silverman, R. L. (1999). *"Where do we turn? What should we do?" Processes to help educators and their students recover from a natural disaster* (Monograph for the Plan for Social Excellence). Retrieved September 15, 2007, from http://eric.ed.gov/ERICWebPortal/recordDetail?accno=ED439524

Tucker, J. (2004). Making difference in the aftermath of the September 11th 2001 terrorist attacks. *Critique of Anthropology, 24*, 34–50.

Watts, M. (2007). Be prepared. *School Planning and Management, 46*, 20–25.

Weathers, F. W., & Litz, B. T. (1994). Psychometric properties of the Clinician-Administered PTSD Scale, CAPS–1. *PTSD Research Quarterly, 5*, 2–6.

Welch, M. (2006). What happens to animals during hurricanes? Teachable moments with extreme weather and animals. *Science Scope, 29*, 14–19.

Zevenbergen, A. A., Sigler, E. A., Duerre, L. J., & Howse, E. (2000). The impact of a natural disaster on classroom curricula. *Journal of Educational Thought, 34*, 285–303.

II

ASSESSING NEED AND FACILITATING COMMUNITY RESPONSE: RESOURCES, SERVICES, AND SUPPORTS

6

SERVICE NEEDS OF CHILDREN AND FAMILIES AFFECTED BY HURRICANE KATRINA

ARIANA SHAHINFAR, TANYA VISHNEVSKY, RYAN P. KILMER,
AND VIRGINIA GIL-RIVAS

It is clear that children are affected by exposure to trauma and that they have unique and specific needs with respect to coping with traumatic exposure. This statement seems obvious today in a world in which news reports are dominated by accounts of terrorism, war, and school violence, and the critical impact these events may have on children's lives is well accepted. Only a few decades ago, however, the importance of addressing children's unique needs in response to trauma was not universally appreciated. In an overview of children and disasters written in the late 1980s, Sugar (1989) noted, "Many disasters involving children have been described with few, if any, remarks about the children. Little or no emotional effect[s] from disasters have been listed by some [investigators]" (p. 164). Furthermore, when those reports did acknowledge symptoms consistent with posttraumatic stress among children, they were often countered by others reporting negative or mixed findings (Sugar, 1989). Since that time, studies involving children exposed to natural disasters (see, e.g., La Greca, Silverman, Vernberg, & Prinstein, 1996; Lonigan, Shannon, Finch,

Funding for the research presented in this chapter was provided by National Institute of Mental Health Grant 1R03MH078197-01 awarded to Virginia Gil-Rivas and Ryan P. Kilmer.

Daugherty, & Taylor, 1991; Proctor et al., 2007; Shaw et al., 1995) have established that the question is not whether disaster trauma affects children, but how much, in what ways, and under what circumstances the effects are mitigated or exacerbated.

It is this third question—that of how disaster trauma can be mitigated or exacerbated for children and families following exposure—that is at the heart of this chapter. More specifically, our focus is on the ameliorating role of social services provided to children and families in a postdisaster environment. Although it is beyond the scope of this chapter to offer a detailed review of the risk and protective factors that contribute to an understanding of children's adjustment following disasters, we know from earlier work that characteristics of the postdisaster recovery environment (e.g., social support to child and family, presence of continued family life stress, disruption of child and family routines) are critical to predicting children's postdisaster stress reactions (Silverman & La Greca, 2002).

In a disaster situation, the Federal Emergency Management Agency (FEMA) and various emergency relief organizations (e.g., the American Red Cross) should ideally be prepared to deal with either providing or supporting the provision of physical shelter and emergency food and medical care. Although these are essential needs, they do not directly address the reestablishment of family life that is crucial to enabling children's psychological and emotional recovery. To the extent that social service and other community-based agencies are relied on in this country to provide families with access to the resources needed to create a stable, healthy, safe environment for children in nonemergency situations, it follows that these agencies would have the capacity to help families reestablish a similar environment following a disaster.

In the case of Hurricane Katrina, repairing the postdisaster environment for children and families was no small task, and the work is ongoing. It has involved the rebuilding of physical environments such as homes, schools, and neighborhoods; provision of opportunities to repair the family economic environment through job availability and transportation; and access to services for dealing with the psychological trauma children and parents experienced during and after the storm. Many social service agencies (including faith-based organizations; see chap. 9 of this volume for an in-depth consideration), primarily at the state and local levels, stepped in to help with these efforts. This chapter examines the child and family service needs that arose following the storm for a portion of the affected population—families that had been displaced to primarily FEMA-sponsored living situations in Baton Rouge and surrounding areas—and how well those needs were met by the available delivery systems through the eyes of both the families and representatives of the service-providing agencies.

Our goal, in part, is to detail the specific successes and failures of service systems in the wake of this particular disaster. Given the unprecedented degree of social disorganization caused by Katrina, however, it would be misplaced to frame this information as an indictment of social service delivery in our nation in general. Rather, the more salient goal before us is to examine the overarching themes present in both the service successes and weaknesses evidenced by Katrina and to use these themes as a springboard for examining how service delivery for children and families may be improved to better meet the needs of those affected by future traumatic events, regardless of the origin and magnitude.

SERVICE NEEDS OF THOSE AFFECTED BY HURRICANE KATRINA

In scrambling to document the plight of those affected by Hurricane Katrina, the Centers for Disease Control and Prevention (CDC) and other organizations dispatched teams to shelters and other temporary housing units following the hurricane to conduct rapid needs assessments (Ridenour, Cummings, Sinclair, & Bixler, 2007; Weisler, Barbee, & Townsend, 2006). General findings included an unsurprising elevation in unemployment and needs for medical care, prescription medication, and mental health assistance. Although these findings provide important information, the assessments that were conducted focused almost entirely on individual adult functioning and needs, independent of family status (Rath et al., 2007). Although the association between parent functioning and child adjustment following exposure to trauma is generally accepted (La Greca & Prinstein, 2002; Lieberman & Knorr, 2007; Scheeringa & Zeanah, 2001; see also chap. 2, this volume), these reports did not address whether and how the individual needs of those surveyed affected family functioning.

In fact, only a handful of reports have centered their focus on children and families as the unit of analysis (Sherrod, 2007). This is an unfortunate oversight when considering that approximately one third of the population of Orleans Parish was under the age of 18 when Katrina struck, and 60% of the households in New Orleans included families (U.S. Census Bureau, 2007). Of those who have attempted to track how families fared through the hurricane and beyond, the consensus is that hurricane-exposed children and parents experienced multiple traumatic events, ranging from witnessing the injury or death of relatives, friends, and neighbors at the hands of the storm to enduring parent–child separation (Scheeringa & Zeanah, 2008; Spell et al., 2008; see also chap. 10, this volume). One study conducted 6 months after Katrina reported that families had moved an average of 3.5 times, and 20%

of school-age children either had not been in school or had missed 10 or more days of school in the prior month (Abramson & Garfield, 2006).

Exposure to Katrina-related trauma and the consequent disruption of family life have been associated with elevated levels of posttraumatic stress disorder (PTSD; Hensley & Varela, 2008; Scheeringa & Zeanah, 2008), internalizing and externalizing problems (Spell et al., 2008), and reactive aggression (Marsee, 2008) among children and youths affected by the hurricane. Further, an investigation of children with a chronic medical condition found that they were significantly more likely to present with medical symptoms and to experience negative psychological consequences from the storm than those without a preexisting chronic medical condition (Rath et al., 2007). Similarly, Weems et al. (2007) found that predisaster trait anxiety predicted post-traumatic stress and generalized anxiety symptoms among youths following the hurricane.

With respect to family functioning, significantly elevated levels of depression and anxiety (Abramson & Garfield, 2006; Scaramella, Sohr-Preston, Callahan, & Mirabile, 2008) and PTSD (Scheeringa & Zeanah, 2008; Spell et al., 2008) among mothers were documented after Katrina. One study found that increased maternal symptomatology was significantly associated with family stress, as indexed by financial strain and neighborhood violence (Scaramella et al., 2008). This maternal symptomatology and family stress have been, in turn, associated with child PTSD (Scheeringa & Zeanah, 2008) and behavior problems (Scaramella et al., 2008; Spell et al., 2008) among families affected by Hurricane Katrina.

UNDERSTANDING POST-KATRINA CHILD AND FAMILY NEEDS IN CONTEXT

In keeping with a bioecological systems approach (Bronfenbrenner, 1983; Bronfenbrenner & Morris, 2006), it is important to focus not only on children's service needs but also on the needs of the family, as they are clearly intertwined. This model (Bronfenbrenner & Morris, 2006; see also Introduction to this volume) posits that there are several nested levels of influence on human growth. The child, with his or her unique biological makeup, is at the center. Moving outward, the direct and transactional effects of individuals in the child's immediate environment are next—parents, siblings, extended family, teachers, and friends. In considering their influence, it is important to account for the ecological circumstances that, in turn, affect these individuals—for example, the parent's workplace and job status, the school environment (including its impact on teachers), and the cultural and community context in which the family operates. In short, development and adaptation occur within the context of dynamic and interconnected systems. As such, myriad aspects of the postdisaster environment need to be explored.

In the case of Hurricane Katrina, many children and families witnessed a collapse at nearly all levels of the ecological system. The home and school contexts were physically destroyed, families were separated, parents lost employment, and children and families were removed from their neighborhoods and social support systems. In short, the usual family, community, and social structures that buoy individuals in a time of crisis were washed away with the storm. Although some families had the resources to escape the devastation, relocate to the homes of family or friends who lived in safer environments, and quickly resume employment and school and family routines, many others were left both physically and psychologically stranded. It is this latter group for whom service delivery was so critical following the hurricane.

The work reported below represents a preliminary inquiry into the nature of those needs, the degree to which they were met, and the needs that remained or were simply not accounted for in preparation for a disaster of this magnitude. The data were collected from interviews with families who had been displaced by the hurricane (Study 1), as well as individuals representing several service agencies in the greater Baton Rouge and New Orleans areas (Study 2).

STUDY 1: INTERVIEWS WITH FAMILIES DISPLACED BY HURRICANE KATRINA

Method

We interviewed 70 adult caregivers who had evacuated their homes as a result of Hurricane Katrina. The interviews were conducted in the Baton Rouge and New Orleans, Louisiana, metropolitan areas and along the Mississippi Gulf Coast as part of a larger effort to assess factors influencing the adaptation of caregiver–child dyads affected directly by the disaster. We conducted baseline interviews approximately 1 year after the hurricane. Participants were recruited via flyers distributed at elementary schools, FEMA-operated trailer parks, service provider agencies, churches, and community-based organizations and via participant referral. Interested individuals were screened to ensure that they met inclusion criteria: (a) they were the primary caregiver (i.e., mainly responsible for the child's care) of a 7- to 10-year-old, and (b) their family had evacuated and/or incurred serious losses as a result of Katrina. Interviews were scheduled at times and locations convenient for caregivers at baseline and follow-up (roughly 22 months postdisaster). Caregivers were reimbursed for their participation. Only data from baseline interviews are reported in this chapter. The institutional review boards of the University of North Carolina at Charlotte and the Louisiana State University approved the study.

Measures

Caregivers reported on family size, household composition, ethnicity, parents' education level, family income, and occupation (see Table 6.1). Caregivers also completed a questionnaire indicating the degree to which their family needed and received a list of 22 services. Fifteen services (see Figure 6.1) related to the needs of the caregiver or the family as a whole (e.g., housing assistance, family therapy, help completing insurance forms), and seven (see Figure 6.2) related to the needs of the 7- to 10-year-old child interviewed for the larger study (e.g., counseling, tutoring for school subjects, medical care). Caregivers were also asked to describe any additional services not on the list

TABLE 6.1
Demographic Characteristics of Caregivers

Characteristic	%
Ethnic background	
African American	78
White, non-Hispanic	15
Native American/Alaskan	3
Multiethnic	4
Marital status	
Married	27
Divorced or separated	30
Never married	37
Widowed	3
Other	3
Education level	
Less than high school	25
High school or equivalency diploma	38
Trade or technical training, some college	17
2-year (AA) or 4-year (BA, BS) college degree	14
Graduate degree (MA, PhD, MD)	6
Employment status	
Employed	67
Unemployed	33
Living situation	
Owned house or apartment	16
Rented house or apartment	37
Lived with relatives	6
Lived in FEMA trailer park	39
Other	2

Note. $n = 70$. FEMA = Federal Emergency Management Agency.

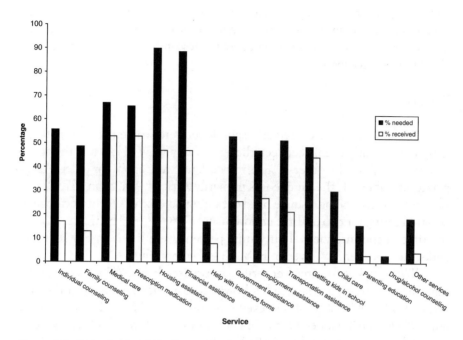

Figure 6.1. Caregiver and family services needed and received.

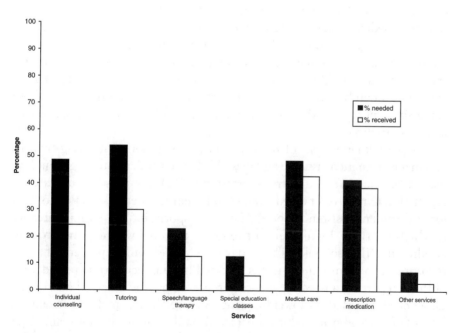

Figure 6.2. Child services needed and received.

and to respond to open-ended questions regarding problems they may have encountered in obtaining needed or desired services. To reduce error and facilitate administration, a trained member of the research team read each question aloud to the participant.

Results

A majority of the caregiver respondents were women (87%), with the sample split nearly evenly between the ages of 20 and 34 (43%) and the ages of 35 and 49 (47%); the other 10% of respondents were age 50 or older. As displayed in Table 6.1, the sample was primarily African American (87%), with most respondents being a single head of household. Sixty percent of caregivers reported caring for two or three children, and 67% reported being employed at the time of the interview. Thirty-nine percent were living in FEMA trailer parks, and another 37% lived in FEMA-assisted housing.

With respect to caregiver service needs (see Figure 6.1), more families reported requiring material needs following the hurricane than any other area assessed, with 90% of those surveyed reporting a need for help with housing and 89% endorsing a need for financial assistance. Across both examples of material needs, just over half (52%) of those reporting the need stated that they had received assistance. A substantial number also reported needs for medical care (67%) and prescription medication (66%). A majority of those reporting medical needs reported having received assistance (80%) by the time of our interview. A third need category, mental health assistance, was also prominent, with 56% reporting a need for individual counseling or therapy for the caregiver and another 49% conveying a need for family counseling or therapy. Unfortunately, these needs were reported as received by only 30% of those expressing a need for individual counseling and 27% of those with a need for family counseling.

Approximately half of respondents (53%) reported needing help to obtain government assistance and reestablish independence through employment assistance (47%) and transportation (51%). For these needs, rates of reported help received ranged from 66% for employment assistance to 49% for government assistance and 41% for transportation. The final category in which relatively high levels of need were reported was help in enrolling children in either school (49%) or day care (30%). Ninety percent of those reporting school enrollment needs reported having received help, and 33% of those reporting a need for day care reported having received assistance. Other needs reported at a lower frequency included help completing insurance forms (17%), parenting education (16%), and drug or alcohol counseling (3%). Unfortunately, these needs were also the least often met, with only 18% of those reporting a need having received parenting education, 8% having received insurance form help, and none having received drug or alcohol counseling.

With respect to caregiver-reported child service needs (see Figure 6.2), the greatest need reported was for tutoring in school subjects (54%), with about half (56%) reporting having received this support. Similar to their self-reported needs, many caregivers reported needs for medical care (49%) and prescription medication (41%) for their children; 88% of medical care needs and 95% of medication needs were reported as met. Needs for mental health services, such as individual child counseling or therapy, were also reported at a high level (49%), with only about half (49%) of those needs reported as met. Finally, school-related child needs, including speech therapy (23% needed) and special education (13% needed), were noted as having been received in 57% and 46% of the cases reporting needs, respectively.

The open-ended item about other needs for either caregiver or child provided illuminating information regarding service gaps for these families. In accord with the results just described, caregivers reiterated that they had the most problems obtaining housing, financial assistance, and transportation. For instance, one caregiver spoke about not being able to return to New Orleans:

> I am trying to go back home, and I would love to go back home. I would like to buy a house back home, but I'm not getting any help. I was a renter when I lived in New Orleans. No one wants to help the renters. Everyone is helping the homeowners.

Although some caregivers acknowledged receiving financial assistance from FEMA and other sources, such as insurance reimbursements, several respondents stated that the financial assistance they were receiving was not enough. As one caregiver explained, "I only got $300 for rent for 1 month. FEMA did not help with my housing. . . . I was denied, and [I] don't know why. I wrote to FEMA, and they still did not help."

Additionally, caregivers discussed their frustrations in trying to obtain many of the services they needed. One caregiver noted, "[Service providers] question you for everything. I had to go through a lot of things before I could get what I needed." Several caregivers talked about not knowing exactly how to obtain services. As one caregiver stated, "I did not know where to go. There was too much red tape."

A number of caregivers reported having difficulty placing their children in the right school and/or obtaining tutoring services. In several instances, caregivers attributed these experiences to discrimination against individuals from New Orleans. As one mother described it, "My child was failing at school, and [the school] didn't provide any help. . . . I really had to advocate for her. [The school] looked down on us because we were from New Orleans."

STUDY 2: INTERVIEWS WITH SOCIAL SERVICE AGENCY REPRESENTATIVES

Method

We conducted the second study to better understand service availability and delivery needs from the perspective of the service providers themselves. Twenty-two leaders of prominent social service agencies working with displaced children and families in Baton Rouge, New Orleans, or West Feliciana, a parish north of Baton Rouge, were contacted during June through August 2007. We contacted potential participants by phone at their place of employment and asked if they were willing to participate in a 30-minute semistructured phone interview regarding their perception of service delivery achievements and gaps for children and families affected by Katrina. If the agency representative was willing to participate, a mutually convenient time was arranged for the interview. All interviews were audiorecorded and transcribed. Participants were provided transcripts of their interviews to review for accuracy.

Of the 22 agency representatives contacted, we were unable to directly reach 11 (50%) (e.g., repeated messages were left but not returned), 7 (32%) expressed interest in the study but were eventually unable to participate because of scheduling difficulties, and 4 (18%) completed the interview. Two participating agency representatives served children and families in the Baton Rouge area, one served the New Orleans area, and one served West Feliciana.

Measures

The semistructured interview began with a request for information regarding the types of services each agency provided and the extent of contact they had had with families affected by Hurricane Katrina. Participants were also asked to provide their impression of delivery adequacy (e.g., how often services were needed and how often needs were met) in the same 15 common social service needs assessed in the caregiver interviews (e.g., counseling or therapy, medical care, housing assistance, financial assistance), allowing for a direct comparison of caregiver and service provider perception. Finally, participants were asked an open-ended question regarding the advice they would have for other organizations facing similar circumstances in the future.

Results

Three of the four participants represented private, nonprofit agencies serving children and families (sometimes in addition to other populations). The fourth participant represented a family service agency overseen by a local public school system. All four reported significant contact with families affected by Hurricane Katrina.

When asked to report on the need for and adequacy of service availability, a clear pattern emerged: All respondents reported that the need for immediate medical care was both highly prevalent and well met by various providers across agencies. One participant credited the mobile medical units that traveled to various FEMA trailer parks as having met immediate, acute medical needs in 90% of the cases, with the other 10% of cases likely reflecting a lack of either willingness to participate or information regarding when and how to obtain the medical services. Another participant praised the efforts of medical treatment teams to connect children and acutely suffering adults with proper care through mobile units but noted that the long-term medical infrastructure had been so damaged (e.g., hospitals were destroyed, "not all physicians came back") that obtaining long-term care for chronic conditions was a problem:

> I meet with a lot of grandparents who are raising their grandchildren. And as they take on the stressors of posthurricane life . . . the very physical demands of parenting children manifest in a lot of challenges to health and wellness. So, you know, you have a grandparent who is having a lot of pain in their legs and they need to figure out what's causing this. Well, those are things that require a specialist, things that are expensive. . . . It's harder to access that kind of care.

In considering the areas in which most service needs for children and families affected by Hurricane Katrina were evident, agency representatives unanimously viewed assistance with finding affordable housing, reliable transportation, and long-term, adequately paying employment as most critical. One agency representative described the situation as follows:

> Housing and transportation are definitely core problems for our area. . . . The cost of housing has escalated dramatically in Baton Rouge since the storm. . . . We had a housing shortage for affordable housing prior to Katrina. Then we added, you know, another 20,000 or 30,000 new households that needed affordable housing.

One agency representative remarked on how the excellent public transportation system in New Orleans before the storm may have paradoxically contributed to a problem for those who remained in or returned to New Orleans. The public system had been decimated, and they were unaccustomed to getting around their city in any other way:

> Well, our streetcars still aren't running. The buses do not seem to be even as dependable as they were before the storm. So I think transportation is a real challenge, especially because . . . there are so many neighborhoods that have not fully come back. So people living in those neighborhoods do need transportation to get to the grocery store.

An agency representative from Baton Rouge observed that cultural barriers may also have contributed to the problem of finding employment for those displaced from New Orleans:

> Culturally, employers are often reluctant to hire evacuees because they fear that they're going to orient and train this person, and then they're going to go back to New Orleans and it's going to be a wasted effort. [Also], a lot of people [from New Orleans] are not accustomed to working these traditional jobs. They're more accustomed to doing odd jobs. In a city like New Orleans that had a huge convention trade . . . there's always somebody catering. There's always somebody setting up convention tables. Always somebody setting up a trade show. And so many people made a righteous living without ever filling out a job application by just doing these odd jobs.

Perhaps most pertinent to families, another representative described the employment problem as one in which minimum wage positions in the service industry were available, but a living wage that a parent needs to support a family was "very hard to come by."

With respect to mental health needs—an area in which caregivers themselves reported pronounced unmet needs—agency representatives presented a mixed picture in which all four interviewees reported availability of services immediately after the hurricane but described challenges in ensuring that those they serve obtained them. As one reported,

> I mean, to me, what I see [is that] there is an abundance of area mental health services, but I don't necessarily say that the needs are being adequately met. . . . The services are there; the challenge is engaging people to access those services.

It is possible that some of this challenge was rooted in the stigma associated with receiving mental health treatment. As one respondent described, "Especially within some socioeconomic groups, [seeking mental health assistance] is viewed as unacceptable."

Another respondent highlighted that although grief and trauma services were available within his organization, it was unclear that all available mental health services were up to the challenge of meeting the particular set of needs associated with the severe trauma following a hurricane of this magnitude:

> I think there's probably varying levels of preparedness to effectively help families reduce grief and trauma reactions within agencies in a city. So some of it is not necessarily, you know, Are there places people can be offered services? but also, Are the services that are being offered up to the challenge of reducing those grief and trauma reactions?

When asked what advice they would give to other organizations facing similar circumstances in the future, agency representatives described themes of hope, preparation, and the importance of providing basic support. As one interviewee phrased it, "Don't just throw your hands up and run out the door." Another reinforced this notion by focusing on the mindset that service providers need to have to continue in their work following a disaster of this scale:

> There's that kind of hope that you need to connect people with to keep going and to continue to live [in circumstances like these]. So, for parents to feel like, you know, I am helping my child function and feel better, for teachers to really see the wonderful gift they're giving to their students by continuing to be here, for all people to really be able to connect with that sense of how they are contributing to a better world—I think that really is the only thing that can keep you [as a service provider] going when there are all these challenges around you all the time.

In addition, agency representatives agreed that better preparation within service agencies would have been helpful. For example, one representative highlighted the importance of having a simple listing of resources within the community on hand before a disaster strikes. For another, agency preparation translated into developing plans and partnerships within the local community services web before another crisis: "The key to being successful is collaboration."

Finally, regardless of the service each agency was designed to provide, there was a unanimous sentiment among agency representatives that offering support for basic needs should not be overlooked. One representative described people's needs for safety and comfort as primary but admitted that bureaucracy "can sometimes get in the way of that." Another added that agencies needed to be prepared to offer support simply by "listening to everybody":

> [Listening] is what a lot of these families wanted. They wanted to tell you what they lost. They wanted to tell you who they couldn't find. Sometimes there's absolutely nothing you can do, but everybody in the organization needs to be prepared to listen.

In a similar vein, one agency representative highlighted that support should be offered not only to those affected by the disaster, but also to providers working to address families' needs:

> I think that it would help the families in the long run . . . if our . . . providers had more help and support . . . in dealing with the crisis—someone to speak with our nurses when they were overwhelmed with a lot of things.

DISCUSSION

Similar to other reports (e.g., Ridenour et al., 2007), we found that requests for immediate medical services and prescription medication were prevalent, but also perhaps the most adequately addressed of all needs in our sample of families, according to caregiver and service agency representative reports. Between 80% (for caregivers) and 88% to 95% (for children) of family medical needs were reported by caregivers as being adequately met. As one agency representative highlighted, however, this assessment of acute medical assistance following the hurricane does not take into account ongoing needs for chronic health care that were either present before the storm or developed as a result of the storm. These chronic needs may include both physical and mental health components. For example, one report estimated that 500,000 people in the New Orleans area will require mental health care in the years following the storm as compared with the 40,000 who accessed those services before Katrina (Weisler et al., 2006; see also Abramson & Garfield, 2006).

The medical infrastructure that existed in New Orleans before the storm, however, is unlikely to return to its prior operating potential in the near future, whether due to an inability to rebuild physical hospital structures or a shortage of medical care professionals, many of whom had not yet returned even 1 year after the storm (Weisler et al., 2006). In one assessment of health care disaster response related to Hurricane Katrina, the authors noted that the most common needs presenting in emergency medical clinics just 2 weeks after the storm related to chronic disease and routine emergency care rather than the direct impact of the hurricane (Millin, Jenkins, & Kirsch, 2006). As the authors highlighted, the problem is that most health care disaster planning does not focus on the management of chronic disorders and resupplying lost routine medications for refills. Offering only acute services may be adequate in smaller scale disasters where people remain close to their "medical homes" (i.e., primary caregivers and related resources) and health care availability is intact, but this approach needs to be reevaluated for future, large-scale emergency situations.

This consideration also applies to the many other service needs families require following a disaster of this magnitude coupled with long-term, sometimes permanent, displacement. For example, the highest reported needs by caregivers—nearly 90%—were for help in obtaining adequate, affordable housing and financial assistance. Unfortunately, only half reported receiving these services nearly 1 year after the hurricane. Needs for employment and transportation assistance were also reported by nearly half of the caregivers yet received in only half of those cases. Agency representatives independently identified housing, transportation, and employment assistance—those areas related to basic household and family functioning and maintenance—as presenting the greatest problems in terms of delivery adequacy.

One area in which there was some disagreement between caregiver and service agency reports was with respect to mental health care. Caregivers reported relatively high needs for individual counseling for themselves (56%) and their children (49%) and for family counseling (49%), yet these needs were reported as being addressed in only 30%, 49%, and 27% of cases, respectively. In their interviews, most agency representatives agreed that mental health needs were often left unmet, but they painted a picture in which mental health services were available, albeit not frequently used by displaced individuals. One reason for this discrepancy may have been a lack of adequate information regarding how and where to obtain mental health services, including appropriate screening or assessment. A second may have been lack of transportation and/or access to child care so that parents could receive individual services. Other barriers agency representatives identified were a lack of available space in which to deliver mental health services in ways that were convenient and accessible to consumers (individuals or families) and the possible stigma associated with seeking mental health services.

CAVEATS

This work is limited in a number of ways. Most obviously, our small sample size, particularly with respect to the service agency representatives, makes it difficult to draw firm conclusions. Rather, our work should be considered as providing "further evidence" in cases in which our findings echo themes uncovered by other researchers and as suggesting avenues for future consideration when our findings are unique in the literature. In addition, our findings may be limited in their generalizability in that the families we interviewed represent a subpopulation of those affected by Hurricane Katrina. Our interviews were conducted primarily with families who had sought shelter and remained in FEMA-sponsored housing within their home region for more than a year. As such, our sample largely does not include those who had the financial and social resources to move into other housing situations following the hurricane. Aside from the obvious advantage of financial resources allowing a family to relocate or rebuild and begin their lives again quickly, the buffering effect of social and emotional resources cannot be underestimated in a time of trauma. For example, Solomon, Bravo, Rubio-Stipec, and Canino (1993) documented emotional support following disaster as playing an important role in moderating the impact of such trauma on adult mental health. Parents who have been exposed to disaster may be especially vulnerable to a lack of social support in that they tend to be the providers of emotional support to family members and, thus, require more resources themselves to maintain this role (Solomon et al., 1993).

In addition, our sample does not reflect those who were able to return to their homes or neighborhoods. It is difficult to gauge whether the present sample would be considered to be more or less at risk as a result of their situation, but it is possible that they represent the more vulnerable of those displaced by the hurricane in that they were unable to regain the sense of place, neighborhood, and community experienced by those who returned to mourn and rebuild with at least some of their neighbors and social support network. Further, our sample does not include those who were unable to access government help following the hurricane. Disturbing reports of undocumented immigrants being encouraged to go to shelters to receive government assistance and instead being sent for deportation hearings were reported in the media following Hurricane Katrina (Terhune & Perez, 2005). As a result, many families—often of Hispanic origin—were left without external assistance at all. In a powerful documentation of this situation, Messias and Lacy (2007) described how such families were often more successful at staying together and helping each other and their neighbors than those who relied on the government to aid them in evacuation.

A further caveat is that our data do not fully permit disaggregation of the service needs that existed before the hurricane from those that were hurricane specific. This question is critical from the perspective of understanding the impact of the hurricane on individual functioning, but it does not minimize the message that children and families who have survived the trauma of a natural disaster of this magnitude will have multiple service needs that require addressing, regardless of origin.

LESSONS LEARNED AND ACTIONABLE RECOMMENDATIONS

There appears to be consensus in the field and empirical support for core foci to support positive mental health and resilience among survivors of mass trauma. These foci include the promotion of a sense of safety, calming, self- and collective efficacy, connectedness, and hope (see, e.g., Hobfoll et al., 2007). However, a great deal of work remains to be done in disseminating these principles to the varied agencies that support primary and secondary trauma response, as well as to policymakers (Benedek & Fullerton, 2007; Fairbank & Gerrity, 2007). In addition, a gap exists with respect to the translation of these foci into actual service delivery that is realistic and relevant across cultures and contexts (Jones, Greenberg, & Wessely, 2007).

Notwithstanding these limitations, we report here for consideration a number of strategies suggested in the literature for improving the degree to which those affected by disaster receive needed mental health services. For example, use of mass media communication and face-to-face outreach and provision of services in neighborhood centers, places of worship, schools, and other community gathering spaces have been identified as important in reaching this population (Gard & Ruzek, 2006). Gard and Ruzek (2006) suggested ensuring that disaster survivors are provided with instrumental and emotional support from family and friends and arranging telephone follow-up at a later date with individuals considered at risk of mental health problems associated with disaster (e.g., those with premorbid conditions). These solutions may be useful in many disaster circumstances, but we again highlight the unique problems presented by Hurricane Katrina in that these solutions do not offer relief for an individual or family displaced to a FEMA trailer, many miles from their home, without television or telephone and with no connection to their neighborhood center, place of worship, or community.

Others have suggested applying frameworks developed for other traumas—for example, school-based interventions—as a model for mental health service delivery to children in cases such as Katrina (e.g., Dean et al., 2008; Osofsky, Osofsky, & Harris, 2007; see also chap. 7, this volume). However, it is unclear how such service delivery would operate when local schools have been destroyed, children have been displaced to communities in which schools may lack resources for trauma support, and school attendance in the new location is disrupted and unpredictable (Abramson & Garfield, 2006).

We would argue that a compelling method of mental health service delivery might be one that follows the mobile medical unit model. This model brings the services to the people who need them, regardless of location and in as many sessions as are required for recovery, and recognizes the challenge of being a parent in need of treatment by offering child care during sessions. This same mobile mental health unit could be equipped with the prescription medication required for treating behavioral and adjustment problems associated with disaster trauma (e.g., depression, anxiety) as well as chronic psychiatric conditions. Part of the problem in obtaining mental health services during Katrina and the disaster's immediate aftermath was that the federal funding available for crisis mental health counseling specified that the resources could not be used to deliver treatment for mental health and behavior disorders, but rather for short-term crisis-intervention sessions and teaching self-help strategies in group settings (Dewan, 2006a). A flexible reallocation of such funding into a model designed to support the long-term needs of individuals following a disaster would certainly serve as a sound starting point in addressing unmet mental health needs.

Although we began this chapter with the express goal of not crafting this report as an indictment of social service delivery in our nation, our work would be incomplete if we did not draw attention to the fact that socioeconomic and racial factors are widely understood to have played a role in the allocation of resources for humanitarian needs before, during, and after Hurricane Katrina (see, e.g., Squires & Hartman, 2006; Stivers, 2007). Whether this problem is described within the context of a preexisting handicap in that certain class and racial groups had limited access to the means with which to evacuate before the storm, or whether the argument is framed as those who found themselves without resources both during and after the storm being neglected because they belonged to groups traditionally discriminated against in American society, it is clear from our data and those of others that the people most in need of services following the hurricane were demographically similar to those most in need in our country in general. Indeed, the poor population disproportionately resided in the areas of New Orleans most vulnerable to natural disaster. In a geographic exploration of stress-related risks, however, Curtis, Mills, and Leitner (2007) showed that it was not simply being poor that predicted vulnerability, but being African American, being female, being a single head of household, having young children in the home, suffering from chronic illness, and being pregnant that also contributed to vulnerability before, during, and after the hurricane. Unfortunately, the data regarding the way in which the federal government handled relief efforts draw a clear and consistent picture of devaluation of those groups most in need (for a thoughtful review, see Stivers, 2007).

Some have examined the culture of aid and social support in this country and found that less educated and Black adult victims of a natural disaster tended to receive less help than did more educated or White victims (Kaniasty & Norris, 1995). Further, others have found that this disparity in treatment is associated with a disparity in mental health outcomes among those displaced by Katrina, such that those who reported a higher level of perceived racial discrimination during the hurricane and greater financial strain after Katrina also evidenced more PTSD symptoms (Chen, Keith, Airriess, Li, & Leong, 2007). Our data point to another interesting pattern of prejudice in that some participants perceived that they had been discriminated against in their new location because of their group membership as a displaced individual from New Orleans. For example, one parent reported feeling that she had to work harder to obtain tutoring assistance for her daughter who was failing academically because the schools were unsympathetic to the plight of evacuees from New Orleans. This sentiment was echoed in our agency representative interviews when one participant highlighted an unwillingness on the part of employers in Baton Rouge to reach out to those affected by the hurricane because they feared that their investment in training evacuees would be wasted when the individuals eventually returned to their homes or perceived a lack of fit between the skills displaced New Orleanians offered (e.g., hospitality, odd jobs) and the available positions.

This phenomenon has also been reported through the media as citywide discrimination against those displaced from New Orleans, which appears to have developed in certain evacuation locations more than others (Dewan, 2006b). Thus, it is possible that the group bias that developed following the hurricane became more complex than the simple racial or socioeconomic divide that was originally thought to have undermined the delivery of help to those in need. It appears that as new group boundaries were drawn, the status of having been displaced by the hurricane and in need of social service assistance may have superseded prior racial or socioeconomic biases and formed a new challenge to those trying to recover.

Although they provided a relatively quick solution to a very difficult problem, FEMA-sponsored housing villages may have contributed to the problem, as social stigma has been hypothesized to be exacerbated by the context of living in segregated, poor, and disordered neighborhoods, independent of the demographic characteristics, individual behaviors of families, and quality of relationships among families living within those neighborhoods (Nation, Perkins, & Hughes, 2007). In short, the social environments in which many displaced individuals and families found themselves following Hurricane Katrina may have fostered a new kind of stigmatization that has only begun to be played out in this society.

A disaster of the magnitude of Katrina provides an unfortunate opportunity to learn lessons about which aspects of humanitarian need were adequately addressed, which were left wanting, and how the nation can better prepare for the needs of children and families in future disasters. Osofsky et al. (2007) highlighted the need to establish and maintain family routines to provide safety, support, and stability for children as soon as possible after the disaster; to educate school and child care personnel about signs of distress; and to develop after-school programs to support displaced children with their academic and social needs to rebuild resilience and self-efficacy. Our data also highlight the need to provide the same opportunities to the caregivers leading the families in which these children live. Parents need access to transportation, housing, and job opportunities to adequately regain their own routines, maintain self-efficacy, and support their children.

As others (see Abramson & Garfield, 2006) have noted, the net effect of family service needs being chronically unmet may not be estimable for many years to come. For example, imbalance in just one area of the child's ecological system—the school—may contribute to reduced academic attainment and lost future economic opportunity during adulthood. The question likely to be addressed in the future with the population of children and families whose lives were disrupted by Hurricane Katrina will be how multiple ecological imbalances affected their growth and development. Although righting each ecological imbalance through concentrated service provision is a noble goal, it was clear from our data that even 1 year after Hurricane Katrina, this goal was not fully realized for many, if not most, services.

Some have suggested stockpiling emergency pharmaceutical supplies and preparing an emergency delivery system so that those displaced by hurricanes have access to medical services and prescriptions anywhere in the country if large-scale population displacement is again required (Millin et al., 2006). This suggestion raises the question of what the social service equivalent of this plan would be for children and families. How can we develop a preventive or rapid-action delivery system that would make housing, transportation, employment, mental health services, and school assistance readily available for families affected by disaster? One example may be found in the operation by some local housing assistance organizations of an ongoing database of available, affordable housing in the region so that people can easily and quickly find a living space that will match their needs. Rather than being solely focused on housing the homeless in a particular community, such a plan enables anyone with a housing crisis to obtain immediate assistance. Because the database is continually updated, the information is available at all times to anyone who needs it—including an influx of displaced individuals. This type of established delivery system would avoid the problems associated with trying to create fresh services in the moment of crisis and could be developed for many different services (e.g., employment, medical and mental health services).

A final aspect to consider is that culture also inadvertently plays a role in how effective or ineffective society may be in dealing with large-scale disaster. In an individualistic culture such as our own, the success or failure of each person is attributed almost exclusively to that individual. In a situation such as the one created by Katrina and its aftermath, this cultural viewpoint results in individual blame—a situation that is clearly unfounded in the case of natural disaster—while absolving society, government, and industry for the situations that gave rise to that vulnerability (Saunders, 2007; Stivers, 2007). Indeed, the social psychological tendency toward "belief in a just world" (Lerner & Miller, 1978) suggests that people place blame directly on victims simply because they have the need to believe in a world in which fairness determines circumstance. Fairness, however, means different things to different people, as views differ depending on one's own unique vantage point (Stivers, 2007).

As many have pointed out, Hurricane Katrina was much more than a natural disaster—it was a social disaster, as preexisting social and structural problems in U.S. society were laid bare by the confluence of bad weather and geographic and social circumstance (Belle, 2006; Moyo & Moldovan, 2008). The question that remains is how mental health professionals can work within the cultural structure to ensure that the needs of families and children are met under such conditions. A powerful set of suggestions for professionals includes building trust before a disaster, maintaining that trust in the delivery of emergency services, knowing the communities whom we are charged with protecting, and developing plans from that knowledge (Carter-Pokras, Zambrana, Mora, & Aaby, 2007). At the heart of these suggestions is the necessity of considering the difficult proposition that we are all vulnerable and that we need to be prepared for the eventuality that we will either need help or be called on to offer help to fellow citizens at some time or another—a proposition not often accepted in American culture, but perhaps the most important lesson from Hurricane Katrina.

REFERENCES

Abramson, D., & Garfield, R. (2006). *On the edge: Children and families displaced by Hurricane Katrina and Rita face a looming medical and mental health crisis* [Electronic version]. Retrieved October 16, 2007, from http://www.ncdp.mailman.columbia.edu/program_special.htm

Belle, D. (2006). Contested interpretations of economic inequality following Hurricane Katrina. *Analyses of Social Issues and Public Policy, 6*, 143–158.

Benedek, D. M., & Fullerton, C. S. (2007). Translating five essential elements into programs and practice. *Psychiatry, 70*, 345–349.

Bronfenbrenner, U. (1983). *Ecology of human development: Experiments by nature and by design.* Cambridge, MA: Harvard University Press.

Bronfenbrenner, U., & Morris, P. A. (2006). The bioecological model of human development. In R. M. Lerner & W. R. Damon (Eds.), *Handbook of child psychology: Vol. 1. Theoretical models of human development* (6th ed., pp. 793–828). Hoboken, NJ: Wiley.

Carter-Pokras, O., Zambrana, R. E., Mora, S. E., & Aaby, K. A. (2007). Emergency preparedness: Knowledge and perceptions of Latin American immigrants. *Journal of Health Care for the Poor and Underserved, 18*, 465–481.

Chen, A. C., Keith, V. M., Airriess, C., Li, W., & Leong, K. J. (2007). Economic vulnerability, discrimination, and Hurricane Katrina: Health among Black Katrina survivors in Eastern New Orleans. *Journal of the American Psychiatric Nurses Association, 13*, 257–266.

Curtis, A., Mills, J. W., & Leitner, M. (2007). Katrina and vulnerability: The geography of stress. *Journal of Health Care for the Poor and Underserved, 18*, 315–330.

Dean, K. L., Langley, A. K., Kataoka, S. H., Jaycox, L. H., Wong, M., & Stein, B. D. (2008). School-based disaster mental health services: Clinical, policy, and community challenges. *Professional Psychology: Research and Practice, 39*, 52–57.

Dewan, S. (2006a, April 18). Evacuee study finds declining health. *New York Times.* Retrieved December 14, 2007, from http://www.nytimes.com/2006/04/18/us/nationalspecial/18health.html

Dewan, S. (2006b, August 24). Storm's escape routes: One forced, one chosen. *New York Times*. Retrieved December 14, 2007, from http://www.nytimes.com/2006/08/24/us/nationalspecial/24katrina.html

Fairbank, J. A., & Gerrity, E. T. (2007). Making trauma intervention principles public policy. *Psychiatry, 70*, 316–319.

Gard, B. A., & Ruzek, J. I. (2006). Community mental health response to crisis. *Journal of Clinical Psychology: In Session, 62*, 1029–1041.

Hensley, L., & Varela, R. E. (2008). PTSD symptoms and somatic complaints following Hurricane Katrina: The roles of trait anxiety and trait sensitivity. *Journal of Clinical Child and Adolescent Psychology, 37*, 542–552.

Hobfoll, S. E., Watson, P., Bell, C. C., Bryant, R. A., Brymer, M. J., Friedman, M. J., et al. (2007). Five essential elements of immediate and mid-term mass trauma intervention: Empirical evidence. *Psychiatry, 70*, 283–315.

Jones, N., Greenberg, N., & Wessely, S. (2007). No plans survive first contact with the enemy: Flexibility and improvisation in disaster mental health. *Psychiatry, 70*, 361–365.

Kaniasty, K., & Norris, F. (1995). In search of altruistic community: Patterns of social support mobilization following Hurricane Hugo. *American Journal of Community Psychology, 23*, 447–477.

La Greca, A. M., & Prinstein, M. J. (2002). Hurricanes and earthquakes. In A. M. La Greca, W. K. Silverman, E. M. Vernberg, & M. C. Roberts (Eds.), *Helping children cope with disasters and terrorism* (pp. 107–138). Washington, DC: American Psychological Association.

La Greca, A. M., Silverman, W. K., Vernberg, E. M., & Prinstein, M. J. (1996). Symptoms of posttraumatic stress after Hurricane Andrew: A prospective study. *Journal of Consulting and Clinical Psychology, 64*, 712–723.

Lerner, M. J., & Miller, D. T. (1978). Just world research and the attribution process: Looking back and ahead. *Psychological Bulletin, 85*, 1030–1051.

Lieberman, A. F., & Knorr, K. (2007). The impact of trauma: A developmental framework for infancy and early childhood. *Psychiatric Annals, 37*, 416–422.

Lonigan, C. J., Shannon, M. P., Finch, A. J., Daugherty, T. K., & Taylor, C. M. (1991). Children's reactions to a natural disaster: Symptom severity and degree of exposure. *Advances in Behaviour Research and Therapy, 13*, 135–154.

Marsee, M. (2008). Reactive aggression and posttraumatic stress in adolescents affected by Hurricane Katrina. *Journal of Clinical Child and Adolescent Psychology, 37*, 519–529.

Messias, D. K. H., & Lacy, E. (2007). Katrina-related health concerns of Latino survivors and evacuees. *Journal of Health Care for the Poor and Underserved, 18*, 443–464.

Millin, M. G., Jenkins, J. L., & Kirsch, T. (2006). A comparative analysis of two external health care disaster responses following Hurricane Katrina. *Prehospital Emergency Care, 10*, 451–456.

Moyo, O., & Moldovan, V. (2008). Lessons for social workers: Hurricane Katrina as a social disaster. *Social Development Issues, 30*, 1–11.

Nation, M., Perkins, D. D., & Hughes, C. (2007). *The sins of darkness: A contextual model of stigma and psychosocial outcomes of children and adolescents of color in disadvantaged neighborhoods*. Manuscript submitted for publication.

Osofsky, J. D., Osofsky, H. J., & Harris, W. W. (2007). Katrina's children: Social policy considerations for children in disasters. *SRCD Social Policy Report, 21*(1), 3–18.

Proctor, L. J., Fauchier, A., Oliver, P. H., Ramos, M. C., Rios, M. A., & Margolin, G. (2007). Family context and young children's responses to earthquake. *Journal of Child Psychology and Psychiatry, 48*, 941–949.

Rath, B., Donato, J., Duggan, A., Perrin, K., Bronfin, D. R., Ratard, R., et al. (2007). Adverse health outcomes after Hurricane Katrina among children and adolescents with chronic conditions. *Journal of Health Care for the Poor and Underserved, 18*, 405–417.

Ridenour, M. L., Cummings, K. J., Sinclair, J. R., & Bixler, D. (2007). Displacement of the underserved: Medical needs of Hurricane Katrina evacuees in West Virginia. *Journal of Health Care for the Poor and Underserved, 18*, 369–381.

Saunders, J. M. (2007). Vulnerable populations in an American Red Cross shelter after Hurricane Katrina. *Perspectives in Psychiatric Care, 43*, 30–37.

Scaramella, L. V., Sohr-Preston, S. L., Callahan, K. L., & Mirabile, S. P. (2008). A test of the family stress model on toddler-aged children's adjustment among Hurricane Katrina impacted and nonimpacted low-income families. *Journal of Clinical Child and Adolescent Psychology, 37*, 530–541.

Scheeringa, M. S., & Zeanah, C. H. (2001). A relational perspective on PTSD in early childhood. *Journal of Traumatic Stress, 14*, 799–815.

Scheeringa, M. S., & Zeanah, C. H. (2008). Reconsideration of harm's way: Onsets and comorbidity patterns of disorders in preschool children and their caregivers following Hurricane Katrina. *Journal of Clinical Child and Adolescent Psychology, 37*, 508–518.

Shaw, J. A., Applegate, B., Tanner, S., Perez, D., Rothe, E., Campo-Bowen, A. E., et al. (1995). Psychological effects of Hurricane Andrew on an elementary school population. *Journal of the American Academy of Child and Adolescent Psychiatry, 34*, 1185–1192.

Sherrod, L. (2007). From the editor. *SRCD Social Policy Report, 21*(1), 2.

Silverman, W. K., & La Greca, A. M. (2002). Children experiencing disasters: Definitions, reactions, and predictors of outcomes. In A. M. La Greca, W. K. Silverman, E. M. Vernberg, & M. C. Roberts (Eds.), *Helping children cope with disasters and terrorism* (pp. 11–33). Washington, DC: American Psychological Association.

Solomon, S. D., Bravo, M., Rubio-Stipec, M., & Canino, G. (1993). Effect of family role on response to disaster. *Journal of Traumatic Stress, 6*, 255–269.

Spell, A. W., Kelley, M. L., Wang, J., Self-Brown, S., Davidson, K. L., Pellegrin, A., et al. (2008). The moderating effects of maternal psychopathology on children's adjustment post-Hurricane Katrina. *Journal of Clinical Child and Adolescent Psychology, 37,* 553–563.

Squires, G. D., & Hartman, C. (Eds.). (2006). *There is no such thing as a natural disaster: Race, class and Hurricane Katrina.* New York: Routledge.

Stivers, C. (2007). "So poor and so Black": Hurricane Katrina, public administration, and the issue of race. *Public Administration Review, 67,* 48–56.

Sugar, M. (1989). Children in a disaster: An overview. *Child Psychiatry and Human Development, 19,* 163–179.

Terhune, C., & Perez, E. (2005, October 3). Roundup of immigrants in shelter reveals rising tensions. *Wall Street Journal.* Retrieved October 4, 2007, from http://online.wsj.com/article/SB112830055169458141.html

U.S. Census Bureau. (2007). *State and county quick facts.* Retrieved November 15, 2007, from http://quickfacts.census.gov/qfd/states/22000.html

Weems, C. F., Pina, A. A., Costa, N. M., Watts, S. E., Taylor, L. K., & Cannon, M. F. (2007). Predisaster trait anxiety and negative affect predict posttraumatic stress in youths after Hurricane Katrina. *Journal of Consulting and Clinical Psychology, 75,* 154–159.

Weisler, R. H., Barbee, J. G., & Townsend, M. H. (2006). Mental health and recovery in the Gulf Coast after Hurricanes Katrina and Rita. *JAMA, 296,* 585–588.

7

IMPLICATIONS OF MAJOR DISASTER FOR EDUCATORS, ADMINISTRATORS, AND SCHOOL-BASED MENTAL HEALTH PROFESSIONALS: NEEDS, ACTIONS, AND THE EXAMPLE OF MAYFAIR ELEMENTARY

RYAN P. KILMER, VIRGINIA GIL-RIVAS,
AND JACQUELINE MACDONALD

We had developed a community within our school. . . . We were a small
school who set out to make every day a day where students and staff "live,
laugh, and learn."
—Jacqueline MacDonald, former principal, Mayfair Elementary School

Hurricane Katrina and its aftermath are widely regarded as constituting
the most severe, damaging, and costly disaster in U.S. history. Of particular
relevance to this chapter, 1,100 schools in Louisiana and Mississippi were
closed following Katrina, with about 830 damaged and 40 completely
destroyed in Louisiana alone (Louisiana Recovery Authority [LRA], 2007;
Osofsky, Osofsky, & Harris, 2007; Save the Children, 2006). Two years later,
educational services remained among the sectors most impacted by disaster-
related events (LRA, 2007).

Hurricane Katrina initially displaced between 1.0 and 1.3 million Gulf
Coast residents, including approximately 372,000 school children (LRA, 2007;
Select Bipartisan Committee to Investigate the Preparation for and Response
to Hurricane Katrina, 2006; U.S. Department of Education, 2005a). This initial evacuation was typically followed by subsequent needs to relocate. The

Preparation of this chapter was supported by National Institute of Mental Health Award R03
MH078197-01 to Virginia Gil-Rivas and Ryan P. Kilmer.

167

movement of children among schools has been found to have detrimental effects (e.g., lower achievement, disciplinary issues; Pane, McCaffrey, Tharp-Taylor, Asmus, & Stokes, 2006), and this high mobility (and lack of stability) brought its share of difficulties for those displaced by Katrina. For example, in relocating and reenrolling, these youngsters not only missed significant school time (Pane et al., 2006), but they also had to learn new patterns of behavior and social expectations at school and adapt to new communities (Madrid, Grant, Reilly, & Redlener, 2006).

Several sources have documented the hurricane-related adversity experienced by these children and their families, including injury or death to family members, separation from caregivers, property and/or major financial loss, and neighborhood damage (Gil-Rivas, Hypes, Kilmer, & Williams, 2007; Hurricane Katrina Community Advisory Group [HKCAG], 2006). For instance, the HKCAG (2006) detailed that nearly 85% of survey respondents from Louisiana, Mississippi, and Alabama reported a significant financial, income, or housing loss, with 36.3% reporting extreme physical adversity and 22.8% reporting extreme psychological adversity; over 40% indicated that they had experienced five or more significant stressors (see also chaps. 2 and 10, this volume). The available evidence suggests that the transitions and challenges have been chronic for many families. In fact, as of late 2007, many families continued to live in temporary housing, experience financial difficulties, and struggle to meet basic needs.

Hurricane Katrina meaningfully altered numerous aspects of life in the affected regions—homes and neighborhoods, social connections, and the accessibility of health and mental health services and supports, to name just a few. Within this context, this chapter focuses on one critical domain of life in any community: the schools. Schools constitute one of the core arenas in which children function, serve as a key source of stability in communities, and are often a prime setting for postdisaster intervention. The sections that follow describe briefly some findings regarding the consequences of disaster for schoolchildren; consider the rationale for school-based response and attention to youngsters' needs following a disaster; describe issues involved in such work within the schools; and focus on the case example of Mayfair Elementary in East Baton Rouge Parish (EBRP), one of the schools reopened to accommodate the influx of families displaced by Hurricane Katrina. Numerous online and print resources detail guidelines and recommendations regarding what schools and school personnel can do after a disaster; however, the description of Mayfair's efforts and the exemplary work of Principal Jacqueline MacDonald is intended to paint a more complete picture of an integrated response that can serve as a model for others. The chapter concludes with additional recommendations for school personnel.

ASSESSING THE IMPACT OF DISASTER ON SCHOOLCHILDREN: BRIEF SUMMARY OF SELECTED FINDINGS

Evidence from prior disasters in this country (see, e.g., Hoven, Duarte, & Mandell, 2003; La Greca, Silverman, Vernberg, & Prinstein, 1996; Pfefferbaum et al., 1999) suggests that although many children cope and adapt effectively following disaster, a sizable proportion of children and youths exhibits a range of mental health consequences. The nature of reactions and effects varies based on a child's developmental level (see detailed descriptions of age-related reactions to trauma, National Child Traumatic Stress Network [NCTSN], n.d.-a) and his or her other resources, but some common reactions among younger schoolchildren include anxiety and worry about the safety of themselves and others, fear of future hurricanes and related events, separation anxiety, clinginess, sleep difficulties, aggression, and regressive behaviors such as temper tantrums and bedwetting (see, e.g., NCTSN, n.d.-a, n.d.-b; Norris, Friedman, Watson, Byrne, et al., 2002; Osofsky et al., 2007). In addition to sadness and anxiety-related difficulties, such as feelings of fear and sleep disturbances, older children and adolescents are also more likely to evidence an increase in problem behaviors and acting out, difficulty concentrating and problems learning, somatic complaints, and withdrawal (e.g., NCTSN, n.d.-a, n.d.-b; Norris, Friedman, Watson, Byrne, et al., 2002; Osofsky et al., 2007).

Beyond those initial reactions, trauma, including disasters, can have a detrimental impact on children's ability to manage normal developmental tasks, which, in turn, may have consequences for their social relationships, academic achievement, and later psychological adjustment (Bosquet, 2004; Margolin & Gordis, 2000). In the longer term, the most commonly reported negative psychological consequences reflect symptoms of posttraumatic stress disorder (PTSD), along with other anxiety-mediated problems and generalized distress, major depression, suicidality, withdrawal, sleep difficulties, problem behaviors, and acting out (e.g., Hoven et al., 2003; Vernberg, La Greca, Silverman, & Prinstein, 1996; Vogel & Vernberg, 1993). Such difficulties, including symptoms of posttraumatic stress, may persist well after the disaster (La Greca et al., 1996; Vogel & Vernberg, 1993). Of particular relevance to the school setting, posttraumatic stress symptoms may contribute to difficulty with attention and concentration and, in turn, may affect school performance.

Prior disaster work has found that aspects of the trauma, such as degree of exposure (e.g., Goenjian et al., 2001), number of secondary risks, and disruption of day-to-day routines, may intensify its negative impact (Lieberman & Van Horn, 2004). However, Katrina is unique among disasters studied in this country, as the adversities related to the hurricane and its aftermath encompass a substantial array of risks, many associated with higher symptom levels, including major personal losses, such as the death of family members; the sheer magnitude of damage and disruption wrought; the degree of exposure to crime, violence, death, and devastation; the large-scale evacuation and displacement; the persistent implications and complications for families (e.g., housing issues) and their uncertain resolution; and the complete disruption, even loss, of neighborhoods, friendships, and linkages with natural support systems (Dewan, 2006; HKCAG, 2006; Lonigan, Shannon, Taylor, Finch, & Sallee, 1994; Norris, Friedman, Watson, Byrne, et al., 2002; Perry & Dobson, n.d.; Vogel & Vernberg, 1993). As such, the impact of Katrina on psychological well-being was expected to be consistent with, if not worse than, the effects found in studies of prior disasters.

In fact, the research involving children affected by Katrina accords with these ideas and prior findings (see Introduction to this volume). Thus, although some children affected directly by Katrina appear to be adapting positively, it is not surprising that hurricane-related events are significantly associated with posttraumatic stress symptoms (e.g., Gil-Rivas et al., 2007; see also chap. 10, this volume) or, more globally, that those affected directly have evidenced high rates of mental health and physical health difficulties (Dewan, 2006; HKCAG, 2006; see also chap. 10, this volume). Such symptoms likely interfere with children's functioning across domains, that is, at home, in school, and with their friends, and these findings underscore the need to mobilize appropriate services and supports to meet their needs.

POSTDISASTER RECOVERY: THE IMPORTANCE OF THE SCHOOL SETTING

Schools are a core element of the fabric of any community. Indeed, they serve as a critical source of continuity, connection, stability, and structure. Exposure to disasters and other traumas can shake the foundation of children's assumptive worlds of safety, protection from harm, and predictability and contribute to loss of trust, meaning, and faith (Goldman, 2002; Klingman & Cohen, 2004; Lieberman & Van Horn, 2004). Because schools can provide a sense of security and normalcy and help reestablish a sense of safety and routine to children and families following a disaster (CDC, 2007; Osofsky et al., 2007), even serving as a secure base for children when family resources are limited (Klingman & Cohen, 2004), numerous authors have highlighted the importance of ensuring that schools are back on line quickly following a disaster (e.g., Klingman & Cohen, 2004; Osofsky et al., 2007). In the case of Katrina, a prime task for many families was getting their children back into school—in many cases, a school different than the one the youngsters knew (Perry & Dobson, n.d.).

In addition to their clear educational mission, schools often are called on to meet the emotional and behavioral needs of students, and, particularly during times of crisis, caregivers rely on schools to protect their children and provide guidance about how to best support them (Jaycox, Morse, Tanielian, & Stein, 2006; Klingman & Cohen, 2004). The New Freedom Commission on Mental Health (2003) noted that "mental health is essential to learning as well as to social and emotional development. Because of this important interplay between emotional health and school success, schools must be partners in the mental health care of our children" (p. 58). In fact, some authors have noted that schools can be the prime community resource for intervention following disaster or trauma, serving as a key locus for assessing students' social and emotional functioning and for providing mental health services, in part because schools are accessible and seen as a natural environment for children and youths and a less stigmatizing setting than a mental health agency, and services can be integrated into the daily routines (e.g., Brown & Bobrow, 2004; Klingman & Cohen, 2004; Kupersmidt, Shahinfar, & Voegler-Lee, 2002; New Freedom Commission on Mental Health, 2003). As such, schools serve as a critical context for action, outreach, and support following a disaster.

More broadly, research on child risk and resilience has also documented the importance of stable, effective schools in the face of adversity (Luthar, Cicchetti, & Becker, 2000; Masten & Coatsworth, 1998; Wyman, Sandler, Wolchik, & Nelson, 2000). Cole et al. (2005) underscored this notion in considering the ways that schools can assist children who have experienced trauma. They noted that school personnel can partner with families and strengthen youngsters' relationships with adults both in and out of school, help children modulate and regulate their emotions and behaviors, and assist them in meeting their potential academically. In sum, the extant literature conveys that a school-based approach, guided by public health principles, is a key means of meeting the needs of children and families after a disaster (Chemtob, Nakashima, & Carlson, 2002; Klingman & Cohen, 2004; Pynoos, Goenjian, & Steinberg, 1998).

WORKING WITHIN THE SCHOOLS FOLLOWING DISASTER: ISSUES AND CHALLENGES

Notwithstanding the potential benefits of a school-based approach following a disaster, the approach is not without obstacles. For example, at a time when it is key for parents and families to collaborate with the school, communicate, and join in postdisaster efforts, the upset related to the trauma may raise issues of trust and leave parents more likely to feel suspicious of the school, question policies, and worry about its capacity to protect children from subsequent harm (Klingman & Cohen, 2004). Such difficulties may be exacerbated by the reality that following a trauma of great magnitude, schools are often unable to respond optimally and to provide the resources and supports that are likely needed (Cole et al., 2005; Jaycox et al., 2007). In addition, even with those means of responding, the infrastructure for communication, support, and action is not always what it could be (Center for Mental Health in Schools [CMHS], 2005a, 2006).

Depending on the nature of the disaster, schools may struggle with such issues as overcrowding; the integration and needs of new (i.e., relocated) students, increases in learning and/or socioemotional problems; and teacher burnout or distress related to the impact of the trauma on school staff, both directly and indirectly (CMHS, 2006; Jaycox et al., 2007). Consequently, following mass trauma or disaster, it is also necessary to ensure that the needs of teachers and staff are addressed (Jaycox et al., 2006; Klingman & Cohen, 2004; see also chap. 1, this volume).

Finally, given the mission and goals of the setting, there may also be a tension between the focus on academics or impending standardized testing and the students' emotional and psychological (or even more basic) needs (Jaycox et al., 2007; Society for Community Research and Action, 2008; see also chap. 5, this volume). Regardless, there is a need to address thoughtfully potential barriers to learning and issues regarding accountability testing, as well as student placement, missing records or paperwork, and the like (e.g., CMHS, 2005a). The next section details selected elements of the approach, actions, and experiences at Mayfair Elementary, in which both students and staff had to grapple with many of these issues.

MAYFAIR ELEMENTARY IN EAST BATON ROUGE PARISH: A CASE EXAMPLE

Many families displaced by Katrina lived temporarily in Baton Rouge, Louisiana, and surrounding areas to escape the devastation left in the storm's wake. The EBRP School System worked to adapt to the influx of thousands of students enrolling in their schools during September 2005. In the first 3 weeks following Katrina, which made landfall on August 29, the system enrolled 4,000 new students, the most of any parish (Pane et al., 2006). Reports noted that as many as 8,000 students were newly registered as "homeless and transient" a month following the hurricane, but only 4,500 to 5,000 of those were attending class (CMHS, 2005b; Kamenetz, 2005). Children and youths relocated after Katrina transitioned out of the EBRP schools throughout the 2005–2006 school year; however, the system ultimately enrolled more than 3,000 new students for the entire year (Pane et al., 2006).

In light of the surge in enrollment, Mayfair Elementary was one of two EBRP schools reopened and dedicated to relocated children and youths. The school enrolled kindergarten through fifth-grade children. The effort at Mayfair Elementary has garnered attention and been described positively in media outlets (see, e.g., Paulson, 2005) for the many approaches staff and administration used not only to meet a range of student needs, but to ensure that the school was a resource for families as well. Principal Jacqueline MacDonald and her staff were innovative in their methods as they worked to help the students cope in the context of their new reality and progress educationally. MacDonald instituted a number of proactive steps to address the multiple needs of her students, over 69% of whom had been classified as at-risk (Louisiana Department of Education, 2006), and end-of-the-year assessments suggested that the students largely made great gains academically. The next paragraphs describe the events at Mayfair in more detail.

Getting Started

MacDonald learned that she would be principal of the new school on a weekend, and Mayfair's first students arrived on Tuesday of the following week, September 12, 2005. In preparing to open, many steps were necessary, and the parish school system had to mobilize significant resources. Indeed, Mayfair's 10 classrooms, library, and cafeteria were empty, so furniture was delivered from the system's surplus warehouse, and other EBRP principals and schools donated supplies and emergency materials to provide aid in the short term. To reach students and their parents, the school system advertised its opening, and representatives visited shelters to encourage families to enroll their children. Because many children lacked necessary records, parents or guardians completed forms and interviews in order to place children in the grade and school best suited to their child's needs. The system had to adapt as well: Notwithstanding the fact that Mayfair students were living throughout the parish, the system provided direct transportation to school, staggering school start times so that buses could pick up the relocated students.

The state department of education placed temporarily two distinguished educators from New Orleans with the school to help set it up and run it. They provided access to the state department and possible contacts, brought knowledge of the New Orleans school structure, and understood the students' experience with the hurricane. With the exception of the principal and school secretary, the school was staffed by teachers and other personnel displaced by Katrina. These teachers knew firsthand what Mayfair's children and families were facing, a beneficial perspective for helping to meet these students' needs. However, it is important to underscore that these teachers were also coping with significant adversity and upheaval, a factor that is considered again in the section "Addressing Socioemotional Concerns."

Guiding Notions

Following a disaster, school principals function in crucial leadership roles. MacDonald, described as "a powerhouse of energy and warmth" and "the school's emotional center" (Paulson, 2005), provided professional leadership during this difficult time that is particularly noteworthy, especially for a new principal. She was guided by several key notions, including (a) an understanding of the need to emphasize the "whole child" (including mental health, educational, and social needs) initially, followed by a focus on transitioning to a more "normal," day-to-day life; (b) a desire to connect with and develop a strong sense of community with the families; and (c) a determination to have the school function as a centralized (and trusted) source of information and dissemination. To that end, she developed a mental health resource list, identified funds for displaced persons, and linked families with community organizations.

Reaching Out

The central office for the EBRP schools provided critical leadership and support. Superintendent Charlotte Placide and Assistant Superintendent Margaret Mary Sulentic-Downing visited often, and in the early weeks, representatives from the system met with parents to assess needs and offer assistance in linking with supports and services.

Support also came from more far-reaching sources. Various forms of media were interested in Mayfair, and to her credit, MacDonald recognized the potential benefit of such attention. Early on, a reporter from the *Christian Science Monitor* came to the school, and the resultant article conveyed the need for supplies and community support (Paulson, 2005). The Associated Press picked up the article, and local and national media (e.g., CNN) covered what was happening in the EBRP schools. This press coverage stimulated an outpouring of support as well as donations and supplies; MacDonald believed that working with the media was fundamental to Mayfair's success.

It is important to note that MacDonald created a list of needed resources based on a parent survey as well as teacher inputs. This list helped ensure that in the face of such widespread need, the school and the families received what they really required and were not overwhelmed with donations that were well intentioned but not well suited to the children, families, or classrooms. Truckloads of supplies and thousands of dollars poured into Mayfair, and soon it was appropriately stocked with materials. According to MacDonald, "Soon our school looked like any other, with ample materials, and teachers teaching, and learning happening in every classroom." Letters of appreciation and pictures were sent out to donors so they could see that their gestures and efforts were being put to good use. To that end, MacDonald set up an e-mail system to provide periodic updates. As donors visited, MacDonald made sure that staff and students had the opportunity to meet them, a step that she reported enhanced students' social skills.

Connecting With Parents and the Community At-Large

MacDonald underscored the need for the school to be seen by the families and community as a place where they could obtain information and services and, of equal importance, where their voices would be heard. She made an effort to be accessible to parents and would meet with them and record anything that would help address their child's needs, a step of great salience because the school could not access the relocated children's files. Caregivers often came for assistance with a range of concerns, from accessing community services or counseling support to securing basic needs.

Mayfair's connection with parents took a meaningful step forward when MacDonald instituted a full-time parent liaison, David Maddox. His position involved holding in-services for parents and students; communicating with parents via newsletters, conferences, and phone calls; and increasing parents' awareness of services and supports throughout Baton Rouge. He surveyed them regarding needs to ensure that his efforts were targeted effectively, and the school provided transportation and child care so parents could attend meetings. In addition, during the year, several organizations, including Save the Children, I-Serve Baton Rouge, and the Parent University set up in-services and information resources for displaced families.

MacDonald worked to facilitate investment by community stakeholders by maintaining an open-door policy with organizations to visit and observe. A sense of community and positive relations were fostered further by events hosted at the school. First, the Southeastern Louisiana School of Nursing put on a health and safety seminar, including a variety of hands-on activities for students and parents, and gave out infant car seats as an incentive to attend. Second, at the end of the year, the Parent University and the EBRP School System coordinated a fair with diverse informational and resource booths that coincided with the school's awards program. Parents received information on a variety of academic and social services and had the opportunity to speak with representatives from the New Orleans School system, the Federal Emergency Management Agency and other hurricane relief agencies, and the EBRP Title 1 Program, which also provided books on the importance of parental involvement in helping students meet their academic potential. Once again, child care and transportation were arranged, and incentives were provided for attendance (e.g., children's books, uniforms). Parents not in attendance received this information when their child brought it home.

The Role of Volunteers

Community support played an invaluable role in the success at Mayfair. Community stakeholders, including churches and faith-based organizations, nonprofits, family or citizen groups, and concerned individuals, donated school supplies, clothing, money, and time. Indeed, volunteers assisted with cleaning the school and beautifying the broader campus, provided assistance in classrooms, and helped parents with specific needs. According to MacDonald, these groups also provided tangible and spiritual support away from school. One church developed a strong bond with teachers and parents and would arrive with snacks, gift cards, and encouragement. Another sponsored a Halloween fair, and the children wore costumes provided by an out-of-state women's group. These events provided another opportunity for parental involvement.

The large volunteer base was of significant benefit, but it also brought to the fore the issue of volunteer screening and monitoring. In turn, all visitors were checked for appropriate authorization and had to complete a volunteer log. In addition, because Mayfair was an open campus, MacDonald implemented strict guidelines such that volunteers would not be permitted to be alone with a student or to take children from classrooms.

Addressing Socioemotional Concerns

Acknowledging children's hurricane-related experiences and the ongoing disruption and adversity, MacDonald sought to establish a safe, nurturing, and caring environment. She worked with a number of organizations to address the socioemotional needs of students. Each program needed to document curriculum plans with research-based strategies submitted to the school before initiating activities, and the EBRP central office approved each program before implementation.

Among the individual and group interventions provided through Mayfair, Save the Children adapted and implemented their psychosocial support program, one that has been used internationally following trauma and disaster. Through this classroom-based program, Save the Children staff met with each grade level for 1 hour three times a week and led hands-on activities (e.g., art, drama, music) that facilitated expression about their experiences. Another agency, I-Care, provided crisis response services. Along with Mayfair's counselor, the I-Care counselor met weekly with children who needed extra attention. Also, Mayfair's counselor incorporated Second Step, a social competence enhancement program (often targeting violence prevention), into weekly classroom lessons. Students learned and practiced problem solving, cooperation, respectful behavior, and anger management. For those with parental consent, another organization conducted a 6-week bereavement program for students. I-Serve Baton Rouge and the Big Buddy program also trained displaced counselors to help Mayfair's teachers and serve the students.

Mayfair personnel reported an additional support of value, one that did not result from formal programming: Schools throughout the country not only donated supplies and funds, but their students wrote encouraging letters to Mayfair's students. Mayfair's children corresponded as part of their curricular goals; the students appeared comforted by knowing that others cared, and they valued the opportunity to show their appreciation. Over time, interested students were encouraged to maintain ongoing correspondence on their own, with parental involvement.

Mayfair's efforts to address psychological and emotional concerns also included the needs of faculty and staff. In the first 4 months of the school year, Save the Children counselors met with faculty during school early dismissals, and faculty were encouraged to attend the various in-services conducted by outside agencies, a particularly relevant step given that many of them had children attending school within the parish. Save the Children's programming, in particular, helped these adults cope with their own issues and concerns related to the storm and its aftermath.

Transition: Attending to Academics

MacDonald maintained a sequential approach to intervention and programming to tailor the school's role and best meet her students' needs. Consequently, the first 2½ months at Mayfair were dedicated to establishing a stable, productive school environment, assessing student and family needs, and creating a vision for the school. Following this initial emphasis on the children's emotional concerns, she saw the need to shift the primary focus and function back to education. As she said, "We're no longer coping; we're now living." Thus, by December 1, supportive programming and counseling were reduced. For example, the Save the Children psychosocial programming was modified to a 30-minute session once a week. Students with ongoing needs continued to receive services, and newly enrolled students were evaluated for needed services by the school counselor and the I-CARE liaison.

The transitory nature of the student body brought its own challenges for the school, as most students enrolled and departed from what MacDonald called "revolving door classrooms" within the span of a few months. The system's focus was to enroll them in permanent schools if the families chose to stay in Baton Rouge, and a prime goal was to prepare the students for the next year and the next level, psychologically, socially, and educationally.

Although the initial weight was placed on support, the school never lost sight of its educational mission. Each child was assessed via standardized instruments that yielded specific reading grade levels as well as competencies and skills not yet mastered in math, science, and social studies. Many Mayfair students were performing at one or even two grade levels below national averages on these measures at entry. To ensure that these students were ready to progress, MacDonald maintained small classes, and each classroom had support staff. School personnel met frequently to discuss strategies and plan. Lesson plans were reviewed in view of curricular components, needed skills, and required timelines. MacDonald emphasized instructional approaches that integrated empirically based strategies, and the EBRP school system central office assigned experienced educators to work with the teachers to help them implement the curriculum. Major decisions were evidence informed. For instance, through evaluation of test scores, classroom observations, and parental input, three grades decided to teach reading across grade level, grouping youngsters based on ability level and teaching basic skills in addition to the standard curriculum. In addition, via e-mails and weekly newsletters, Mayfair's staff kept abreast of professional development opportunities in the parish, focusing on technology, differentiated instruction, and classroom management. These three areas became focal points in the effort to help students succeed.

Notwithstanding her desire to connect with the community and meet the needs of the families displaced by Katrina, MacDonald described tension in having to say no to some offers of support as she put in place processes to help the children reach the next level academically. She had to strike a balance between serving as a support for families and the community, meeting basic needs and teaching the whole child, and ensuring that students learned and developed or enhanced needed skills. In turn, she sought guidance from experienced administrators, and these mentors assisted her not only in setting up Mayfair but in incorporating the system's strategic initiatives. Her efforts were successful: Under MacDonald's leadership, Mayfair's students demonstrated significant gains on key academic indicators.

The Mayfair Experience Comes to an End

At the end of the 2005–2006 school year, the school population had dwindled, and the EBRP central office decided to close Mayfair. A meeting was arranged with parents, many of whom wanted to keep Mayfair open, and all parents were notified of the school closing via a letter. The remaining students were assigned to other schools in the system, and staff kept parents informed via newsletters and phone calls.

MacDonald also notified community partners, agencies, and volunteers of Mayfair's closing and her plans for the materials donated over the course of the year. She assured them that she would send the materials to schools that were taking students enrolled at Mayfair, after she had contacted principals to assess their needs. Similarly, with the school system's support, MacDonald worked to allocate surplus monies to the schools receiving the majority of Mayfair's students. Furthermore, the library's newly donated books were largely given to schools in New Orleans.

Finally, active folders and test data were sent to schools in which Mayfair students were enrolled for the 2006–2007 school year, and MacDonald contacted principals to provide additional information regarding the children's needs. She sent letters to parents, providing her contact information and detailing how to enroll their children for the coming year. She had done what she could to facilitate the transition.

As the year came to an end, MacDonald reflected,

> We left with the knowledge that we had been true to the initiatives that our school system had set for all our schools and felt proud that we had involved our community to meet the needs of our families. Schools often wonder why the community is not involved. I have learned that you only need to share the specific goals and needs, and the community will step forward. We had developed a community within our school. This could not have happened if we had not had the support of various people within the EBRP School System, the community, parental involvement, and a strong faculty and staff who understood the ever-changing needs of our students and helped reach our goals and objectives. We were a small school who set out to make every day a day where students and staff "live, laugh and learn." It was an incredible, positive year.

LESSONS LEARNED AND ACTIONABLE RECOMMENDATIONS

The work of Jacqueline MacDonald and her staff at Mayfair Elementary can serve as a model for other schools and districts responding to future disasters. Many demonstration or model projects yield successes primarily because of extraordinary individuals at the helm, and indeed, one should not underestimate MacDonald's value and impact as principal of the school. Although her individual characteristics certainly cannot be easily duplicated, it is possible to consider and use the steps she took, the model she employed, and her philosophy about her school and her students.

In addition, resources abound for school personnel, including those providing diverse guidelines and recommendations regarding how to talk to students and help youngsters cope, what to "look for" in determining if a child needs to be referred for services, and other suggestions for helping children adapt following a disaster. The sections that follow consider several steps that school personnel can consider as they strive to meet the needs of their students.

Principals and Administrators

Principals and other administrators play a critical role in the aftermath of disaster. As illustrated by the Mayfair example, administrators can provide necessary leadership, establish and communicate a guiding philosophy and strategy for action, and set the tone for their school's response. They can serve as rudders for their schools, helping to steer them in the desired direction.

As the school attempts to reestablish routines and get back on line after a disaster, a first step is ensuring safety, stability, and structure. As others in this volume have described (see, e.g., chaps. 8 and 12, this volume), the use of Psychological First Aid (NCTSN & National Center for PTSD, 2006) is often a necessary acute intervention to reduce distress in the immediate aftermath of a disaster. In parallel, given the often pronounced needs following a disaster, principals can create strategies for tapping into resources from the community and disaster relief organizations. This may also be a fruitful time to think flexibly about ways to use volunteers to meet students' and schools' needs and to put in place mechanisms for deploying resources and person power where they are most needed (CMHS, 2005a).

Whether to build capacity before disaster strikes or to obtain needed resources, services, and supports should a disaster occur, principals can work to identify mechanisms to secure funding (such as those offered through the U.S. Department of Education's Readiness and Emergency Management for Schools program; see U.S. Department of Education, n.d.). Overall, it is crucial to develop plans that address the multiple and ongoing needs of students, as well as their families and school staff, for the short- and long-term aftermath of a disaster (CMHS, 2005a; Klingman & Cohen, 2004). The available evidence (see, e.g., Jaycox et al., 2007) suggests that efforts were uneven following Katrina, with schools generally mobilizing effectively to meet the needs of students in the immediate aftermath but lacking the resources, planning, or intent (e.g., not perceiving a need for ongoing services) to implement services for the longer term. Indeed, all too often following a disaster, efforts are fragmented and circumscribed, focusing solely on immediate crisis response rather than on longer-term effects that may function as obstacles to teaching, learning, and well-being among those affected (CMHS, 2005a; 2006).

In that vein, consistent with the work of MacDonald at Mayfair, numerous authors have advocated taking steps to support parents and caregivers themselves, including sponsoring parent gatherings so that they can meet, connect, and support one another and organizing supportive activities more explicitly designed to address parental needs and concerns (Klingman & Cohen, 2004; U.S. Department of Education, 2005b). In fact, evidence suggests that interventions that target children alone may be of limited effectiveness if the needs of the family system are not addressed; more specifically, Norris, Friedman, and Watson (2002) noted that providing care and support to parents may be among the most effective ways to meet the needs of children.

Furthermore, given the circumstances of many disasters, including Katrina, it is also necessary to recognize that teachers may have been affected directly and that they may have to cope and adapt in the face of not only the initial trauma, but also the secondary trauma and challenges inherent in trying to support and be available for their students (see chaps. 1 and 5, this volume). In a study of student displacement following Katrina conducted by the RAND Gulf Policy Institute, principals of schools with high numbers of newly enrolled displaced students reported that their teachers exhibited higher levels of stress than in prior years, as well as more work fatigue and higher absenteeism (Pane et al., 2006). Teachers and school staff will likely benefit from extra support and resources, both in addressing their own needs and in identifying strategies to assist their students or engage new (i.e., relocated) students (e.g., Pane et al., 2006; U.S. Department of Education, 2005b).

More globally, deciding about the implementation of preventive interventions and/or other programming is salient for both principals and school mental health staff. Although there is not a "right" answer per se, any intervention through the schools must take into account the children and youths' developmental level, special needs, and, critically, culture (Klingman & Cohen, 2004; Osofsky et al., 2007; Shen & Sink, 2002). Local school personnel must not accept uncritically programs that are offered; rather, they must evaluate carefully potential programs and have input into their implementation. It is necessary to create a clear policy for organizing service providers who wish to intervene and provide assistance, paying particular attention to children representing special populations or for whom services may be difficult to access (e.g., rural families, children in poverty or housing projects; see La Greca, Silverman, Vernberg, & Roberts, 2002). School personnel sometimes discover that it can be difficult to import a program into their school setting; beyond the need to ensure that the program is culturally competent and a "good fit" for that context, it may require significant time, money, and other resources to ensure that those implementing programs are trained appropriately and that the program is conducted in a manner consistent with the principles and method behind its documented effectiveness (Society for Community Research and Action, 2008).

A number of postdisaster programs for children have been developed, including several for use in the school setting. La Greca and her colleagues

(La Greca, Vernberg, Silverman, Vogel, & Prinstein, 2001, La Greca, Sevin, & Sevin, 2005) have developed multiple resources for use following disaster. Moreover, in a RAND Corporation publication, Jaycox and others identified numerous school-based programs for students who have experienced disaster and/or other trauma, including programs identified as promising and evidence supported by the NCTSN. Although describing these programs is beyond the scope of this chapter (see Jaycox et al., 2006), such programs largely seek both to reduce behavioral and emotional difficulties related to the disaster and to build or enhance competencies that appear to relate to or foster resilience (Jaycox et al., 2006). Such evidence-informed curricula for students (i.e., regarding stress, trauma, and coping) can be profitably implemented in schools, but other relevant and effective school-based programming (e.g., cooperative learning or buddy programming; social skills building; stress management; supportive programs for parents, teachers, and students) does not have to be disaster specific (Donnelly et al., 2006; Society for Community Research and Action, 2008).

If principals, school mental health professionals, or others choose to implement such a program, they must also determine how to identify and select student participants. As Jaycox et al. (2006) noted, there are four main methods: (a) referral by teacher or counselor, (b) parent nomination or request, (c) targeted school screening, and (d) general school screening (see March, Amaya-Jackson, Murray, & Schulte, 1998, and Pullins, McCammon, Lamson, Wuensch, & Mega, 2005, for discussions of screening approaches, as well as comparisons of findings using different methods). In considering referral and screening options, school-age youngsters are generally considered to be the optimal informants (Saylor & Deroma, 2002), particularly for internalizing concerns (e.g., shy, anxious, depressed, withdrawn), though research has also suggested that some children may minimize their reactions to protect their overly taxed caregivers (Gurwitch, Sitterle, Young, & Pfefferbaum, 2002).

School Mental Health Professionals

For school psychologists, counselors, social workers, and other mental health professionals, in addition to providing one-on-one counseling, a primary emphasis of their work following disaster is at the level of the system (e.g., helping identify and implement interventions, developing screening strategies, working with teachers). Indeed, a salient step is to seek training or continuing education in trauma mental health (e.g., Evans & Oehler-Stinnett, 2006) and, using this knowledge, to help teachers understand the range of children's reactions to trauma, ensure that they are aware of signs that may suggest more serious difficulty, and facilitate the development of strategies for responding to children's needs (Osofsky et al., 2007; Shen & Sink, 2002; U.S. Department of Education, 2005b). In some cases, it may be necessary to seek the support and guidance of professionals outside the school who have expertise in the issues students face and the capacity to provide hands-on, practical advice for teachers and other school personnel. Indeed, it is critical to look beyond the school and collaborate with community partners, mental health agencies, disaster relief organizations, and others to ensure that services are available to address the diverse needs of students, including those with special needs (U.S. Department of Education, 2005b). In these efforts, professionals must ensure that they minimize bureaucratic red tape and facilitate student and family access to needed services (U.S. Department of Education, 2005b).

Although it is crucial to strive to meet students' needs in the immediate aftermath of disaster, it is also necessary to strategize about how to best address student (and staff) concerns in the long term (CMHS, 2006). In that context, in addition to considering intervention and programming options and working to ensure that interventions are strengths based and enhance students' sense of belonging, it is important to develop or use natural and informal supports in the school and community.

Teachers

Following a disaster, one of the best ways teachers can help students is by taking care of themselves (Jaycox et al., 2007; NCTSN, n.d.-b). In so doing, they will be better able to maintain their energy and their own resources to provide appropriate support. Although the teacher–student relationship is a professional one and it is necessary to maintain boundaries, teachers should feel free to demonstrate caring, empathize with their students' experiences, and be available (U.S. Department of Education, 2005b). Attending to the needs of the whole child, as conveyed in the example of Mayfair Elementary, can help children feel more secure and facilitate both positive adaptation and school success. In fact, social support has been found to relate to less severe or reduced levels of PTSD symptomatology following disaster (e.g., La Greca et al., 1996; Vernberg et al., 1996). Although parents and friends tend to be the primary sources of such support and coping assistance (see, e.g., Cauce, Reid, Landesman, & Gonzales, 1990; Prinstein, La Greca, Vernberg, & Silverman, 1996), teachers can also offer emotional support and help children take steps to reestablish routines and familiar roles in their lives (e.g., Klingman & Cohen, 2004). In research on child resilience, connections with caring extrafamilial support sources and positive identification models have consistently been linked with positive adjustment in the face of adversity (see, e.g., Luthar et al., 2000; Werner & Smith, 1992; Wyman et al., 2000); the schools constitute a natural support system that can provide such positive relational contacts. In that spirit, to the degree possible, it is often of great utility for teachers to extend support to parents and, of particular import, to keep them informed (Klingman & Cohen, 2004).

In the classroom, as numerous sources have conveyed (e.g., NCTSN, n.d.-b; Perry & Dobson, n.d.), although lesson plans may have to be modified, teachers are encouraged to maintain structure and predictability, resume normal patterns, and reestablish routines. If new students join a classroom as a result of the disaster, steps are warranted to ensure that they feel welcomed and to foster connectedness (U.S. Department of Education, 2005b). The need for structure, consistency, and clarity is salient on the discipline front as well, though during a trying time characterized by disruption, transition, and adversity, marshaling resources necessary for patience and compassion is also important. Although it is necessary to monitor children for adverse reactions or meaningful changes in their performance or behavior (see, e.g., Osofsky et al., 2007), a focus on strengths, competencies, and needs for mastery can be particularly useful at this time (Cole et al., 2005; Tedeschi & Kilmer, 2005).

Teachers can also fruitfully provide opportunities for students to express their feelings and reactions in a way that is contained and appropriate for the class setting; such activities can serve as a framework for listening to and discussing student questions and concerns and sharing age-appropriate factual information about the disaster (NCTSN, n.d.-b; Perry & Dobson, n.d.; Shen & Sink, 2002; U.S. Department of Education, 2005b). As Buchanan, Casbergue, and Baumgartner describe in chapter 5 of this volume, one approach is to incorporate aspects of the experience into the curriculum (see University of Illinois Extension Disaster Resources, n.d., for suggestions for how to do so). Such activities and lessons can be integrated into elements of a range of core curricular subjects, including science, writing, reading, and art, and can provide a framework through which students can consider their experiences and, perhaps, further process or work to make meaning of the events. The American Psychological Association (n.d.) recommended creating positive connections by developing classroom projects that increase opportunities for teamwork and respect, and multiple sources (e.g., U.S. Department of Education, 2005b) have noted that teachers can help identify opportunities to assist others affected by the disaster, including group activities to help their school, neighborhood, or others in the community. Such prosocial activities can not only help the students feel as though they are "doing something," but also increase their perceived sense of community (NCTSN, n.d.-b).

Although the focus of the present chapter has been on postdisaster response, the evidence suggests that predisaster planning and infrastructure development can greatly facilitate efficient and effective implementation of postdisaster services and supports. Following Katrina, the schools whose personnel had received crisis response training reportedly were able to respond more effectively than schools whose personnel had not had such training (CMHS, 2005a). They were seemingly better able to meet the needs of the many students and staff who had to move to new schools and to address the socioemotional concerns of youngsters and teachers (CMHS, 2005a, 2006). In contrast, some educators have noted that they and their principals "winged it" or, in some cases, "ignored the situation out of ignorance" (name withheld, personal communication, May 23, 2006). In some cases, administrators and school personnel may have felt that implementing these strategies interfered with their efforts to follow education policy and/or meet the education standards set by the state and federal governments (see chap. 5, this volume).

Considering the longer term, school systems' central office administrators and school principals would benefit from training relevant to a range of emergency and disaster situations, with planning encompassing the elucidation of communication, support, and resource networks. Such efforts are essential for meeting the socioemotional needs of children while achieving the academic goals outlined by current educational policies. To that end, Klingman and Cohen (2004) described a seven-level model for school-based postdisaster preventive intervention, a systematized approach that may be of utility to educators.

Some authors have raised valid issues about recommending school-based services when, for example, schools have been destroyed or lack resources for necessary programming or support (e.g., Abramson & Garfield, 2006). Nevertheless, in studies of child development and adaptation, effective schools were among the factors identified as holding the potential to serve a "protective" function and facilitate positive adjustment despite adversity (Masten & Coatsworth, 1998; Wyman et al., 2000) or, more broadly, promote wellness and healthy adjustment (Cowen, 1994). Indeed, others (e.g., Cowen, 1994) have argued that schools can influence children not only through academics but also through "affective lessons, taught through the functional dynamics of human relationships" (Ryan & Stiller, 1991, p. 116), which can help foster prosocial behaviors, interpersonal competencies, and relationships. In light of this potential influence, the critical school context may be fruitfully targeted as a setting for action in disaster's aftermath, particularly when parental and family resources for coping have been overly taxed. In future disasters, the potential positive impact (and success in preventing difficulties and promoting healthy adaptation) of school systems' efforts will be optimized by large-scale planning for the long term that considers necessary resources, training, and infrastructure and ensures that processes are documented and necessary linkages are in place (CMHS, 2006; Jaycox et al., 2007). Such steps will be more likely to yield maximal benefit for children, youth, and families following disaster.

REFERENCES

Abramson, D., & Garfield, R. (2006). *On the edge: Children and families displaced by Hurricanes Katrina and Rita face a looming medical and mental health crisis.* New York: Columbia University Mailman School of Public Health. Retrieved December 30, 2008, from http://www.ncdp.mailman.columbia.edu/files/On%20the%20Edge%20L-CAFH%20Final%20Report_Columbia%20University.pdf

American Psychological Association. (n.d.). *Fact sheet: Fostering resilience in response to terrorism: For psychologists working with children.* Retrieved November 23, 2007, from http://www.apa.org/psychologists/pdfs/children.pdf

Bosquet, M. (2004). How research informs clinical work with traumatized young children. In J. D. Osofsky (Ed.), *Young children and trauma: Intervention and treatment* (pp. 301–325). New York: Guilford Press.

Brown, E. J., & Bobrow, A. L. (2004). School entry after a community-wide trauma: Challenges and lessons learned from September 11th, 2001. *Clinical Child and Family Psychology Review, 7,* 211–221.

Cauce, A. M., Reid, M., Landesman, S., & Gonzales, N. (1990). Social support in young children: Measurement, structure, and behavioral impact. In B. R. Sarason, I. G. Sarason, & G. R. Pierce (Eds.), *Social support: An interactional view* (pp. 64–94). New York: Wiley.

Center for Mental Health in Schools, University of California at Los Angeles. (2005a). *Special ENEWS: Lessons learned so far (11/22/05)—Disaster aftermath.* Retrieved April 21, 2007, from http://smhp.psych.ucla.edu/pdfdocs/enews/ENEWS(11-22-05).pdf

Center for Mental Health in Schools, University of California at Los Angeles. (2005b). *Special ENEWS: Periodic update (10/20/05)—Disaster aftermath.* Retrieved April 21, 2007, from http://smhp.psych.ucla.edu/pdfdocs/enews/ENEWS(10-20-05).pdf

Center for Mental Health in Schools, University of California at Los Angeles. (2006, July 12). *End of the school year update on the aftermath of the hurricanes.* Retrieved December 1, 2007, from http://smhp.psych.ucla.edu/pdfdocs/enews/ENEWS(7-12-06).pdf

Centers for Disease Control and Prevention. (2007). *Healthy youth! Health topics: Crisis preparedness and response.* Retrieved April 21, 2007, from http://www.ced.gov/HealthYouth/crisis/index.htm

Chemtob, C. M., Nakashima, J., & Carlson, J. G. (2002). Brief treatment for elementary school children with disaster-related posttraumatic stress disorder: A field study. *Journal of Clinical Psychology, 58,* 98–112.

Cole, S. F., Greenwald O'Brien, J., Gadd, M. G., Ristuccia, J., Wallace, D. L., & Gregory, M. (2005). *Helping traumatized children learn: Supportive school environments for children traumatized by family violence.* Boston: Massachusetts Advocates for Children.

Cowen, E. L. (1994). The enhancement of psychological wellness: Challenges and opportunities. *American Journal of Community Psychology, 22,* 149–179.

Dewan, S. (2006, April 18). Evacuee study finds declining health. *New York Times.* Retrieved November 30, 2007, from http://www.nytimes.com/2006/04/18/us/nationalspecial/18health.html

Donnelly, W. O., Miller, A. C., Young, L., Jones, G., Reeve, C. C., & La Greca, A. M. (2006). Recreating home after disaster: Challenges for Katrina's kids. *Child, Youth, and Family Services Advocate, 29,* 1–4.

Evans, L., & Oehler-Stinnett, J. (2006). Children and natural disasters: A primer for school psychologists. *School Psychology International, 27,* 33–55.

Gil-Rivas, V., Hypes, A., Kilmer, R. P., & Williams, J. (2007, November). *Child resources and children's PTS symptoms post-Hurricane Katrina.* Poster presented at the 23rd Annual Meeting of the International Society for Traumatic Stress Studies, Baltimore.

Goenjian, A. K., Molina, L., Steinberg, A. M., Fairbanks, L. A., Alvarez, M. L., Goenjian, H. A., & Pynoos, R. S. (2001). Posttraumatic stress and depressive reactions among Nicaraguan adolescents after hurricane Mitch. *American Journal of Psychiatry, 158,* 788–794.

Goldman, L. (2002). The assumptive world of children. In J. Kauffman (Ed.), *Loss of the assumptive world: A theory of traumatic loss* (pp. 193–202). New York: Brunner-Routledge.

Gurwitch, R. H., Sitterle, K. A., Young, B. H., & Pfefferbaum, B. (2002). The aftermath of terrorism. In A. M. La Greca, W. K. Silverman, E. M. Vernberg, & M. C. Roberts (Eds.), *Helping children cope with disasters and terrorism* (pp. 327–357). Washington, DC: American Psychological Association.

Hoven, C. W., Duarte, C. S., & Mandell, D. J. (2003). Children's mental health after disasters: The impact of the World Trade Center attack. *Current Psychiatry Reports, 5,* 101–107.

Hurricane Katrina Community Advisory Group. (2006). *Overview of baseline survey results.* Retrieved November 22, 2007, from http://hurricanekatrina.med.harvard.edu/pdf/baseline_report%208-25-06.pdf

Jaycox, L. H., Morse, L. K., Tanielian, T., & Stein, B. D. (2006). *How schools can help students recover from traumatic experiences: A tool kit for supporting long-term recovery* (Tech. Rep. 413). Santa Monica, CA: RAND Corporation. Retrieved April 3, 2007, from http://www.rand.org/pubs/technical_reports/2006/RAND_TR413.pdf

Jaycox, L. H., Tanielian, T. L., Sharma, P., Morse, L., Clum, G., & Stein, B. D. (2007). Schools' mental health responses following Hurricanes Katrina and Rita. *Psychiatric Services, 58,* 1339–1343.

Kamenetz, A. (2005, October 2). Dispersed and unequal: New Orleans children are abandoned again, this time in Baton Rouge schools. *Village Voice.* Retrieved November 23, 2007, from http://www.villagevoice.com/news/0540,kamenetz,68414,6.html

Klingman, A., & Cohen, E. (2004). *School-based multisystemic interventions for mass trauma*. New York: Kluwer Academic/Plenum Publishers.

Kupersmidt, J. B., Shahinfar, A., & Voegler-Lee, M. E. (2002). Children's exposure to community violence. In A. M. La Greca, W. K. Silverman, E. M. Vernberg, & M. C. Roberts (Eds.), *Helping children cope with disasters and terrorism* (pp. 381–401). Washington, DC: American Psychological Association.

La Greca, A. M., Sevin, S. W., & Sevin, E. (2005). *After the storm: A guide to help children cope with the psychological effects of a hurricane*. Retrieved November 22, 2007, from http://www.7-dippity.com/other/After_The_Storm_(Special_Edition_2005).pdf

La Greca, A. M., Silverman, W. K., Vernberg, E. M., & Prinstein, M. J. (1996). Symptoms of posttraumatic stress in children after Hurricane Andrew: A prospective study. *Journal of Consulting and Clinical Psychology, 64,* 712–723.

La Greca, A. M., Silverman, W. K., Vernberg, E. M., & Roberts, M. C. (2002). Children and disasters: Future directions for research and public policy. In A. M. La Greca, W. K. Silverman, E. M. Vernberg, & M. C. Roberts (Eds.), *Helping children cope with disasters and terrorism* (pp. 405–423). Washington, DC: American Psychological Association.

La Greca, A. M., Vernberg, E. M., Silverman, W. K., Vogel, A. L., & Prinstein, M. J. (2001). *Helping children cope with disasters: A manual for professionals working with elementary school children*. Retrieved November 21, 2007, from www.psy.miami.edu/child/helping_children_cope.html

Lieberman, A. F., & Van Horn, P. (2004). Assessment and treatment of young children exposed to traumatic events. In J. D. Osofsky (Ed.), *Young children and trauma: Intervention and treatment* (pp. 111–138). New York: Guilford Press.

Lonigan, C. J., Shannon, M. P., Taylor, C. M., Finch, A. J., & Sallee, F. R. (1994). Children exposed to disaster: II. Risk factors for the development of posttraumatic symptomatology. *Journal of the American Academy of Child and Adolescent Psychiatry, 33,* 94–105.

Louisiana Department of Education. (2006). *Planning, analysis, and information resources: Students—public school—multiple statistics—sites (2005–2006)*. Retrieved November 23, 2007, from http://www.doe.state.la.us/lde/pair/2289.html

Louisiana Recovery Authority. (2007). *Moving beyond Katrina and Rita: Recovery data indicators for Louisiana*. Retrieved November 18, 2007, from http://www.lra.louisiana.gov/assets/twoyear/Indicators082107.pdf

Luthar, S. S., Cicchetti, D., & Becker, B. (2000). The construct of resilience: A critical evaluation and guidelines for future work. *Child Development, 71,* 543–562.

Madrid, P. A., Grant, R., Reilly, M. J., & Redlener, N. B. (2006). Challenges in meeting immediate emotional needs: Short-term impact of a major disaster on children's mental health: Building resiliency in the aftermath of Hurricane Katrina. *Pediatrics, 117,* S448–S453.

March, J. S., Amaya-Jackson, L., Murray, M. C., & Schulte, A. (1998). Cognitive–behavioral psychotherapy for children and adolescents with post-traumatic stress disorder after a single-incident stressor. *Journal of the American Academy of Child and Adolescent Psychiatry, 37,* 585–593.

Margolin, G., & Gordis, E. B. (2000). The effects of family and community violence on children. *Annual Review of Psychology, 51,* 445–479.

Masten, A. S., & Coatsworth, J. D. (1998). The development of competence in favorable and unfavorable environments. *American Psychologist, 53,* 205–220.

National Child Traumatic Stress Network. (n.d.-a). *Age-related reactions to a traumatic event.* Retrieved April 9, 2009, from http://www.nctsnet.org/nctsn_assets/pdfs/age_related_reactions.pdf

National Child Traumatic Stress Network. (n.d.-b). *Teacher guidelines for helping students after a hurricane.* Retrieved April 9, 2009, from http://www.nctsnet.org/nctsn_assets/pdfs/teachers_guidelines_talk_children_hurricanes.pdf

National Child Traumatic Stress Network, & National Center for PTSD. (2006). *Psychological first aid: Field operations guide* (2nd ed.). Retrieved December 1, 2007, from http://www.nctsn.org/nctsn_assets/pdfs/pfa/2/psyfirstaid.pdf

New Freedom Commission on Mental Health. (2003). *Achieving the promise: Transforming mental health care in America: Final report.* (DHHS Publication No. SMA-03-3832). Rockville, MD: Author.

Norris, F., Friedman, M., & Watson, P. (2002). 60,000 disaster victims speak: Part II. Summary and implications of the disaster mental health research. *Psychiatry, 65,* 240–260.

Norris, F., Friedman, M., Watson, P., Byrne, C., Diaz, E., & Kaniasty, K. (2002). 60,000 disaster victims speak: Part I. An empirical review of the empirical literature, 1981–2001. *Psychiatry, 65,* 207–239.

Osofsky, J. D., Osofsky, H. J., & Harris, W. W. (2007). Katrina's children: Social policy considerations for children in disasters. *Society for Research in Child Development Social Policy Report, 21,* 1–18.

Pane, J. F., McCaffrey, D. F., Tharp-Taylor, S., Asmus, G. J., & Stokes, B. R. (2006). *Student displacement in Louisiana after the hurricanes of 2005: Experiences of public schools and their students* (Tech. Rep. 430). Santa Monica, CA: RAND Gulf States Policy Institute, RAND Corporation.

Paulson, A. (2005, September 28). At school for storm evacuees, hugs before homework. *Christian Science Monitor.* Retrieved April 21, 2007, from http://www.csmonitor.com/2005/0928/p01s04-ussc.html

Perry, B. D., & Dobson, C. (n.d.). *The impact of Katrina on children: Special comments for educators.* Houston, TX: ChildTrauma Academy. Retrieved April 2, 2007, from http://www.childtrauma.org/CTAMATERIALS/Educators_Katrina_05.pdf

Pfefferbaum, B., Nixon, S. J., Tucker, P. M., Tivis, R. D., Moore, V. L., Gurwitch, R. H., et al. (1999). Posttraumatic stress responses in bereaved children after the

Oklahoma City bombing. *Journal of the American Academy of Child and Adolescent Psychiatry, 38,* 1372–1379.

Prinstein, M. J., La Greca, A. M., Vernberg, E. M., & Silverman, W. K. (1996). Children's coping assistance: How parents, teachers, and friends help children cope after a natural disaster. *Journal of Clinical Child Psychology, 25,* 463–475.

Pullins, L. G., McCammon, S. L., Lamson, A. S., Wuensch, K. L., & Mega, L. (2005). School-based post-flood screening and evaluation: Findings and challenges in one community. *Stress, Trauma, and Crisis, 8,* 229–249.

Pynoos, R. S., Goenjian, A. K., & Steinberg, A. M. (1998). A public mental health approach to the post disaster treatment of children and adolescents. *Child and Adolescent Psychiatric Clinics of North America, 7,* 195–210.

Ryan, R. M., & Stiller, J. (1991). The social contexts of internalization: Parent and teacher influences on autonomy, motivation, and learning. In R. P. Pintrich & M. L. Maehr (Eds.), *Advances in motivation and achievement: Vol. 7. Goals and self-regulatory processes* (pp. 115–149). Greenwich, CT: JAI Press.

Save the Children. (2006, September). *Katrina response: Protecting the children of the storm* (Issue Brief No. 2). Westport, CT: Save the Children Federation.

Saylor, C., & Deroma, V. (2002). Assessment of children and adolescents exposed to disaster. In A. M. La Greca, W. K. Silverman, E. M. Vernberg, & M. C. Roberts (Eds.), *Helping children cope with disasters and terrorism* (pp. 35–53). Washington, DC: American Psychological Association.

Select Bipartisan Committee to Investigate the Preparation for and Response to Hurricane Katrina. (2006). *A failure of initiative: Final report of the Select Bipartisan Committee to Investigate the Preparation for and Response to Hurricane Katrina* (U.S. House of Representatives). Retrieved November 22, 2007, from http://www.gpoaccess.gov/katrinareport/mainreport.pdf

Shen, Y.-J., & Sink, C. A. (2002). Helping elementary-age children cope with disasters. *Professional Counseling, 5,* 322–330.

Society for Community Research and Action. (2008). *How to help your community recover from disaster: A manual for planning and action.* Manuscript in preparation.

Tedeschi, R. G., & Kilmer, R. P. (2005). Assessing strengths, resilience, and growth to guide clinical interventions. *Professional Psychology: Research and Practice, 36,* 230–237.

University of Illinois Extension Disaster Resources. (n.d.). *Children, stress, and natural disasters: School activities for children.* Retrieved April 21, 2007, from http://web.extension.uiuc.edu/disaster/teacher/csndactx.html

U.S. Department of Education. (2005a). *New support for families and areas affected by Hurricane Katrina.* Retrieved November 17, 2007, from http://hurricanehelpforschools.gov/0916-factsheet.pdf

U.S. Department of Education. (2005b). *Tips for helping students recovering from traumatic events.* Washington, DC: Author. Retrieved April 21, 2007, from http://www.ed.gov/parents/academic/help/recovering/recovering.pdf

U.S. Department of Education. (n.d.). *Readiness and emergency management for schools technical assistance center: FY 2009 REMS grant application.* Retrieved April 8, 2009, from http://rems.ed.gov/index.cfm?event=GrantApp

Vernberg, E. M., La Greca, A. M., Silverman, W. K., & Prinstein, M. J. (1996). Prediction of posttraumatic stress symptoms in children after Hurricane Andrew. *Journal of Abnormal Psychology, 105,* 237–248.

Vogel, J. M., & Vernberg, E. M. (1993). Task force report: Part I. Children's psychological responses to disasters. *Journal of Clinical Child Psychology, 22,* 464–484.

Werner, E. E., & Smith, R. S. (1992). *Overcoming the odds: High risk children from birth to adulthood.* Ithaca, NY: Cornell University Press.

Wyman, P. A., Sandler, I., Wolchik, S. A., & Nelson, K. (2000). Resilience as cumulative competence promotion and stress protection: Theory and intervention. In D. Cicchetti, J. Rappaport, I. Sandler, & R. P. Weissberg (Eds.), *The promotion of wellness in children and adolescents* (pp. 133–184). Thousand Oaks, CA: Sage.

8

SOCIAL AND COMMUNITY RESPONSES: ASSESSING RELATIONSHIPS AMONG ENVIRONMENTAL SUPPORTS IN CHILD AND CAREGIVER ADJUSTMENT FOLLOWING A HURRICANE

R. ENRIQUE VARELA, LAUREN HENSLEY-MALONEY, AND ERIC M. VERNBERG

Major hurricanes such as Katrina and Rita undoubtedly affect the lives of many children, adolescents, and their families. The impact of such storms on family members may be influenced by several factors, including the degree of exposure, the time elapsed since the storm, personality traits, preexisting psychopathology, postdisaster life stressors, and the amount of environmental support that is available and used (Silverman & La Greca, 2002; Vernberg & Varela, 2001). The present chapter focuses on the impact of social and community responses on the environments of children and their caregivers at all levels, with special consideration of these responses in the context of Hurricanes Katrina and Rita. In addition, we offer some suggestions on how to improve responses to future hurricanes.

Social and community responses refer to services provided in a broad and systematic fashion by organizations at the local, state, or national level as well as informal assistance provided by individuals such as family members, peers, teachers, and other community members. Disaster-related interventions vary widely, depending on features such as timing in relation to the disaster, content and form of the interventions, severity of exposure experienced by those targeted, and characteristics of individual participants (Vernberg, 2002).

Typologies of disaster exposure and recovery phases have been proposed based on common psychological responses (e.g., heroic, honeymoon, disillusionment, reconstruction; National Institute of Mental Health, 1990) and on the chronology of disaster-related events (Vernberg, 2002). Given the unusual scope and nature of Hurricane Katrina, we discuss the role of social and community responses in the context of a broad chronological typology that includes four phases: (a) planning, (b) impact, (c) short-term adaptation, and (d) long-term adaptation (Vernberg, 2002; Vernberg & Vogel, 1993). The *planning phase* refers to the time before the disaster, during which preparations for dealing with the disaster take place. The *impact phase* is when the disaster is actually occurring. The *short-term adaptation phase* refers to the period after the disaster subsides and assessment of losses and planning for recovery occur. In the *long-term adaptation phase*, the need for crisis-oriented interventions decreases and environmental conditions begin to stabilize as schools, businesses, and local governments begin to function again.

Even with this chronological typology, in which the phases of disaster and recovery are broadly constructed, recovery from Hurricane Katrina remains difficult to categorize because of its magnitude. For instance, it is difficult to identify clearly when the impact phase was over because of the widespread flooding and extended social turmoil that followed. Three years after the hurricane, normally well into long-term adaptation when the need for crisis interventions greatly decreases, some families in the Gulf Coast region continued to struggle to reestablish residential, educational, and occupational stability (Pope & Vanacore, 2008). Acknowledging these difficulties in categorization, we discuss the role of social and community support in the adjustment of children and their caregivers following hurricanes.

CHILD AND FAMILY CONSIDERATIONS
IN THE PLANNING PHASE

Adequate planning for meeting the needs of families (i.e., evacuation, sheltering, mental and medical health services) in the event of a hurricane warning is a major challenge for many coastal regions. Families with children present special challenges in terms of anticipating the needs of minors in the process of evacuation and sheltering (Vernberg, 2002). From a psychological perspective, some of these needs involve safety and comfort. Given the important roles attachment figures play in regulating children's distress during times of stress (Cook et al., 2005), it is important to ensure that youths are not separated from caregivers or are reunited quickly with family members if separation is unavoidable. Within shelters, consideration must be given to providing some means of preserving family boundaries and routines, such as encouraging families to eat and sleep together and providing protected areas for parenting activities and age-appropriate recreation (e.g., Vernberg & Field, 1990).

Other considerations relate to providing realistic options for families to heed evacuation warnings. Many barriers to evacuation and shelter use are related to the limited resources of those living in poverty (e.g., lack of transportation, poor evacuation options). In the cases of Katrina and Rita, for example, a survey of New Orleans residents who were eventually moved to Houston-area shelters indicated that they were disproportionately from low-income, minority households and lacked the means to evacuate (Brodie, Weltzien, Altman, Blendon, & Benson, 2006). Almost half of respondents in this survey reported having one or more children under 18, and about a third had children with them in the shelter.

Unfortunately, the widely publicized problems with safety and a lack of basic provisions in some shelter sites in New Orleans in the days and weeks following Katrina (e.g., Brodie et al., 2006) probably did little to increase confidence among evacuees. Communicating information about shelters in a clear, credible manner to low-income residents can be facilitated by involving families and community leaders in the planning process, thereby tailoring plans to the unique needs of individual neighborhoods. Refining evacuation plans during the predisaster phase may limit hurricane exposure and thus decrease the risk for negative outcomes such as physical injury and psychological maladjustment (Vernberg, 2002).

CHILD AND FAMILY CONSIDERATIONS IN THE IMPACT PHASE

Community responses are crucial during the first few hours and days following a hurricane, when the most important objectives are to fulfill safety concerns and meet the primary needs of a large group of people. Mass communications about what to do and not do during a storm and in its immediate aftermath are often used to disseminate important information. The overriding goal of such mass communications is to prevent widespread panic by providing timely and accurate information. Although such efforts often rely on electronic channels of communication (e.g., Web sites, television, radio), printed materials may also be necessary either because of power outages or because large numbers of people may not have access to electronic media following the storm. Other challenges of postdisaster communication include ensuring that materials are available at a variety of literacy levels; reflect the diversity of languages spoken; and present information that is sensitive to the specific climate, culture, and changing needs of the affected area (Vanderford, Nastoff, Telfer, & Bonzo, 2007).

Ideally, these communications would also address concerns related to children and caregivers. For example, information on strategies for caregivers about how to respond to children's increased needs for comfort and security and how to protect them from further trauma exposure could be provided. It is important that information about resources for reporting and locating missing family members and about efforts to provide rescue and relief to those in need be readily accessible. One dissemination challenge involves identifying the sources of information most often used by families.

In addition to providing information to survivors, government and community agencies face the task of providing survivors with shelter and food. Families often need access to specialized foods that their children tolerate and accept. For infants and toddlers, this need may be particularly acute. Concerns about basic necessities are likely to disrupt children's sense of security and normalcy. Caregivers may also feel stress about their inability to provide for their children, which may interfere with their ability to emotionally support their children (Shelby & Tredinnick, 1995).

The wide dissemination of basic provisions after a disaster can be challenging. This was particularly true in New Orleans given the widespread flooding in the immediate aftermath of Katrina. Even though supplies may have been available for distribution, these could not reach a large segment of the population because of impassable roads and safety concerns (Huus, 2006). Agencies such as the Federal Emergency Management Agency (FEMA), the National Guard, the Red Cross, and the Salvation Army (American Red Cross, 2006; Defense Logistics Agency, 2005; Salvation Army, 2006) were eventually successful in distributing food and water to the majority of the remaining population. Stockpiling basic supplies before a major storm and considering alternative ways of availing survivors ahead of time may facilitate effective distribution of emergency supplies.

Personal safety constitutes another basic need. Children especially need to feel that their environment is safe and their caregivers will provide protection from external harmful agents (Shelby & Tredinnick, 1995). Unfortunately, following Hurricane Katrina, reports of murder, rape, and looting in New Orleans abounded, although several sources later determined that much of the reported violence was exaggerated (e.g., Rosenblatt & Rainey, 2005). Accurate reporting by the media would help children feel safer in post-disaster areas. If violence or other disturbing content is to be shown on television, news organizations would be justified in warning viewers of the material's unsuitability for children.

Addressing the medical and mental health needs of survivors is also of great importance. Because children may have difficulties verbalizing their medical or mental health concerns compared with adults, extreme stress can exacerbate preexisting problems (Silverman & La Greca, 2002; Sledjeski,

Speisman, & Dierker, 2008). In addition, some individuals may experience increased somatic or physical discomfort or illness as an indirect result of mental anguish (e.g., Campo, Jansen-McWilliams, Comer, & Kelleher, 1999). Other individuals may express psychological distress by voicing physical complaints, a tendency that may be especially prevalent in African American and Hispanic cultures (e.g., Kingery, Ginsburg, & Alfano, 2007; Varela et al., 2004; Varela, Sanchez-Sosa, Biggs, & Luis, 2008) and among individuals of low socioeconomic status (e.g., Escobar, Rubio-Stipec, Canino, & Karno, 1989). An increase in physical symptoms in response to traumatic experiences has been documented in children and adults (Bailey et al., 2005; Escobar, Canino, Rubio-Stipec, & Bravo, 1992; Gobble, Sweeny, & Fishbein, 2004; Shaw, 2003). Hensley and Varela (2008) found that 20% of a sample of 302 sixth and seventh graders reported four or more somatic symptoms, suggesting "problematic somatization," up to 7 months following Hurricane Katrina. The number of somatic symptoms experienced was positively associated with the level of hurricane exposure.

Because of the destruction of medical facilities and the evacuation or loss of medical personnel, obtaining emergency or routine medical care can be extremely difficult for families in disaster-affected areas. The health of children and their caregivers may be in jeopardy because of supply shortages, long-term loss of electricity, and the inability to transport patients to receive specialized care (Weisler, Barbee, & Townsend, 2006). For example, Children's Hospital of New Orleans was not damaged by the storm or flooding but eventually evacuated all of its patients because of an electrical power shortage. The damage to health care facilities not only deprived residents of care in New Orleans and surrounding areas but was also responsible for the death of a reported 215 residents and patients (Davis & Johnson, 2005; Weisler et al., 2006).

The provision of mental health services is vital to the recovery of any area stricken by a disaster (Silverman & La Greca, 2002). Immediate goals of such services are to engage survivors in mental health discussion, increase their perception of safety and comfort, normalize their emotions, gather information about their most pressing needs and concerns, help families devise plans to meet their immediate needs, provide information about healthy coping methods, and link families with community-based mental health services for further assistance (Brymer et al., 2006). Clearly presented information about common signs of maladaptive coping in adults and children can alert survivors to early warning signs that further intervention is needed, possibly minimizing future psychological maladjustment (Vernberg, 2002). Additionally, the normalization of common reactions to trauma, as well as suggestions on how to deal with such reactions, can reduce worry and frustration experienced by caregivers as they struggle to care for their children (Vernberg & Vogel, 1993).

National organizations such as FEMA, the Red Cross, and the Disaster Response Network provide mental health services following disasters. The Disaster Response Network consists of state-organized groups of psychologists who are formally trained in disaster interventions and are willing to be called on by the Red Cross in the event of a disaster (American Psychological Association, 2007). Unfortunately, even with various agencies aiding the Gulf Coast region, mental health problems were and continue to be a serious issue in the greater New Orleans area (Mack, 2008). For example, in a survey conducted by the Centers for Disease Control and Prevention (2006) 7 weeks after Katrina, 50% of respondents indicated a possible need for mental health assistance, and 26% reported that at least one member of the household needed mental health counseling, whereas less than 2% of those in need were actually receiving counseling. Mental health providers responding to natural disasters are most effective when they can quickly and accurately identify individuals who may be in need of immediate, intensive emergency services (Vernberg, 2002).

Psychological First Aid (PFA; Brymer et al., 2006) is a program recommended by the Red Cross that provides actionable recommendations for mental health providers (Gard & Ruzek, 2006). Survivor engagement and education are core elements of the PFA framework that have particular relevance to provision of services to children and families. The first step of PFA, engagement, may be done through disseminating information via mass communication channels, meeting face to face with hurricane survivors, working with local community groups to reach their members through informal networking or more formal presentations, and even going door to door.

From a PFA framework, survivor education involves providing educational presentations, conversations, and materials; these interventions may be less stigmatizing for some individuals than seeking more personalized mental health services (Gard & Ruzek, 2006). Informal social networks (e.g., extended family, church organizations, coworkers) can provide information about the best ways to access community support, greatly reducing the stress levels of families. This kind of support during the disaster and its immediate aftermath can provide an outlet for individuals to voice their feelings and opinions without the bureaucracy of more structured responding agencies and may be useful in normalizing individuals' needs and fears. Informal social networks can be a resource for families needing extensive individualized guidance, which may be difficult for mental health professionals to provide immediately following a disaster. Many families were separated in the aftermath of Hurricane Katrina because it was unclear where to receive evacuation assistance and transportation out of the city was limited (Brodie et al., 2006). In such cases, in which existing social networks have been scattered by the disaster, it is important to set up places for survivors to meet and receive informal social support.

CHILD AND FAMILY CONSIDERATIONS IN THE
SHORT-TERM ADAPTATION PHASE

In the weeks after a disaster, relief efforts supplying primary needs (e.g., shelter, water, food) usually start to function more effectively. Community organizations that may have been unable to reach survivors during the impact phase are usually able to enter disaster areas by this time, and larger organizations have usually established a consistent operating system. During this phase, community responses begin to move away from providing mass information and instrumental aid and are able to focus on meeting the needs of individual survivors and targeting those who seem to be having the most trouble getting back on their feet (Vernberg, 2002).

For instance, at this time services may include helping families transition from shelters to more permanent housing and normal routines. Providing children with safe activities could allow parents to focus on dealing with immediate needs, such as home reconstruction, insurance claims, and reclaiming jobs. It bears mention that in the New Orleans area, short-term adaptation phase activities lasted months rather than weeks because of widespread flooding that prevented people from returning to the area. The ability of disaster response to move successfully from responding to the acute needs of a large group to the more focused task of identifying individuals and families needing ongoing and more personalized intervention largely depends on a successful and time-efficient response during the impact phase.

Government and community organizations continue to provide services during the short-term adaptation phase, but services decrease as more survivors resume their former lives or begin to build new, postdisaster lives. Services depending on large amounts of volunteer support such as shelters and meal kitchens generally empty and close their doors, while services requiring less staffing, such as financial support and telephone hotlines, continue. Importantly, during this phase, the provision of face-to-face services begins to depend heavily on local community and occupational organizations (either in the disaster area or in areas with disaster evacuees) and less on national organizations. National organizations begin to take on a supportive rather than a direct-provider role and may support smaller community organizations by providing financial assistance through grants or supplying them with materials such as psychological treatment manuals or construction equipment. Direct financial aid and employment assistance are very important services as survivors begin to rebuild their lives. Medical needs continue as survivors, especially those returning to sparsely populated disaster areas, may have difficulty finding adequate medical care after shelters close. As services and delivery methods change, it is important for both national and local organizations to keep survivors informed of opportunities for continuing aid.

Although service providers may be scarce, many families are still in need of assistance during the short-term adaptation phase. Caregivers may experience stress and frustration over unemployment, difficulty securing long-term shelter, and lack of services such as child care in disaster-stricken areas. As the immediate shock and trauma dissipate, the postimpact phase is a critical time for families in terms of preparing for long-term adjustment.

As needs for shelter and sustenance become less of a focus during the short-term adaptation phase, the mental health of disaster survivors becomes more of a priority. The PFA framework continues to be a resource during this phase, but the focus shifts from immediate crisis reduction to the facilitation of adaptation and adjustment. For survivors who may be struggling with mostly disaster-related adjustment issues, PFA supports the use of brief crisis-focused intervention (Gard & Ruzek, 2006). In one to three sessions, a mental health professional offers emotional support, education about and normalization of specific responses to disasters, personalized coping support and advice, and help with generating solutions to practical and emotional problems (Gard & Ruzek, 2006). If additional support is needed, a referral can be made.

There are special considerations in helping children and adolescents adjust to a postdisaster climate. Adults can help to foster continuity (Omer & Alon, 1994) in the lives of young survivors to maximize their likelihood of adaptive adjustment. Important strategies include reopening schools, having children perform chores ordinarily expected of them, and maintaining pre-disaster standards for behavior at home and school. As normal roles and routines are resumed, adults can also encourage youths to process the events of the storm by helping them explore the meaning of the disaster and construct views of their experience that enable them to acknowledge the effects of the disaster on their lives without feeling emotionally overwhelmed or personally defined by the event (Vernberg, 2002).

In the weeks following a disaster, mental health professionals—those previously employed by the schools and others—may enter schools in disaster areas or in areas with large numbers of evacuees to help students process traumatic events and rebuild their lives. Helpful activities may include encouraging students to discuss hurricane-related events, ongoing stressors, and ways that they may contribute to the rebuilding process (NCTSN & NCPTSD, 2005). Mental health professionals may consult with administrators and teachers about the most effective ways to respond to a disaster at school, which may include addressing general mental health topics and coping strategies in presentations to large numbers of students, holding group sessions for students who have suffered significant loss or who have been identified as having difficulty coping with disaster-related events, and offering private counseling sessions. Vernberg (2002) discussed some possible negative outcomes of school-based mental health interventions. Potential concerns include exposing students to new troubling images; provoking inappropriate self-disclosure; and encouraging a decrease in self-control, possibly due to relaxed school rules. Issues concerning school interventions following natural disasters, including Katrina, are discussed in chapters 5 and 7 of this volume.

Feelings of anxiety, sadness, numbness, anger, loss, being out of control, disorientation, and general negative affect have been observed in adult survivors of natural disasters (Freedy, Shaw, Jarrell, & Masters, 1992; Phifer & Norris, 1989). Contrary to previous beliefs that children are generally unaffected by disasters, the literature suggests that the reactions of young survivors may in fact be very significant, though symptoms may differ from their older counterparts (e.g., Shelby & Tredinnick, 1995). In their fieldwork with young survivors of Hurricane Andrew (which made landfall in South Florida, 1992), Shelby and Tredinnick (1995) noted that many children presented with preoccupation with death, regression, nightmares, increased fear of nonhurricane objects and situations, and decreased behavioral control. It is important to note that these authors stressed that the impact of psychological maladjustment did not affect individuals alone but extended to families and other loved ones, potentially disrupting family functioning. For example, they found a decrease in positive parent–child interactions and an increase in negative parental views of their children as overly needy and prone to misbehavior. Though there is still much to learn about psychological adjustment following disasters, social support reduces the chances that an individual will develop severe mental health consequences. Notably, low social support has been associated with increased psychological distress, PTSD, depression, and anxiety in adults (Acierno, Ruggiero, Kilpatrick, Resnick, & Galea, 2006; Sattler et al., 2002; Solomon, 1985).

Social support is also an important protective factor for young survivors, as illustrated by Hardin, Weinrich, Weinrich, Hardin, and Garrison (1994), who found that adolescents who had low perceived social support following Hurricane Hugo (which made landfall in North and South Carolina, 1989) were more likely to experience anger and depression. Following Hurricane Andrew, elementary schoolchildren who perceived low levels of social support 3 months after the storm reported significantly more PTSD symptoms 7 and 10 months after the hurricane (La Greca, Silverman, Vernberg, & Prinstein, 1996). Vernberg, La Greca, Silverman, and Prinstein (1996) examined different sources of social support following Hurricane Andrew and concluded that it is important for children to have support from multiple sources (teachers, classmates, parents, close friends) to ensure the fulfillment of different support needs.

One way adults can provide social support to children is to be available to discuss the event and related feelings (see chaps. 2 and 3, this volume). The resumption of predisaster activities affords children opportunities to interact with peers and adults (e.g., teachers and coaches) who can function as sources of support by listening and sharing their own experiences (e.g., Prinstein, La Greca, Vernberg, & Silverman, 1996). The ideal scenario would be to have children involved in activities they were undertaking before the storm (e.g., sports, karate lessons, scouting). This involvement, of course, would depend largely on the postdisaster environment and available organizations to conduct such activities. Facilitating a rapid return to school is another way to increase support opportunities for children, as school-based mental health professionals often provide individual and group counseling sessions for students having difficulty adjusting (Vernberg, 2002).

In Orleans Parish, the parish most affected by the storm and subsequent flooding, evacuees were not allowed to return to their homes until 2 months after the hurricane. Although some were able to remain in their homes, most did not have habitable homes and were forced to find alternatives or to return to their evacuation site. During the evacuation and the return home, families were separated, daily routines were disrupted, and in many instances living conditions were overcrowded (Brodie et al., 2006). Children of families who were living in this parish had to begin school in the middle of the semester or spend the year at schools in other parishes because the Orleans schools were not open. In all, these disruptions may have prevented individuals from obtaining adequate social support.

Mental health difficulties were and continue to be pronounced following Hurricane Katrina for both adults and children (e.g., Mack, 2008). In Hensley and Varela's (2008) sample of 302 sixth and seventh graders in the New Orleans area, 71% reported at least some PTSD symptoms, with 12% reporting severe or very severe symptoms, 7 months following the hurricane. Social environmental conditions following the hurricane were likely contributors to poor adjustment. In this study, 85% of the youths evacuated New Orleans in advance of the hurricane, 57% had to change schools on return to the city, and 42% reported difficulty seeing their old friends. Additionally, Quigley (2006) reported that 4 weeks after Katrina, evacuees had registered in all 50 states and in 18,700 zip codes, and 60,000 evacuees were more than 750 miles away from home. Families that evacuated had to develop social networks in their new places of residence, even if temporary. They had to establish new community linkages and somehow regain a sense of connectedness to their new environment. The mixed government reports of when families would be allowed to return to New Orleans likely only increased the uncertainty and stress experienced by these families.

Given the impact of natural disasters on family functioning and the wealth of literature indicating the importance of social support, clinicians may consider interventions that involve the entire family in the treatment process (e.g., Prinstein et al., 1996; Solomon, 1985) and should strongly encourage survivors to maintain connections with social support networks and to build new networks where old ones have dissolved. This proposition may be challenging, considering that families are likely more concerned with securing basic necessities. In the case of Hurricane Katrina, finding new employment was also a realistic concern for many of the evacuees because the time frame for the mandatory evacuation was unknown for weeks, and even on return to the New Orleans area, previous employment was not guaranteed (Dolfman, Wasser, & Bergman, 2007).

Nonetheless, mental health providers in disaster-stricken areas and those outside of disaster areas who are working with evacuees can encourage families to build and strengthen their social support networks. Providers can recommend that survivors seek out others with whom they feel a connection (e.g., people of the same age, cultural background, profession) and make friends with those who did not experience the disaster. Mental health professionals can also educate parents and teachers about how to provide more effective social support and how to foster more effective support among classmates and peers. Finally, being alert to survivors who may need more intensive therapeutic intervention will increase the chances that these individuals receive the best care possible in a timely manner (Vernberg, 2002). Following these guidelines will help clinicians promote psychological adjustment among children and families during this phase (Vernberg, 2002).

CHILD AND FAMILY CONSIDERATIONS IN THE LONG-TERM ADAPTATION PHASE

Following severe disasters, government and community agencies often continue to provide aid. However, such aid may not be sufficient to meet the needs of those affected because local service providers may not yet have resumed their job responsibilities when health professionals who have volunteered their time begin leaving the affected area (Vernberg, 2002). Furthermore, government or community-based financial assistance may be provided for a limited amount of time and may expire during the long-term adaptation phase (Vernberg, 2002). The services survivors receive at this phase may depend greatly on their determination and ability to seek out help. In terms of mental health, there is no longer the urgency to meet the needs of large numbers of people within a short time frame, and service providers can move beyond brief, disaster-focused counseling to tailoring interventions to address a wide range of survivor needs (Vernberg, 2002). Individuals experiencing significant impairment in psychological functioning at this stage are likely to need long-term intervention.

Findings from Hurricane Katrina indicate that survivors were still experiencing significant life disruption months after the storm. For example, approximately 100,000 people continued to reside in FEMA trailers 10 months after the storm (FEMA, 2006). In terms of health care availability, only 23% of primary care physicians had returned to the greater New Orleans area 8 months after the hurricane, and only 11% of psychiatrists continued to operate (Pope, 2006). The Katrina Assistance Project, which was funded by the Substance Abuse and Mental Health Services Administration and provided more than 1,200 mental health professionals, ended after 11 months because of federal mandates that funding be used only for short-term crisis management (Robert T. Stafford Act, 1988; Weisler et al., 2006).

Government and community relief agencies still operating in this phase can be more effective in service provision if they use many forms of media to keep survivors aware of existing opportunities and eligibility requirements for receiving aid (Vanderford et al., 2007). Making public transportation accessible could also increase the likelihood that families in need are able to tap into available resources. In terms of mental health care, following up to the greatest extent possible with those identified as needing further assessment and long-term care in previous phases of intervention is a priority. Thorough assessments and clinical interviews can be used to determine the severity of symptoms and their relation to disaster-related experiences and to devise an appropriate treatment plan (Gard & Ruzek, 2006).

CULTURAL AND INDIVIDUAL CONSIDERATIONS IN SOCIAL AND COMMUNITY RESPONSES

Hurricane Katrina, perhaps more than any other crisis in recent history, has turned the world's attention to the effects of individual characteristics such as race, economic status, and age on received support following a disaster. Differences in how individuals from diverse backgrounds experience natural disasters may begin even before any particular storm develops and warnings or evacuation orders are given. For example, properties in low-income areas may be at particular risk for flooding or mudslides following hurricanes. The Okeechobee Hurricane in Florida in 1928 caused many fatalities among migrant farm communities (Kleinberg, 2003). This destruction was blamed on poorly constructed levees surrounding the low-income area, and discussions continue about racial and economic disparities in damage caused by the hurricane (Kleinberg, 2003). Following Hurricane Katrina, media outlets from around the globe reported that many residents in the New Orleans area believed that racial inequality was to blame for the failure of levees causing severe devastation in the Lower Ninth Ward of New Orleans, a largely African American neighborhood (e.g., Another Flood That Stunned America, 2005).

In addition to risks economically disadvantaged populations may face in terms of neighborhood location and maintenance, research indicates that these individuals may be less likely to evacuate than more affluent individuals. Bates (1963) found that higher income families were more likely to evacuate before Hurricane Audrey hit Louisiana and Texas in 1957, most likely because they were able to afford to go to hotels out of harm's way. Similarly, Gladwin and Peacock (1997) found that low-income and elderly or disabled households were less likely to evacuate than other households. Transportation difficulties and lack of information about where to find low-cost shelters may be primary obstacles during evacuation periods (Gladwin & Peacock, 1997). Often, by the time mandatory evacuation orders are issued, finding transportation out of the threatened areas is difficult. In addition, marginalized individuals may have a distrust of government and social service agencies that could impede their willingness to evacuate (Gladwin & Peacock, 1997).

Low-income residents may also be at a disadvantage during the impact and postimpact phases of intervention because they are often reliant on free services provided by government and community agencies (Vernberg, 2002). Individuals without the means to seek out private sources of assistance (e.g., contacts living far away, private loans, access to savings accounts) are at the mercy of the often overcrowded and overwhelmed service areas at shelters and other community help stations (Brodie et al., 2006). Additionally, a report on Hurricane Katrina by the U.S. House of Representatives (2006) noted that by the time evacuation orders were received, many caretaking facilities needing buses and/or ambulances for evacuation were unable to find such services, fuel and rental cars were in short supply, and many forms of public transportation had been shut down.

Mental health providers may find it useful to explore issues related to culture and race before implementing a treatment plan. For example, the experience of racism may be an additional stressor in an individual's life and add to his or her vulnerability to maladjustment in the aftermath of a disaster (Rabalais, Ruggiero, & Scotti, 2002). Data collected after Hurricane Hugo indicated that race, education, and age moderated the impact of disaster exposure on the amount of postdisaster aid received from a variety of sources (Kaniasty & Norris, 1995). For instance, individuals with higher education reported receiving more tangible support than those with lower levels of education. Similarly, many individuals believed that economic and racial inequality were responsible for the slow response time of rescue efforts in several mostly African American, low-income neighborhoods in the greater New Orleans area following Katrina (Weems et al., 2007). Moreover, residents of New Orleans were more likely to report discrimination than residents in other Gulf Coast regions (e.g., Mississippi) following the hurricane (Weems et al., 2007).

For ethnic groups such as African Americans and Hispanics, who may already be dealing with challenges related to their minority status (e.g., discrimination), social support in the form of positive family relationships, a strong sense of community, and spirituality may be particularly important (Gonzales & Kim, 1997). Weems and colleagues (2007) found that perception of discrimination was related to increased PTSD symptoms in ethnic minorities following Hurricane Katrina. Finally, service providers should strive to be aware of and respect cultural beliefs about natural disasters (e.g., some religious groups expressed the belief that Hurricane Katrina was punishment from God) as well as preferences for help seeking (e.g., African Americans may prefer to seek mental health counseling from religious leaders; Aderibigbe, Bloch, & Pandurangi, 2003).

LESSONS LEARNED AND ACTIONABLE RECOMMENDATIONS

Planning Phase

The most important recommendation for those wishing to minimize adjustment difficulties after a disaster is to thoroughly prepare. By ensuring that public service messages are preplanned to the greatest extent possible, available in a variety of languages and literacy levels, as specific as possible to regional climates and cultures, and not entirely dependent on technology, agencies will be more effective in communicating with the public during and after disasters. Government and national disaster relief agencies can form partnerships with local community agencies and professionals before disaster strikes so that immediate action can be taken in the event that disaster areas are unreachable to outsiders. Preexisting and rehearsed plans for providing public transportation are likely to prevent poorly coordinated evacuation efforts if a mass evacuation is necessary. It would be most beneficial if hospitals and other medical care facilities have their own evacuation plans in place, including predisaster contracts with public transportation or ambulatory services in case these are needed. Improvements regarding evacuation orders and options were made and exercised during preparation for Hurricane Gustav, which hit Louisiana in September 2008. With no local shelters available, nearly 2 million Gulf Coast residents were successfully evacuated by plane, train, and bus in preparation for Gustav, with officials allowing up to 36 hours more time for evacuation than was allowed before Katrina (Fiore, 2008).

Some challenges that may interfere with implementation of plans at the preimpact phase include lack of funding for initiatives and poor coordination across agencies in developing plans. After Katrina, citizen-driven neighborhood associations in New Orleans have taken on the informal role of monitoring the efforts of government agencies in preplanning for future hurricanes (e.g., Broadmoor Improvement Association, 2008). In addition, these associations have sought funding for planning initiatives through federal grants and private foundations, both independently and in collaboration with local government agencies.

Mental health service providers interested in becoming involved in disaster relief efforts need to obtain training in advance so that they are prepared to mobilize immediately after or even before a disaster to provide relief as quickly as possible. Mass distribution of materials about common reactions to natural disasters and warning signs that professional intervention is needed is one effective way to prepare to reach many people in the immediate aftermath of a disaster (Vernberg, 2002). The training of mental health responders should include how to manage one's own response to witnessing destruction, how to prioritize cases given a large group of people with varying needs, how to encourage clients to use social support, how to work with clients experiencing extreme reactions to trauma, how to decide whether further referrals are necessary, and how to work with individuals of varying cultural backgrounds and levels of openness to mental health interventions (Gard & Ruzek, 2006; Vernberg, 2002). Mental health networks and associations such as the NCTSN or the American Psychological Association can take a proactive role in providing training to members who may be first responders following a disaster. Local governments in areas at risk for natural disasters (e.g., Florida and the Mississippi and Louisiana Gulf Coasts) could also allocate funds to pay for training of local mental health providers.

Local governments should ensure that all individuals, including those who live in high-risk areas, benefit from preparation efforts. For example, reinforcing the notion that transportation will be provided for everyone and ensuring that instructions are accessible and understandable in a variety of languages will increase the likelihood that low-income and non-English-speaking residents will evacuate.

Impact Phase

Government and community service agencies need to continue to ensure that public health announcements are clear and relevant to the target population during the impact phase. National service agencies operating in affected areas should concentrate on organization and efficiency. Relief workers can be most effective by placing priority on treating emergency situations while educating the public about how to handle more common physical and mental ailments. PFA is an important tool in providing mental health services, and the most relevant elements in this and following phases are survivor outreach and education.

Short-Term Adaptation Phase

Government and national community service agencies need to increase their focus on helping local agencies prepare to take over disaster relief efforts during the short-term adaptation phase, in preparation for the waning of direct services provided by outside organizations that usually begins in the postimpact phase. Helping survivors find employment can promote self-sufficiency as free services such as food and medical care decrease during this period. Mental health services may shift to more personalized interventions, and brief crisis-focused therapy is advocated by PFA guidelines to help survivors (Gard & Ruzek, 2006). Referrals should be made for those needing more intensive treatment once it is feasible, and emergency cases should continue to receive immediate intervention.

Long-Term Adaptation Phase

As opportunities for disaster-related aid decrease, widespread advertisement through media outlets of existing opportunities will increase the chances that those who need these services have access to them (Vanderford et al., 2007). During the long-term adaptation phase, mental health practitioners need to thoroughly evaluate referrals made during previous phases and form individualized treatment plans so as to most effectively address psychological difficulties (Vernberg, 2002).

CONCLUDING REMARKS

A number of factors influence the relationship between exposure to frightening and highly disruptive events such as a major hurricane and children's developmental outcomes. From an ecological perspective, children's proximal influences, including the ability of caretakers to cope well with the disaster, have a major impact on their adjustment in a posttrauma environment. In turn, social and community responses to a family's needs exert a significant effect on the entire family's coping abilities in the short-term aftermath and long after the disaster. At highest risk of maladaptive responses are families and children with low economic, emotional, and social resources and poor access to community and social offerings of aid before and after a disaster occurs. Although more efficient evacuations prior to Hurricanes Gustav and Ike present hope that as a society we are learning from our past experiences, the fact that families are still struggling to reestablish their lives more than 3 years after Hurricanes Katrina and Rita shows that we need to do a better job at responding to the needs of those most vulnerable to the effects of major storms.

REFERENCES

Aderibigbe, Y. A., Bloch, R. M., & Pandurangi, A. (2003). Emotional and somatic distress in eastern North Carolina: Help-seeking behaviors. *International Journal of Social Psychology, 49*, 126–141.

Acierno, R., Ruggiero, K. J., Kilpatrick, D. G., Resnick, H. S., & Galea, S. (2006). Risk and protective factors for psychopathology among older versus younger adults after the 2004 Florida hurricanes. *American Journal of Geriatric Psychiatry, 14*, 1051–1059.

American Psychological Association. (2007). *Disaster Response Network fact sheet.* Retrieved December 2, 2007, from http://www.apa.org/practice/drnindex.html

American Red Cross. (2006). *A year of healing: The American Red Cross response to hurricanes Katrina, Wilma, and Rita.* Retrieved June 25, 2007, from http://www.redcross.org/images/pdfs/Katrina_OneYearReport.pdf

Another flood that stunned America. (2005, September 4). *U.S. News & World Report.* Retrieved November 6, 2008, from http://www.usnews.com/usnews/news/articles/050912/12leadall.b.htm

Bailey, B. N., Delaney-Black, V., Hannigan, J. H., Ager, J., Sokok, R. J., & Covington, C. Y. (2005). Somatic complaints in children and community violence exposure. *Journal of Developmental & Behavioral Pediatrics, 26*, 341–348.

Bates, F. L. (1963). *The social and psychological consequences of a natural disaster: A longitudinal study of Hurricane Audrey.* Washington, DC: National Academy Press.

Broadmoor Improvement Association. (2008). *Emergency preparedness.* Retrieved November 8, 2008, from http://broadmoorimprovement.com/node/92

Brodie, M., Weltzien, E., Altman, D., Blendon, R. J., & Benson, J. M. (2006). Experiences of Hurricane Katrina evacuees in Houston shelters: Implications for future planning. *American Journal of Public Health, 96*, 1402–1408.

Brymer, M., Jacob, A., Layne, C., Pynoos, R., Ruzek, J., Steinberg, A., et al. (2006). *Psychological First Aid field operations guide* (2nd ed.). Los Angeles: National Child Traumatic Stress Network and National Center for PTSD.

Campo, J. V., Jansen-McWilliams, L., Comer, D. M., & Kelleher, K. J. (1999). Somatization in pediatric primary care: Association with psychopathology, functional impairment, and use of services. *Journal of the American Academy of Child and Adolescent Psychiatry, 38*, 1093–1101.

Centers for Disease Control and Prevention. (2006). Assessment of health related needs after hurricanes Katrina and Rita: Orleans and Jefferson Parishes, New Orleans area, Louisiana, October 17–22, 2005. *Morbidity and Mortality Weekly Report, 55*, 38–41.

Cook, A., Spinazzola, J., Ford, J., Lanktree, C., Blaustein, M., Cloitre, M., et al. (2005). Complex trauma in children and adolescents. *Psychiatric Annals, 35*, 390–398.

Davis, R., & Johnson, K. (2005, October 16). Louisiana looks into 215 Katrina deaths. *USA Today*. Retrieved June 27, 2007, from http://www.usatoday.com/news/nation/2005-10-16-la-katrina-investigation_x.htm

Defense Logistics Agency. (2005). *Defense Supply Center Philadelphia annual report*. Retrieved June 25, 2007, from http://www.dscp.dla.mil/AnnualReport/annrep05

Dolfman, M. L., Wasser, S. F., & Bergman, B. (2007). The effects of Hurricane Katrina on the New Orleans economy. *Monthly Labor Review Online, 130*. Retrieved November 6, 2008, from http://www.bls.gov/opub/mlr/2007/06/art1 exc.htm

Escobar, J. I., Canino, G., Rubio-Stipec, M., & Bravo, M. (1992). Somatic symptoms after a natural disaster: A prospective study. *American Journal of Psychiatry, 149*, 965–967.

Escobar, J. I., Rubio-Stipec, M., Canino, G., & Karno, M. (1989). Somatic Symptom Index (SSI): A new and abridged somatization construct: Prevalence and epidemiological correlates in two large community samples. *Journal of Nervous and Mental Disease, 177*, 140–146.

Federal Emergency Management Agency. (2006, June 16). *Hurricane Katrina recovery update: Week 41*. Washington, DC: Author. Retrieved July 2, 2007, from http://www.fema.gov/news/newsrelease.fema?id=27080

Fiore, F. (2008, September 2). FEMA says it's applying Hurricane Katrina lessons to Gustav. *Los Angeles Times*. Retrieved November 8, 2008, from http://www.latimes.com/news/nationworld/nation/la-na-fema2-2008sep02,0,7688528.story

Freedy, J. R., Shaw, D. L., Jarrell, M. P., & Masters, C. R. (1992). Towards an understanding of the psychological impact of natural disaster: An application of the conservation of resources stress model. *Journal of Traumatic Stress, 5*, 441–454.

Gard, B. A., & Ruzek, J. I. (2006). Community mental health response to crisis. *Journal of Clinical Psychology: In Session, 62*, 1029–1041.

Gladwin, H., & Peacock, W. G. (1997). Warning and evacuation: A night for hard houses. In W. Peacock, B. Morrow, & H. Gladwin (Eds.), *Hurricane Andrew: Ethnicity, gender and the sociology of disasters* (pp. 52–74). London: Routledge.

Gobble, R., Sweeny, C., & Fishbein, M. (2004). The impact of the September 11, 2001 terrorist attacks and aftermath on the incidence of recurrent abdominal pain syndrome in children. *Clinical Pediatrics, 43*, 275–277.

Gonzales, N., & Kim, L. (1997). Stress and coping in an ethnic minority context. In S. A. Wolchik & I. N. Sandler (Eds.), *Handbook of children's coping: Linking theory and intervention* (pp. 481–511). New York: Plenum Press.

Hardin, S. B., Weinrich, M., Weinrich, S., Hardin, T. L., & Garrison, C. (1994). Psychological distress of adolescents exposed to Hurricane Hugo. *Journal of Traumatic Stress, 7*, 427–440.

Hensley, L. S., & Varela, R. E. (2008). PTSD symptoms and somatic complaints following Hurricane Katrina: The role of trait anxiety and anxiety sensitivity. *Journal of Clinical Child and Adolescent Psychology, 37*, 542–552.

Huus, K. (2006, May 31). *Here come the storms as FEMA rushes reforms*. Retrieved November 6, 2008, from http://www.msnbc.msn.com/id/12978598/

Kaniasty, K., & Norris, F. H. (1995). In search of altruistic community: Patterns of social support mobilization following Hurricane Hugo. *American Journal of Community Psychology, 23*, 447–477.

Kingery, J. N., Ginsburg, F. S., & Alfano, C. A. (2007). Somatic symptoms and anxiety among African American adolescents. *Journal of Black Psychology, 33*, 363–378.

Kleinberg, E. (2003). *Black cloud: The great Florida hurricane of 1928*. New York: Carroll & Graf.

La Greca, A. M., Silverman, W. K., Vernberg, E. M., & Prinstein, M. J. (1996). Symptoms of posttraumatic stress in children following Hurricane Andrew: A prospective study. *Journal of Consulting and Clinical Psychology, 64*, 712–723.

Mack, S. (2008, May 5). *State of mind: A shortage of mental health professionals puts New Orleans' psychological recovery at risk*. Retrieved November 6, 2008, from http://www.bestofneworleans.com/dispatch/2008-05-06/healthfeat.php

National Institute of Mental Health. (1990). *Training manual for human service workers in major disasters* (DHHS Publication No. ADM 90-538). Washington, DC: U.S. Government Printing Office.

Omer, H., & Alon, N. (1994). The continuity principle: A unified approach to disaster and trauma. *American Journal of Community Psychology, 22*, 273–287.

Phifer, J. F., & Norris, F. H. (1989). Psychological symptoms in older adults following natural disaster: Nature, timing, duration, and course. *Journal of Gerontology, 11*, 9207–9217.

Pope, J. (2006, April 26). New Orleans is short on doctors, dentists; city becomes eligible for recruitment help. *New Orleans Times-Picayune*, p. B1.

Pope, J., & Vanacore, A. (2008, August 23). 3 years later Katrina is reshaping area's life. *New Orleans Times-Picayune*. Retrieved March 31, 2009, from http://www.nola.com/news/index.ssf/2008/08/3_years_later_katrina_is_resha.html

Prinstein, M. J., La Greca, A. M., Vernberg, E. M., & Silverman, W. K. (1996). Children's coping assistance: How parents, teachers, and friends help children cope after a natural disaster. *Journal of Clinical Child Psychology, 25*, 463–475.

Quigley, B. (2006). *Six months after Katrina: Who was left behind then and who is being left behind now?* Washington, DC: Center of Concern. Retrieved June 27, 2007, from http://www.coc.org/index.fpl/1090/article/3678.html

Rabalais, A., Ruggiero, K. J., & Scotti, J. R. (2002). Multicultural issues in the response of children to disasters. In A. M. La Greca, W. K. Silverman, E. M. Vernberg, & M. C. Roberts (Eds.), *Helping children cope with disasters and terrorism* (pp. 73–99). Washington, DC: American Psychological Association.

Robert T. Stafford Disaster Relief and Emergency Assistance (Stafford) Act, 42 U.S.C. §5121, 1988.

Rosenblatt, S., & Rainey, J. (2005, September 27). Katrina rumors. *Los Angeles Times*. Retrieved July 2, 2007, from http://www.latimes.com/news/printedition/asection/la-na-rumors27sep27,0,5536446.story?track=hpmostemailedlink

Salvation Army. (2006). *Salvation Army reflects on largest disaster response ever at one-year anniversary of Hurricane Katrina*. Retrieved June 25, 2007, from http://www1.salvationarmy.org/usw%5Cwww_usw.nsf/vw-news/2A147D78BC387D3A882571D8005CDE1D?opendocument

Sattler, D. N., Preston, A. J., Kaiser, C. F., Olivera, V. E., Valdez, J., & Schlueter, S. (2002). Hurricane Georges: A cross-national study examining preparedness, resource loss, and psychological distress in the U.S. Virgin Islands, Puerto Rico, Dominican Republic, and the United States. *Journal of Traumatic Stress, 15*, 339–350.

Shaw, J. A. (2003). Children exposed to war/terrorism. *Clinical Child and Family Psychology Review, 6*, 237–246.

Shelby, J. S., & Tredinnick, M. G. (1995). Crisis intervention with survivors of natural disaster: Lessons from Hurricane Andrew. *Journal of Counseling & Development, 73*, 491–497.

Silverman, W. K., & La Greca, A. M. (2002). Children experiencing disasters: Definitions, reactions, and predictors of outcomes. In A. M. La Greca, W. K. Silverman, E. M. Vernberg, & M. C. Roberts (Eds.), *Helping children cope with disasters and terrorism* (pp. 11–33). Washington, DC: American Psychological Association.

Sledjeski, E. M., Speisman, B., & Dierker, L. C. (2008). Does number of lifetime traumas explain the relationship between PTSD and chronic medical conditions? Answers from the National Comorbidity Survey—Replication (NCS–R). *Journal of Behavioral Medicine, 31*, 341–349.

Solomon, Z. (1985). Stress, social support and affective disorders in mothers of pre-school children: A test of the stress-buffering effect of social support. *Social Psychiatry, 20*, 100–105.

U.S. House of Representatives. (2006). *A failure of initiative: Final report of the Select Bipartisan Committee to investigate the preparation for and response to Hurricane Katrina*. Washington, DC: Author.

Vanderford, M. L., Nastoff, N., Telfer, J. L., & Bonzo, S. E. (2007). Emergency communication challenges in response to Hurricane Katrina: Lessons from the Centers for Disease Control and Prevention. *Journal of Applied Communication Research, 35*, 9–25.

Varela, R. E., Sanchez-Sosa, J. J., Biggs, B. K., & Luis, T. M. (2008). Anxiety symptoms and fears in Hispanic and European American children: Cross-cultural measurement equivalence. *Journal of Psychopathology and Behavioral Assessment, 30*, 132–145.

Varela, R. E., Vernberg, E. M., Sanchez-Sosa, J. J., Riveros, A., Mitchell, M., & Mashunkashey, J. (2004). Anxiety reporting and culturally associated interpretation biases and cognitive schemas: A comparison of Mexican, Mexican

American, and European American families. *Journal of Clinical Child and Adolescent Psychology, 33*, 237–247.

Vernberg, E. M. (2002). Intervention approaches following disasters. In A. M. La Greca, W. K. Silverman, E. M. Vernberg, & M. C. Roberts (Eds.), *Helping children cope with disasters and terrorism* (pp. 55–72). Washington, DC: American Psychological Association.

Vernberg, E. M., & Field, T. (1990). Transitional stress in children and adolescents moving to new environments. In S. Fisher & C. L. Cooper (Eds.), *On the move: The psychology of change and transition* (pp. 127–151). Chichester, England: Wiley.

Vernberg, E. M., La Greca, A. M., Silverman, W. K., & Prinstein, M. J. (1996). Prediction of posttraumatic stress symptoms in children after Hurricane Andrew. *Journal of Abnormal Psychology, 105*, 237–248.

Vernberg, E. M., & Varela, R. E. (2001). Posttraumatic stress disorder: A developmental perspective. In M. W. Vasey & M. R. Dadds (Eds.), *The developmental psychopathology of anxiety* (pp. 386–406). New York: Oxford University Press.

Vernberg, E. M., & Vogel, J. (1993). Interventions with children following disasters. *Journal of Clinical Child Psychology, 22*, 485–498.

Weems, C. F., Watts, S. E., Marsee, M. A., Taylor, L. K., Costa, N. M., Cannon, M. F., et al. (2007). The psychological impact of Hurricane Katrina: Contextual differences in psychological symptoms, social support, and discrimination. *Behavior Research and Therapy, 45*, 2295–2306.

Weisler, R. H., Barbee, J. G., & Townsend, M. H. (2006). Mental health and recovery in the Gulf Coast after Hurricanes Katrina and Rita. *JAMA, 296*, 585–588.

9

THE ROLES OF FAITH-BASED ORGANIZATIONS AFTER HURRICANE KATRINA

BRENDA PHILLIPS AND PAMELA JENKINS

Historically, religious and faith-based organizations (FBOs) have made up an important part of the social and cultural infrastructure of New Orleans, and before Hurricane Katrina, the numerous congregations represented a critical touchstone in the everyday life of most citizens. New Orleans was, and remains, a diversely religious city in which a wide range of cultures attend worship services routinely. On their day of religious celebration, people would drive to the congregation of their youth—a reflection of deep loyalty to spiritual roots. Now, after the storm, people are driving from Baton Rouge, Louisiana; Houston, Texas; or Jackson, Mississippi to attend their home congregations in New Orleans.

Local churches also had a long history of supporting the community by addressing nondisaster problems such as housing and poverty. In the year before the storm, predominantly African American congregations through the Total Community Action Faith Collaborate added disaster preparedness to

Data gathered through the support of National Science Foundation Grant BCS 0554925 were used for this chapter. We thank Jeanette Sutton for suggestions related to this chapter. The findings are those of the authors and do not necessarily represent those of the National Science Foundation or others mentioned here. The authors contributed equally to the preparation of this chapter; the order of authorship is arbitrary.

their educational plans, one of the first efforts to target African American congregations. Another such initiative, Operation Brother's Keeper, involved collaboration among the American Red Cross, a local public university, and several congregations. Operation Brother's Keeper, funded by Baptist Community Ministries, worked to educate parishioners about evacuation. Operation Brother's Keeper also partnered with congregations north of Interstate 10, the "line" below which survival would be seriously compromised. Katrina severed citizens from these meaningful, faith-based networks and sources of support. Yet, the spiritual core of the city and the FBOs that would arrive from outside would serve as a source of renewal during the recovery.

This chapter describes the faith-based response to the greatest urban disaster in U.S. history and is the first to document the full range of efforts. In a context in which many deemed government response delayed and inadequate, the faith-based sector responded in a broad-based and overwhelming manner. Local denominations, dramatically affected by the storm, responded in new and often creative ways, and national organizations stretched their resources to meet a broad array of needs across an extensive geographic area.

We define *faith-based organizations* as social units linked to religious traditions, such as disaster-specific organizations like Presbyterian Disaster Assistance or the Mennonite Disaster Service, or more general organizations like Catholic Charities or the Ananda Marga Universal Relief Team. FBOs represent crucial linkages between families, policies, programs, and—ultimately—response and recovery to disasters. Because so many families lack resources for mitigating and preparing for disaster, they face difficulties with evacuation transportation, shelter needs, short-term housing, and long-term reconstruction. Federal assistance programs, for example, provide a maximum $28,800 grant to low-income families, hardly enough to rebuild a home. FBOs provide knowledge, labor, and building supplies to those lacking adequate federal assistance.

To describe FBOs' relevance to disasters, the sections that follow situate the chapter in the context of New Orleans, examine the limited literature available to date, explain our data sources and methodology, and reveal how FBOs operate in a disaster context. A narrative section then outlines the broad range of faith-based response and recovery activities observed in New Orleans after Hurricane Katrina. Response functions included rescue, reunification, sheltering, meeting of cultural and special needs, donations management, cleanup, and medical and dental services. Recovery functions included salvage work, addressing of unmet needs, case management, counseling, funding, volunteer labor and housing, rebuilding, reestablishment of households, transitional needs, satellite services, child care, political participation, community organizing, partnerships, and economic development. Finally, we identify recommendations for policy, practice, and future research.

We offer this chapter from two perspectives and note our two voices in the text. Pamela Jenkins offers an insider's point of view reflecting knowledge gained from personal and professional activity within the communities of New Orleans. Brenda Phillips brings an outsider's understanding supported by observations from Hurricane Katrina volunteers and researchers.

HURRICANE KATRINA: "THIS ONE IS DIFFERENT"

Disaster researchers tell us that the scale, scope, and magnitude of an event matter. Typically, disasters disrupt the daily routine of communities, forcing closures of businesses, schools, and health care facilities for varying amounts of time (Quarantelli, 1998). Catastrophic events overwhelm regional capacities to respond and tax national and federal organizations. Indeed, organizations may not be able to function in a catastrophic context (Quarantelli, 2006).

Further, it is clear from recent national inquiries (e.g., General Accountability Office, 2006a, 2006b; U.S. House of Representatives, 2006) that Katrina included multiple disasters, including the preevent evacuation, the hurricane, the levee failures, and the inadequate response and recovery effort. Evacuees relocated across all 50 states, though most remained concentrated in those closest to home (Metropolitan Policy Program at Brookings & Greater New Orleans Community Data Center, 2008). Families often evacuated in extended family units, with several generations traveling together. As the floodwaters receded, residents slowly returned in an uneven fashion. As an indicator of loss and the strong familial ties people have to New Orleans, evacuees situate their loss not only with their homes but within the overall impact on the extended family, or the few family members who have a house left experience the burden of taking in multiple generations. It has been difficult for many evacuees to reconnect to their original congregations, social networks, and places of support. Life is strained for the people of New Orleans and for its faith-based sector. Only 43.1% of local pre-Katrina worship centers were back operating well after the hurricane (Day, 2007); all faiths were affected, without exception.

Commencement of any disaster recovery process is often marked by the arrival of national FBOs, which contribute key resources, personnel, and experience. Though these organizations are often unheralded, disaster recovery would not be possible for many communities without them. As we watched from our varying perspectives—flood survivor, researcher, and volunteer—several things became clear: (a) This recovery would extend beyond the 18-month period during which the Federal Emergency Management Agency (FEMA) typically provides resources, (b) the leadership of national organizations would have to rethink where they would set up and how they would attempt to meet needs, and (c) the nature of the affected and widely evacuated populations (poor, urban, many elderly and disabled) would mean that FBOs would play an even more pivotal role than is usual in disaster recovery. As we sat in recovery meetings or interviewed organizational representatives during our research, we heard one phrase repeatedly: "You know, this one is different." According to Jenkins,

> Local faith-based organizations, which would normally contribute resources to a community crisis, struggled to survive. Local congregations lost their buildings, staff, and members. Staff and congregational members lost their homes and their jobs as well as functionally meaningful social and spiritual ties to each other. Yet every type of faith and faith-based organization came to the Gulf Coast. Often members of a congregation would come to the area and go back and report on their experience, and others would follow. Campus Crusaders for Christ lived for a year in City Park in the middle of New Orleans. Retired couples from the Mennonites and Baptists, among others, left their homes for up to 2 years to live in New Orleans and supervise volunteer crews. As they returned, members of local congregations hosted volunteer crews, organized work projects, and provided cooking, sleeping, and laundry facilities. It was overwhelming— visible, moving symbols of people and organizations stepping into the remnants of our lives and working to restore our city, our neighborhoods, our lives.

ROLES OF FAITH-BASED ORGANIZATIONS: A LITERATURE REVIEW

In this section, we consider the relationship between faith and volunteerism in disaster contexts. Studies have revealed that altruistic or "helping" behavior is a norm in disaster situations, even in situations in which death is imminent (Johnson, 1988; Johnson, Feinberg, & Johnston, 1994) or there is deep uncertainty about how to respond, such as the evacuation of the World Trade Center in 1993 (Aguirre, Wenger, & Vigo, 1998). Nelson and Dynes (1976) uncovered "pronounced differences" between ordinary and emergency contexts. They suggested that religious organizations provide frameworks through which social participation is facilitated.

Sutton (2003) found that some local FBOs responding in New York City after the terrorist attacks of September 11, 2001 (9/11) experienced organizational changes, such as increasing their volunteer base to meet a perceived need. FBOs that experience such adaptive change tend to become more structurally flexible to address unmet needs and to work effectively in unfamiliar contexts. FBOs represent valued assets, and "recognition of the work and leadership of congregations should lead to the inclusion of local [FBOs] in community recovery plans" (Sutton, 2003, p. 424).

Religious entities have historically organized and participated in disaster contexts in a variety of ways. One form of interreligious organization that has become increasingly common after disaster is called "interfaith," an umbrella-type structure that typically works ecumenically across a community (National Voluntary Organizations Active in Disaster [NVOAD], 2006). Ross (1980; see also Ross & Smith, 1974), studying noncatastrophic disasters, found that interfaith organizations require time and effort to emerge, stabilize, establish work domains, and meet goals.

New organizational structures usually emerge where community coordination fails, when authority remains ambiguous, and/or when unmet needs arise (Drabek, 1986; Parr, 1970; Quarantelli et al., 1983; Tierney, Lindell, & Perry, 2001). For new efforts, groups, or organizations to emerge, key social conditions must exist, including predisaster ties, resources, and a legitimizing social setting (Quarantelli et al., 1983), all of which were undermined by Katrina. Conditions that inhibit social and political equality may also affect emergence, such as when those leading recovery fail to meet the needs of historically disenfranchised or excluded groups (Neal & Phillips, 1990; Phillips, 1993). Large sectors of the Gulf Coast population met those criteria (Cutter, 2006). To illustrate, FEMA failed to provide adequate numbers of wheelchair-accessible trailers. Although FBOs provided assistance with building ramps, an advocacy-based lawsuit (*Brou et al. v. Federal Emergency Management Agency et al.*) resulted in the development of a new system to identify and meet needs. In addition, repopulation and rebuilding remain uneven across New Orleans, with low-income and minority neighborhoods lagging. In these areas, FBOs and community-based partnerships have had to advocate for reconstruction, provide resources, and launch rebuilding. In short, the stage was set for great need as well as challenging conditions that would potentially thwart the emergence and establishment of local efforts such as interfaith alliances.

Consequently, recovery committees of varying kinds formed across many of the communities affected. Many committees struggled to form in a context in which travel remained difficult and both the normal volunteer cadre and faith communities remained dispersed across the nation. Dozens of FBOs entered the communities and made significant commitments. Non-local FBOs set up partnerships with local congregations, worked with recovery committees, and partnered with community organizations.

To summarize, religion provides positive reinforcement for participation and offers an organizational vehicle through which meaningful social exchange can occur. In the catastrophic context following Hurricane Katrina, it would not be unreasonable to assume that the massive flooding would undermine the ability of the faith-based sector to participate. Yet FBOs played a crucial role in preparing New Orleans to help people come home.

DATA SOURCES AND METHODOLOGY

In this chapter, we draw on a variety of data sources. First, we rely on our insights as volunteers and community activists as a way to contextualize and bring to life the faith-based community's response. We also acknowledge insights generated from participatory processes including meeting with ministers, congregations, and faith-based community organizations and providing direct services (e.g., meals, cleaning equipment, and clothing) to clients, parishioners, and congregations. We have taken care to exclude data gained through the private conversations that took place in volunteer environments and to use only general insights from public sources, open events, annual reports of FBOs, and local newspaper accounts. Use of such publicly available reports, also known as *unobtrusive measures*, is common practice in traditional disaster research (Stallings, 2001; Webb, Campbell, Schwartz, Sechrest, & Grove, 1981).

Additional data came from a study on shelters funded by the National Science Foundation; this effort included qualitative interviews with more than 80 shelter managers across Texas, Louisiana, and Mississippi. To gather these data, we amassed a database of nearly 1,000 shelter locations, then conducted random sampling to identify a representative set of Red Cross and non–Red Cross shelters. About half of the Red Cross shelters opened in worship centers but were operated by trained Red Cross staff and volunteers.

To summarize, we draw on three main data sources: participation, unobtrusive measures available from FBO Web sites and newspapers, and interviews. This use of multiple methods represents a traditional strategy called *triangulation* that can enhance the credibility and trustworthiness of the analysis (Erlandson, 1993; Lincoln & Guba, 1985; Webb et al., 1981). We conducted basic data analysis efforts based on Spradley's (1980) developmental research sequence that uncovers cultural domains—in this instance, the domains of FBO involvement.

FAITH-BASED ORGANIZATIONS AND DISASTERS

Emergency managers divide their respective tasks into four overlapping phases called the *comprehensive emergency management cycle* (FEMA, 2007; National Governors Association, 1978). These phases include (a) mitigation projects designed to reduce future risks; (b) preparedness efforts that include education, planning, and training; (c) response efforts that focus on saving lives; and (d) recovery work such as rebuilding. Traditionally, FBOs participate during the response and recovery periods. For example, when a disaster occurs, the Southern Baptist Men's Association arrives with trucks of cooking equipment and shower facilities. The Church of the Brethren provides child care so that families can begin household recovery. Lutheran Disaster Response sets up long-term rebuilding projects. Most major denominations have established, national-level disaster programs.

During the 1980s and 1990s, FBOs became increasingly organized and specialized and began to network inter-organizationally. To illustrate, the National Voluntary Organizations Active in Disaster formalized its efforts in January of 1978 to coordinate, cooperate, and communicate disaster education, mitigation, and outreach efforts (for more information, see http://www.nvoad.org/history). A wide number of national FBOs participate as members, including Catholic Charities USA, Christian Reformed World Relief Committee, Presbyterian Church (USA), and United Jewish Communities. Statewide and even local Voluntary Organizations Active in Disaster (VOADs) developed as well. Areas with repetitive hazards tend to have more active state-level VOADs.

The value of a well-trained VOAD with participating FBOs was evident in the 1999 Oklahoma tornado outbreak. A historic storm that spawned widely destructive F5-level tornados occurred on May 3, a Monday evening. By Wednesday morning, the Oklahoma VOAD had convened its first meeting in the Oklahoma Civil Defense and Emergency Management offices. By Friday, the Adventists had organized a massive donations warehouse. Within the warehouse, AmeriCorps volunteers sorted and organized items while U.S. Department of Housing and Urban Development personnel provided database expertise and faxed inventory lists to FBOs and the American Red Cross. Goodwill and Second Harvest served as distribution centers.

What has become apparent in the past 20 years is that FBOs, as part of the disaster volunteer sector, have developed a specialized division of labor, one that can be counted on in the aftermath of major disasters. The creation of the Federal Response Plan in the early 1990s, which later morphed into the National Response Framework, yielded more formalized coordination and connection. The National Response Framework groups functional needs into emergency support functions (ESFs); volunteer organizations and FBOs work under ESF 6. This ESF is typically managed by a FEMA staff member called the *voluntary agency liaison*, who serves as a critical staff linkage between federal efforts and FBOs.

Faith-Based Organization Response After Hurricane Katrina

In the first 10 days after Katrina, we witnessed a massive FBO effort in which congregations served public need by opening shelters, feeding the displaced, providing clothing and other goods, and generally caring for many of the displaced residents across dozens of states. They provided safe harbor and gave refuge to tens of thousands who had lost homes, loved ones, neighborhoods, and entire cities to the storm and flood.

The first VOAD meeting, which included many FBOs, occurred at the Baton Rouge Catholic Charities office 1 week after the hurricane, with an overflowing crowd in attendance. The Louisiana VOAD and FEMA voluntary agency liaisons organized the meeting, informed FBOs of the location, secured snacks and beverages, organized a directory of those in attendance, and provided expertise and insights. A number of organizations new to disaster response attended, such as local Muslim and Buddhist organizations, as well as a local National Guard unit recently back from Iraq.

The majority of local FBOs appeared to be involved in managing shelters and donations. The more experienced national organizations discussed where to set up projects, a difficult decision to make considering the widespread destruction. Within a few weeks after the storm, most national and some local FBOs had found desk space at FEMA's Baton Rouge headquarters, where they coordinated under ESF 6 and organized rebuilding projects. Under the National Response Framework, resources are provided to responding agencies and organizations, including computers, telephones, supplies, and, of particular importance, information and a place to meet. Regular teleconferences connected participating organizations to foster collaboration. FEMA also generated a listserv for participating organizations that included a daily situation report. Phillips described the structure as follows:

> As one of those FBO volunteers, I was grateful for the framework that FEMA and especially the voluntary agency liaisons provided. I was touched by how people I had interviewed as a university researcher for previous disasters now viewed me as one of them and went out of their way to ensure my integration into the process. I felt like I was part of the FBO and VOAD "family" that I had observed as a researcher, and they willingly and patiently helped me with everything. The time and care they gave to the survivors was humbling.

With national FBOs participating in the structure developed by VOAD, Hurricane Katrina was met with many different types of response that were connected, in varying degrees, to a larger institutional structure. Because of the severity of the storm, many of the FBOs met unexpected needs during the response phase. A number of faith-based shelter managers that we visited in Mississippi indicated that they had taken boats into flooded areas to rescue people from their homes, driven them to shelter, provided first aid, and assisted them with temporary housing. Typically, the American Red Cross opens shelters as part of their congressional mandate. The evacuation of New

Orleans, coupled with massive Gulf Coast damage, overran Red Cross capabilities. Data gathered under a project funded by the National Science Foundation indicate that at least 40% were faith based, non–Red Cross shelters ranging from local churches opening their doors to massive, community-wide efforts supported by multiple denominations.

Faith-based shelters provided comprehensive services to those who were displaced. To illustrate, one Mississippi Baptist church took in a multigenerational family from New Orleans. Because most families expected to be gone from their homes only a few days, they did not have sufficient clothing or funds. As the days progressed and it became clear that all of the family's generations had lost their homes, the church found rental housing so all could stay in the same apartment complex. The church paid the rent for 6 months on all of the units; provided food, furniture, and clothing; and assisted the family in finding local employment. The teenager in the family enrolled at a local college. We found this extensive support, with attention to a range of basic needs, not the least bit unusual in faith-based sheltering services.

Among the variety of services FBOs provided to displaced persons, reuniting families and loved ones emerged as a novel yet crucial function. Faith groups offered several types of reunification services. First, shelters established lists of residents and posted or shared the names. Second, they enabled families to search for missing loved ones on Web sites and provided access to computing services; in addition, volunteers searched Web sites to aid residents. Third, they worked to reunite those from their own congregations through phone calls, e-mails, and other means, even hiring people to help find missing persons. Fourth, FBOs provided funds to purchase bus and airplane tickets and even drove families to distant locations.

Katrina brought members of many different racial and ethnic groups together. From our shelter research, it was clear that the first few days were challenging. Primarily because of media accounts of crime and violence within the Superdome, some providers were fearful and uncertain about persons arriving from New Orleans. Within a week, however, both shelter staff and residents settled down and began to build relationships. Indeed, Mississippi shelter managers and residents often described their experiences as being "like family," although this experience was not necessarily the norm across all shelters.

Many faith-based shelters also tried to address cultural differences, especially those revolving around diet and food. Understanding such cultural needs is important because familiar foods offer comfort and a small sense of continuity amid uncertainty and upheaval. A familiar diet is especially important for children because few children will eat unfamiliar foods, and those who do so may develop digestive problems.

One Mississippi church shelter faced challenges in trying to provide culturally appropriate food for Vietnamese American families. The church found a way for these families to cook their own fish. When the families left, they constructed a handmade sign from spare wood, electrical tape, and nails that spelled out "Thanks you." A predominantly White church housing primarily African American residents worked with local African American businesses to bring in culturally specific beauty and skin care products. In one Louisiana shelter, the manager arranged for Cajun foods to be served on Saturday nights. The length of stay for shelter residents was ultimately much longer than anyone could anticipate, and this cultural sensitivity was important.

One Muslim organization involved in its first disaster response sought out Muslim sisters and brothers in traditional shelters and brought them to the local mosque. Imagine, for example, being faced with the ubiquitous ham and white-bread sandwiches in a shelter; indeed, this group faced a tough choice between eating whatever food became available and honoring their religious prohibition on eating pork. Involving a variety of FBOs in outreach efforts can assist with the identification of and attention to spiritual and cultural issues and help avoid complications from dilemmas such as that faced by Muslim evacuees. As one Muslim woman said to us, "Just let us walk through the shelter in our traditional shalwar qamiz. . . . Muslim women will approach us."

Moreover, as shelter stays lengthened, providing for special needs, usually under the purview of the American Red Cross, became part of the faith-based response for a time. In Louisiana, "Deaf churches" provided context in a world in which those who were Deaf lacked the signs to explain and understand how their community had been ravaged; church staff rescued Deaf residents from flooded areas. Other denominations tried to reach out as well. For example, the United Jewish Communities provided social services to low-income elderly persons. Overall, however, according to our interviews with shelter managers operating in faith-based locations, meeting special needs proved especially challenging. In many cases, because they lacked resources or experienced volunteers, they inappropriately sent persons with disabilities to Red Cross special needs shelters.[1]

The immediate medical needs in the Katrina-affected areas were much greater than anyone could imagine. Local Episcopalians, with support from their national counterpart, worked with the St. Thomas Louisiana State University Health Clinic to support its pediatric program and helped to fund a mobile medical unit. Tzu Chi Buddhists sent a mobile dental van to Houston. Volunteers from Operation Blessing and Ananda Marga Universal Relief

---

[1]*Special needs* are those that may require additional planning and expertise, such as when people need medical support or supervision. People with disabilities should be accommodated in general populations shelters per Americans With Disabilities Act recommendations rather than in special needs shelters, and thus it was inappropriate to send someone who could not hear or had a mobility disability to a special needs shelter when they should have been accommodated in a general populations shelter.

Team entered shelters and neighborhoods. Many of these programs continued giving health aid more than 2 years later.

The giving, as in any disaster, also took the form of donations. Donations can become a significant problem after a disaster when massive amounts of unsolicited items pour into an area, requiring the redirection of personnel to sort, organize, distribute, and store the materials (Neal, 1994). Fortunately, the Adventists secured a massive warehouse and worked to inventory items and make the list accessible nationally through an online inventory control system. Multiple waves of volunteers, who arrived with their own travel trailers, provided warehouse support and other key resources. A local National Guard unit assisted with warehouse logistics and transportation. Across all affected states, local denominations collected, organized, and distributed food, clothing, toys, and diapers to individuals and organizations. Despite the clear need for a range of items (e.g., beds, wheelchairs, diapers), the abundant donations, particularly used clothing, would become a problem for FBOs and community organizations everywhere. As Kevin Brown, director of Trinity Christian Community Center, remarked, "Used clothes are the last thing people want when they have no place to put them." Brown used a donated circus tent to house all the donations behind his center. Eventually, he replaced all the old clothes with new clothes donated by corporations from around the world.

At the same time that these organizations were receiving goods, they were busy helping with supplies for a massive cleanup. The Salvation Army (among dozens of other faith-based and non-faith-based organizations) worked with several local congregations and national denominations to distribute cleaning supplies, food, and water. These sites stayed open for months as people returned to the city at different times to begin gutting and salvaging their houses. Other smaller FBOs also provided cleaning supplies. Residents from Louisiana parishes and Mississippi counties would often come across a small truck from a congregation with members standing on the side of the road distributing water, snacks, and cleaning supplies.

Faith-Based Organization Recovery Efforts

The recovery period marks the beginning of efforts to return people to a stable household in which they can cook, sleep, and care for each other, a place from which no additional moves are necessary (Quarantelli, 1982). In more typical disasters, organizations may expect to stay in place for up to 2 years during the rebuilding process. With Katrina, however, the needs will linger far longer. USA Today (Szabo, 2007) conservatively estimated that well in excess of half a million faith-based volunteers worked on approximately 53,000 Gulf Coast homes within the first 2 years after the storm, activity that has continued.

FBOs have taken both routine and nontraditional avenues to help rebuild the city. As with the immediate response, FBOs found new ways of working in this recovery period. Unlike fires or earthquakes, many buildings and homes were left standing but were filled with mud, mold, and damaged contents. Communities could rebuild, but first they had to salvage their belongings, decide what could be saved, and gut their homes. Throughout the area, national organizations, congregations from other states, and local FBOs began the process of salvaging and gutting houses for their congregation members and the community at-large. FBOs such as the Nazarenes sent week-long mission teams to don protective clothing and sort through the structural and material remains of strangers' lives. FBO volunteers worked in high temperatures and humidity to rip out drywall, ceilings, and insulation; remove nails; bleach studs; and tenderly wash family china. Throughout the city, numerous signs bore "Catholic Charities," "Trinity Christian Community Center," or the names of other FBOs in front of gutted houses, businesses, or community centers.

Volunteer labor—including the thousands who came and continue to come to the area—was a major factor in accomplishing this work. Most aid typically arrives in the first few weeks after a disaster. However, the majority of volunteer effort is needed 6 to 12 months later, or, in the case of Katrina, even years later. Presbyterian Disaster Assistance, for example, set up six large tent cities for Katrina volunteers across Louisiana and Mississippi in 2007 (http://www.pcusa.org/pda). Other Presbyterian churches hosted mission teams, providing their own self-contained beds, cooking facilities, showers, and projects. The Presbyterians are only one of a range of faiths working in such a manner across the Gulf Coast. USA Today's survey (Szabo, 2007) indicated that the Southern Baptist Convention had sent more than 175,000 volunteers, Habitat for Humanity supported more than 71,000, and Nazarene Disaster Response provided more than 15,000.

Nearly 2 years later, gutting and salvaging work continued, with tens of thousands of homes remaining to be done—a process normally completed within a few months in most disasters. By the 3rd year, when most communities have returned to a sense of normalcy, uneven recovery and a housing shortage characterizes New Orleans: "The pace of home renovations and demolitions has slowed by half as compared to last year. . . . Rising rents, now 46% higher than before the storm, threaten the ability of many essential service workers to afford housing, as wages are not keeping pace" (Brookings Institution, 2008, p. 7).

Although dozens of FBOs have participated in the rebuilding process to date, the efforts of the Mennonite Disaster Service illustrate well how the faith-based sector contributes. Mennonite Disaster Service often selects the most marginalized and impoverished communities and families to support, particularly elderly individuals, persons with disabilities, and single parents. Mennonite Disaster Service sets up its own volunteer centers with available or imported housing. A volunteer project director handles setup, work crews, and case management. Work teams typically come for a week at a time, eat in a common kitchen, and sleep in group quarters. The main offices of the Mennonite Disaster Service provide daily support for decision making, problem solving, and funding. Further, Catholic Charities is working with the city of New Orleans and others to rebuild low-income housing. Trinity Christian Community Center is also involved in neighborhood development, acquiring property, rebuilding homes, and providing these homes to former residents.

In many cases, rebuilding homes is not the end of FBOs' involvement. Returning a family to their residence, one that has been obliterated by a tornado or inundated by floodwaters, requires more than physical construction. Families need appliances, furniture, bedding, clothing, food, and more to reestablish a household routine. Organizations like the Salvation Army, Goodwill, St. Vincent de Paul, and Second Harvest offer specific items and services. Their participation is crucial because the majority of donations arrive, unsolicited, in the immediate aftermath. Storing those items until families can return—perhaps years later, as is the case for many families following Katrina—is an important role.

Beyond Paint and Drywall

The gutting, salvaging, rebuilding, and reconstruction are critical elements in recovery, but the psychological and emotional needs are just as important. The loss and stress of rebuilding in a devastated area take an enormous toll on individuals and families, and there are a number of examples of the faith-based response to this ongoing experience. For instance, as recovery efforts unfold, local and national organizations often form partnerships designed to identify and meet the needs of those who would otherwise "fall through the cracks." NVOAD (2006) indicated that these efforts can take several forms and names; most commonly, they are known as *unmet needs committees* or *interfaith committees*. For example, after the 1989 Loma Prieta earthquake in California, the Watsonville Area Interfaith Disaster Relief formed to help those who were having trouble rebuilding their homes. This organization facilitated local reconstruction by serving as a vehicle for funds, communication, and coordination. In 2006, the Louisiana Interchurch organization formed to foster a holistic vision of recovery across the denominations. In a typical unmet needs committee, local and national organizations hear a caseworker present a family's needs, then offer to provide appropriate assistance. For any given family, a dozen organizations or more might participate in securing the necessary resources, expertise, transportation of materials, labor, and funding to rebuild. This process has been unfolding slowly in Louisiana parishes.

A particular kind of disaster case management has developed to assist people affected by Katrina. Most families have never had to build a home, particularly not in a situation with so many potential complications. Families have often had to make very quick decisions about whether to gut or tear down their damaged property. Families might face specific and circumscribed decisions, such as replacement of household appliances, or major decisions, such as rebuilding from the ground up, while living hundreds of miles away from the work site. Case management, in which case workers help families through the recovery experience, often unfolds through a combination of local FBOs, voluntary organizations, and experienced social service providers. Typically, communities find, train, and maintain a cadre of case managers, which can be exceptionally difficult, and turnover may be high. Working with traumatized disaster victims facing extraordinary adversity requires experience and local knowledge; these qualifications are often in short supply.

Until Katrina, case managers usually adapted or created case management forms and processes. After Katrina, the United Methodist Committee on Relief (UMCOR) created intake, assessment, and recovery planning forms, as well as processes for implementation, assessment, closure, and monitoring. UMCOR also sponsored a Web site designed to assist case managers. UMCOR's efforts represent the first national endeavor to support case managers so they may better assist their clients. UMCOR has been supported through a creative interfaith effort that included the Episcopal Church. Locally, the Louisiana Interchurch and other local FBOs are providing support to case managers.

Another example of a desperate need in New Orleans centers on child care. The Church of the Brethren has historically provided certified Disaster Child Care program support for affected families. Without such help, families cannot get back to work or negotiate the cumbersome processes involved in rebuilding homes. The Mennonites, for example, are working with a local nonprofit, Goodworks, to create capacity for child care providers. Together with this nonprofit, they wrote a U.S. Department of Education grant application that allows for the training of local people to open small day care centers. The Lutheran Disaster Response has organized Camp Noah, featuring week-long recovery experiences for children in kindergarten through sixth grade. Daily activities and therapy are organized around themes of preparedness, evacuation, temporary housing, and hope.

In Katrina's aftermath, many secular organizations and FBOs coalesced to provide support for survivors (e.g., American Red Cross Access to Care program). Louisiana Spirit (see chap. 10, this volume), which began in the aftermath of Hurricanes Katrina and Rita, offers recovery counseling services free of charge throughout the state. Through its providers, the federally funded, state-operated program has made almost 2 million counseling contacts with Louisiana residents. In addition to individual counseling, Louisiana Spirit offers group counseling for first responders and others affected by the hurricanes. Many of the Louisiana Spirit contracts went to FBOs such as Catholic Charities.

Not surprisingly, in the midst of disaster, church life continues. Funerals are held, baptisms are scheduled, and people still get married. People move into and out of temporary homes and into permanent housing. Life transition services are provided by FBOs, such as when Ananda Marga meets evacuees at their temporary trailers and provides welcome kits. FBOs often host house "blessings" when they turn over the keys to the family, home at last and free from further moves. A religious symbol may be offered to the family or placed on the wall, and holy items such as a Bible or a Quran may be given to the family. Blessings and dedications represent the culmination of weeks to years of efforts, with tremendous emotion and satisfaction among those present. Families and volunteers may very well stay in touch beyond the blessing, forming long-term friendships. The service to the families does not go unrewarded; representatives of diverse denominations report that family members who received assistance often volunteer in new events.

When families come home, they may face limited worship opportunities. Katrina destroyed massive numbers of worship locations, and congregants have remained dispersed. New Orleans' local churches established satellite branches in various locations where ministers and evacuees temporarily dwelled. Pastors evolved into the old "circuit rider" ministers, traveling by airplane rather than horseback to maintain the spiritual welfare and social connections of the community. For example, the New Orleans Franklin Avenue Baptist Church, which had more than 7,000 members before Katrina, offers services in Houston, Baton Rouge, and New Orleans. Moreover, denominations have shared resources in response to the devastation. Some church buildings house more than five congregations each Sunday. Spiritual support is, of course, a critical element of the faith-based efforts, and it takes a number of forms. Perhaps most commonly, organizations offer both direct and indirect spiritual support through prayer. A National Day of Prayer has been held, and Web sites, newsletters, and direct appeals for both general and specific prayer have been used. FBOs working on rebuilding projects list prayer concerns on their Web sites and may list a prayer request for a particular individual or family.

Beyond the Collection Plate

To pay for all these projects, FBOs have provided millions of dollars to hundreds of efforts. Nearly all FBOs involved in the response and recovery have given grants, jointly funded various initiatives, and worked to main-stream money into the organizations working locally. Here, we highlight several unique funding efforts that are making a local difference—programs that fill needs that are not typically recognized. For example, the storm and its aftermath destroyed three domestic violence programs below Interstate 10 in Louisiana. In response, Catholic Charities, which ran the only battered women's shelter in Orleans Parish, began to rethink how to provide services in the aftermath of the disaster. Because of their work, in collaboration with the city and the state, this organization is in the process of receiving federal funding to collaboratively build a Family Justice Center. Many others, such as the Tzu Chi Buddhists, have directed funds into the hands of victims through gift cards. Recognizing that those in need require more than a home for psychological and social recovery, United Jewish Communities gave money to help build a New Orleans playground.

Though FBOs typically focus on families, houses, and rebuilding, Katrina destroyed places of work and created or worsened poverty conditions. FBOs stepped in to help with these needs. The United Jewish Communities, recognizing a highly vulnerable population, funded job training for seniors. The Mennonite Central Committee partnered with the Mennonite Disaster Service to offer microloans for reestablishing local and home-based businesses. These endeavors were just the beginning of the additional roles FBOs have undertaken following Katrina.

Rebuilding the infrastructure of the city meant that the congregations stepped out into more secular relationships and partnerships. For example, congregations that still have their buildings and infrastructure are often serving many purposes. In New Orleans, the local Unitarian Universalist building hosts many community organizations and work groups that consistently meet in this still gutted-out structure. Other congregations or FBOs, such as Trinity Christian Community Center, also house community meetings, community development organizations, and after-school programs.

Following the storm, many organizations began to work on their disaster plans. For example, during 2006–2007, a number of stakeholders working with elderly evacuees started meeting to outline the issues, underscoring the vulnerability of this group. Because of the slow recovery, the elderly population remaining in New Orleans are less able to prepare and plan for the next storm. Critical players in this process include Catholic Charities and Operation Brother's Keeper.

It is not surprising that the politics of New Orleans altered in the wake of the storm. The greatest changes involve not the mayor's office but the City Council, school board, and levee boards. The City Council was nearly completely changed, the levee boards were reduced to two, and the Orleans Parish School Board lost control of all but four schools to private charter schools and the state-run Recovery School District. The 2006 mayoral election created a setting for the religious community to play an unusual role. Reverend Tom Watson, head of the Greater New Orleans Coalition of Ministers and one of the most powerful African American ministers in New Orleans and the South, ran in the primary for mayor. Historically, religious leadership in New Orleans has played a role in highlighting issues of concern in the city, including crime, education, and housing. Reverend Watson and other spiritual leaders again stepped out into the secular world within their spiritual context. Instead of supporting a mayoral candidate or city council candidate, however, they became candidates themselves (Lee, 2006).

LESSONS LEARNED AND ACTIONABLE RECOMMENDATIONS

It is not surprising that the faith community continues to play a major role in a city where FBOs are so strong. National-level FBOs are always involved in disaster recovery across the nation, though not to the extent seen following Katrina. Local congregations, although struggling to return, are determined to contribute. It is clear that FBOs represent crucial resources for recovery. However, all of this effort is not without criticism. Some local FBOs thought that not enough of the money was channeled to their efforts, whereas others thought there was too much focus on the faith-based aspect of service provision. Regardless, the response from the largest organization to the smallest congregation helped to steer the course of recovery.

Further, the experience of Katrina highlights just how integrated congregations are within their communities. Beyond the traditional responses (i.e., food, clothing, supplies, spiritual needs), these organizations became even more embedded in these communities when they addressed issues of housing, employment, medical care, and the comprehensive services necessary for families to return home, provide for themselves, and repopulate a devastated city. In the sections that follow, we reflect on these insights and provide recommendations for future efforts. We conclude with suggestions for necessary research to observe fully the ways in which FBOs participate in all phases of disasters.

Recommendations for Faith-Based Organizations

Katrina nearly destroyed local faith-based capacity to respond. To ensure that local congregations are prepared for a disaster, a number of actions can be taken. For example, national FBOs should encourage local congregations to become more disaster resilient, as doing so would increase their ability to respond after a disaster. Strategies for disaster resiliency might include efforts to protect the congregation's physical facilities, staff, and parishioners. For example, local congregations should write and practice disaster plans. Buildings, offices, and homes could be assessed for structural weaknesses, and efforts could be made to mitigate potential damage and to develop a plan to house staff if their homes are damaged. Local congregations can also offer training for specific skills. Predisaster training that would translate well to postdisaster environments includes repair projects at worship centers, congregate care facilities (e.g., faith-based children's homes), and the homes of elderly or disabled parishioners. Outreach efforts could include distributing educational materials and holding workshops for disaster preparedness. The National Organization on Disability offers an educational outreach program, Congregations Who Care Prepare, and disability-specific brochures on disaster preparedness (http://www.nod.org).

Because FBOs help those at highest risk, they might prepare in advance to do so. FBOs that open shelters, for example, should plan and train for special needs populations—for example, by creating shelter intake and discharge procedures and preparing staff to accommodate persons with special needs. FBOs may be wise to preestablish local partnerships with other providers to address needs often not met after a disaster, such as those experienced by battered women and children, seniors in need of transportation, or families requiring child care. Case management to assist survivors through the recovery process often involves FBOs, so training to do this work in a sensitive, professional capacity can be done in advance.

Interfaith alliances often emerge after a disaster. Local clergy can preestablish such efforts by integrating disaster planning into local ministerial alliances. For example, FBOs and interfaith committees usually organize and distribute donations, so a plan to manage this effort should be written and in place before disaster strikes. Likewise, interfaith committees' rebuilding efforts operate best with preplanning and training. FBOs can also volunteer for local disaster organizations such as the VOAD, Red Cross, and others to build effective interpersonal working relationships, enjoy access to disaster-specific training, and become part of the local disaster team available for a response. These other partners bring expertise and resources to the efforts described above and can assist with integrating FBOs into the local, state, and federal response and recovery efforts.

Recommendations for Emergency Management Practice and Policy

Because FBOs represent such a useful and extensive resource, emergency managers who organize disaster mitigation, preparedness, response, and recovery activities should take advantage of this valuable asset. As a starting point, the NVOAD Web site provides links to information about national disaster organizations and state VOADs. FEMA also offers free online courses on voluntary organizations, including FBOs, at their independent study Web site (http://training.fema.gov/IS/crslist.asp). FBOs can provide labor, skills, and support to underresourced emergency management offices at the local and state levels. To maximize these resources, emergency managers and other officials involved in handling disasters should invite FBOs to their meeting and planning sessions and to disaster exercises and trainings. Such cross training fosters more effective partnerships because people learn how their roles and responsibilities fit together. Educating representatives from the FBO sector about the practice of emergency management can help managers identify areas in which local congregations might provide support.

The information and experiences summarized here can also inform and guide aspects of local and national policy. The National Response Framework would benefit by informing all agencies participating in all emergency support functions about the capacities and resources of FBOs and other voluntary organizations. A number of FBOs, for example, provided health care after Katrina, which might be integrated in ESF 8 regarding public health. Similarly, FBOs could help convene neighborhoods to talk about recovery visions, typically part of the responsibility of ESF 14, which normally does not involve FBOs. Indeed, citizens might feel more comfortable with FBO involvement, particularly in communities characterized by spiritual depth.

The American Red Cross and FEMA should work with FBOs to develop effective sheltering strategies for future events, particularly for evacuees representing diverse cultures and with varying special needs, an effort with which some FBOs struggled. The role of the FEMA voluntary agency liaison should be supported further with resources and staffing, as it represents a crucial integrative position linking unmet needs with experienced organizations and their resources. These partnerships need to be strengthened over time so that in the next disaster, federal and relief aid is coordinated with FBOs.

Remaining Research Questions

Until this analysis, scholars have not identified the many ways in which FBOs participate in disaster response and recovery. Yet many questions remain, suggesting that the scant research on FBO involvement must be expanded. As this chapter represents the first overview, it would be helpful to identify the full range of ways in which FBOs contribute to disaster response and recovery. Moreover, because of the catastrophic consequences of Katrina, the functions identified here may not be typical. Sutton (2003) found that FBOs adapt structurally following a disaster. Could it also be true that FBOs adapt functionally as well? Are FBOs organizational chameleons, able to meet needs as they arise and then flex back into normal operations? Our work suggests that

Parr (1970) and Quarantelli et al. (1983) were correct that organizations address unmet needs and that organizational emergence occurs in some combination of new structures and new tasks. In our study, most organizations existed rather than emerged. What we observed most commonly was a form of function-based emergence, or the taking on of new tasks, similar to Dynes's (1970) characterization of how extending organizations (those that exist before the disaster but grow in size and take on new tasks) operate in disasters.

Yet prior studies have taken place during more typical disasters. How does the Katrina context influence functional adaptation? Further, are there consequences of this functional adaptation, particularly for FBO missions, structure, funding, volunteers, and staff or for federal response and recovery? Should there be such consequences, given that catastrophic events are not typical of the disasters to which most agencies and organizations respond? Finally, should consideration be given to the role that FBOs play, primarily in response and recovery, when mitigation and preparedness efforts have a greater chance of reducing the impact of disasters? Could the energies and resources of FBOs be directed toward disaster reduction efforts?

New Orleans will remain a research site for perhaps decades to come. A number of questions remain that might be examined longitudinally. For example, the number of legal and undocumented immigrants has increased. Some of these immigrants need services, including translation, housing, and employment. Several local FBOs are responding. What will the continued role of the FBOs be with the newest immigrant populations? Does Katrina represent a turning point in local FBO activity that will continue? Crime rates, including homicide and other forms of crime, are also on the rise. Disaster-related crime, such as the theft of copper tubing and wiring from homes and businesses, has appeared. Domestic violence, suicide, and mental illness rates are rising. Will FBOs view this work as part of their mission to help create safer, healthier communities?

In New Orleans, housing of any kind remains the greatest unmet need, although affordable housing—an issue in many communities before a disaster but especially so in this city—is the biggest challenge. How long will FBOs participate in housing recovery efforts? At what point do efforts at postdisaster housing recovery cease and those consistent with predisaster initiatives return? How do FBOs negotiate their role in this transition?

The nearly immeasurable loss is how the waters washed away much of the indigenous neighborhood life—music, food, relationships. As FBOs work in New Orleans, their volunteers and staff learn about local cultures, fostering an intercultural exchange. How will that exchange influence FBOs? Will FBOs see a role for themselves in sustaining local cultures through their work, as the many volunteers working on building housing in the Musicians' Village are doing?

What Does This Mean for the Future?

Faith-based organizations were not the only organizations to respond to the storm in novel ways. Community organizations with no official religious ties are working tirelessly to meet some of the same needs as FBOs. Katrina and the government response at all levels left a void that many rushed to fill. We are not, in any way, advocating the reduction of the government role in future disasters. Instead, we argue that the embeddedness and connections that FBOs offer constitute a successful model to be documented, evaluated, and perhaps replicated in other disasters.

When disasters disrupt social structure, FBOs usually play a role centered on restoring the social institution of the family through rebuilding homes and providing related social services. However, the catastrophic nature of this event destroyed elements necessary for families to return: jobs, schools, health care, child care, places of worship, parks, opportunities to participate in the political system, and more. FBOs were required to think through their efforts holistically, understanding that this time, it would take more than lumber and labor to serve those in need. In short, FBOs began completely rebuilding entire communities rather than single homes.

If disasters disrupt normal routines, then catastrophic events undermine the stability and functioning of society. Religion traditionally functions to bring people together and serves to unite people through shared social bonds (Durkheim, 1912). FBOs support that function in a disaster context as well; in a catastrophic context, FBOs help restore entire societies. Thus, this chapter discussed how congregations and FBOs participated in the recovery by examining the ways they shored up social institutions (e.g., family, jobs, education, political participation, and the religious institutions themselves) and helped restore shared social bonds and functioning. Indeed, after Katrina, FBOs engaged in a broad range of traditional and nontraditional efforts to serve humanity. We close with an observation by Jenkins:

> This is only the beginning of the story. As local congregations struggle to return or make decisions whether to return, they have to decide how they are going to rebuild not just the physical structures, but also their communities. Further, a number of local FBOs received substantial financial, technical, and personal support from their national organizations. It will become crucial for local organizations to define their relationship to these national organizations. Local organizations need to mediate between what national organizations say they can do versus what the local organizations are able to articulate as what they need in a post-Katrina world. Everything in New Orleans is different. The floodwaters have receded. Yet the faithful return and remain.

REFERENCES

Aguirre, B., Wenger, D., & Vigo, G. (1998). A test of the emergent norm theory of collective behavior. *Sociological Forum*, *13*, 301–320.

Americans With Disabilities Act, Title 42, chapter 126, §§ 12101–12213 and Title 47, chapter 5, §§ 225 and 611, U.S.C. (1990).

Brookings Institution. (2008). *The New Orleans Index anniversary edition: Three years after Katrina.* Retrieved November 7, 2008, from http://www.brookings.edu/reports/2007/08neworleansindex.aspx

Metropolitan Policy Program at Brookings & Greater New Orleans Community Data Center. (2008, August). *New Orleans index: Tracking the recovery of New Orleans & the Metro Area: Anniversary edition: Three years after Katrina.* Washington, DC, and New Orleans, LA: Authors.

Brou et al. v. Federal Emergency Management Agency et al., U.S. Dist. Ct. No. 06-0838 (E.D. Louisiana, 2006).

Cutter, S. (2006, June 11). *The geography of social vulnerability: Race, class, and catastrophe.* Retrieved March 30, 2009, from http://understandingkatrina.ssrc.org/Cutter/

Day, W. (2007). [Faith-based organization return rates]. Unpublished data, New Orleans Baptist Theological Seminary, New Orleans, LA.

Drabek, T. E. (1986). *Human system responses to disaster.* New York: Springer-Verlag.

Durkheim, E. (1912). *The elementary forms of religious life.* New York: Oxford University Press.

Dynes, R. (1970). *Organized behavior in disaster.* Lexington, MA: Heath Lexington Books.

Erlandson, D. (1993). *Doing naturalistic inquiry.* Beverly Hills, CA: Sage.

Federal Emergency Management Agency. (2007, May 24). *IS-1 Emergency Manager: An orientation to the position.* Retrieved March 30, 2009, from http://training.fema.gov/EMIWeb/IS/is1.asp

General Accountability Office. (2006a, March 8). *Hurricane Katrina: GAO's preliminary observations regarding preparedness, response, and recovery.* Retrieved June 7, 2007, from http://www.gao.gov/new.items/d06442t.pdf

General Accountability Office. (2006b, June 8). *Hurricanes Katrina and Rita: Coordination between FEMA and the Red Cross should be improved for the 2006 hurricane season.* Retrieved June 7, 2007, from http://www.gao.gov/new.items/d06712.pdf

Johnson, N. (1988). Fire in a crowded theater. *International Journal of Mass Emergencies and Disasters*, *6*, 7–26.

Johnson, N., Feinberg, W. E., & Johnston, D. M. (1994). Microstructure and panic. In R. Dynes & K. Tierney (Eds.), *Disasters, collective behavior, and social organization* (pp. 168–189). Newark: University of Delaware Press.

Lee, T. (2006, April 10). Tom Watson: He's preaching city unity, healing. *New Orleans Times-Picayune*. Retrieved November 20, 2007, from http://www.nola.com/frontpage/t-p/index. ssf?/base/news-5/114464966694290.xml

Lincoln, Y., & Guba, E. (1985). *Naturalistic inquiry*. Beverly Hills, CA: Sage.

National Governors Association. (1978). *Comprehensive emergency management*. Washington, DC: Author.

National Voluntary Organizations Active in Disaster. (2006, October). *Long-term recovery manual*. Available at http://www.nvoad.org/NewsInformation/Planning Documents/tabid/83/Default.aspx

Neal, D. M. (1994). Consequences of excessive donations in disaster: The case of Hurricane Andrew. *Disaster Management, 6*, 23–28.

Neal, D., & Phillips, B. (1990). Female-dominated local social movement organizations in disaster–threat situations. In G. West & R. Blumberg (Eds.), *Women and social protest* (pp. 243–255). New York: Oxford University Press.

Nelson, L. D., & Dynes, R. (1976). The impact of devotionalism and attendance on ordinary and emergency helping behavior. *Journal for the Scientific Study of Religion, 15*, 47–59.

Parr, A. (1970). Organizational response to community crises and group emergence. *American Behavioral Scientist, 13*, 424–427.

Phillips, B. D. (1993). Cultural diversity in disasters. *International Journal of Mass Emergencies and Disasters, 11*, 99–110.

Quarantelli, E. L. (1982). *Sheltering and housing after major U.S. disasters*. Newark: University of Delaware, Disaster Research Center.

Quarantelli, E. L. (Ed.). (1998). *What is a disaster?* London: Routledge.

Quarantelli, E. L. (2006, June 11). *Catastrophes are different from disasters: Some implications for crisis planning and managing drawn from Katrina*. Retrieved March 30, 2009, from http://understandingkatrina.ssrc.org/Quarantelli

Quarantelli, E. L., Neal, D. M., Green, K., Ireland, E., McCabe, S., Phillips, B., & Hutchinson, D. (1983). *Emergent citizen groups in disaster preparedness and recovery activities*. Newark: University of Delaware, Disaster Research Center.

Ross, A. (1980). The emergence of organizational sets in three ecumenical disaster recovery organizations. *Human Relations, 33*, 23–29.

Ross, A., & Smith, S. (1974). *The emergence of an organizational and an organization set: A study of an interfaith disaster recovery group* (Preliminary Paper No. 16). Newark: University of Delaware, Disaster Research Center.

Spradley, J. (1980). *Participant observation*. New York: Holt, Rinehart & Winston.

Stallings, R. (Ed.). (2001). *Methods of disaster research*. Philadelphia: Xlibris, International Research Committee on Disasters.

Sutton, J. (2003). A complex organizational adaptation to the World Trade Center disaster: An analysis of faith-based organizations. In J. L. Monday (Ed.), *Beyond*

September 11: An account of post-disaster research (pp. 405–428). Boulder, CO: Natural Hazards Center. Retrieved June 7, 2007, from http://www.colorado.edu/hazards/publications/sp/sp39/sept11book_ch16_sutton.pdf

Szabo, L. (2007, July 18). Faith rebuilds house and soul. *USA Today*, pp. 1–2.

Tierney, K., Lindell, M., & Perry, R. (2001). *Facing the unexpected*. Washington, DC: Joseph Henry Press.

U.S. House of Representatives. (2006). *A failure of initiative*. Retrieved June 7, 2007, from http://www.gpoaccess.gov/katrinareport/mainreport.pdf

Webb, E. J., Campbell, D. T., Schwartz, R., Sechrest, L., & Grove, J. B. (1981). *Nonreactive measures in the social sciences*. Boston: Houghton Mifflin.

III

WHAT LESSONS HAVE BEEN LEARNED? CONCLUSIONS, IMPLICATIONS, AND RECOMMENDATIONS

10

THE AFTERMATH OF HURRICANE KATRINA: MENTAL HEALTH CONSIDERATIONS AND LESSONS LEARNED

JOY D. OSOFSKY, HOWARD J. OSOFSKY, MINDY KRONENBERG, AND TONYA CROSS HANSEL

Despite the lessons learned from experiences during and after the terrorist attacks of September 11, 2001 (9/11), the Oklahoma City bombing in 1995, and recent destructive hurricanes in Florida, the response to Hurricane Katrina was grossly inadequate. Neither the City of New Orleans, the State of Louisiana, nor the federal government was prepared to respond to the disaster and the damage caused by the hurricane and the flooding. The inadequate response continued in the immediate aftermath, and the nation watched as the crisis deepened. Unlike most disasters, which have a circumscribed period of crisis followed by gradual recovery, progress and recovery following Hurricane Katrina remain slow. Factors contributing to problems with recovery relate to the extent of devastation, displacement of families and other supports, job loss, lack of clarity about rebuilding, and questions about the federal commitment to supporting adequate levee and coastal protection.

We thank the Trauma Team faculty in the Department of Psychiatry at Louisiana State University Health Sciences Center for their dedication and courageous work in the aftermath of Hurricane Katrina. This project was partially funded by Substance Abuse and Mental Health Administration Grant 5U79SM6203 to the Louisiana Rural Trauma Services Center, Baptist Community Ministries, and Louisiana Spirit through our work with the Louisiana Crisis Counseling Program.

Reflecting both limited economic resources and the typical response to hurricanes along the Gulf Coast, many people chose not to evacuate and were then trapped in their homes or in the Superdome. Patients, doctors, nurses, staff, and family members were stranded at hospitals without power and with limited food and supplies. First responders faced conflicting loyalties—the need to care for their own families versus their commitment to the responsibilities of their positions and colleagues. Despite flooded headquarters, police districts, and firehouses, and disabled or destroyed equipment, first responders struggled valiantly to evacuate New Orleans and the metropolitan area and to protect the city. Family members, unfortunately, were sometimes separated; with inadequate space for all in rescuing helicopters, parents hesitantly but desperately handed over their children, hoping to keep them safe. The immediate and continuing response to the disaster can rightfully be characterized as chaotic.

BACKGROUND

The first and second authors of this chapter, Joy D. Osofsky and Howard J. Osofsky, worked at the Command Center and in New Orleans with city, state, and national leaders and volunteers from around the country, providing help and advice as requested and needed in an atmosphere filled with concern and uncertainty. Since the initial days after Hurricane Katrina, these authors, along with the Department of Psychiatry at Louisiana State University Health Sciences Center (LSUHSC), have taken on multiple roles for the state Office of Mental Health (OMH) and metropolitan New Orleans. Given the background and long-standing experience of the authors and the Department of Psychiatry faculty related to trauma, disaster, and terrorism, including work with first responders and children and families, the Office of Mental Health of the Louisiana State Department of Health and Hospitals requested that Howard J. Osofsky serve as clinical director of the overall behavioral health crisis response and for Louisiana Spirit, the state crisis counseling program; OMH requested that Joy D. Osofsky serve as clinical director for child and adolescent services for Louisiana Spirit.

During the days immediately following Hurricane Katrina, Mayor Ray Nagin requested that the LSUHSC team provide direct services for New Orleans first responders and their families who had lost so much; heavily devastated St. Bernard Parish followed with a similar request. LSUHSC faculty have provided Psychological First Aid (Brymer et al., 2006; see also chaps. 8 and 12, this volume), crisis intervention, and resilience building—that is, support to build on strengths and respond to adversity in healthy and constructive ways. The LSUHSC Trauma Team provided outreach in nontraditional settings, including on the streets; at temporary headquarters, districts, and fire stations; and on cruise ships housing first responders and their families. The team provided services for children and adolescents in schools, preschools, and child care centers (including Head Start and Early Head Start) serving displaced children and those returning to metropolitan New Orleans. Faculty continued to identify needs and provide resilience-building and psychoeducational services for children and adolescents.

We (Joy and Howard Osofsky) vividly remember our initial return to our beloved city after Mayor Nagin's request, each of us in separate state police cars, surrounded by armed police for protection and taken by a circuitous route to enter the still-flooded city. With so much devastation and destruction, we were overwhelmed not only with sadness but also by the suffering, bravery, and commitment of those with whom worked. We knew that our city would never be the same and that we must help in the response, recovery, and rebuilding.

A few of our first remembrances include trudging through water to City Hall and walking up to the ninth floor (no elevator or central air conditioning) to meet with ranking New Orleans police officers in a temporary office. They interrupted their meeting and wanted to talk with us about two respected officers who had just committed suicide. We remember entering the Sheraton Hotel on Canal Street, where some police were quartered before the cruise ships arrived, and having to be cleared by security guards who we were told would shoot anyone who was not properly accompanied. We recall meeting a ranking police officer, diabetic and without insulin, who refused to leave his position because of his sense of duty and responsibility; later, almost in diabetic shock, he had to be taken for an emergency evaluation to the one operating hospital in the city.

In the aftermath of Hurricane Rita, which hit during the third week in September, a ranking police officer asked us to come into the totally evacuated city. As we sat with him in front of Harrah's Casino, feeling like we were in a deserted Wild West city, another officer on medical leave asked for our help. He had been awaiting a transplant before the storm but insisted on reporting for duty. With the stress of the disaster, he had resumed smoking and, as a result, could not be retained on the transplant list. He was very worried and wondered whether we could help him stop smoking. In the staging area for emergency response in the evacuated city, a woman fell to her knees, crying "thank God!" when she saw us. She pleaded with us to help her as her quadriplegic son's motorized chair and equipment were in their flooded house in an area where passes were not allowed. Without the chair, he was confined to bed and would deteriorate both physically and emotionally. Fortunately, the police officers we were with volunteered to retrieve what she needed.

We also remember a first responder, himself on a roof, threatening to jump. He had just learned that his wife, who had evacuated with their child, would not return. Their marriage was over. He tearfully described loving her and their child and felt that without them, his life was not worth living. We were able to help him through the crisis. Finally, we remember a first responder who was a single parent and whose daughter was displaced to another community. She worried that even when she received her paycheck, she would not know how to send money to her daughter. She was torn between her responsibility to her child and her loyalty to her colleagues.

PSYCHOLOGICAL EFFECTS OF HURRICANE KATRINA ON CHILDREN AND ADOLESCENTS

It is important to recognize that most children and adolescents cope successfully and demonstrate adaptive coping skills following traumatic exposure. Masten (2001) described the ordinary magic of resilience, and Benight and Bandura (2004) referred to such responses as defining self-efficacy. At the same time, data from a number of studies demonstrate higher incidences of emotional, behavioral, developmental, and academic difficulties following traumatic exposure (Cicchetti & Toth, 1997; Eckenrode, Laird, & Doris, 1993; Goenjian et al., 2005; Mollica et al., 2004; Osofsky, 1997, 2004; Pfefferbaum, Nixon, & Krug, 1999).

Following natural disasters, children and adolescents experience stress reactions, increased risk of psychological disorders, and behavioral difficulties. The reason for these problems is that children's typical supports may not be available following a disaster. Bronfenbrenner (1979), in his ecological systems theory, viewed the child's development within the context of the system of relationships that form his or her environment. The interaction between factors in children's maturing biology, their immediate family and community environment, and the society in which they live guides their development. Bronfenbrenner observed that changes and conflicts in one layer ripple through and affect other layers.

Katrina affected multiple systems, leading to multiple such ripples. Following Katrina, most children were displaced from their homes, and many were separated from their families; even if they were with their families, they frequently were living in very crowded conditions. Almost all children were in new and unfamiliar schools, were not with and could not communicate with their friends, and did not have the usual routines and supports that are so important for psychological health. These changes affected children's social and emotional development and mental health. When elevated mental health symptoms meet criteria for a disorder, posttraumatic stress disorder (PTSD) and mood disorders (Briere & Elliot, 2000; De Bellis & Van Dillen, 2005) are the most commonly diagnosed. Children demonstrate symptoms similar to those of adults in addition to developmentally specific symptoms such as regression, separation anxiety, clinginess, increased aggression, and withdrawal.

Surveys of 8,226 children and adolescents carried out 6 months after 9/11 focused national attention on the impact of trauma exposure on children, with data showing considerably elevated rates of PTSD, major depression, separation anxiety, phobia, conduct disorder, and alcohol use (Hoven, Duarte, & Mandell, 2003). Nearly two thirds of the children had experienced exposure to trauma before 9/11 (Schaffer et al., 1996). Further trauma exposure can reawaken previous traumas and contribute to current symptoms. Other literature supports the finding that children who have experienced previous loss or trauma are at higher risk of mental health problems than those without such histories (Bowlby, 1973; Goenjian et al., 2005; Laor et al., 1997; Osofsky, 2004; Pynoos, Steinberg, & Piacentini, 1999; Vernberg, La Greca, Silverman, & Prinstein, 1996).

With a disaster of the proportions of Hurricane Katrina, which brought so much loss, separation, slowness of recovery, continuing displacement, and lack of support, outcomes for children are influenced significantly by family stability and support factors. In reaction to a different disaster, but focusing on family issues, Laor, Wolmer, and Cohen (2001) assessed the long-term consequences of a 1991 SCUD missile attack in Israel for children as a function of family factors, including maternal psychological functioning and family cohesion. Laor et al. studied 81 children ages 8 to 10 years whose homes were damaged in the missile attack. They examined stress, internalizing (withdrawal, depressive reactions), externalizing (aggressive, acting out behaviors), and posttraumatic stress symptoms (e.g., avoidance of thinking about the trauma, reexperiencing the event through language or play, numbing of affect, and hypervigilance). Greater symptom severity was associated with being displaced, living in a family with inadequate cohesion, and having a mother with poor psychological functioning. Parents were found to be less emotionally available to the children because of their own traumatization. Younger children evidenced more symptoms than older children.

Other studies (e.g., Beardslee et al., 1988; Shalev et al., 1998; Silverstein, Augustyn, Cabral, & Zuckerman, 2006) have also shown that if parents or caregivers are not doing well because of the circumstances of their own lives, depression, other mental disorder, or prior exposure to violence, their young and adolescent children may experience increased distress and symptoms. These parents, like those described by Laor et al. (2001), may have been less emotionally available to their children.

In attempting to understand the effects of the hurricane and flooding on children and adolescents in New Orleans, it is helpful to consider the previous studies on populations affected by a hurricane. Sutker, Corrigan, Sundgaard-Riise, Uddo, and Allain (2002) and Smith and Freedy (2000) found that previous exposure to trauma predicted an increase in symptoms following a hurricane. Gittelman (2003) found that living in a shelter and under stress for an extended period predicted increased emotional problems. Following hurricanes and flooding, higher incidences of PTSD, major depressive disorder, and symptoms consistent with both disorders have been observed (Assanangkornchai, Tangboonngam, & Edwards, 2004; Briere & Elliot, 2000; Fullerton & Ursano, 2005; La Greca, Silverman, Vernberg, & Prinstein, 1996; Norris, Murphy, Baker, & Perilla, 2004; North, Kawasaki, Spitznagel, & Hong, 2004; Shelby & Tredinnick, 1995; Vernberg et al., 1996).

This literature is helpful because it may enhance understanding not only of factors that may contribute to more symptomatic and problematic reactions but also of factors that may lead to resilience (Luthar, 2003). For example, shelters (if children and families must live in them) could be designed to provide activities for children and on-site child care so that children can play and experience more "normal" behaviors and support and parents who are also traumatized can receive respite. For displaced families living in transitional communities, community centers, recreational areas, and supports for children and families would make a significant difference in adjustment. Finding permanent housing for displaced families faster and developing a plan for rebuilding that minimizes bureaucratic red tape are crucial for reestablishing stability in families' lives.

ROLE OF FIRST RESPONDERS IN A DISASTER

Hurricane Katrina highlighted the crucial role of first responders in times of disaster, as well as the enormous stress that they and their families face. First responders are required to meet the challenges of the community—maintaining safety, rescuing and saving lives, and helping to evacuate those with special needs. Frequently, neither first responders nor their organizational structures have made adequate plans for their families, including evacuation, shelter, temporary financial resources, medical care, communication, and other necessary support. Following Hurricane Katrina, first responders struggled to perform their duties to serve and protect, with disruptions of facilities and infrastructure, difficulties in communication, lack of equipment, problems with evacuation, increased work-related medical risks, a populace under stress, and the need to make painful triage decisions. Compounding the stress of their work responsibilities during and after the hurricane, first responders were separated from their families and often, because of difficulties with communication, did not know about their well-being and safety.

Given the severity of the crisis, during the initial weeks following Katrina, LSUHSC psychiatry faculty focused on meeting the immediate needs, and giving Psychological First Aid (Brymer et al., 2006) and crisis response to first responders and their families. Eighty percent of first responders in New Orleans suffered severe or irreparable damage to their homes (Kronenberg et al., 2008). Those who did not lose their homes often suffered survivor guilt because so many of their colleagues had lost so much. Family members were living in other communities, at times sharing crowded facilities, separated from relatives and friends. When first responders had a limited period of time off, they had to commute long distances to be with their families, trying to meet the needs of spouses or partners and children while exhausted and pressured themselves. With their many work responsibilities to keep citizens safe and continually respond to emergency situations, the personal problems caused by the hurricane made their lives that much more stressful.

First responders need additional training in responding to community distress and community psychosocial needs during times of crisis and in preparing their own families to ensure safety and improved communication. At the local, state, and federal levels, a heightened state of preparedness for disasters is needed. At the local level, preparedness means having equipment to respond despite the elements, which, in the case of Hurricane Katrina and the breach of the levees, caused flooding. At the state level, preparedness means having an organized response in place to help a city by coordinating activities with needed federal help. At the federal level, preparedness means being responsive immediately with sensitivity to the area being served, despite the role that politics may play. When a disaster strikes, human lives need to be saved and cities helped despite geography; political influence in the state; or racial, ethnic, and socioeconomic composition.

An appreciation and understanding of culture and context need to be incorporated into the training of aid workers and program responses to victims of disasters. Cultural competence is important so that those intervening can function within the context of behaviors and beliefs of members of diverse populations in local communities. In the New Orleans metropolitan area, there is much diversity in race, ethnicity, and socioeconomics. Multigenerational family, kinship, and faith-based ties are very important components of life. New Orleans, the hub of the region, is a community with much history and character but also a legacy of racism and poverty. Within New Orleans, a majority of the population is African American and has a Protestant affiliation. The population of the adjacent, and highly devastated, St. Bernard and Plaquemines parishes is primarily White, with a Catholic affiliation. In general, these communities are composed of hardworking blue collar families who are employed in factories working in the petrochemical and fishing industries.

Before Hurricane Katrina devastated New Orleans in August 2005, the reported poverty level was 23%, which was considerably higher than the national average of 13%. Following Katrina, 70% or more of students in all three parishes were eligible for free or reduced-cost school lunches (Osofsky, Osofsky, & Harris, 2007). Yet when the children and adolescents who were forced to evacuate returned to metropolitan New Orleans, they were relieved, despite the continuing stresses, to be back in their communities, where they felt better understood and more comfortable.

CHILDREN OF FIRST RESPONDERS ON THE CRUISE SHIPS

About 2 weeks after the storm, two cruise ships arrived at Julia Street Harbor in New Orleans to provide temporary housing for first responders and family members who were able to return to New Orleans and to neighboring St. Bernard Parish; approximately 95% of first responders from St. Bernard Parish had lost their homes (Louisiana Long-Term Community Recovery Team, 2006). Joy D. Osofsky and Howard J. Osofsky lived with the first responders on one of the ships. A senior social worker on our LSUHSC faculty, whose home was heavily damaged, also lived on one of the ships to coordinate behavioral health activities. The LSUHSC Department of Psychiatry and Pediatrics Trauma Team faculty, with specific knowledge and training in working with traumatized children and families, was equipped to provide supportive services for first responders and to help develop services for their returning children. The authors recognized that to support *resilience*—that is, the ability to recover in the face of adversity and adjust to misfortune or change—it was crucial to establish some sense of normalcy and routine in the now "abnormal" world. Forty-five children and adolescents returned when the cruise ships docked in New Orleans. Our team worked diligently with the New Orleans Police Department (NOPD), New Orleans Fire Department, New Orleans Health Department, the Federal Emergency Management Agency (FEMA), and the Coast Guard to encourage children to return and to allow them to live on the ships with their families. The authors also worked with the departments of education and district superintendents in neighboring parishes so that the children would be able to go to school. They firmly believed that first responders and their families would be stronger and more resilient if, despite the ongoing stresses, they were able to be together. By February 2006, as many as 780 children were living on these ships at any time.

Faculty and trainees, joined by Substance Abuse and Mental Health Services Administration (SAMHSA) volunteers, provided services on the decks and in the cafeteria and recreation areas. Temporary offices were established on the cruise ships, wherever space was available, to provide support, help families with day-to-day problems, help them regain stability and security, foster resilience, and build a sense of community. For example, many families felt isolated from their extended families and friends who were displaced to other states. Therefore, the team went beyond usual mental health services and worked with the ship staff to set up movie nights, Saturday activities for children, and other usual activities, such as religious services on the boats. Further, the team provided child care and respite for parents, arranged for school enrollment for children together with departments of education and the NOPD, and provided after-school and weekend services and activities.

The children were pleased to be reunited with their parents. However, initially many appeared dazed and unsettled. Young children were clingy and did not want to be out of their parents' sight. Children of every age missed friends and relatives. Cell phones and the Internet, when they became available, helped considerably. Children worried about pets, especially if they did not know their whereabouts. Older adolescents missed normal peer activities. They worried about graduation and getting into college, as well as whether student loans would be available if they had missed the deadlines to apply. Some wondered whether jobs would be available, whether they could move in with friends, and whether they should or could leave their families, as they had planned, to attend college. Children, even older youths, despite seeing pictures of the devastated areas, were convinced that their homes were OK and just needed to be swept up and organized again.

Charles Currie, director of SAMHSA, came to New Orleans 2 weeks after the ships were docked to review the status of the crisis response and to help determine what additional services were needed. The team was able to share with him the results of the screening needs assessment that had been carried out with 71 of the initially returning children. The screening instrument used was the National Child Traumatic Stress Network (NCTSN) Hurricane Assessment and Referral Tool for Children and Adolescents (NCTSN, 2005), with modifications in wording suggested by local stakeholders to be responsive to ethnic and racial diversity of the populations as well as differences in socioeconomic background. In addition, school system administrators and personnel and LSUHSC faculty adapted the wording of questions to make them more familiar and user friendly so that youths in the 4th through 12th grades could complete the instrument themselves. The assessment measure helped the team learn more about the children's functioning and needs.

A few stories from the cruise ships:

- The older brother of a 5-year-old girl, who acted as her "protector," told us how well she was doing, but with eyes down, she sadly described missing friends and a sense that students at her new school did not like her.

- A 5-year-old boy rode out the storm at the Superdome with his grandparents, who now worried about his withdrawn behavior. While at the Superdome, he turned 6 and did not understand why his father, a first responder, did not bring a birthday cake as expected (his family was initially concerned about whether his father was alive; he was alive but trapped and could not communicate with his family). The boy gradually described how scary it was to be at the Superdome and even on the cruise ship.
- A female first responder tearfully cried, "Please, make it go away; I just want to be able to do my washing and ironing and make a home for my daughter." Her home was destroyed and her possessions lost. We discussed both the difficult realities and her continuing importance as a parent and a role model. She then reflectively quoted Martin Luther King and described her ability to rely on his words in helping to reestablish her own strength.
- A mother with two young children, one of whom was severely developmentally disabled and being wheeled by his "big" brother (who was also just a child), initially did not make eye contact with our social worker or talk with other parents. She began to brighten after the social worker arranged for special services for her child; she had believed that this could not again be a reality. As she began to take better care of herself, she offered to teach the social worker about hair grooming.

WORKING WITH CHILDREN AND ADOLESCENTS IN SCHOOLS

On the basis of a long-standing collaborative relationship, during the weeks immediately following Katrina, the late Cecil Picard, superintendent of the Louisiana State Board of Education, requested that Joy D. Osofsky and Howard J. Osofsky help meet the needs of students, parents, and school personnel in devastated parishes and work with the department of education in developing a mental health component for Project SERV (School Emergency Response to Violence). Joy D. Osofsky also played a key role in establishing the interface and collaboration between Project SERV and Louisiana Spirit.

In early October 2005, the Osofskys and the LSUHSC Trauma Team established what has evolved into an extremely meaningful relationship with the newly established post-Katrina St. Bernard Unified School District. St. Bernard Parish was the most heavily affected parish and was almost completely destroyed by the flooding. All of the schools were flooded, and most were totally destroyed. A toxic oil spill led to further questions as to whether the parish could be resettled. Doris Votier, the courageous superintendent of the St. Bernard School System (later honored with the John F. Kennedy 2007 Profile in Courage Award), believed that the school system should serve as the center of the rebuilding and recovery of the community and that there must be a functioning school system if people were to return to the parish. We volunteered to work with Votier and Associate Superintendent Beverley Lawrason as they started their school in temporary modular trailers and classrooms. We all agreed that more mental health support would be very important because so many children and families had experienced much trauma. When the St. Bernard school system reopened, pre-Hurricane Katrina principals returned as teachers with necessary reductions in salary. Administrators, teachers, and students alike lived in tents or trailers in St. Bernard Parish or with relatives, some commuting 4 hours daily to be able to return to their school. Initially, the Unified School District expected about 150 students to return; instead, 350 returned. By January 2006, 1,600 had returned. Votier was determined to have a functioning school building by January 2006. Although FEMA respected her determination, their guidelines and regulations would have delayed necessary structural changes until May or June of 2006. Votier persisted and obtained contracts to follow her timetable. Chalmette High School, one of three high schools in the parish before the storm, was reopened as a unified school on schedule in January 2006 with not only high school students, but elementary and preschool students as well. The school was very crowded, and modular classrooms and trailers were still needed, but the spirit and commitment were palpable.

From the beginning, Votier, Lawrason, and the teachers worried about how their students and families were doing, how much they had lost, and how they were currently living. Administrators, teachers, and other school employees worried that at the end of the day, students would leave their school buses and go into darkened areas, as power and light had not yet returned to the parish. Using temporary structures, they provided hot lunches to returning students, knowing that this might be their only hot meal for the day. One child said, when served a hot spaghetti and meatball lunch, "We have real food!"

The superintendent's office asked that we collaborate with them to screen all students returning to the school to identify service needs and provide services to students with difficulties. We obviously could not refuse; both the need and the motivation were so high. What has evolved is a lifelong friendship and collaboration. Early in our work in St. Bernard schools, a fine and overworked member of our faculty asked, "How can I volunteer the extra time needed in St. Bernard Parish?" The next day, he described a student who needed to be evaluated. Although the student had clear mental health symptoms, his main concern was, "How do I help rebuild my parish?" The faculty member, like others on our team, never again questioned the extra work. We cannot emphasize too much the dedication and inspiring work of the administration and teachers within this school district; they consistently demonstrated devotion to students and a commitment to education and supportive services.

The LSUHSC Department of Psychiatry's dedicated Trauma Team simultaneously reached out to Orleans and Plaquemines parishes. The then-president of the Orleans Parish School Board, Reverend Torin Sanders, asked for help in October 2005. Because of the already failing schools, after Katrina the state legislature placed most of the schools in the New Orleans Public Schools (NOPS) into a new Recovery School District under the Louisiana State Board of Education. The remaining NOPS schools lost key administrative and school facilities, but in 2005–2006, five schools reopened. With repair of buildings and hiring of staff, NOPS currently operates 18 schools, including regular and charter schools. President Sanders's successor and current president of the school board, Phyllis Landrieu, has been untiring in opening quality schools, working with the Charter and Recovery Schools, and developing the Greater Achievement Program, a new quality facility to provide education and community-based comprehensive services for children ages 0 to 5 and their families (VanDenBerg & Grealish, 1996). In the fall of 2006, the Trauma Team collaborated with NOPS in screening all returning students and developing supportive services.

Many other schools throughout the region have turned to LSUHSC for support and services. For example, in January 2006, the Sisters of the Holy Family opened the MAX School, which brought together three high-achieving Catholic schools in New Orleans to provide ongoing education to their students. Two of the three schools operating before Hurricane Katrina were unusable, so they combined the schools for the first year. Over the years, this Catholic order of predominantly African American clergy has provided fine educations for African American students, many of whom have become leaders in the community. Although facilities were limited, dedication to education remained paramount. The order has now reopened the three schools, one in a borrowed school building.

Many families who evacuated from New Orleans because of the hurricane had no home or job to which they could return. However, these families did return to the city, and they cited allowing their child to return to their pre-Katrina school as a primary reason for doing so. Although the area was devastated, schools served as a safe haven in the midst of the crisis. The children were able to reconnect with their friends and have a sense of normalcy when they were in school. Many families reported that their children were happier when they returned to New Orleans and their schools because they no longer felt like outsiders. They shared stories of strength but also feelings of being rejected in many of the schools they attended in other communities. They poignantly shared being teased for being "trailer trash" and missing the culture, including the food, in New Orleans. Although they were appreciative of the schools that took them in, many did not feel accepted in other communities.

Unfortunately, some adolescents were living on their own with little supervision because of family circumstances, crowding in trailers, and limited options for displaced families. Counselors and teachers described worrisome behaviors in both elementary and older students, including an inability to pay attention in class, disruptive behaviors, changes in behaviors and friendships, and risk taking. They mentioned adolescents being unable to talk with their parents because of the parents' traumatization and stress interfering with their being emotionally available to listen to their children. Schools recognized that they needed additional support for their students, teachers, and families to address the stresses created by the traumatic experiences and the ongoing recovery process. The older children had little to do after school, and substance use and risky sexual behaviors were common. Younger children showed disruptive and aggressive behaviors, withdrawal, inability to concentrate, and depression. Training school personnel, local providers, and others to recognize "red flag" behaviors can be extremely helpful.

UNDERSTANDING THE EXPERIENCES AND NEEDS OF CHILDREN AND ADOLESCENTS

The NCTSN's (2005) Hurricane Assessment and Referral Tool for Children and Adolescents was useful in gathering data about experiences and reactions of the youths returning to the New Orleans metropolitan area. The schools gathered the data in collaboration with LSUHSC, and respondents represented a cross-section of all children affected, primarily those returning to the most heavily affected areas. The results were used to help respond to needs (e.g., promoting resilience) and develop services (e.g., psychotherapeutic interventions) to support the children and adolescents.

In the first year, 2005–2006, the screen was administered to 2,585 children and adolescents in the 4th through 12th grades in Orleans and St. Bernard Parishes, all of whom had been displaced, and in St. John Parish, a parish that received many displaced children. The sample was 44% White, 46% African American, and 4% Hispanic, with the remainder (6%) other ethnic and racial groups. The mean age of the students was 14.60 years ($SD = 2.45$), and the sample was approximately evenly divided between boys and girls. At the time of the survey, 55% reported living with both parents and 38% with either their mother or father. They reported that they had attended as many as nine schools ($M = 2.13$, $SD = 0.93$). Some of the experiences children had during the hurricane are shown in Table 10.1.

Many children reported trauma symptoms consistent with PTSD and depression, with 77% of students endorsing at least one symptom. The most frequently reported symptoms were worry (45%), trying to avoid thinking about the hurricane (35%), and becoming upset when thinking about hurricane-related experience (30%). Substantial proportions of children also reported difficulty concentrating (28%), said that "nothing is fun anymore" (26%), and noted somatic complaints such as increased headaches or stomachaches (24%). More than a third of the children reported depression, loneliness (many missed friends), sadness, and anger. Forty-nine percent of the children and adolescents met the norm-based cutoff for referral for mental health services.

As mentioned earlier, there is considerable support in the trauma literature indicating that children who have experienced previous trauma or loss are at higher risk for mental health problems. Thirty-eight percent of the children surveyed reported having experienced previous trauma or loss; a greater proportion of these students met the NCTSN cutoff for referral for mental health services, $\chi^2(1) = 5.26$, $p = .022$.

All of the children who met the cutoff for mental health referral were seen in consultations with LSUHSC clinicians. Children were also evaluated if they exhibited significant behavior or emotional problems at school or at home and were referred by school personnel or parents. Most of the children who were referred had experienced multiple traumas, including interpersonal and hurricane-related events. Social workers, psychologists, and psychiatrists provided individual psychotherapy using a variety of evidence-based techniques depending on the child's age and symptomatology. Many of the children and families were in long-term treatment for a year or more. Following therapy, children demonstrated reduced symptoms of depression and anxiety

TABLE 10.1
Fourth- Through 12th-Grade Students' Experiences
Related to Hurricane Katrina

Experience	%
Student was injured in the storm.	5
Student had family members who were injured.	21
Student had family members who were killed.	13
Student saw neighborhood destroyed or damaged.	94
Student was separated from caregiver.	34
Student's toys and clothes were destroyed or damaged.	68
Student was separated from pet.	34
At least one parent was unemployed because of hurricane.	43

and were able to function well in school and at home. In addition, the LSUHSC program provided each school with a report on the experiences and symptomatology of their student body so that the school could offer appropriate mental health services.

Psychological First Aid (see chaps. 8 and 12, this volume) was widely utilized for individual and classroom interventions focused on supporting teachers, helping children and families stabilize and connect with social support systems, and providing education for teachers and parents on trauma and its effects. Evidence-based individual and group trauma-informed interventions and services were brought to school settings including Trauma Focused Cognitive Behavioral Therapy (Cohen, Deblinger, Mannarino, & Steer, 2004) and Cognitive Behavioral Intervention for Trauma in Schools (Jaycox, 2004; Stein et al., 2003). During groups, students in 7th through 12th grades shared stories about their experiences and helped each other problem solve how to cope with fears. Resilience-building group programs, including Healing After Trauma Skills (Gurwitch & Messenbaugh, 2001), were also initiated in classrooms, after school, and in summer programs, Through learning collaboratives with NCTSN colleagues, we have been providing training to providers in the community on trauma-focused individual, group, and family-oriented services that are evidence based and promising.

We also collected NCTSN Hurricane Assessment and Referral Tool data during 2005–2006 from 760 younger children in collaboration with Head Start, prekindergarten, and first- through third-grade classes. Because these children were too young to fill out the screen themselves, it was modified for parental report. Parents reported that their children attended as many as five schools or centers because of the displacement ($M = 1.87$, $SD = 0.94$, range = 1–9). When children returned, they had to live in trailers, tents, or crowded quarters with relatives or friends. Parental unemployment, according to data from the NCTSN screener, was (and remains) very high in these families' communities. Although the percentage of unemployment has decreased, family disruption continues, with some families separated because of employment in other cities in Louisiana and out of state. Related to additional risk, 17% of the parents reported that their children had experienced previous loss or trauma, such as loss of a relative or exposure to community or domestic violence. Some of the hurricane experiences of children in Head Start, prekindergarten, and first- through third-grade classes are shown in Table 10.2. (We recognize that parents tend to underreport symptoms of their children's exposure to trauma; Martinez & Richters, 1993.)

For these younger children, the parent reports indicated that 32% of the children met the cutoff for mental health services. The most common behaviors reported, quite understandably, were clinginess and separation anxiety. Fifty-two percent of children exhibited PTSD or depressive symptoms.

TABLE 10.2

Head Start, Prekindergarten, and First- Through Third-Grade Students'
Experiences Related to Hurricane Katrina

Experience	%
Child witnessed injury of family member.	5
Child was in new school or center.	82
Child witnessed destruction to community.	38
Child witnessed destruction to home.	77
Child was separated from caregiver.	16
Child was living somewhere different than before storm.	77
Child lived in at least one crowded shelter.	18
Child was living in shelter 6 months after hurricane.	6
At least one parent was unemployed because of hurricane.	76

About 38% of the parents responded that they would like their child to speak to a counselor. These parents understood that even young children are affected by trauma; the high percentage of parents requesting help may also relate to their own desire to talk to a counselor about their feelings of post-hurricane depression and anxiety. The LSUHSC trauma team, in collaboration with schools, provided trauma-focused treatment services in school and after-school resilience-building activities. For younger children and parents, supportive services were provided, as well as trauma-informed and evidence-based Child–Parent Psychotherapy (Cicchetti & Toth, 1997; Lieberman & Van Horn, 2005).

Although these data provide a picture of the mental health status of children returning to the New Orleans area, they do not tell us how well displaced children who did not return were doing in their new environments. Some continued living in difficult, crowded situations and in transitional living communities. Family and economic problems continued, and many of the children and adolescents felt unwelcome in new schools. They missed their familiar environment and may have been doing worse. Others, especially if their families had relocated successfully and had homes, employment, and schools, may have been adapting well and doing better than children who had returned. It is likely that children whose families would have liked to return but could not for economic reasons and lack of housing may have had more problems. Although some of the children we screened continued to live in trailers, relatively little data are available about how they have fared. Anecdotal reports indicate increased violence in at least some trailer communities, as well as rivalries between children and adolescents displaced from New Orleans and those living in the receiving areas (see Center for Empowered Decision Making & Common Health Action, 2006; Osofsky et al., 2007).

LESSONS LEARNED AND ACTIONABLE RECOMMENDATIONS

Perhaps the most important lesson learned from our experiences during and in the aftermath of Hurricane Katrina is that the United States has no clearly articulated disaster plan for children, adolescents, and families and that such a plan needs to be developed (Osofsky et al., 2007). To date, the disaster response in this country has not built adequately on experiences from previous disasters, such as the Oklahoma City bombing and the 9/11 terrorist attacks. Further, for children and adolescents, the response has not been based on sound developmental principles. Issues related to the effects of separating children from their families need to be incorporated in planning. In addition, supports need to be set up for children of different ages, including child care and play situations for younger children, activities with peers for older children and adolescents, support and respite for stressed parents, and activities that include and support both parents and children.

In establishing a national plan that meets the needs of children, adolescents, and families, it is crucial that efforts be made to understand the cultural and economic issues and special needs within communities so that the national plan can be appropriately implemented at the local level. Cultural traditions vary, and activities that are supportive for some groups may not be for others. It is crucial to meet children and parents at their own level related to their needs, expectations, and comfort. At least some volunteers after disasters need to have developmental knowledge and sensitivity to be able to flexibly support children and families in environments in which there is much disruption and chaos. They must be aware of their role in providing temporary support, as most are deployed for only about 2 weeks following a disaster, and of children's and families' needs for ongoing stability and support.

In preparation for disaster response, it is important to have a well-trained cadre of mental health providers with knowledge of developmental considerations in trauma; a practice directorate, including screening and counseling approaches and Psychological First Aid; and trauma-focused, evidence-based therapeutic practices. This knowledge is crucial during the crisis and recovery to build resilience and provide necessary services for children and adolescents. If communities do not have such expertise and resources, there should be agencies available to immediately provide these resources following a disaster.

On the basis of the experience with Hurricane Katrina, there needs to be a plan in place to ensure that children are evacuated safely with their parents or caregivers. During the evacuation of metropolitan New Orleans following Katrina, there were multiple stories of children and parents being separated. With limited resources, well-meaning parents and rescue workers had to make difficult choices about whom to evacuate; thus, at times, parents and children were separated on different buses or helicopters when leaving the city. The attachment literature (e.g., Bowlby, 1973) is grounded in the potential deleterious effects of separation of children and parents; yet without a plan for another major disaster, these types of separations will occur again. Disaster plans need to recognize the attachment needs of children, especially in times of crisis, and prioritize the need for parents to stay with their children at all times to provide a sense of security and reduce long-term mental health sequelae.

Special needs populations, such as children with developmental or medical disabilities, children in foster care, and children who themselves or whose parents have mental health difficulties, must be addressed. A plan should be in place to provide medical records to families of special needs children and to ensure that the continuing support and immediate services that are required be planned for in advance and put in place.

Safety, stability, support, and the reestablishment of routines for children need to be addressed as soon as possible after the disaster. In many communities, as we saw clearly in devastated St. Bernard Parish, the efficient rebuilding and reopening of schools are essential to the recovery of the community. Child care facilities are also essential to recovery. Both contribute to the reestablishment of routines and stability and provide family and community support. Without functioning schools and child care facilities, families could not have returned to St. Bernard Parish, even when family and work responsibilities required that they do so. Creative, "out-of-the-box" plans are needed for recovery, as disasters can result in an abnormal environment for some time. As we have seen, creative thinking can expand the mission of schools to serve children's social, emotional, and mental health needs following a disaster.

Most children and adolescents are resilient in response to disasters. However, we need to support their resilience by creating a normal environment as rapidly as possible. Recognizing students' strengths and providing Psychological First Aid and resilience-building and leadership-enhancing services will support positive contributions, decrease risk-taking behaviors, and have a beneficial impact on others. Resilience-building and leadership-enhancing activities allow children to take control and effectively change their environment. Following a disaster, both children and adults may feel helpless; however, when individuals are successful in achieving goals, their self-efficacy increases. Children ought to be encouraged to express their needs and when possible, encouraged to work together to achieve their goals. One such example occurred when children who were distressed about combining schools and about the loss of trees, grass, and flowers planted a beautiful flower garden with colors representing each of their former schools; they described feelings of hopefulness and their ability to make a difference as they memorialized their schools and planted for the future.

Recovery workers need to recognize the importance of family; friends; pets; and normal age-appropriate activities, such as play and after-school activities. A serious problem observed after Katrina was that many of the typical supporters of children and adolescents, including parents, relatives, teachers, and friends, were also displaced and traumatized, so it was more difficult for them to be emotionally available. As noted, adolescents sometimes reported that they felt they could not talk to their parents because their parents were so burdened and preoccupied with coping with loss, rebuilding, and trying to support their families.

It is essential to recognize the importance of family and family-oriented services. As with other disasters, Hurricane Katrina amply demonstrated the stresses on families—displacement, losses, economic difficulties, over-crowding—and the resultant decline in emotional availability, increased arguments, use and abuse of alcohol and drugs, marital conflict, and even divorce (Hurricane Katrina Community Advisory Group, 2006; Kessler, Galea, Jones, & Parker, 2006; Osofsky et al., 2007). As noted, when parents of younger children requested services for their children, they often were also indicating their own need for support. When parents are not emotionally available to children, additional child and family mental health services are of utmost importance. Mental health services and supports for parents and caregivers must not be ignored. When the parents and caregivers are cared for, they are able to reaffirm their roles as protectors and nurturers of their children. Children with caregivers who are emotionally healthy are most likely to be resilient in the face of disaster.

Mental health professionals who respond to disasters need a firm understanding of attachment theory and the effects of trauma on a young child's sense of safety. We found it best to offer services immediately, gearing the services to the needs that are most important during the crisis and recovery. We also found that collaborative community-based services, including services offered in schools, were far superior to traditional clinic- or office-based therapeutic services. Children and families were appreciative of and more comfortable participating in resilience-building and therapeutic services integrated into schools and other community settings.

We have learned how important it is to bring awareness building, education, and training to the community with developmentally informed, trauma-focused interventions in the aftermath of a disaster. Many well-meaning providers and volunteers are not sufficiently trained to respond sensitively and appropriately to those suffering from trauma and loss. First responders should have training in meeting community psychosocial needs and should know about available resources to support the community and to meet the needs of their own families. Teachers, nurses and counselors, early childhood providers, medical and mental health professionals, and parents should be offered educational workshops about the psychological effects of trauma, red flags indicating the need for help, and the impact of development on the manifestation of symptoms. They also need to be helped with stresses they may be experiencing in their lives, including vicarious traumatization. We have conducted basic and advanced trauma education for parents, school personnel, child care professionals, primary care professionals, and pediatricians at conferences and via telecommunication. We have provided education for mental health professionals at conferences and in learning collaboratives. On the basis of our experience, each group welcomes the opportunity to gain additional training and consultation to build capacity and sustainability of quality services.

It is crucial to focus not only on the disaster but also on the recovery. In the aftermath of Hurricane Katrina, because of the extent of the devastation and difficulties in the response at the local, state, and federal levels, the New Orleans metropolitan area, including three heavily devastated parishes, suffered major disruptions in infrastructure and systems of care. To rebuild takes leadership, energy, and motivation in addition to financial support.

Finally, the issue of vicarious traumatization and burnout among first responders, teachers, parents, community leaders, and other service providers must be taken into account with a disaster of the proportions of Katrina. The losses of so many in the population were great, and progress has been so very slow. We must provide support for those who are rebuilding, teaching and supporting children and adolescents, and caring for others. Self-care is a crucial aspect of recovery and one that has been a difficult lesson to learn for many within the affected areas. Self-care is necessary not only for children, adolescents, and families but also for leaders to support their strength and resilience.

REFERENCES

Assanangkornchai, S., Tangboonngam, S., & Edwards, J. (2004). The flooding of Hai Tai: Predictors of adverse emotional responses to a natural disaster. *Stress and Health, 20,* 81–89.

Beardslee, W. R., Keller, M. B., Lavori, P. W., Klerman, G. K., Dorer, D. J., & Samuelson, H. (1988). Psychiatric disorder in adolescent offspring of parents with affective disorder in a non-referred sample. *Journal of Affective Disorders, 15,* 313–322.

Benight, C. C., & Bandura, A. (2004). Social cognitive theory of posttraumatic recovery: The role of perceived self-efficacy. *Behaviour Research and Therapy, 42,* 1129–1148.

Bowlby, J. (1973). *Attachment and loss: Vol. 2. Separation: Anxiety and anger.* New York: Basic Books.

Briere, J., & Elliot, D. (2000). Prevalence, characteristics, and long-term sequelae of natural disaster exposure in the general population. *Journal of Traumatic Stress, 13,* 661–679.

Bronfenbrenner, U. (1979). *The ecology of human development: Experiments by nature and design.* Cambridge, MA: Harvard University Press.

Brymer, M., Jacobs, A., Layne, C., Pynoos, R., Ruzek, J., Steinberg, A., et al. (2006, July). *Psychological First Aid: Field operations guide* (2nd ed.). Available at http://www.nctsn.org and http://www.ncptsd.va.gov

Center for Empowered Decision Making & Common Health Action (2006, September). *Prepare for the children: A critical phase of recovery: Meeting summary; opportunities and next steps.* Retrieved April 10, 2009, from http://www. commonhealthaction.org/Prepare%20for%20the%20Children%20Strategy %20Report%20Sept%2006.pdf

Cicchetti, D., & Toth, S. L. (1997). *Developmental perspectives on trauma: Theory, research and intervention.* Rochester, NY: University of Rochester Press.

Cohen, J., Deblinger, E., Mannarino, A., & Steer, R. (2004). A multisite, randomized controlled trial for children with sexual abuse related PTSD symptoms. *Journal of the American Academy of Child and Adolescent Psychiatry, 43,* 393–402.

De Bellis, M. D., & Van Dillen, T. (2005). Childhood post traumatic stress disorder: An overview. *Child and Adolescent Psychiatric Clinics of North America, 14,* 745–772.

Eckenrode, J., Laird, M., & Doris, J. (1993). School performance and disciplinary problems among abused and neglected children. *Developmental Psychology, 29,* 53–62.

Fullerton, C. S., & Ursano, R. J. (2005). Psychological and psychopathological consequences of disasters. In J. J. Lopez-Ibor, G. Christodoulou, M. Maj, N. Sartorius, & A. Okasha (Eds.), *Disasters and mental health* (pp. 13–36). New York: Wiley.

Gittelman, M. (2003). Disasters and psychosocial rehabilitation. *International Journal of Mental Health, 32,* 51–69.

Goenjian, A. K., Walling, D., Steinberg, A. M., Karayan, I., Najarian, L. M., & Pynoos, R. (2005). A prospective study of posttraumatic stress and depressive reactions among treated and untreated adolescents 5 years after a catastrophic disaster. *American Journal of Psychiatry, 162,* 2302–2308.

Gurwitch, R. H., & Messenbaugh, A. K. (2001). *Healing after trauma skills: A manual for professionals, teachers, and families working with children after trauma/disaster.* Retrieved June 5, 2006, from http://www.nctsnet.org/nctsn_assets/pdfs/edu_ materials/HATS2ndEdition.pdf

Hoven, C. W., Duarte, C. S., & Mandell, D. J. (2003). Children's mental health after disasters: The impact of the World Trade Center attack. *Current Psychiatry Reports, 5,* 101–107.

Hurricane Katrina Community Advisory Group. (2006, August 29). *Overview of baseline survey results: Hurricane Katrina Community Advisory Group.* Retrieved April 10, 2009, from www.hurricanekatrina.http://www.hurricanekatrina.med. harvard.edu/pdf/baseline_report%208-25-06.pdf

Jaycox, L. (2004). *Cognitive behavioral intervention for trauma in schools.* Longmont, CO: Sopris West Educational Services.

Kessler, R. C., Galea, S., Jones, R. T., & Parker, H. A. (2006). Mental illness and suicidality after Hurricane Katrina. *Bulletin of the World Health Organization, 84,* 930–939.

Kronenberg, M., Osofsky, H. J., Osofsky, J. D., Many, M., Hardy, M., & Arey, J. (2008). First responder culture: Implications for mental health professionals providing services following a natural disaster. *Psychiatric Annals, 38,* 114–118.

La Greca, A., Silverman, W., Vernberg, E., & Prinstein, M. (1996). Symptoms of posttraumatic stress in children after Hurricane Andrew: A prospective study. *Journal of Consulting and Clinical Psychology, 64,* 712–723.

Laor, N., Wolmer, L., & Cohen, D. J. (2001). Mothers' functioning and children's symptoms 5 years after a SCUD missile attack. *American Journal of Psychiatry, 158,* 1020–1026.

Laor, N., Wolmer, L., Mayes, L., Gershon, A., Weizman, R., & Cohen, D. (1997). Israeli preschool children under SCUDs: A 30-month follow-up. *Journal of the American Academy of Children and Adolescent Psychiatry, 36,* 349–356.

Lieberman, A. F., & Van Horn, P. (2005). *Don't hit my mommy: A manual for child–parent psychotherapy with young witnesses of family violence.* Washington, DC: Zero to Three Press.

Louisiana Long-Term Community Recovery Team. (2006). *St. Bernard Parish— Disaster impact and needs assessment.* Retrieved April 10, 2009, from http://www.louisianaspeaks-parishplans.org/IndParishHomepage_BaselineNeedsAssessment.cfm?EntID=13

Luthar, S. S. (Ed). (2003). *Resilience and vulnerability: Adaptation in the context of childhood adversities.* New York: Cambridge University Press.

Martinez, P., & Richters, J. E. (1993). The NIMH Community Violence Project: II. Children's distress symptoms associated with violence exposure. *Psychiatry, 56,* 22–35.

Masten, A. (2001). Ordinary magic: Resilience processes in development. *American Psychologist, 56,* 227–238.

Mollica, R. F., Lopes Cardozo, B., Osofsky, H. J., Raphael, B., Ager, A., & Salama, P. (2004). Mental health in complex humanitarian emergencies. *Lancet, 364,* 2058–2067.

National Child Traumatic Stress Network. (2005). *Hurricane Assessment and Referral Tool for Children and Adolescents.* Retrieved October 10, 2005, from http://www.nctsnet.org/nctsn_assets/pdfs/intervention_manuals/referraltool.pdf

Norris, F., Murphy, A., Baker, C. K., & Perilla, J. L. (2004). Postdisaster PTSD over four waves of a panel study of Mexico's 1999 flood. *Journal of Traumatic Stress, 17,* 283–292.

North, C. S., Kawasaki, A., Spitznagel, E. L., & Hong, B. A. (2004). The course of PTSD, major depression, substance abuse, and somatization after a natural disaster. *Journal of Nervous and Mental Disease, 192,* 823–829.

Osofsky, J. D. (Ed.). (1997). *Children in a violent society*. New York: Guilford Press.

Osofsky, J. D. (Ed.). (2004). *Young children and trauma: Intervention and treatment*. New York: Guilford Press.

Osofsky, J. D., Osofsky, H. J., & Harris, W. W. (2007). Katrina's children: Social policy considerations for children in disasters. *Social Policy Reports, 21*, 3–19. Retrieved May 5, 2007, from http://www.srcd.org/spr.html

Pfefferbaum, B., Nixon, S. J., & Krug, R. S. (1999). Clinical needs assessment of middle and high school students following the 1995 Oklahoma City bombing. *American Journal of Psychiatry, 156*, 1069–1074.

Pynoos, R., Steinberg, A., & Piacentini, J. (1999). A developmental model of childhood traumatic stress and intersection with anxiety disorders. *Biological Psychiatry, 46*, 1542–1554.

Schaffer, D., Fisher, P., Dulcan, M. K., Davies, M., Piacentini, J., Schwab-Stone, M. E., et al. (1996). The NIMH Diagnostic Interview Schedule for Children Version 2.3 (DISC–2.3): Description, acceptability, prevalence rates and performance in the MECA study. *Journal of the American Academy of Child and Adolescent Psychiatry, 35*, 865–877.

Shalev, A. Y., Freedman, S., Peri, T., Brandes, D., Sahar, T., Orr, S. P., et al. (1998). Prospective study of posttraumatic stress disorder and depression following trauma. *American Journal of Psychiatry, 155*, 630–637.

Shelby, J. S., & Tredinnick, M. G. (1995). Crisis interventions with survivors of natural disaster: Lessons from Hurricane Andrew. *Journal of Counseling and Development, 73*, 491–497.

Silverstein, M., Augustyn, M., Cabral, H., & Zuckerman, B. (2006). Maternal depression and violence exposure: Double jeopardy for child school functioning. *Pediatrics, 118*, 792–800.

Smith, B. W., & Freedy, J. R. (2000). Psychosocial resource loss as a mediator of the effects of flood exposure on psychological distress and physical symptoms. *Journal of Traumatic Stress, 13*, 349–357.

Stein, B., Jaycox, L., Kataoka, S., Wong, M., Tu, W., Eliot, M., et al. (2003). A mental health intervention for school children exposed to violence: A randomized controlled trial. *JAMA, 290*, 603–611.

Sutker, P. B., Corrigan, S. A., Sundgaard-Riise, K., Uddo, M., & Allain, A. N. (2002). Exposure to war trauma, war-related PTSD, and psychological impact of subsequent hurricane. *Journal of Psychopathology and Behavioral Assessment, 24*, 25–37.

VanDenBerg, J., & Grealish, E. M. (1996). Individualized services and supports through the Wraparound Process: Philosophy and procedures. *Journal of Child and Family Studies, 5*, 7–21.

Vernberg, E., La Greca, A., Silverman, W., & Prinstein, M. (1996). Prediction of posttraumatic stress symptoms in children after Hurricane Andrew. *Journal of Abnormal Psychology, 105*, 237–248.

11

COMMUNITY RESILIENCE AND WELLNESS FOR CHILDREN EXPOSED TO HURRICANE KATRINA

BETTY PFEFFERBAUM, ROSE L. PFEFFERBAUM, AND FRAN H. NORRIS

Hurricane Katrina, a Category 3 hurricane, initiated a series of crises—created and perpetuated, in part, by failures of government and poor leadership at multiple levels (Senate Committee on Homeland Security and Governmental Affairs, 2006; U.S. House of Representatives, 2006)—that resulted in a disaster of unparalleled magnitude with numerous human-caused as well as natural elements. In some areas, whole communities were destroyed, raising questions about recovery and about the wisdom of rebuilding. The construct of community resilience was garnering professional attention before Katrina but remained primarily at a conceptual stage, with applications largely untested. In the context of Katrina and its massive destruction of community infrastructure, the issue of community resilience has taken on new meaning.

This research was supported by Grant N00140510629 from the U.S. Department of Homeland Security through the National Consortium for the Study of Terrorism and Responses to Terrorism, and by Grant 5 U79 SM57278-03 from the Substance Abuse and Mental Health Services Administration (SAMHSA) through the Terrorism and Disaster Center of the National Child Traumatic Stress Network. Any opinions, findings, and conclusions or recommendations in this document are those of the authors and do not necessarily reflect views of the U.S. Department of Homeland Security or SAMHSA.

In this chapter, we describe childhood wellness and wellness approaches, explore the construct of community resilience as applied to Hurricane Katrina, and identify child-supporting resilience strategies for disaster readiness. The impact of disasters on children, families, the programs and systems that serve and influence children, and the community and society at-large can be viewed within the bioecological framework proposed by Bronfenbrenner and colleagues (see, e.g., Bronfenbrenner & Morris, 1998). This framework places the child within nested and interacting systems and processes that foster or impede development and adaptation. As such, models of community resilience and child wellness fit within the bioecological framework. We rely on a general understanding of what occurred primarily in New Orleans, rather than on specific empirical data that the behavioral and social sciences are only now delivering, as we elaborate and link theoretical concepts of community resilience and child wellness in relation to this catastrophe.

THE CHILDREN OF NEW ORLEANS

An amalgam of customs and traditions, its own idiom, and distinct food and music characterized the proud and rich culture of New Orleans. Even before Katrina, children in New Orleans and the surrounding areas were among the poorest in the nation. More than 30% of Louisiana children under the age of 6, and almost 20% of children age 6 and older, lived in poor families. A disproportionate number of these children were African American. Almost 20% of poor children in Louisiana did not have health insurance (National Center for Children in Poverty, 2005). For poor children living in New Orleans, Katrina meant the deterioration of an already fragile existence. Resources were unevenly distributed, and many of the parishes most seriously affected by Katrina hosted inadequate educational and social systems (Campanella, 2006). Such conditions, typically exacerbated by disasters, suggest that New Orleans may not have been healthy before Katrina. The unfolding service needs of children and families are suggested by recent post-Katrina studies, which have documented the hurricane-related experiences, ongoing adversities, and mental health needs of children and youths affected by Katrina (see, e.g., Osofsky, Osofsky, & Harris, 2007; see also Introduction and chaps. 1, 6, and 10, this volume).

WELLNESS

Psychological wellness is not merely the absence of disease. It represents one end of a continuum, with pathology at the other end, and is determined by the presence of behavioral and psychological markers. Behavioral markers of wellness include wholesome health habits, effective interpersonal relationships, and mastery of developmentally appropriate tasks. Psychological markers include self-efficacy, empowerment, and a sense of belonging (Cowen, 1994, 2000b). Psychological wellness is not captured in the moment but must be enduring (Cowen, 2000a). Many children who are not sick cannot be classified as psychologically well (Cowen, 1994).

Children's psychological wellness incorporates competence, empowerment, and resilience. *Competence* is "a pattern of effective performance in the environment, evaluated from the perspective of development in ecological and cultural context" (Masten & Coatsworth, 1995, p. 724). It is the "demonstrated acquisition and further development of knowledge and skills" (Bronfenbrenner & Morris, 1998, p. 803) including intellectual, physical, social, and emotional knowledge and skills. Cowen (2000a) defined competence as doing correctly and well that which one should be doing. Acquiring relevant competencies is "the single most important pathway that children have to empowerment," the second component of wellness, which entails a sense of control over their own future (Cowen, 2000a, p. 87). *Resilience*—the ability of children to adapt, master their environment, and influence their own fate—is the third component of psychological wellness (Cowen, 2000a; see also Luthar, Cicchetti, & Becker, 2000; Masten, 2001). Ideally, attention is given to competence, empowerment, and resilience across developmental stages. Special effort is needed following a disaster, when the child's competence and empowerment are likely to be compromised and resilience is likely to be challenged.

Consistent with the bioecological framework (e.g., Bronfenbrenner & Morris, 1998), Cowen (1994, 2000a) identified five crucial, "mutually enhancing" (Cowen, 1994, p. 159) pathways to wellness—attachment, competencies, favorable environments, empowerment, and coping skills—all of which must be considered within the context of family and community. The attachment that Cowen envisioned is primarily that of young children with their caretakers, but attachment is essential to the development of healthy relationships both within families and beyond. Attachment can be affected by the environment both directly and indirectly through its influence on the caretaker and family. Competencies in cognition and interpersonal relationships derive in part from attachment but also are influenced by other experiences during the child's formative years and by training focused on one or multiple skills. Attachment and competencies provide important foundations for other aspects of development and the other pathways to wellness. For example, attachment and acquired competencies may increase the child's sense of efficacy and empowerment. Empowerment entails command over one's life (Cowen, 1994) and focuses squarely on the child's position within the social environment to address issues such as the injustice of prejudice and poverty (Cowen, 2000a). As a pathway to wellness, favorable environments include settings and situations that reinforce wellness, promote empowerment, support equity, provide opportunity, and inspire hope. Finally, the ability to cope with life stress across settings promotes wellness (Cowen, 1994).

Multiple factors and systems within the bioecological framework influence psychological wellness at each stage of child development. These include, for example, individual disposition, experience, transactions, and environmental conditions. Contributions to psychological wellness grow in complexity as children mature because the number and importance of systems in which they interact increase over time (Cowen, 2000a). Family and early experiences are the primary influences on wellness in infants and young children. Family, peers, and the school environment exert key influence throughout childhood. Work, social, and community factors are more important later (Cowen, 1994, 2000a). Thus, the individual child's community enlarges and changes over time, suggesting the increased importance of community influences as the child ages. It would be a mistake, however, to discount the impact of community factors during infancy and early childhood, even if primarily indirect, because the social environment has implications for maternal and family health and adjustment, which directly influence the development, health, and welfare of infants and young children.

Threats to wellness exist at many levels and occur throughout the child's development. Wellness may be undermined by personal and family problems, such as insecure attachments, poor physical health, inappropriate role models, and negative self-concepts; the failure to be taught or acquire needed skills and competencies; and social forces such as lack of opportunity and social injustice (Cowen, 2000a). These came into play for many of the children of New Orleans when, in the wreckage of Katrina, many families functioning on the margin before the storm were torn apart, schools were destroyed, and societal supports vanished.

INDIVIDUAL AND COMMUNITY RESILIENCE

Resilience refers to the ability to adapt successfully to adversity, trauma, and threat. It involves attitudes, behaviors, and skills that can be cultivated, taught, and practiced (American Psychological Association Task Force on Resilience in Response to Terrorism, n.d.; R. L. Pfefferbaum et al., 2008; Reissman, Klomp, Kent, & Pfefferbaum, 2004). Transient distress and even dysfunction may be expected in the postdisaster environment even among individuals on the trajectory of resilience. It is not the absence of adversity and distress that characterizes resilience; rather, it is the ability to recover and progress that is its hallmark. Resilience is not an end state but a dynamic process of interdependent forces—at the individual, family, group, and community levels—that continually shape and reshape the organism (see, e.g., Luthar et al., 2000; Masten, 2001).

Community resilience has been described as the ability of social units to mitigate the effects of hazards and to initiate recovery activities that limit social disruption and the effects of future events (Bruneau et al., 2003). More than individual coping, community resilience involves interactions as a collective unit. Members of resilient communities address problems together through intentional, collective analysis and behavior (Brown & Kulig, 1996–1997; Kulig, 2000; B. J. Pfefferbaum, Reissman, Pfefferbaum, Klomp, & Gurwitch, 2007; R. L. Pfefferbaum et al., 2008). Community resilience consists of both reactive and proactive elements that join recovery from adversity with individual and group efforts to transform their environments to mitigate future problems or events. Thus, community resilience is not simply the return to homeostasis, but rather implies a potential to grow from adversity that derives, in part, from deliberate, meaningful cooperation and action (Brown & Kulig, 1996–1997; Kulig, 2000; B. J. Pfefferbaum et al., 2007). Resilience may entail regaining and/or maintaining stability when stability is warranted. When stability is not possible or when adverse conditions persist, resilience is expressed in the ability to change and adapt (Longstaff, 2005). Indeed, in some situations, failure to change could represent a lack of resilience.

Community Resilience Factors

A number of factors associated with community resilience have been identified (B. J. Pfefferbaum et al., 2007; R. L. Pfefferbaum et al., 2008). These factors, described in this section with special emphasis on their importance for children and families, include connectedness, commitment, and shared values; participation; structure, roles, and responsibilities; resources; support and nurturance; critical reflection and skill building; communication; and disaster prevention and mitigation, preparedness, and response.

For most children, school is the primary community agency where these factors are expressed. Typically situated in local neighborhoods, schools provide a nidus of belonging and socialization, structure, information sharing and communication, resource exchange, and social support for entire families. Schools figure prominently in disasters because services located there can reach large segments of the population and reactions can be normalized in a developmentally appropriate context (see chaps. 1 and 7, this volume).

Connectedness, Commitment, and Shared Values

Community membership suggests a sense of belonging to a place or a group of people with shared history, laws, interests, and social mores. Children and families feel connected if they perceive themselves to be valued by others and if their needs are fulfilled through affiliation with the community and community organizations. Schools, for example, provide a venue for establishing connections through the pursuit of education and enrichment. A strong commitment to the community contributes to communication, consensus building, and collaboration, which are vital in disaster preparedness and response. Communities that embrace diversity among members may be better able to address the needs of children and families in the face of adversity. What we know about New Orleans suggests that residents feel connected to and identify with the community, but the degree to which this connection translates into consensus building and collaboration within neighborhoods and across the metropolis is unclear.

Participation

Participation of children and families in community activities and processes may intensify their sense of belonging. Schools and community programs may detect and address the child and family issues and needs of their members. Disaster preparedness and response depend on broad-based participation to reach potentially affected individuals. Opportunities for involvement should be sensitive to the interests, ability, and diversity of children and families. When participation is viewed as important, individuals are likely to take pride in their contributions and derive increased benefit from involvement, thus helping the community respond to the needs of children and families during and in the aftermath of disasters as well as those needs that occur more regularly. The poverty and racial discrimination that have characterized much of New Orleans likely served to disfranchise large segments of the population (see, e.g., Center for Social Inclusion, 2006).

Structure, Roles, and Responsibilities

Communities include individuals, families, schools, other organizations, and systems that link to form overlapping networks. Structure, roles, and responsibilities create the capacity for mitigation of and timely response to disasters, thereby diminishing adverse secondary consequences for children and families. Formal and informal associations are key to establishing priorities and resolving issues. Disasters create chaos and uncertainty, requiring able and responsive leadership; effective teamwork; transparent organizational structures; and well-defined roles, responsibilities, and lines of authority in response and recovery. Traditional roles and responsibilities expand and adapt in the face of disasters. For example, faith-based organizations assume a major role in counseling and support services to enhance hope and provide solace (see chap. 9, this volume), and school personnel take on mitigation, needs assessment, and outreach functions (see, e.g., chaps. 1 and 7, this volume). Structural elements must permit sufficient flexibility to address unfore-seen threats and vulnerabilities. Communities also must manage relations with external government and social agencies that contribute to disaster management. Katrina revealed poor leadership and coordination at multiple levels and across many organizations within New Orleans, the state of Louisiana, and the federal government (Gheytanchi et al., 2007; Senate Committee on Homeland Security and Governmental Affairs, 2006; U.S. House of Representatives, 2006).

Resources

A community's resources include those belonging to its members and those attached to the community itself. In addition to raw materials, resources include the physical infrastructure and machinery of the community, includ-ing built structures such as parks, libraries, movie theaters, and shopping malls, where children are likely to congregate. Human resources include the labor force of agencies serving children and families; expertise and leadership for personal, family, and community development; and underlying sentiment that instills hope and creates the will to improve community well-being. Relationships and support systems within a community, as well as character-istics such as cohesion, constitute social resources. Resilient communities acquire, mobilize, allocate, and use resources effectively to meet community goals associated with children and families. Infrastructure and systems must be able to endure and respond appropriately to a range of potential disasters and secondary adversities with sufficient resources substituting for and com-plementing each other to maintain essential community operations.

Resilience is likely to require ongoing investment in physical, human, and social capital, which may include, for example, improvements in schools and health facilities, job training, and neighborhood development. Resources in New Orleans before Katrina were inadequate and were not equitably distrib-uted, creating pockets of poverty, diminished opportunity, and hopelessness. In the year 2000, nearly 10% of the labor force was unemployed, and 28% of res-idents were living in poverty (U.S. Census Bureau, 2000). This hurricane-prone environment, in which evacuation would become an important route to safety, was further characterized by a lack of personal transportation in more than half of poor households, including nearly 60% of poor Black households and 65% of poor elderly households (Sherman & Shapiro, 2005).

Support and Nurturance

Support and nurturance contribute to resilience at community and indi-vidual levels. Supportive and nurturing communities help members achieve goals and address the needs of children and families regardless of background or socioeconomic status. For example, social service networks, agencies, and organizations such as Boys and Girls Clubs may enhance children's self-concepts, instill hope, and empower children and families and the institutions that serve them. Communities should grow more resilient as they attend to basic human needs and the environment in which their members live and work and through the process of locating, acquiring, and equitably distributing resources.

In resilient communities, support mechanisms provide early and ongoing assessment and assistance for vulnerable populations like children and socially disadvantaged persons before, during, and in the aftermath of disasters. Support for children and families is sustained through crises and buffers the personal, social, and economic losses that accompany adversity. Any evidence of support and nurturance for impoverished minority populations that may have existed in New Orleans faded from view in the Katrina evacuation process; many residents in neighborhoods of extreme poverty were unaware of the severity and scale of the looming disaster, had no private transportation, and lacked social networks outside the city that could provide shelter and assistance (see, e.g., Berube & Katz, 2005).

Critical Reflection and Skill Building

Resilient communities recognize and address issues, needs, and problems; develop structures to identify, collect, analyze, and use information; and plan, manage, and evaluate activities and programs in support of children and families. Critical reflection about values, their own history, and the experiences of others, along with an analysis of resources, should permit formal and informal community leaders to reason, set goals, make decisions, and develop and implement disaster management strategies. Resilient communities assess their performance, study their successes and failures, support skill building at individual and systemic levels, and learn from adversity. Learning, accommodation, and growth may lead to enhanced capacity to serve children and families. The communal analytic skills and behaviors needed to prepare New Orleans for a disaster of Katrina's magnitude were sorely lacking, and lessons learned were unheeded in preparation for and response to this catastrophe (Gheytanchi et al., 2007; U.S. House of Representatives, 2006).

Communication

Clear, timely, accurate, and effective communication among members and across boundaries is vital to disaster preparedness and response. Effective communication requires common meanings and understandings, openness, and honesty. Children and families and the organizations that serve them should have opportunities to identify and articulate their needs and views, especially in support of diverse groups, needs, and opinions. Open and productive communication can foster trust in leadership and increase the likelihood that children and families will participate in and comply with directives during community disasters. Sufficient redundancy in communication channels can help to ensure timely resource mobilization in response to threats. Ineffective communication, coupled with problematic evacuation, left New Orleans and its residents susceptible to Katrina's destruction (Gheytanchi et al., 2007; Senate Committee on Homeland Security and Governmental Affairs, 2006; U.S. House of Representatives, 2006).

Disaster Prevention and Mitigation, Preparedness, and Response

Resilient communities that seek to protect children and families take deliberate steps to prevent and mitigate, prepare for, and respond to disasters. Prevention and mitigation include activities to avoid or control an incident, to decrease risks to people and property, and to diminish potential or actual adverse effects associated with an event. Preparedness involves efforts to prevent adverse consequences and to assemble resources to respond. It is an ongoing process that identifies threats, assesses vulnerabilities, and determines resource requirements. Disaster response addresses the direct, short-term effects of an incident, including efforts to limit further damage during or immediately after a disaster, to support basic human needs of children and families, and to maintain the social, economic, and political structure of the affected community. The relatively short-term response phase transitions to a longer period of recovery and reconstruction during which children and families begin to rebuild their lives and their community. New Orleans, the state of Louisiana, and the federal government failed miserably in mitigation, preparedness, and response, despite having knowledge of the potential devastation that a hurricane of Katrina's magnitude could cause and fair warning of its approaching path (U.S. House of Representatives, 2006). How well the community rebuilds and recovers remains to be seen.

Relationship Between Personal and Community Resilience and Wellness

The child develops within nested environments of interconnected and interacting systems—family, school, neighborhood, and larger community. The community, along with other communities, is in turn nested in the larger society and linked through institutions, structures, networks, and processes such as state and federal agencies, transportation systems, communication channels, the media, and national policy (Riley & Masten, 2005). Together, the child and these nested environments form the ecological context for development and adaptation (see e.g., Bronfenbrenner & Morris, 1998).

Child wellness depends on individual, family, and social factors. Understanding the environment is essential to understanding wellness. Customs and social norms influence and set standards for behavior, thus determining, in part at least, the child's fit in the environment (Kelly, 2000).

Community characteristics that create risk or promote protection for children include, for example, economic conditions, community resources and services, and social support. That such characteristics are important to personal resilience, as well as indicators and determinants of community resilience, suggests a link between the child's personal resilience and community resilience. Yet although community resilience may enhance personal resilience, children who exhibit resilience often reside in adverse environments. In fact, resilient children may be identified because of their adaptation within these surroundings. Furthermore, just as a community is not defined solely in terms of child, family, or even organizational characteristics, a community is not resilient simply because it comprises resilient individuals. Community resilience, like personal resilience, is a process that becomes apparent through challenge and change. Community resilience is neither necessary nor sufficient for personal resilience. Nonetheless, it is difficult to imagine resilience in a multigenerational community that fails to address the needs of its children.

Population Wellness and Community Resilience

Norris, Stevens, Pfefferbaum, Wyche, and Pfefferbaum (2008) recommended that population wellness serve as an indicator of community adaptation. Wellness is measured by the absence of psychopathology, healthy patterns of behavior, and adequate role functioning at home, school, and work (Norris et al., 2008). Further, population wellness represents community-level adaptation as reflected by a high prevalence of wellness in the community, as well as high and nondisparate levels of mental and behavioral health, role function, and quality of life in constituent populations (Norris et al., 2008). The parishes most severely affected by Katrina were among the most socially vulnerable before the disaster, a factor that may impede recovery (Cutter et al., 2006). With high rates of poverty (National Center for Children in Poverty, 2005), with inadequate and inequitably distributed educational and social services (Campanella, 2006) before Katrina, and with many of the children who have returned to New Orleans qualifying for referral to mental health services (Osofsky et al., 2007), the community cannot be considered well. These realities—reflecting a dearth of individual and communal resources that poses a major challenge to community resilience—are complicated by limited familiarity with mental health issues among non–mental health care professionals, a lack of integration between community health and mental health, stigma associated with mental illness and treatment, and a limited evidence base for culture-specific disaster mental health services. Such realities call for the adoption of a holistic wellness perspective for communities as well as individuals, including increased integration of mental, physical, and public health services (R. L. Pfefferbaum et al., 2008).

Recognizing that adverse events cannot be prevented, a framework of resilience or wellness must direct attention to how, and how well, these events are addressed. Inaction or a passive response, especially when there are indications "that certain actions can prevent damage and/or promote wellness," is a betrayal of children and the community just as deliberate, thoughtful, and planned efforts to "forestall predictable misfortune" (Cowen, 2000a, p. 89) are evidence of the value we place on children and the community. The response to Katrina exposed how shallow these values are, at least for some children and some communities. The approximately 100,000 New Orleans residents who had not evacuated by the time Katrina struck depict a "social rather than a natural disaster" (Napier, Mandisodza, Andersen, & Jost, 2006, p. 58) in which thousands of poor, mostly Black residents were left stranded for days without food, water, or transportation. The poorest areas of the city had not been notified of mandatory evacuation other than by standard radio and television broadcasts, and transportation out of the city had not been provided, even though most poor households had no means of personal transportation (Napier et al., 2006). These facts suggest a community lacking in attributes associated with resilience—connectedness, commitment, and shared values; strong and responsive leadership; clear organizational structures; well-defined roles, responsibilities, and lines of authority; support and nurturance; effective communication; and disaster management. Ultimately, the course and process of the community's recovery will tell the story of its resilience.

COMMUNITY RESILIENCE AS A PREPAREDNESS STRATEGY

Community resilience strategies require community-level interventions that are multidimensional, operate across multiple settings, and join individual change tactics with environmental approaches (Wandersman & Florin, 2003). Community resilience interventions focus on systems and take into consideration families, schools, workplaces, organizations, and community structures (Fullilove & Saul, 2006). A variety of stakeholders are needed to deliver these interventions, including (but not limited to) media outlets, schools, libraries, social service agencies, local businesses and unions, public health and emergency management professionals, and local and state governments, as well as youth-serving, faith-based, volunteer, cultural, and fraternal organizations.

Norris et al. (2008) outlined five broad resilience strategies for disaster preparedness. They recommended that communities decrease risk and resource inequities, engage members in mitigation, create organizational links, enhance and protect social support, and plan for the unexpected. R. L. Pfefferbaum et al. (2008) identified a similar set of actions with notable additions: using a holistic wellness approach and promoting a conscious awareness of community resilience. We review these strategies in application to children and families and link them to Katrina.

Risk and Resources

Resource considerations include not only the paucity or destruction of resources before, during, and after a disaster but also disparities in resource availability, risk, and social vulnerability (Norris et al., 2008; R. L. Pfefferbaum et al., 2008). Disaster exposure is not random, nor is it evenly distributed (Cutter, Boruff, & Shirley, 2003). Some geographic regions and certain population groups are at heightened risk of exposure and adverse outcomes (Somasundaram & van de Put, 2006). Poor communities lacking in both individual and communal resources, a solid economic foundation, and strong leadership are at increased risk of adversity and diminished community resilience following a disaster (R. L. Pfefferbaum et al., 2008). Individuals in greatest need of support may have the least access to it; thus, economic and social resources, essential to community resilience and disaster response, must be acquired and shared to reduce risk and address social vulnerability associated with disaster (Norris et al., 2008). Hurricane Katrina dramatized the importance of scarcity, resource inequities, and the needs of the most defenseless populations. In general, children are considered especially susceptible to the adverse consequences of disasters, and children with preexisting problems are likely to suffer even more. Certainly, Katrina statistics suggest this to be the case as the gap between those who are socially secure and those who are most fragile undoubtedly widened in this disaster.

Recognizing and reducing inequities before an event would enhance disaster preparedness and reduce the kind of inequities—reflected in poverty and racism—revealed so vividly by Hurricane Katrina. Deliberate efforts are required to identify, develop, and distribute the resources necessary to address social, environmental, and economic vulnerability. It is too soon to ascertain the potential resilience of New Orleans as it selects for and accommodates shifts in demographics, adjusts to geographic hazards and realities, and modifies its physical and built environment in the coming years. The verdict on how well the community addresses resource disparities and how well it treats its children over time—especially its poor and minority children— also awaits determination.

The future of New Orleans after Katrina will be influenced by its ability to establish a solid economic base with sufficient resources to provide for the needs of the community. Critical reflection and skill building, one of eight factors associated with community resilience (B. J. Pfefferbaum et al., 2007; R. L. Pfefferbaum et al., 2008), combined with problem-solving and social and political action, will be necessary for accumulation and equitable distribution of resources (Norris et al., 2008).

Community Engagement and Participation in Mitigation

In the face of many competing needs, disaster preparedness is commonly not a priority for either the general public or the government. This was obvious with Hurricane Katrina, when much of the populace disregarded evacuation warnings and when it became clear that the government had ignored evidence that the levees in New Orleans could not withstand a hurricane the magnitude of Katrina. For the public, failure to engage in preparedness may stem from denial, underestimated risks, and a false sense of security; it may also result from more focused attention to other real and pressing problems of everyday life. Competing priorities, failure to accurately estimate capacity and potential need, and ambiguity in responsibility are among the numerous factors in the government's failure to focus on disaster preparedness (Auf der Heide, 1989; R. L. Pfefferbaum et al., 2008).

Community resilience can be enhanced through the engagement and participation of community residents (Norris et al., 2008; R. L. Pfefferbaum et al., 2008). Efforts to build community solidarity and cohesion will have a greater likelihood of success to the extent that community members are knowledgeable about local resources, interact with local organizations and social networks, and help shape communal processes, especially insofar as these efforts are driven by the priorities and preferences of community members. Member investment in the community—social and psychological, though not necessarily financial—is often essential for the sustainability of community development programs (Fullilove & Saul, 2006).

Describing New York after the terrorist attacks of September 11, 2001, Fullilove and Saul (2006) portrayed the community as harboring "a spectrum of opportunities for healing" (p. 175) in members with diverse strengths, talents, skills, occupations, and ages. Healing, they wrote, is a creative process resulting "from the synergy of various community actors" (p. 175) working toward a common purpose. The capacity for communal healing to emanate from the engagement of local residents has been severely compromised in the case of New Orleans following Katrina, with increased marginalization of already vulnerable groups and the slow return or loss of former residents, altered sociocultural landscape, and diminished socioeconomic conditions (see, e.g., Campanella, 2006, and Miller & Rivera, 2007, for a discussion of the importance of sociocultural and socioeconomic landscapes with respect to post-Katrina New Orleans). Although one should not expect those whose lives were ravaged by Katrina to attend, in the near term, to a common purpose other than meeting the basic human needs of self and family, a community resilience framework suggests that recovery for New Orleans will require the "reweaving of social connections" disrupted by Katrina (Fullilove & Saul, 2006, p. 176). In a city burdened by racism and with neighborhoods of extreme poverty, enhanced social connectedness will likely depend on community development that generates opportunities for work, access to services, and the availability of quality schools.

In making the case for public engagement in planning for bioterrorism response, Glass and Schoch-Spana (2002) recommended that public and civic organizations be enlisted to implement public health measures, that communities invest in outreach and communication, and that planning and intervention reflect the values and priorities of affected populations. Additionally, community members should assess and address their own vulnerability to hazards, improve their own problem-solving abilities, and identify and connect with networks that provide information and assistance (Brown & Kulig, 1996–1997; Coles & Buckle, 2004; Longstaff, 2005; Norris et al., 2008; B. J. Pfefferbaum et al., 2007). Community Emergency Response Teams (CERTs) and similar programs provide opportunities for individuals to learn about threats and vulnerabilities and to develop skills to address personal and communal emergencies. Traditionally neighborhood based, CERTs are increasingly being formed in workplace settings and schools. Children can and should be engaged in age-appropriate activities as well. In fact, information and materials provided to children in school can reach families as part of disaster preparedness, resilience, and wellness campaigns.

Organizational Links and Networks

Preexisting organizational relationships and networks, coalitions, and cooperative agreements are key to mobilizing emergency response and disaster support services (Norris et al., 2008). Disaster preparedness and response for children are commonly located in the school setting (see chaps. 1 and 7, this volume); however, school systems tend to be closed except to known and trusted partners (Norris et al., 2008), and schools are burdened by many agendas and have little time and few resources to devote to disaster preparedness. Disaster preparedness should include efforts to establish relationships and official collaborative agreements with state education authorities, with school districts in local regions, and with individual schools in communities and neighborhoods. Information about and models for school crisis plans are readily available through federal and state governments (see, e.g., U.S. Department of Education Office of Safe and Drug-Free Schools, 2007). School crisis planning and drills provide opportunities for involvement of local public health and emergency management officials who bring resources schools may lack. Contact can be initiated by public officials or schools either before or after an event. Without data, it is unclear the extent to which interorganizational relationships and links existed in New Orleans before Katrina. The catastrophic nature of this disaster may well have destroyed pre-existing networks as well as those that were tenuous.

Organizational links and networks can be built around mutual concerns and specific issues, including disaster preparedness and management. Representation on boards and committees, information and resource sharing, cosponsorship of community events, support for professional and practitioner associations, and involvement in coalitions are methods for developing and strengthening bonds among organizations and within networks. Coalitions involving schools and parent–teacher groups with local businesses, human service organizations, and emergency management agencies also provide a mechanism for clarifying needs and developing solutions to community problems such as school crisis planning. Such coalitions furnish evidence of broad support for a cause, encourage involvement in compelling issues without requiring an organization or individual to assume sole responsibility, reduce duplication of effort, and increase power and influence through joint action. Successful coalitions mobilize various community sectors to accomplish their goals. As such, they are natural vehicles for building community resilience (Wandersman & Florin, 2003).

Networks extend beyond the community into the larger society. The federal disaster and emergency management program is illustrative in its establishment of a hierarchy of responsibility based on an understanding that disasters are local and that response requires the involvement of people who are familiar with and who will remain in the community after rescue and recovery efforts are complete. Thus, the federal model assigns initial and primary official responsibility for disaster management to the local government. When local resources are inadequate, state government assists. Federal assistance is available if state and local resources are insufficient. The Katrina response in New Orleans was not well coordinated within the community or in relation to the larger society. Children and other especially vulnerable populations suffered as a result.

Social Support

Social support, measured in multiple ways and derived from various sources, has been shown to predict disaster outcome in children (Udwin, Boyle, Yule, Bolton, & O'Ryan, 2000; Vernberg, La Greca, Silverman, &

Prinstein, 1996). For example, Vernberg et al. (1996) found that children's self-reported access to support from teachers and classmates was significant in predicting outcome in elementary school students 3 months after Hurricane Andrew (which made landfall in South Florida, 1992). Udwin and colleagues (2000) found that severity and duration of posttraumatic stress disorder (PTSD) were determined in part by the availability of social support and support from school in young adults who developed PTSD related to a shipping disaster experienced during their adolescence.

Disaster interventions should protect and enhance existing social supports, which, for children, occur in families and extended families, schools, Boys and Girls Clubs, faith-based and neighborhood organizations, and various child-serving agencies. Well-functioning social networks inform members about each other's needs and about available resources, and they may facilitate equitable distribution of resources. Unfortunately, altruism and cohesion, which may be abundant in the initial aftermath of a disaster, do not endure across disaster phases (Norris et al., 2008). Thus, overt efforts may be necessary to create and build social support in the context of disaster response.

The importance of fostering naturally occurring social supports in the aftermath of disasters is of concern in the post-Katrina environment because much of the social support system was destroyed in the flood or dismantled with the mass displacement. In some instances, families were torn apart, shattering the most important support system for children. The result has been a damaged social infrastructure in a reconfigured community with altered demographics (Cutter et al., 2006; Osofsky et al., 2007) and networks. Naturally occurring support that resides in families, friends, rituals, and traditions can be buttressed in the aftermath of catastrophic events by the following:

- material assistance;
- accessible, affordable, and responsive community services provided through existing and new organizations that arise to address the needs of survivors;
- information on coping provided through the media, community meetings, religious sermons, newsletters, and fact sheets that are widely disseminated through, for example, schools, libraries, recreation centers, health clinics, faith-based organizations, fast food restaurants, and grocery stores; and
- intensified public health and safety measures.

Schools are an effective setting for serving children and reaching families (see chaps. 1 and 7, this volume), but they are likely to need an infusion of resources to perform regular tasks and also meet increased demands following a disaster. Programs aimed at assisting caretakers are likely to be better attended if child care services are provided. Campaigns that teach about disaster reactions can reduce the stigma associated with mental health services and promote greater and more appropriate use of such services. Cross-training of human service personnel that enables them to recognize signs of emotional distress can foster improved information and referral services. Employee assistance programs can build coping and crisis management skills and address conflict resolution and anger management. These programs will be more effective if workplace adjustments are enacted to accommodate personal needs of workers and their families.

A Holistic Wellness Approach

In keeping with the general approach to disaster mental health, R. L. Pfefferbaum et al. (2008) suggested that community resilience activities be based on a holistic wellness approach rather than an illness model. A wellness approach focuses on promoting effective coping and health-seeking behaviors, restoring functioning, understanding traumatic stress, and improving emotional as well as physical health (Friedman, 2005). It must not, however, exclude services and supports for those who suffer serious or incapacitating reactions to disasters. These individuals, who may have preexisting conditions, typically need traditional health and mental health care that must be part of a system of disaster services.

Wellness enhancement is focused on full populations rather than on children who have developed disorders, for whom clinical interventions might be appropriate, or on those at risk for problems, for whom disease prevention might be appropriate (Cowen, 1994). Clinical interventions, provided by licensed individuals, are remedial in nature and delivered after a problem occurs, reactive in their focus on diagnosis and treatment of children with disorders, and guided by legal formalities of the clinician–patient relationship such as consent, confidentiality, record keeping, and malpractice. Wellness enhancement has the potential to promote success in young children early in life and to provide more protections against a variety of maladaptive outcomes than clinical interventions specifically focused on those conditions (Cowen, 2000b).

Wellness enhancement joins risk detection and prevention efforts as more promising approaches than those instituted after problems have emerged (Cowen, 2000b). Like primary prevention, the promotion of wellness is proactive rather than reactive (Cowen, 1994), but it is broader than and encompasses prevention (Cowen, 2000b). Wellness and prevention, both important in fostering positive child development, share a focus on increasing adaptation. They differ in approach, populations addressed, and timing (Cowen, 1994). Primary prevention aims "to forestall dysfunction" (Cowen, 1973, p. 433) by decreasing rates of the occurrence of disorders in the population over long periods of time. In practice, primary prevention is, in many instances, simply disease prevention in those known to be at risk of a specific condition (Cowen, 1994, 2000b). A wellness approach assumes that adaptation is on a continuum rather than that people are either well or sick, at risk or not at risk (Cowen, 1994). A wellness approach focuses more on healthy beginnings than on later damage control (Cowen, 2000b), and it assumes that wellness immunizes against a variety of adverse outcomes (Cowen, 1994). Thus, wellness approaches are consistent with community resilience strategies that focus on improving the child's environment as a way of promoting general health and adaptation. The potential for wellness to safeguard against multiple threats makes it particularly appealing in preparing for an all-hazards environment, in which any of the many natural, human-caused, or technological disasters may occur.

Cowen (2000a) maintained that families, schools, and the educational process are key to enhancing wellness in the context of threats and deficiencies stemming from the absence of essential early factors or from the failure to acquire basic skills and competencies. For example, efforts to enhance attachment and communication in young children may provide protection from later emotional problems (Cowen, 2000b). Similarly, school readiness prepares children for educational success both academically and socially, and these in turn promote later success in the workforce and socially. Wellness enhancement promotes, but does not guarantee, adaptive results. The child will confront challenges associated with development and life stresses (Cowen, 2000b). When social injustices deprive children of opportunity and hope, the community and society's institutions, policies, and practices can be validating and enabling (Cowen, 2000a). Thus, proactive wellness enhancement was indicated for the children of New Orleans before Katrina and should become part of ongoing work to build community resilience.

Disaster Planning and Management

The events of Katrina and its aftermath illustrate the crucial significance of disaster planning and management. A bipartisan Senate subcommittee concluded that human suffering "continued longer than it should have because of—and was in some ways exacerbated by—failure of government at all levels to plan, prepare for, and respond aggressively to the storm" and that "these failures were not just conspicuous; they were pervasive" (Senate Committee on Homeland Security and Governmental Affairs, 2006, p. 2). Gaps in information and communication were critical (U.S. House of Representatives, 2006). Miscommunication discouraged both individual and family action and government response (Gheytanchi et al., 2007). Although disaster management typically requires state and local governments to identify problems and needs and to request federal support, catastrophic disasters like Katrina necessitate greater initiative by the federal government. All levels of government were faulted for being inflexible, for failure to learn from prior experience and from preparedness exercises, for failure to effectively implement components of the National Response Plan, and for poor coordination among agencies (U.S. House of Representatives, 2006).

It is imperative that communities develop flexible community emergency plans that include effective risk communication using trusted sources of information and that recognize the potential for unforeseen and unknown events (Longstaff, 2005; Norris et al., 2008; R. L. Pfefferbaum et al., 2008). Norris and colleagues (2008) emphasized the almost universal existence of uncertainty following disasters. The uncertainty that arose as Katrina unfolded over days and weeks is remarkable given what was known before the event from weather forecasts, studies documenting problems with the levee system, simulation exercises, and local demographics.

Among the great lessons of Hurricane Katrina is the importance of disaster management. Insufficient attention and follow-through characterized all four disaster management phases—prevention and mitigation, preparedness, response, and recovery. Community resilience can support disaster prevention and mitigation through involvement of residents in risk assessment, participation in planning (e.g., evacuation planning), and identification of potential barriers to the implementation of plans such as location of homebound residents and lack of transportation. The proximity of community members to neighborhood situations and the importance of their support in the execution of and compliance with plans make their involvement in, and contributions during, the prevention and mitigation phase particularly consequential, as was demonstrated so clearly by the lack thereof in Katrina.

Community preparedness requires knowledge of existing structures, roles, and responsibilities as well as critical reflection and skill building (R. L. Pfefferbaum et al., 2008). As part of a preparedness tactic, public deliberation can "harness citizens' collective wisdom and judgment" (Schoch-Spana, Franco, Nuzzo, & Usenza, 2007, p. 13) to help identify opportunity costs, set priorities, address ethical issues, and inform complex policy decisions. Effective communication channels and social support networks can expedite the flow of information, raise awareness, and provide instruction in personal and family preparedness. For New Orleans, attention to diversity of community members and an appreciation of customs and traditions would facilitate, and are likely essential to the success of, local preparedness efforts.

If accustomed to working together, local associations and agencies, organized volunteer responders, professionals and practitioners, and formal and informal leaders can serve as a crisis communication network for timely transmission of information during the response phase of disaster management (Schoch-Spana et al., 2007). Another resilience-building response strategy would incorporate Psychological First Aid (Norris & Stevens, 2007; see also chaps. 8 and 12, this volume)—a universal intervention with principles that are applicable to virtually all interactions in a disaster setting—into disaster response efforts of public health, medical, emergency management, and mental health personnel.

The failure to effectively use the organizational structure and incident command system in place as part of the National Response Plan clearly interfered with the ability of New Orleans to respond to and recover from Katrina. Critical analysis of this failure can contribute to resilience building for New Orleans as well as communities across the nation. Community resilience aids disaster recovery both immediately and over the longer term through connectedness, commitment, and shared values of residents who can assist individuals in the aftermath of a disaster, contribute to their support when external resources cease to be available, and participate in rebuilding lives and infrastructure.

Problem-solving approaches should encourage innovation and local variation in preparedness, response, and recovery (Norris et al., 2008). Disaster planning and management must recognize the unique vulnerability and needs of children (National Advisory Committee on Children and Terrorism, 2003).

Conscious Awareness of Community Resilience

Community resilience involves deliberate collective action to transform the environment to mitigate future problems (B. J. Pfefferbaum et al., 2007; R. L. Pfefferbaum et al., 2008). Raising awareness about community resilience is a strategy that itself may encourage citizen participation and engagement (R. L. Pfefferbaum et al., 2008). This is no less true for children than it is for adults, and it may take shape in public education for both. Awareness does not guarantee that resource inequities will be addressed, that organizations will collaborate, or that plans will be practiced, but it may be a first step in engagement and participation and in augmenting social support networks. The media have a potential role in making resilience relevant.

Although differences in many parameters make it difficult to identify and develop specific community resilience strategies with general application across communities (R. L. Pfefferbaum et al., 2008), for any community it is helpful to assess assets and identify opportunities and to use community strengths to address community challenges. This process can be facilitated by and, in turn, facilitates the development of a conscious awareness of community resilience.

CONCLUSION

Community resilience takes on critical importance in the context of Hurricane Katrina and its damage to the physical infrastructure, breakdown of social support systems, lack of public accountability, and continued questions regarding the community's very survival. The inadequacy of prevention, mitigation, preparedness, and response to this disaster triggered a cascade of ill-fated leadership decisions. The result was an evacuation and displacement of massive proportion, total destruction of the infrastructure in some areas, delayed return of basic services, and unrelenting hardship. The future of New Orleans will be determined, in large part, by its attention to community restoration and renewal, which can be fostered through the implementation of resilience-building strategies.

Disasters like Hurricane Katrina are traumatic events, collectively experienced, with prolonged consequences for the structure and functioning of the community itself as well as for individuals and families. Difficulties associated with accessing public and private support and in navigating the bureaucracy that emerges following a disaster often contribute to persistent distress and demoralization. Children are especially susceptible, with the potential for enduring effects across developmental trajectories. They deserve our attention during all phases of disaster management.

REFERENCES

American Psychological Association Task Force on Resilience in Response to Terrorism. (n.d.). *Fact sheet: Fostering resilience in response to terrorism: A fact sheet for psychologists working with adults.* Retrieved June 28, 2007, from http://www.apa.org/psychologists/pdfs/adults.pdf

Auf der Heide, E. (1989). *Disaster response: Principles of preparation and coordination.* Retrieved October 24, 2008, from http://orgmail2.coe-dmha.org/dr/flash.htm

Berube, A., & Katz, B. (2005, October). *Katrina's window: Confronting concentrated poverty across America.* Washington, DC: Brookings Institution. Retrieved October 18, 2008, from http://www.brookings.edu/~/media/Files/rc/reports/2005/10poverty_berube/20051012_Concentratedpoverty.pdf

Bronfenbrenner, U., & Morris, P. A. (1998). The bioecological model of human development. In W. Damon & R. M. Lerner (Eds.), *Handbook of child psychology: Vol. 1. Theoretical models of human development* (pp. 793–828). New York: Wiley.

Brown, D. D., & Kulig, J. C. (1996–1997). The concept of resiliency: Theoretical lessons from community research. *Health and Canadian Society, 4,* 29–50.

Bruneau, M., Chang, S. E., Eguchi, R. T., Lee, G. C., O'Rourke, T. D., Reinhorn, A. M., et al. (2003). A framework to quantitatively assess and enhance the seismic resilience of communities. *Earthquake Spectra, 19,* 733–752.

Campanella, T. J. (2006). Urban resilience and the recovery of New Orleans. *Journal of the American Planning Association, 72,* 141–146.

Center for Social Inclusion. (2006, August). *The race to rebuild: The color of opportunity and the future of New Orleans.* New York: Center for Social Inclusion. Retrieved October 24, 2008, from http://www.centerforsocialinclusion.org/PDF/racetorebuild.pdf

Coles, E., & Buckle, P. (2004). Developing community resilience as a foundation for effective disaster recovery. *Australian Journal of Emergency Management, 19,* 6–15.

Cowen, E. L. (1973). Social and community interventions. *Annual Review of Psychology, 24,* 423–472.

Cowen, E. L. (1994). The enhancement of psychological wellness: Challenges and opportunities. *American Journal of Community Psychology, 22,* 149–179.

Cowen, E. L. (2000a). Community psychology and routes to psychological wellness. In J. Rappaport & E. Seidman (Eds.), *Handbook of community psychology* (pp. 79–99). New York: Kluwer Academic/Plenum.

Cowen, E. L. (2000b). Psychological wellness: Some hopes for the future. In D. Cicchetti, J. Rappaport, I. Sandler, & R. P. Weissberg (Eds.), *The promotion of wellness in children and adolescents* (pp. 477–503). Washington, DC: Child Welfare League of America.

Cutter, S. L., Boruff, B. J., & Shirley, W. L. (2003). Social vulnerability to environmental hazards. *Social Science Quarterly, 84,* 242–261.

Cutter, S. L., Emrich, C. T., Mitchell, J. T., Boruff, B. J., Gall, M., Schmidtlein, M. C., et al. (2006). The long road home: Race, class, and recovery from Hurricane Katrina. *Environment Science & Policy for Sustainable Development, 48,* 8–20.

Friedman, M. J. (2005). Every crisis is an opportunity. *CNS Spectrums, 10,* 96–98.

Fullilove, M. T., & Saul, J. (2006). Rebuilding communities post-disaster in New York. In Y. Neria, R. Gross, & R. D. Marshall (Eds.), *9/11: Mental health in the wake of terrorist attacks* (pp. 164–177). Cambridge, England: Cambridge University Press.

Gheytanchi, A., Joseph, L., Gierlach, E., Kimpara, S., Housley, J., Franco, Z. E., et al. (2007). The dirty dozen: Twelve failures of the Hurricane Katrina response and how psychology can help. *American Psychologist, 62,* 118–130.

Glass, T. A., & Schoch-Spana, M. (2002). Bioterrorism and the people: How to vaccinate a city against panic. *Clinical Infectious Diseases, 34,* 217–223.

Kelly, J. G. (2000). Wellness as an ecological enterprise. In D. Cicchetti, J. Rappaport, I. Sandler, & R. P. Weissberg (Eds.), *The promotion of wellness in children and adolescents* (pp. 101–131). Washington, DC: Child Welfare League of America.

Kulig, J. C. (2000). Community resiliency: The potential for community health nursing theory development. *Public Health Nursing, 17,* 374–385.

Longstaff, P. H. (2005). *Security, resilience, and communication in unpredictable environments such as terrorism, natural disasters, and complex technology*. Retrieved October 24, 2008, from http://pirp.harvard.edu/pubs_pdf/longsta/longsta-p05-3.pdf

Luthar, S. S., Cicchetti, D., & Becker, B. (2000). The construct of resilience: A critical evaluation and guidelines for future work. *Child Development, 71*, 543–562.

Masten, A. S. (2001). Ordinary magic. *American Psychologist, 56*, 227–238.

Masten, A. S., & Coatsworth, J. D. (1995). Competence, resilience, and psychopathology. In D. Cicchetti & D. J. Cohen (Eds.), *Developmental psychopathology: Vol. 2. Risk, disorder, and adaptation* (pp. 715–752). New York: Wiley.

Miller, D. S., & Rivera, J. D. (2007). Landscapes of disaster and place orientation in the aftermath of Hurricane Katrina. In D. L. Brunsma, D. Overfelt, & J. S. Picou (Eds.), *The sociology of Katrina* (pp. 141–154). Lanham, MD: Rowman & Littlefield.

Napier, J. L., Mandisodza, A. N., Andersen, S. M., & Jost, J. T. (2006). System justification in responding to the poor and displaced in the aftermath of Hurricane Katrina. *Analyses of Social Issues and Public Policy, 6*, 57–73.

National Advisory Committee on Children and Terrorism. (2003, June). *Recommendations to the Secretary*. Retrieved August 7, 2006, from http://www.bt.cdc.gov/children/PDF/working/Recommend.pdf

National Center for Children in Poverty. (2005, September). *Child poverty in 21st century America: Child poverty in states hit by Hurricane Katrina* (Fact Sheet 1). Retrieved June 27, 2007, from http://nccp.org/publications/pdf/text_622.pdf

Norris, F. H., & Stevens, S. P. (2007). Community resilience and the principles of mass trauma intervention. *Psychiatry, 70*, 320–328.

Norris, F. H., Stevens, S. P., Pfefferbaum, B., Wyche, K. F., & Pfefferbaum, R. L. (2008). Community resilience as a metaphor, theory, set of capacities, and strategy for disaster readiness. *American Journal of Community Psychology, 41*, 127–150.

Osofsky, J. D., Osofsky, H. J., & Harris, W. W. (2007). Katrina's children: Social policy considerations for children in disasters. *Social Policy Report, 21*, 3–19.

Pfefferbaum, B. J., Reissman, D. B., Pfefferbaum, R. L., Klomp, R. W., & Gurwitch, R. H. (2007). *Building resilience to mass trauma events*. In L. S. Doll, S. E. Bonzo, D. A. Sleet, J. A. Mercy, & E. N. Haas (Eds.), *Handbook of injury and violence prevention* (pp. 347–358). New York: Springer Science+Business Media.

Pfefferbaum, R. L., Reissman, D. B., Pfefferbaum, B., Wyche, K. F., Norris, F. H., & Klomp, R. W. (2008). Factors in the development of community resilience to disasters. In M. Blumenfield & R. J. Ursano (Eds.), *Intervention and resilience after mass trauma* (pp. 49–68). Cambridge, England: Cambridge University Press.

Reissman, D. B., Klomp, R. W., Kent, A. T., & Pfefferbaum, B. (2004). Exploring psychological resilience in the face of terrorism. *Psychiatric Annals, 33*, 627–632.

Riley, J. R., & Masten, A. S. (2005). Resilience in context. In R. D. Peters, B. Leadbeater, & R. J. McMahon (Eds.), *Resilience in children, families, and communities* (pp. 13–25). New York: Kluwer Academic/Plenum.

Schoch-Spana, M., Franco, C., Nuzzo, J. B., & Usenza, C. (2007). Community engagement: Leadership tool for catastrophic health events. *Biosecurity and Bioterrorism: Biodefense Strategy, Practice, and Science, 5*, 8–25.

Senate Committee on Homeland Security and Governmental Affairs. (2006, May). *Hurricane Katrina: A nation still unprepared.* Retrieved October 24, 2008, from http://www.gpoaccess.gov/serialset/creports/katrinanation.html

Sherman, A., & Shapiro, I. (2005, September). *Essential facts about the victims of Hurricane Katrina.* Washington, DC: Center on Budget and Policy Priorities. Retrieved October 18, 2008, from http://www.cbpp.org/9-19-05pov.pdf

Somasundaram, D. J., & van de Put, W. A. C. M. (2006). Management of trauma in special populations after a disaster. *Journal of Clinical Psychiatry, 67*, 64–73.

Udwin, O., Boyle, S., Yule, W., Bolton, D., & O'Ryan, D. (2000). Risk factors for long-term psychological effects of a disaster experienced in adolescence: Predictors of post traumatic stress disorder. *Journal of Child Psychology and Psychiatry, 41*, 969–979.

U.S. Census Bureau. (2000). [U.S. Census database]. Available at http://factfinder.census.gov/home/saff/main.html?_lang-en

U.S. Department of Education Office of Safe and Drug-Free Schools. (2007, January). *Practical information and crisis planning: A guide for schools and communities.* Retrieved October 18, 2008, from http://www.ed.gov/admins/lead/safety/emergencyplan/crisisplanning.pdf

U.S. House of Representatives. (2006). *A failure of initiative: Final report of the Select Bipartisan Committee to investigate the preparation for and response to Hurricane Katrina.* Retrieved October 24, 2008, from http://www.gpoaccess.gov/serialset/creports/katrina.html

Vernberg, E. M., La Greca, A. M., Silverman, W. K., & Prinstein, M. J. (1996). Prediction of posttraumatic stress symptoms in children after Hurricane Andrew. *Journal of Abnormal Psychology, 105*, 237–248.

Wandersman, A., & Florin, P. (2003). Community interventions and effective prevention. *American Psychologist, 58*, 441–448.

12

LESSONS LEARNED FROM KATRINA AND OTHER DEVASTATING HURRICANES: STEPS NECESSARY FOR ADEQUATE PREPAREDNESS, RESPONSE, AND INTERVENTION

WENDY K. SILVERMAN, ANDREA ALLEN, AND CLAUDIO D. ORTIZ

> We learn from history that we learn nothing from history.
> —Georg Wilhelm Friedrich Hegel, c. 1800
>
> Those who cannot learn from history are doomed to repeat it.
> —George Santayana, c. 1905
>
> When will they ever learn? When will they ever learn?
> —Pete Seeger, c. 1961

In the context of Hurricane Katrina, we can all only hope that Hegel will be proved wrong, that Santayana will be proved right, and that the answer to Seeger's question is that we have *now* learned lessons from Katrina and other devastating hurricanes. Finally! One step toward moving this hope closer to reality is by our providing our perspective in this chapter on some of the key lessons that can be learned from Katrina and other devastating hurricanes. We also offer concrete steps for promoting adequate preparedness, response, and intervention.

The precise number of youths affected by hurricanes is unknown and difficult to estimate. The International Federation of Red Cross and Red Crescent Societies (IFRC) indicated that approximately 2.5 billion people worldwide were affected by natural disasters between 1996 and 2005. In the western hemisphere alone, an estimated 59.1 million people were affected by natural disasters between 1996 and 2005 (IFRC, 2006). A substantial proportion are likely to have been children and adolescents. Although young people have been the forgotten victims of natural disasters, including hurricanes (Osofsky, 2007), we have had the opportunity to collaborate with others to assist in delivering mental health recovery services to young hurricane victims.

Specifically, we collaborated with others to assist youths who were exposed to the 2004 Florida hurricanes, Charley, Frances, and Ivan; the 2005 Florida hurricane, Wilma; and Katrina in New Orleans in 2005. In addition, Wendy K. Silverman conducted a series of studies with La Greca and colleagues in the aftermath of Hurricane Andrew, which struck South Florida in 1992 (La Greca, Silverman, Vernberg, & Prinstein, 1996; La Greca, Silverman, & Wasserstein, 1998; Vernberg, La Greca, Silverman, & Prinstein, 1996).

Our discussion in this chapter of lessons learned draws not only on our direct hands-on research and mental health service delivery experiences but also on research findings of other investigative teams studying youths' reactions to Hurricane Andrew (Shaw et al., 1995) and Hurricane Hugo, which struck the Carolinas in 1989 (Lonigan, Anthony, & Shannon, 1998; Lonigan, Shannon, Finch, Daugherty, & Taylor, 1991; Lonigan, Shannon, Taylor, Finch, & Sallee, 1994). Recent research conducted with children and adolescents after Hurricane Katrina (Weems et al., 2007) also informs the present discussion. We begin with a brief overview of what the empirical research (i.e., the studies just cited) indicates regarding children's and adolescents' reactions to hurricanes. This overview serves as the backdrop for the steps that we suggest later in the chapter with respect to preparedness, response, and intervention.

CHILDREN'S REACTIONS TO HURRICANES: A BRIEF OVERVIEW

In discussing children's reactions, it is important to first consider the issue of timing (Valent, 2000). In the context of natural disasters, including hurricanes, individuals' reactions can be assessed during one or more of the following five phases: (a) *preimpact*, the time period before a disaster; (b) *impact*, when the event occurs; (c) *recoil*, immediately after the event; (d) *postimpact*, days to weeks after the event; and (e) *recovery and reconstruction*, months or years after the event (Silverman & La Greca, 2002). In the recoil and postimpact phases, acute stress reactions such as a sense of shock and high levels of distress and fear are not uncommon (National Child Traumatic Stress Network [NCTSN] & National Center for Posttraumatic Stress Disorder [NCPTSD], 2006; Pynoos & Nader, 1988). In the hurricane disaster area, most of the empirical research has focused on youths' reactions during the recovery and reconstruction phase. It is this research that we summarize next, followed by a brief discussion of factors that have been found to predict these reactions in youths.

Common Reactions in Youths

The most common reactions displayed by children and adolescents during the recovery and reconstruction phases are posttraumatic stress reactions, particularly posttraumatic stress symptoms (PTSS; e.g., La Greca et al., 1996, 1998; Lonigan et al., 1994, 1998; Nolen-Hoeksema & Morrow, 1991; Russoniello et al., 2002; Swenson et al., 1996; Weems et al., 2007). With respect to PTSS, using the Posttraumatic Stress Disorder Reaction Index for Youth (Frederick, 1985), La Greca et al. (1996) assessed PTSS at three assessment points (3 months, 7 months, and 10 months postdisaster) in 442 third- through fifth-grade children exposed to Hurricane Andrew. Although the findings indicated that the children's ratings of PTSS declined over time, a substantial percentage of children continued to report severe or very severe PTSS: 29.8% at 3 months, 18.1% at 7 months, and 12.5% at 10 months following the disaster. Other studies have described similar patterns (Lonigan et al., 1991, 1994). In addition, children who reported moderate to very severe levels of PTSS in the immediate hurricane aftermath were more likely to suffer symptom persistence (La Greca et al., 1996).

Factors Predicting Child Reactions

Factors predicting children's reactions to hurricanes have been discussed within the context of a conceptual model (e.g., La Greca et al., 1996; Silverman & La Greca, 2002; Vernberg et al., 1996) in which variables associated with reactions are organized into four domains: (a) aspects of the exposure (e.g., life threat), (b) preexisting characteristics of the child (e.g., predisaster functioning), (c) characteristics of the postrecovery environment (e.g., social support), and (d) the child's psychological resources (e.g., coping strategies).

Exposure

Severity or intensity of the individual's exposure to the hurricane has been the most consistently found significant predictor of PTSS in the short term and over time. For example, on the basis of children's responses to a questionnaire designed to assess for level of exposure to life-threatening experiences (e.g., "Did you get hurt during the hurricane?") and loss/disruption experiences (e.g., "Was your home badly damaged or destroyed by the hurricane?"), children who reported high levels of such exposure were most likely to report PTSS and to show symptom persistence (La Greca et al., 1996; Vernberg et al., 1996).

Preexisting Characteristics

Knowledge about preexisting child characteristics that may predict symptom persistence exists mainly because investigators have been in the serendipitous position of having gathered prehurricane data on youth samples, allowing for a comparison of youth functioning before and after the storm (e.g., La Greca et al., 1996; Weems et al., 2007). La Greca et al. (1998), for example, found that prehurricane anxiety levels in a sample of elementary schoolchildren (Grades 4–6) significantly predicted PTSS. Using the Revised Children's Manifest Anxiety Scale (RCMAS; Reynolds & Richmond, 1985), the authors found that high levels of child anxiety symptoms assessed 15 months before Hurricane Andrew (i.e., the preimpact phase) significantly predicted high levels of child PTSS 3 months after the hurricane. More recently, Weems et al. (2007), using the trait version of the State–Trait Anxiety Inventory for Children (Spielberger, 1973), found that high levels of trait anxiety in 52 youths ages 5 to 16 years, assessed on average 17 months before exposure to Hurricane Katrina, significantly predicted PTSS on the Child PTSD Checklist (Amaya-Jackson, McCarthy, Newman, & Cherney, 1995), as well as symptoms of generalized anxiety disorder and major depression using the Revised Child Anxiety and Depression Scale (Chorpita, Yim, Moffit, Umemoto, & Francis, 2000).

Using a cross-sectional design, Lonigan et al. (1994) assessed anxiety using the RCMAS in youths ages 9 to 19 years 3 months following Hurricane Hugo, along with hurricane impact factors (e.g., location during storm, subjective severity of exposure, home damage) and demographic variables (i.e., gender, age, race), to determine significant predictors of PTSS, assessed using the Reaction Index for Children (Frederick, 1985). Findings indicated that of all the variables assessed, youth anxiety was the strongest predictor of PTSS: Youths who had anxiety scores higher than the sample median on the RCMAS reported more PTSS and were more likely to meet diagnostic criteria for PTSD than youths who scored below the median.

Although they studied children exposed to an earthquake, not a hurricane, Asarnow et al.'s (1999) findings warrant mention because they are consistent with the above-cited studies. Youths ages 8 to 18 years were administered the child version of the Schedule for Affective Disorder and Schizophrenia (Orvaschel & Puig-Antich, 1987) and the RCMAS 18 months before exposure to the 1994 Northridge earthquake in Los Angeles. Results indicated that having a predisaster anxiety disorder diagnosis and elevated RCMAS scores predicted youth PTSS 1 year after the earthquake.

In addition to preexisting anxiety levels, hurricane researchers have examined the role of demographic characteristics. The findings have been inconsistent. Some studies have found that child gender significantly predicts youth PTSS (i.e., girls are more likely than boys to show PTSS; Lonigan et al., 1991; Vernberg et al., 1996), but other studies have not identified sex differences (e.g., La Greca et al., 1996, 1998). In terms of ethnicity, Vernberg et al. (1996) found that ethnicity was not significantly related to children's PTSS; La Greca et al. (1996) found that Hispanic and African American children reported higher levels of PTSS than European American children over time. In light of the scant and inconsistent existing research, it is critical that further research be conducted on how membership in a minority group affects young people's perceptions of hurricane exposure and its impact. Given the other traumas and negative life events associated with minority status, including poverty and discrimination, racial and ethnic minority youths and families would appear to have additional challenges to cope with after being exposed to a devastating hurricane.

Postrecovery Environment

A number of variables have been examined as predictors of children's reactions following natural disasters. Most common has been level of social support. In studies by Vernberg et al. (1996) and La Greca et al. (1996), children completed the Social Support Scale for Children and Adolescents (Harter, 1985) to assess their perceptions of social support from four sources: parents, classmates, teachers, and close friends. Low levels of perceived social support from classmates and teachers predicted high levels of child PTSS 3 months after exposure to Hurricane Andrew. Seven and 10 months after exposure to the hurricane, low levels of perceived social support from classmates and from parents continued to predict high levels of PTSS, but perceived low levels of social support from teachers did not.

Another postrecovery environment variable studied has been stressful life events. Garrison et al. (1995) administered a modified version of the Life Events Checklist (Johnson & McCutcheon, 1980) to adolescents ages 12 to 17 years 6 months after exposure to Hurricane Andrew. Results indicated that lifetime exposure to violent events, as well as exposure to undesirable events (events not specified) since the hurricane, were both significantly related to adolescent PTSS. Similarly, using the Life Events Schedule (Coddington, 1972), La Greca et al. (1996) found that number of stressful life events experienced since Hurricane Andrew was significantly related to PTSS in children 7 months after hurricane exposure.

In the aftermath of natural disasters, including hurricanes, the media coverage is incessant. We are not aware of studies that have examined the effects of media coverage on youths' reactions following hurricanes. However, studies following the terrorist attacks of September 11, 2001 (9/11; Saylor, Cowart, Lipovsky, Jackson, & Finch, 2003), and the 1995 Oklahoma City bombing (Pfefferbaum et al., 2000, 2003) revealed a positive and significant relation between the amount of child exposure to media coverage and child PTSS. This relation was observed among children (i.e., sixth graders) who were exposed to media coverage only (not the disaster itself), suggesting that adverse reactions emerge even when children are not exposed directly to the event. Given these findings in the aftermath of terrorist events, it is important for future research to determine whether similar patterns are found in the aftermath of hurricanes.

Finally, although it is plausible to suspect that parents' psychosocial functioning and levels of psychopathology can influence their children's posthurricane reactions, there is scarce research on this issue (see chaps. 2 and 3, this volume). Prior research (Swenson et al., 1996) found that mothers' distress in the aftermath of Hurricane Hugo was associated with the persistence of their children's postdisaster emotional and behavioral difficulties.

Child Psychological Resources

As far as the authors are aware, children's coping strategies are the only child psychological resources that have been studied (La Greca et al., 1996; Russoniello et al., 2002; Vernberg et al., 1996). In these studies, the 15-item Kidcope (Spirito, Star, & Williams, 1988) has been the measure used to assess children's coping. In the series of studies by La Greca and colleagues (La Greca et al., 1996; Vernberg et al., 1996), a principal components analysis was conducted on the Kidcope, yielding four factors: positive coping, blame and anger, wishful thinking, and social withdrawal. Results indicated that blame and anger, although the least reported by the children, were most predictive of elevated PTSS 2 months after Hurricane Andrew and continued to predict elevated PTSS 7 and 10 months later (La Greca et al., 1996). Using the original 10-factor structure of the Kidcope derived by Spirito et al. (1988), Russoniello et al. (2002) found that in the aftermath of Hurricane Floyd, which struck North Carolina in 1999, children who reported using the following five coping strategies had elevated PTSS: social withdrawal, blaming others, self-criticism, problem solving, and emotional regulation difficulties.

Summary of Findings on Children's Reactions to Hurricanes

Although as many as 30% of children report PTSS 3 months after a severe hurricane, a decline in PTSS occurs with the passage of time (La Greca et al., 1996; Vernberg et al., 1996). Research further indicates that children who report mild PTSS in the early aftermath of a hurricane recover well. Children who report moderate to very severe levels of PTSS after exposure to a hurricane, however, are more likely to suffer symptom persistence (La Greca et al., 1996). In addition, level of exposure, preexisting child characteristics (e.g., anxiety), the child's postrecovery environment (e.g., social support), and the child's psychological resources (e.g., coping) are the most consistently observed predictors of persistent youth PTSS following hurricanes. These findings, taken together, serve as the backdrop for the subsequent discussion regarding lessons learned for preparedness, response, and intervention.

PREPARING CHILDREN AND ADOLESCENTS BEFORE HURRICANES STRIKE

For accounts of the failures of the response systems, both local and national, with respect to preparation before and during Katrina (i.e., the preimpact and impact phases), the reader is referred to sources about this disaster (e.g., Cooper & Block, 2006; Curiel, 2006; Gheytanchi et al., 2007; Von Winterfeldt, 2006). With respect to preparation materials for use with children and adolescents before a hurricane strikes, several Web-based materials exist, including materials from the American Psychological Association, the National Institute of Mental Health, the U.S. Department of Homeland Security, the Federal Emergency Management Agency (FEMA), the American Red Cross, and NCTSN. These predisaster preparatory materials focus on helping children return to their daily predisaster routines and provide useful facts and educational information about the nature of hurricanes, how to prepare for them, and how to handle hurricane-related disruptions. Additionally, developmentally sensitive suggestions are offered to parents on how to encourage children to talk about their hurricane-related concerns. Also included in some of these materials (e.g., NCTSN's Web site) is useful information about the psychological effects of hurricanes on children and families, such as heightened anxiety and PTSS. Suggestions to the media on how to cover hurricanes and disasters in a sensitive manner also are provided.

Although such psychoeducational information might serve a useful preparatory function, as far as we know, no one has tested whether such information increases children's and parents' knowledge. Also untested is whether such information translates into behavior change efforts, as well as whether such information mediates reductions in children's and parents' stress reactions. Based on knowledge garnered from other public health information campaigns (e.g., smoking, teenage pregnancy), if hurricane preparatory resources are to be helpful, they need to be designed to meet particular target groups' needs and existing beliefs (e.g., Fishbein, Hall-Jamieson, Zimmer, von Haeften, & Nabi, 2002). In line with the contextual approach of Bronfenbrenner (1979, 1989), for example, youths' needs, such as their emotional reactions to the potential threat of a disaster, could be met by actively involving proximal influences, such as family members, school personnel, and peer groups, in preparedness activities. In considering more distal potential influences, youths' needs could be met by integrating preparedness programs within the community and raising awareness about disaster preparedness within the culture at-large. Such an approach, of course, would also carefully consider and include cultural and ethnic issues that may be unique or salient to the specific group with which one is working.

In addition to the above types of psychoeducational materials, which can be provided in a universal fashion to children and their families, work involving developing materials for selective interventions is under way. For example, with support from the Terrorism and Disaster Center (led by Betty Pfefferbaum) of the NCTSN and in collaboration with Annette La Greca and Robert Pynoos, we have been developing and gathering preliminary data on a Resilience-Building Screen. The screen was designed to identify children who may be at risk of impairing negative reactions to the cues and signals of disasters before a personal experience with disaster occurs (Silverman, La Greca, & Ortiz, 2004). The Resilience-Building Screen's development is based on the previously cited studies regarding the most commonly found predictors of enduring posthurricane child traumatic stress reactions, and the screen's items map onto each of these predictors/variables. Data analyses for this project are currently in progress.

Our objective is empirically to devise a screening instrument that will be successful in identifying children who might benefit from a predisaster Resilience-Building Training program, a program that we also are in the midst of developing. Such a program would focus on enhancing those domains (i.e., the variables assessed on the Resilience-Building Screen) in which children were found to be deficient (e.g., coping strategies), so that children would be better prepared to manage their reactions relating to hurricanes during the various phases (e.g., preimpact, postimpact).

RESPONDING TO CHILDREN AND ADOLESCENTS IN THE SHORT-TERM AFTERMATH

Similar to the preimpact phase, scarce empirical research has been conducted on responding to children and adolescents in the immediate and postimpact (i.e., days to weeks) phases of severe hurricanes. However, two approaches are available: (a) critical incident stress debriefing (CISD), the development of which has not been generally empirically informed; and (b) Psychological First Aid, which is more empirically informed.

Critical Incident Stress Debriefing

CISD was initially conceived for use with emergency workers. Survivors attend a debriefing session within days of the critical incident, such as a severe hurricane, to vent, discuss, and process their experiences (Everly, Flannery, & Eyler, 2001; Mitchell & Everly, 2006). Although CISD training is widely available, with more than 40,000 individuals receiving training every year (McNally, 2004), CISD has been a subject of discussion and controversy in the disaster literature on adults (Bisson, Jenkins, Alexander, & Bannister,

1997; Hobbs, Mayou, Harrison, & Worlock, 1996; Mayou, Ehlers, & Hobbs, 2000; McNally, 2004) and youths (Yule, 2001). The controversy centers on CISD's potential iatrogenic effects and its possible inattention to the complex set of reactions displayed by youths in the aftermath of disasters (La Greca, 2008; Mayou et al., 2000).

Few studies have evaluated the effectiveness of CISD with children and adolescents. In the only youth randomized controlled trial that we could locate, Stallard et al. (2006) assigned 158 youths ages 7 to 18 years who had been admitted to a hospital emergency department following a motor vehicle accident to CISD or to a comparison control condition (i.e., group discussion of non-accident-related events). The findings indicated a decline in youths' rates of PTSD and symptoms of depression; however, no significant differences were found between the two groups. Although this study represents a laudable initial empirical effort, the debriefing format was administered 4 weeks after the youths' accidents rather than in the immediate aftermath of the event (e.g., Mitchell, 1983). Thus, whether this study is an evaluation of CISD is questionable. Because of the potential for iatrogenic effects of CISD, we cannot currently recommend CISD as a strategy to alleviate youths' psychological distress in the immediate aftermath of a traumatic event.

Psychological First Aid

In the wake of 9/11, mental health experts convened and recommended the development of a comprehensive mental health response approach for use with youths and adults who have been exposed to disaster or terrorist events and who report an increased level of distress in the immediate aftermath. Federal funding was provided, and the NCTSN and the NCPTSD (2006) spearheaded the development of the Psychological First Aid manual.

Designed to be delivered by first responders and disaster response workers in emergency settings, such as shelters, in a single session or over multiple sessions, Psychological First Aid is currently the "acute intervention of choice" (NCTSN & NCPTSD, 2006). Between its Fall 2005 posting on the NCTSN and the NCPTSD's Web sites and Fall 2007, the Psychological First Aid manual was downloaded more than 25,000 times, and several thousand hard copies were distributed during trainings (M. Brymer, personal communication, July 16, 2007). In addition to the development of the NCTSN/NCPTSD manual, other agencies have developed Psychological First Aid approaches (e.g., the American Red Cross) or have adapted the NCTSN/NCPTSD model (e.g., the Medical Reserve Corps). Also, a manual on using Psychological First Aid in schools during disasters, crises, or emergencies is available through the U.S. Department of Homeland Security's Ready America campaign.

The principles of Psychological First Aid are based on research showing that a return to predisaster levels of functioning is typical for individuals who have been exposed to a traumatic event and that supporting these individuals' strengths and competence can help foster resilience (Pynoos & Nader, 1988). Psychological First Aid is structured around eight "Core Actions" (NCTSN & NCPTSD, 2006); the manual includes suggestions for both adults and youths:

1. Core Action 1 involves suggestions about contact and engagement, focusing on how to respond to trauma survivors in an appropriate and compassionate fashion.
2. Core Action 2, safety and comfort, centers around reestablishing disaster survivors' sense of safety (e.g., physical and emotional comfort).
3. Core Action 3 provides information on how to help stabilize survivors who are overwhelmed emotionally by the traumatic experience; the steps include grounding strategies that involve deep breathing methods.
4. Core Action 4 centers on information gathering. Survivors' needs for individualized services are elicited, and concerns regarding the extent of the traumatic exposure are identified (e.g., a youth's reaction to the death of a family member, family disruption, or loss or destruction of home).
5. Core Action 5 focuses on providing survivors with practical assistance to help address their needs. For example, youths are offered suggestions on how to access resources to meet their most pressing needs, such as locating loved ones who are lost.
6. The purpose of Core Action 6 is to help survivors identify and draw on available social support. Youths, for example, are encouraged to seek support from family members, friends, community centers, and spiritual or religious organizations.
7. In Core Action 7, information on coping with common immediate postdisaster stress reactions (e.g., bothersome thoughts about the traumatic experience, physiological arousal) is provided, and strategies for reducing such stress are offered (e.g., relaxation, exercise, journaling).
8. Finally, Core Action 8 emphasizes the necessity of providing parents and/or caregivers with necessary additional services or referrals for their child in the future.

Although Psychological First Aid appears to be based on stronger theoretical and empirical groundings than CISD, further empirical research is needed to support both approaches. It remains an empirical question whether youths who receive Psychological First Aid show improved recovery or a quicker return to normative functioning than youths who do not receive it. We recognize that the chaos and disruption of severe hurricanes render conducting research in their aftermath highly challenging; nevertheless, the need for such research is of considerable public health significance. As La Greca (2008) noted, the NCTSN/NCPTSD (2006) Psychological First Aid manual is fairly lengthy (189 pages), which can lead to some apprehension among potential users. On the more positive side, the eight core actions do not involve psychological counseling per se and thus can be delivered by trained paraprofessional disaster workers.

INTERVENING WITH CHILDREN AND ADOLESCENTS IN THE LONG-TERM AFTERMATH

As noted at the beginning of this chapter, the authors have been involved in efforts to intervene with children and adolescents in the reconstruction and recovery phases following the 2004 and 2005 Florida hurricanes, as well as Hurricane Katrina. Before we describe these efforts, it is important to note that studies conducted in the reconstruction and recovery phases following hurricanes are scarce.

Research on Children and Adolescents Following a Disaster

One postdisaster study involved a nonrandomized school-based intervention that compared Brief Trauma/Grief Focused Psychotherapy ($n = 35$; two individual and four classroom sessions) with no treatment ($n = 29$) 3 years after the devastating 1988 earthquake in Armenia (mean age = 13.2 years; Goenjian et al., 1997, 2005). Another study was a nonrandomized school-based intervention that compared a classroom-based School Reactivation Program, a combination of psychoeducation and cognitive–behavioral therapy (CBT) delivered to 202 youths 9 to 17 years old 4 to 5 months after a devastating earthquake in Turkey in 1999 (Wolmer, Laor, Dedeoglu, Siev, & Yazgan, 2005). In addition, a multiple-baseline design study evaluated an exposure-based CBT intervention with 17 children and adolescents who displayed PTSD (average duration = 1.5–2.5 years) after a single traumatic incident (e.g., car accident, shooting, accidental injury) or disaster-related incident (e.g., severe storm, fire; March, Amaya-Jackson, Murray, & Schulte, 1998).

It is not possible to draw firm inferences from any of these studies, given methodological limitations. As a whole, however, the findings suggest that providing psychosocial intervention can be helpful. The study by Goenjian et al. (1997, 2005), which included a no-treatment comparison condition, further suggests that psychosocial intervention is better than not providing any intervention. (See Jaycox, Morse, Tanielian, and Stein, 2006, for a review of school-based studies.)

Chemtob, Nakashima, and Hamada (2002) conducted a randomized controlled trial on children exposed to Hurricane Iniki, which struck the Hawaiian island of Kauai in 1992. After screening 3,864 second through sixth graders for high levels of PTSS 2 years after Hurricane Iniki, 248 children (6.4%) with elevated PTSS were randomly assigned to consecutively treated cohorts (children awaiting treatment served as wait-list controls). Within each cohort, children were randomly assigned to either individual or group treatment. In groups of four to eight, children were provided with developmentally sensitive, structured therapy exercises over four weekly sessions. Though play, art, and therapeutic discussions, the treatment sessions focused on helping children master disaster-related psychological challenges, including (a) regaining a sense of safety and addressing feelings of helplessness, (b) addressing the significance of losses and renewing attachments, (c) expressing disaster-related anger, and (d) achieving closure about the disaster in order to move forward. Treated children reported significant reductions in PTSS that were maintained at 12-month follow-up, with no significant differences between the group and individual treatment approaches. Interestingly, children in the group condition were more likely to complete treatment than children in the individual condition.

Salloum and Overstreet (2008) tested a 10-week manualized community-based intervention for 56 children 7 to 12 years of age who experienced grief from a recent death (duration of grief > 1 month) or trauma 4 months following Hurricane Katrina (score of 25 or higher on the University of California at Los Angeles PTSD Reaction Index; Steinberg, Brymer, Decker, & Pynoos, 2004). The authors noted that because of ethical concerns in withholding treatment in a postdisaster environment, randomly assigning children to alternative treatments or alternative treatment modalities represents a more reasonable approach to conduct rigorous research (Chemtob et al., 2002). Thus, children were randomly assigned to either an individual or group treatment format that focused on psychoeducation about grief and trauma reactions, increase in affective and cognitive expression through the development of a coherent trauma narrative, and adaptive coping strategies. Children in both the individual and group treatments showed significant decreases in PTSS, as well as depression and grief symptoms, with no significant difference found between the two formats. The study represents an important effort in working with children following a devastating hurricane; however, because the follow-up was, on average, only 20 days, it will be necessary to learn more about how these children fare over time.

Given the scarcity of hurricane intervention studies, it is worthwhile to note that in the broader child and adolescent trauma treatment research literature, a review and meta-analysis of 21 studies published between 1993 and 2007 revealed that interventions that involve components of cognitive–behavioral therapy were more efficacious in reducing trauma reactions in youths than non-CBT therapies (Silverman et al., 2008). Although there are variants of CBT (Silverman et al., 2008), trauma-focused CBT was found to have the highest level of empirical support. The core treatment components of trauma-focused CBT include psychoeducation, management of anxiety, trauma and loss reminders, trauma narration and organization, cognitive and affective labeling and processing, problem solving regarding safety and relationships, parent skill building and behavioral management, emotional regulation, and support of youths to resume negatively affected developmental competencies (Amaya-Jackson & DeRosa, 2007). We now briefly describe our efforts to intervene with children and adolescents in the reconstruction and recovery phases following the 2004 and 2005 Florida hurricanes as well as the devastating Hurricane Katrina in 2005.

Adolescent and Child Component Therapy

Adolescent and Child Component Therapy (ACT; Saltzman et al., 2005) emerged as a product of Project Recovery, funded by the Substance Abuse and Mental Health Services Administration (SAMHSA) and the State of Florida in response to the four hurricanes (Charley, Frances, Ivan, and Jeanne) that struck Florida between August 13 and September 26, 2004. In total, the hurricanes led to an estimated $20 billion in damages and significant loss of life (Caputo, 2004). Children affected by Florida Hurricane Wilma in 2005 also were recipients of ACT (see Allen, Saltzman, Brymer, Oshri, & Silverman, 2006).

Although the evaluation of ACT is in progress, Brymer and Steinberg's (2007) final report to the State of Florida on Project Recovery is noteworthy. A large majority of youth participants lost their homes and had observed their neighborhood ruined, indicating that the population was screened appropriately and contained a large proportion of youths who would benefit from trauma-informed services. The outcome measures were all consistent in providing empirical support for the intervention's effectiveness. There were significant pre- to postintervention reductions in posttraumatic stress and depressive and anxiety reactions. Posttraumatic stress reactions fell from a moderate to a very mild range; depressive reactions fell from clinical to subclinical levels. Reductions also were found on general anxiety reactions and specific anxiety factors. Youths' maladaptive coping styles also were significantly reduced. These findings support the core treatment components of ACT.

Strength After Trauma

Strength After Trauma (StArT; Saltzman et al., 2007) was developed to address the needs of youths who continued to report disaster-related distress in the aftermath of Hurricane Katrina.[1] These youths were still residing either in the New Orleans area or in Texas, having relocated after the storm. The horrors inflicted by Katrina have been discussed in previous chapters in this volume (see, e.g., Introduction, chap. 1). In the aftermath of one of worst natural disasters in this country's history, an intervention such as StArT was sorely needed for the affected Hurricane Katrina youths. At the time of this writing, the program and its evaluation are ongoing.

StArT's training format was based on a somewhat more structured approach than ACT in that it followed the format of a learning collaborative model. Developed by the Institute for Healthcare Improvement (2003), the learning collaborative model aims to enhance implementation efforts by actively involving practitioners, providing skills-based training, and allowing trainings to be infused by the needs and experiences of the practitioners who are implementing the intervention. StArT training has been provided over the course of three 2-day learning sessions over 9 to 12 months. During implementation of the training material, ongoing expert consultation and feedback via telephone conferences have been provided. Given the more intensive approach to the learning collaborative model used in StArT, it has required a substantial time commitment on behalf of the practitioners. Whether the approach used in StArT leads to improved outcomes relative to the less intensive approach used in ACT will be of interest once the evaluative aspects of both projects are completed.

SOCIOCULTURAL AND ETHICAL CONSIDERATIONS IN WORK WITH CHILDREN AND ADOLESCENTS FOLLOWING A HURRICANE

In this section we discuss the importance of two additional issues we believe are particularly important to consider when working with children and adolescents in the context of severe hurricanes: (a) showing sensitivity to youth development, culture, and socioeconomic status (SES) and (b) attending to ethical issues.

---

[1]Silverman and Allen (2006) also developed the Kids Dealing With Disasters (KiDD) manual with support from the Terrorism and Disaster Center. Because implementation of KiDD is pending, our focus here is on ACT and StArT.

Sensitivity to Youth Development, Culture, and Socioeconomic Status

As with any intervention used with young people, it is important to ensure that both the content and process of the intervention are delivered in a developmentally appropriate way. In the ACT and StArT manuals, and especially during the trainings, sample language is provided to help adapt the manuals for different age groups. For example, practitioners are instructed to use vocabulary that is appropriate to the children's development (e.g., "stay away" vs. "avoid," "feeling funny or weird in our body" vs. "physiological symptoms," "things we say to ourselves" vs. "cognitions"). They are also cautioned to ensure that the examples provided are sensitive to developmental level (e.g., "playing with other kids" vs. "hanging out with friends"). Similarly, in discussing access to social support resources in StArT, adolescents are provided with information about six different types of social support (emotional support, social connection, feeling needed, advice and information, physical assistance, material assistance). Younger children, however, are simply asked questions such as, "Who can you talk to when you are feeling worried or sad?" and "Who helps you do things like homework or fix a broken toy?"

Similar efforts are made to ensure that the processes used to communicate the main ideas and therapeutic procedures consider the children's developmental needs. For example, with younger children, greater emphasis is typically placed on using visual stimuli, such as drawing figures on the blackboard, drawing or writing out key concepts on the board, and asking the children to repeat back some of the main session points.

It is of equal importance to ensure that the content and process of the intervention are delivered in a manner that is sensitive to the youths' cultural milieu. It can be particularly challenging to develop trusting relationships with disaster-exposed youths and families of ethnic or racial minority groups, in part because mental health providers often are from the majority culture. Thus, the chance for distrust between the parties is increased. Breaking through this distrust by developing an understanding of the cultural mores and customs of the group with which one is working is incumbent on all mental health professionals who intend to deliver disaster mental health services.

In Psychological First Aid, for example, providers are encouraged to consider survivors' cultural backgrounds when considering grief and spiritual issues and to seek guidance from community religious or clerical leaders regarding customs and traditions. Providers are further encouraged to be aware of cultural customs such as those relating to eye contact and personal space and to intervene accordingly depending on how these customs may vary across cultures.

Regarding SES-related issues, many families treated with ACT and StArT reported increased financial stressors in the aftermath of the storm, including losing employment, living in more crowded conditions, and feeling singled out for living in a FEMA trailer. Hurricane survivors who were forced to relocate to Texas reported having lost a sense of community specific to New Orleans (e.g., Cajun cuisine, Mardi Gras). In the manuals and trainings, practitioners were encouraged to be cognizant of these issues and to attend to them, as necessary, in their work with youths.

Much of the ACT and StArT module content focuses on proximal needs of the particular child, such as the child's primary relationships with parents and peers. The manuals and trainings place emphasis on ensuring that the delivery of the different modules was sensitive to each child's ecological context (Bronfenbrenner, 1979, 1989). When developing trauma narratives, for example, practitioners are encouraged to explore how children's disaster experiences and reactions are influenced by parents' or caregivers' postdisaster loss (e.g., lack of employment). Ensuring that ACT and StArT are implemented by clinicians who live in the affected communities and are familiar with the culture enhances the ecological strength of the modules.

Ethical Issues

Although attending to ethical issues pervades all psychological work, in the context of disasters, certain ethical issues are likely to be particularly salient. In the context of the Resilience-Building Screen and the Resilience-Building Training, mentioned earlier, if students are selected for intervention on the basis of their score on the screen, there is the possibility that the selected students will be stigmatized, an issue that practitioners need carefully to consider. One alternative is to provide the training to all students in the school, regardless of how they score on the screen, thereby circumventing any potential stigmatization, especially given that all children could potentially benefit from such training. In this scenario, the screen would still be useful for evaluating whether children who were found to be deficient in particular domains via the screen improved following the training.

When implementing Psychological First Aid, ethical issues pertaining to confidentiality and privacy also bear mentioning. In the chaos of the immediate postdisaster environment, for example, it may prove highly challenging (if not impossible) to find space in a crowded shelter to provide services in a setting that is confidential and private enough for survivors to feel comfortable discussing personal issues.

When implementing interventions such as those described in the ACT and StArT manuals during the reconstruction and recovery phase, some key points relating to the research process warrant further consideration. Given that research evidence suggests that individuals' decisional abilities can be adversely affected following trauma exposure (Rosenstein,

2004), it is important to ascertain whether potential participants are able to provide informed consent. They may or may not be able to do so (Collogan, Tuma, Dolan-Sewell, Borja, & Fleischman, 2004), and one way to ascertain whether they can is by having individuals independent from the research team and/or interveners assist in more intensive and thorough evaluations of parents' or caregivers' and children's decision-making abilities (Rosenstein, 2004).

In one of the few studies we could locate on the issue of trauma victims' reactions to research participation, Ruzek and Zatzick (2000) conducted 1-hour interviews with 117 survivors of motor vehicle accidents (ages ranged from 14 to 61 years; 10 were adolescents ages 14–18 years). Specifically, while still receiving treatment for their injuries in the hospital, participants were asked questions about their experiences with previous traumatic events; their physical health and psychological health, including substance use; and their level of satisfaction regarding the quality of medical care received. When subsequently asked about their reactions to participating in this research study, 75% of participants reported deriving "some benefit" from being part of the study, and 95% reported that participation was more beneficial than not and that given the choice, they would participate again (Ruzek & Zatzick, 2000). On the more negative side, "unwanted thoughts" and feeling "emotionally upset" were reported by 30% and 12% of participants, respectively, and 19% indicated that they felt they could not say no to participating in the research project. Given this study's focus on motor vehicle accident survivors and the predominance of adult participants, it is not clear whether these findings would generalize to child and adolescent participants in hurricane disaster research. This question warrants further study.

LESSONS LEARNED AND ACTIONABLE RECOMMENDATIONS

In preparing youths before hurricanes strike, it is critical to ensure that children and adolescents are provided with psychoeducational information in a developmentally and culturally sensitive manner. The type of information most likely to be useful to youths in this phase includes facts and educational information about the nature of hurricanes, ways to prepare for them, and methods for handling hurricane-related disruptions. Providing developmentally and culturally sensitive suggestions to assist parents in talking with their children about hurricane-related issues, including how to encourage their children to share their concerns, can be helpful.

In terms of responding to youths' needs in the short-term aftermath of a hurricane, normalizing their experiences, providing comfort, increasing their coping strategies, and offering assistance and information about resources to help promote a safe return to predisaster routines are most critical. In addition, although Psychological First Aid requires systematic empirical evaluation, we would still recommend this approach over CISD because the former is based on empirically informed practices with respect to addressing youths' immediate postdisaster reactions. Regarding long-term intervention strategies, CBT-based psychosocial treatments are most highly recommended. We await the empirical findings that emerge from the ACT and StArT interventions before we provide recommendations for their use.

Have lessons been learned in the aftermath of Hurricane Katrina and the severe hurricanes that have preceded it? We believe so. Before Katrina, the field had learned about youths' persistent reactions to hurricanes, particularly PTSS, and also had identified factors most predictive of PTSS (La Greca et al., 1996; Lonigan et al., 1991, 1998; Vernberg et al., 1996). Since Hurricane Katrina, systematic and empirically informed efforts have been undertaken based on the earlier research to devise strategies to identify children at risk of developing symptoms should a future disaster strike (i.e., the Resilience-Building Screen and the Resilience-Building Program). Prior research findings also have guided efforts to develop and to begin to evaluate empirically informed interventions for use in the immediate aftermath of hurricanes, such as Psychological First Aid, as well as in the long-term aftermath, such as ACT and StArT.

In conclusion, in response to Pete Seeger's question noted at the chapter's beginning, we hope this chapter has provided the answer: Much indeed has been learned about ways to help children and adolescents before and after severe hurricanes, but there is much that remains to be learned.

REFERENCES

Allen, A., Saltzman, W. R., Brymer, M. J., Oshri, A., & Silverman, W. K. (2006). An empirically informed intervention for children following exposure to severe hurricanes. *Behavior Therapist, 6,* 118–124.

Amaya-Jackson, L., & DeRosa, R. R. (2007). Treatment considerations for clinicians in applying evidence-based practice to complex presentations in child trauma. *Journal of Traumatic Stress, 20,* 379–390.

Amaya-Jackson, L., McCarthy, G., Newman, E., & Cherney, M. S. (1995). *Child PTSD Checklist.* Durham, NC: Duke University Medical Center.

Asarnow, J., Glynn, S., Pynoos, R. S., Nahum, J., Guthrie, D., Cantwell, D. P., et al. (1999). When the Earth stops shaking: Earthquake sequelae among children diagnosed for pre-earthquake psychopathology. *Journal of the American Academy of Child and Adolescent Psychiatry, 38,* 1016–1023.

Bisson, J. I., Jenkins, P. L., Alexander, J., & Bannister, C. (1997). Randomized controlled trial of psychological debriefing for victims of acute burn trauma. *British Journal of Psychiatry, 171,* 78–81.

Bronfenbrenner, U. (1979). *The ecology of human development.* Cambridge, MA: Harvard University Press.

Bronfenbrenner, U. (1989). Ecological systems theory. *Annals of Child Development, 6,* 187–249.

Brymer, M. J., & Steinberg, A. M. (2007). *Project Recovery final evaluation: Adolescent and Child Component Therapy for Youth.* Los Angeles: National Center for Child Traumatic Stress, University of California at Los Angeles and Duke University.

Caputo, M. (2004, November 13). State's storm cost: $42 billion. *Miami Herald.* p. B1.

Chemtob, C., Nakashima, J., & Carlson, J. (2002). Brief treatment for elementary school children with disaster-related post traumatic stress disorder: A field study. *Journal of Clinical Psychology, 58,* 99–112.

Chemtob, C. M., Nakashima, J. P., & Hamada, R. S. (2002). Psychosocial intervention for postdisaster trauma symptoms in elementary school children: A controlled community field study. *Archives of Pediatric and Adolescent Medicine, 156,* 211–216.

Chorpita, B. F., Yim, L., Moffitt, C., Umemoto, L. A., & Francis, S. E. (2000). Assessment of symptoms of DSM–IV anxiety and depression in children: A revised child anxiety and depression scale. *Behaviour Research and Therapy, 38,* 835–855.

Coddington, R. D. (1972). The significance of life events as etiological factors in the disease of children: A study of a normal population. *Journal of Psychosomatic Research, 16,* 205–213.

Collogan, L. K., Tuma, F., Dolan-Sewell, R., Borja, S., & Fleischman, A. R. (2004). Ethical issues pertaining to research in the aftermath of disaster. *Journal of Traumatic Stress, 17,* 363–372.

Cooper, C., & Block, R. (2006). *Disaster: Hurricane Katrina and the failure of homeland security.* New York: Times Books.

Curiel, T. J. (2006). Murder or mercy? Hurricane Katrina and the need for disaster training. *New England Journal of Medicine, 355,* 2067–2069.

Everly, G. S., Jr., Flannery, R. B., Jr., & Eyler, V. (2001). Sufficiency analysis of an integrated multicomponent approach to crisis intervention: Critical incident stress management. *Advances in Mind–Body Medicine, 17,* 174–181.

Fishbein, M., Hall-Jamieson, K., Zimmer, E., von Haeften, I., & Nabi, R. (2002). Avoiding the boomerang: Testing the relative effectiveness of antidrug public service announcements before a national campaign. *American Journal of Public Health, 92,* 238–245.

Frederick, C. (1985). Selected foci in the spectrum of posttraumatic stress disorder. In J. Laube & S. A. Murphy (Eds.), *Perspectives on disaster recovery* (pp. 110–131). Norwalk, CT: Appleton-Century-Croft.

Garrison, C. Z., Bryant, E. S., Addy, C. L., Spurrier, P. G., Freedy, J. R., & Kilpatrick, D. G. (1995). Posttraumatic stress disorder in adolescents after Hurricane

Andrew. *Journal of the American Academy of Child and Adolescent Psychiatry, 34,* 1193–1201.

Gheytanchi, A., Joseph, L., Gierlach, E., Kimpara, S., Housely, J., Franco, Z. E., et al. (2007). The dirty dozen: Twelve failures of the Hurricane Katrina response and how psychology can help. *American Psychologist, 62,* 118–130.

Goenjian, A. K., Karayan, I., Pynoos, R. S., Minassian, D., Najarian, L. M., Steinberg, A. M., et al. (1997). Outcome of psychotherapy among early adolescents after trauma. *American Journal of Psychiatry, 154,* 536–542.

Goenjian, A. K., Walling, D., Steinberg, A. M., Karayan, I., Najarian, L. M., & Pynoos, R. S. (2005). A prospective study of posttraumatic stress and depressive reactions among treated and untreated adolescents 5 years after a catastrophic disaster. *American Journal of Psychiatry, 162,* 2302–2308.

Harter, S. (1985). *Manual for the Social Support Scale for Children and Adolescents.* Denver, CO: Author.

Hobbs, M., Mayou, R., Harrison, B., & Worlock, P. (1996). A randomized controlled trial of psychological debriefing for victims of road traffic accidents. *British Medical Journal, 313,* 1438–1439.

Institute for Healthcare Improvement. (2003). *The Breakthrough Series: IHI's collaborative model for achieving breakthrough improvement* (IHI Innovation Series White Paper). Boston: Author. Available at http://www.ihi.org/IHI/Results/White Papers/TheBreakthroughSeriesIHIsCollaborativeModelforAchieving+ BreakthroughImprovement.htm

International Federation of Red Cross and Red Crescent Societies. (2006). *World disasters report: Focus on neglected crises.* Bloomfield, CT: Kumarian Press.

Jaycox, L. H., Morse, L. K., Tanielian, T., & Stein, B. D. (2006). *How schools can help students recover from traumatic experiences: A tool kit for supporting long-term recovery.* Santa Monica, CA: RAND Corporation. Retrieved December 12, 2007, from http://www.rand.org/pubs/technical_reports/2006/RAND_TR413.pdf

Johnson, J. H., & McCutcheon, S. M. (1980). Assessing life stress in older children and adolescents: Preliminary findings with the Life Events Checklist. In I. G. Sarason & C. D. Spielberger (Eds.), *Stress and anxiety* (pp. 111–127). Washington, DC: Hemisphere.

La Greca, A. M. (2008). Interventions for posttraumatic stress in children and adolescents following natural disasters and acts of terrorism. In M. C. Roberts, D. Elkin, & R. Steele (Eds.), *Handbook of evidence-based therapies for children and adolescents: Bridging science and practice* (pp. 137–157). New York: Springer-Verlag.

La Greca, A. M., Silverman, W. K., Vernberg, E. M., & Prinstein, M. J. (1996). Symptoms of posttraumatic stress in children after Hurricane Andrew: A prospective study. *Journal of Consulting and Clinical Psychology, 64,* 712–723.

La Greca, A. M., Silverman, W. K., & Wasserstein, S. B. (1998). Children's predisaster functioning as a predictor of posttraumatic stress following Hurricane Andrew. *Journal of Consulting and Clinical Psychology, 66,* 883–892.

Lonigan, C. J., Anthony, J. L., & Shannon, M. P. (1998). Diagnostic efficacy of posttraumatic symptoms in children exposed to disaster. *Journal of Clinical Child Psychology, 27,* 255–267.

Lonigan, C. J., Shannon, M. P., Finch, A. J., Daugherty, T. K., & Taylor, C. M. (1991). Children's reactions to a natural disaster: Symptom severity and degree of exposure. *Advances in Behaviour Research and Therapy, 13,* 135–154.

Lonigan, C. J., Shannon, M. P., Taylor, C. M., Finch, A. J., Jr., & Sallee, F. R. (1994). Children exposed to disaster: II. Risk factors for the development of post-traumatic stress symptomatology. *Journal of the American Academy of Child and Adolescent Psychiatry, 33,* 94–105.

March, J. S., Amaya-Jackson, L., Murray, M. C., & Schulte, A. (1998). Cognitive–behavioral psychotherapy for children and adolescents with posttraumatic stress disorder after a single incident stressor. *Journal of the American Academy of Child and Adolescent Psychiatry, 37,* 585–593.

Mayou, R. A., Ehlers, A., & Hobbs, M. (2000). Psychological debriefing for road traffic accidents: Three-year follow up of a randomized controlled trial. *British Journal of Psychiatry, 176,* 589–593.

McNally, R. J. (2004). Psychological debriefing does not prevent posttraumatic stress disorder. *Psychiatric Times, 21.* Retrieved March 30, 2009, from http://www.psychiatrictimes.com/display/article/10168/54486?pageNumber=1

Mitchell, J. T. (1983). When disaster strikes: The critical incidence stress debriefing process. *Journal of Emergency Medical Services, 8,* 36–39.

Mitchell, J. T., & Everly, G. S., Jr. (2006). Critical incident stress management in terrorist events and disasters. In L. A. Schein, H. I. Spitz, G. M. Burlingame, P. R. Muskin, & S. Vargo (Eds.), *Psychological effects of catastrophic disasters: Group approaches to treatment* (pp. 425–480). New York: Haworth Press.

National Child Traumatic Stress Network & National Center for PTSD (NCPTSD). (2006). *Psychological First Aid: Field operations guide* (2nd ed.). Los Angeles and White River Junction, VT: Authors.

Nolen-Hoeksema, S., & Morrow, J. (1991). A prospective study of depression and posttraumatic stress symptoms after a natural disaster: The 1989 Loma Prieta earthquake. *Journal of Personality and Social Psychology, 61,* 115–121.

Orvaschel, H., & Puig-Antich, J. (1987). *Schedule for affective disorders and schizophrenia for school-age children, epidemiological version.* Palo Alto, CA: Social Ecology Laboratory.

Osofsky, J. (Ed.). (2007). *Young children and trauma.* New York: Guilford Press.

Pfefferbaum, B., Seale, T. W., Brandt, E. N., Pfefferbaum, R. L., Doughty, D. E., & Rainwater, S. M. (2003). Media exposure in children one hundred miles from a terrorist bombing. *Annals of Clinical Psychiatry, 15,* 1–8.

Pfefferbaum, B., Seale, T. W., McDonald, N. B., Brandt, E. N., Rainwater, S. M., Maynard, B. T., et al. (2000). Posttraumatic stress two years after the Oklahoma City bombing in youths geographically distant from the explosion. *Psychiatry, 63,* 358–370.

Pynoos, R. S., & Nader, K. (1988). Children who witness the sexual assaults of their mothers. *Journal of the American Academy of Child and Adolescent Psychiatry, 27*, 567–572.

Reynolds, C. R., & Richmond, B. O. (1985). *Revised Children's Manifest Anxiety Scale (RCMAS)*. Los Angeles: Western Psychological Services.

Rosenstein, D. L. (2004). Decision-making capacity and disaster research. *Journal of Traumatic Stress, 17*, 373–381.

Russoniello, C. V., Skalko, T. K., O'Brien, K., McGhee, S. A., Bingham-Alexander, D., & Beatley, J. (2002). Childhood posttraumatic stress disorder and efforts to cope after Hurricane Floyd. *Behavioral Medicine, 28*, 61–71.

Ruzek, J. I., & Zatzick, D. F. (2000). Ethical considerations in research participation among acutely injured trauma survivors: An empirical investigation. *General Hospital Psychiatry, 22*, 27–36.

Salloum, A., & Overstreet, S. (2008). Evaluation of individual and group grief and trauma interventions of children post disaster. *Journal of Clinical Child and Adolescent Psychology, 37*, 495–507.

Saltzman, W. R., Layne, C. M., Pynoos, R., Silverman, W. K., Lester, P. E., Allen, A., et al. (2005). *Adolescent and Child Component Therapy for trauma: Enhanced services, Project Recovery*. Los Angeles: National Child Traumatic Stress Network.

Saltzman, W. R., Silverman, W. K., Allen, A., Brymer, M. J., Layne, C. M., Pynoos, R. S., et al. (2007). *StArT: Strength After Trauma: A modular intervention for children and adolescents affected by hurricanes*. Los Angeles: National Child Traumatic Stress Network.

Saylor, C. F., Cowart, B. L., Lipovsky, J. A., Jackson, C., & Finch, A. J., Jr. (2003). Media exposure to September 11: Elementary school students' experiences and posttraumatic symptoms. *American Behavioral Scientist, 46*, 1622–1642.

Shaw, J. A., Applegate, B., Tanner, S., Perez, D., Rothe, E., Campo-Bowen, A. E., et al. (1995). Psychological effects of Hurricane Andrew on an elementary school population. *Journal of the American Academy of Child and Adolescent Psychiatry, 34*, 1185–1192.

Silverman, W. K., & Allen, A. (2006). *KiDD: Kids Dealing With Disasters: An empirically-informed intervention for use with children, hurricane adaptation*. Oklahoma City, OK: Terrorism and Disaster Center.

Silverman, W. K., & La Greca, A. M. (2002). Children experiencing disasters: Definitions, reactions, and predictors of outcomes. In A. M. La Greca, W. K. Silverman, E. M. Vernberg, & M. C. Roberts (Eds.), *Helping children cope with disasters and terrorism* (pp. 11–34). Washington, DC: American Psychological Association.

Silverman, W. K., La Greca, A. M., & Ortiz, C. D. (2004, July). *Resilience building in children prior to traumatic exposure: Screening considerations*. Symposium presented at the 112th Annual Convention of the American Psychological Association, Honolulu, HI.

Silverman, W. K., Ortiz, C. D., Viswesvaran, C., Burns, B. J., Kolko, D. J., Putnam, F. W., et al. (2008). Evidence-based psychosocial treatments for children and adolescents exposed to traumatic events. *Journal of Clinical Child and Adolescent Psychology, 37,* 156–183.

Spielberger, C. D. (1973). *Manual for the State–Trait Anxiety Inventory.* Palo Alto, CA: Consulting Psychologists Press.

Spirito, A., Star, L. J., & Williams, C. (1988). Development of a brief coping checklist for use with pediatric populations. *Journal of Pediatric Psychology, 13,* 555–574.

Stallard, P., Velleman, R., Salter, E., Howse, I., Yule, W., & Taylor, G. (2006). A randomized controlled trial to determine the effectiveness of an early psychological intervention with children involved in road traffic accidents. *Journal of Child Psychology and Psychiatry, 47,* 127–134.

Steinberg, A. M., Brymer, M. J., Decker, K., & Pynoos, R. S. (2004). The UCLA PTSD Reaction Index. *Current Psychiatry Reports, 6,* 96–100.

Swenson, C. C., Saylor, C. F., Powell, M. P., Stokes, S. J., Foster, K. Y., & Belter, R. W. (1996). Impact of a natural disaster on preschool children: Adjustment 14 months after a hurricane. *American Journal of Orthopsychiatry, 66,* 122–130.

Valent, P. (2000). Disaster syndrome. In G. Fink (Ed.), *Encyclopedia of stress* (Vol. 1, pp. 706–709). San Diego, CA: Academic Press.

Vernberg, E. M., La Greca, A. M., Silverman, W. K., & Prinstein, M. J. (1996). Prediction of posttraumatic stress symptoms in children after Hurricane Andrew. *Journal of Abnormal Psychology, 105,* 237–248.

Von Winterfeldt, D. (2006). Using risk and decision analysis to protect New Orleans against future hurricanes. In R. J. Daniels, D. F. Kettle, & H. Kunreuther (Eds.), *On risk and disaster: Lessons from Hurricane Katrina* (pp. 27–41). Philadelphia: University of Pennsylvania Press.

Weems, C. F., Pina, A. A., Costa, N. M., Watts, S. E., Taylor, L. K., & Cannon, M. F. (2007). Predisaster trait anxiety and negative affect predict posttraumatic stress in youth after Hurricane Katrina. *Journal of Consulting and Clinical Psychology, 75,* 154–159.

Wolmer, L., Laor, N., Dedeoglu, C., Siev, J., & Yazgan, Y. (2005). Teacher mediated intervention after disaster: A controlled three-year follow-up of children's functioning. *Journal of Child Psychology and Psychiatry, 46,* 1161–1168.

Yule, W. (2001). When disaster strikes—The need to be "wise before the event": Crisis intervention with children. *Advances in Mind–Body Medicine, 17,* 191–196.

EPILOGUE:
MEETING THE NEEDS
OF CHILDREN, FAMILIES, AND
COMMUNITIES FOLLOWING DISASTER

RYAN P. KILMER AND VIRGINIA GIL-RIVAS

As this volume prepares to go to press, nearly 3 years after we identified a framework and plan for the book, the mismanagement of the preparation for and response to Hurricane Katrina is still referenced in the media. Critically, however, we can already count some successes in the lessons learned following Katrina. Indeed, the 2008 hurricane season saw efforts at early communication and systematic, well-coordinated preparation and evacuation plans put into action in the days preceding Hurricanes Gustav and Ike (e.g., Scallan, 2008). With thoughts of Katrina's devastation fresh on their minds—and evidence of its damaging effects still visible in places—millions heeded the warnings and evacuated in advance of Gustav, which threatened the Gulf Coast and New Orleans (e.g., Schleifstein, 2008); an estimated 2 million evacuated southern Louisiana alone (Salmon & Hedgpeth, 2008). By many accounts, the readiness plans, in principle and execution, were an undeniable success at the federal, state, and local levels. They were viewed as, essentially, everything that should have been in place 3 years before.

Preparation of this chapter was supported by National Institute of Mental Health Award R03 MH078197-01 to Virginia Gil-Rivas and Ryan P. Kilmer.

In the days following Gustav, however, the shine came off some of those reports, as others highlighted negative or potentially negative repercussions. For one, media reports described failings in the evacuation plan and a process that resulted in differential treatment and substandard shelter conditions for some of Louisiana's poorest families ("Never Again," Again, 2008). Moreover, some analysts worried about the implications of Gustav for subsequent evacuations. That is, in this case, although some residents remained in their homes, the public, in large numbers, responded appropriately to warnings, taking necessary precautions and evacuating promptly. Yet Gustav deviated from its anticipated path, and although Baton Rouge faced high winds and some coastal parishes were flooded, the area was largely spared the damage that had been projected. The storm and flooding, although notable, did not approximate the level of severity predicted or feared. That result left many experts concerned that citizens may experience "hurricane fatigue" as a result of the emotional and financial strain associated with evacuation efforts. In turn, they feared, Gulf Coast residents may not be as responsive to future warnings or calls to evacuate (Gray, 2008).

Some of those fears were realized later in the season as Hurricane Ike approached the Texas coast. Estimates of a massive storm surge led to unequivocal warnings and mandatory evacuation orders (e.g., Canadian Broadcasting Company, 2008). Although many residents of coastal Texas and other communities along the Gulf Coast evacuated, an estimated 21% to 40% of the more than 57,000 residents of Galveston, Texas, did not (Associated Press, 2008; Casselman, 2008; "Hurricane Ike," 2008), putting themselves and, in turn, first responders at unnecessary risk.

Nevertheless, steps were taken to mobilize necessary personnel and resources as the storm approached and to coordinate efforts both before it made landfall and in its aftermath (e.g., Federal Emergency Management Agency [FEMA], 2008a). Indeed, what the 2008 hurricane season reinforced is that as a country, the United States has the capacity to prepare, communicate, and plan; the challenge lies in ensuring proper implementation of plans and well-targeted use of resources, as well as the appropriate response of the public.

Although such readiness planning is critical, the prime foci of this volume center on response, recovery, and the steps necessary to meet the needs of children, families, and communities following disaster. This emphasis was stimulated by the manifold failures following Katrina, which have been well documented (e.g., Gheytanchi et al., 2007; Grunwald, 2007); in fact, many families continue to struggle to meet basic needs, even 3 years later (Dewan, 2008; Fernandes, 2008).

Responses clearly need to be coordinated and collaborative, taking into account the larger ecologies in which children and families function. Doing so would be consistent with a prior Surgeon General's call to develop services that go beyond a "focus on the 'identified client' to embrace the community, cultural, and family context" (U.S. Department of Health and Human Services, 1999, p. 186). As Katrina demonstrated, disasters have the potential to disrupt every level of an individual's ecology, and if the objective is to enhance the well-being of those affected, responses need to be comprehensive in targeting these levels and influences.

Although the recommendations in the present volume vary in their scale, complexity, and reach, not every warranted action has to be major; sometimes relatively small steps can make a substantial difference. As one case in point, we reflect back on our meetings with children and families displaced by the hurricane. We met with many individuals and families, some eligible to participate in our research study, some not, in the trailer parks established by FEMA and elsewhere. Many such meetings occurred in the largest park, known as Renaissance Village, outside of Baker, Louisiana (the first families moved into the Village on October 7, 2005, and the last moved out on June 17, 2008; FEMA, 2008b). Some meetings took place in families' trailers, some in the large "community tent" near the center of the nearly 600-trailer compound.

Some reports have noted that the tent was provided by charitable organizations and that FEMA had not established a community meeting area because the intent was for the park to be temporary. Regardless, this open-walled tent was the site of community meetings, housed various faith-based events, and was intended as a place for residents to come together. In our many visits to the park, however, primarily during the summer of 2006, we were struck by the fact that, with few exceptions, only a handful of people were typically found in the tent. After spending even a few minutes in the sweltering heat and humidity of Louisiana's summer, it became clear why that was the case: The tent was inadequately cooled by a large, loud fan or two, and the individual trailers were largely air-conditioned. Consequently, many families spent a great deal of time isolated in their trailers and did not benefit from the potential social connectedness, support, and even sense of community they might have forged with other evacuees. The well-intentioned setup of the tent could have been vastly improved by some relatively minor modifications, including walls for the tent and a cooling system, that could have fostered relatedness and support, two critical elements in promoting well-being following disaster. The tent's physical structure reduced the likelihood of its purpose being realized.

As we look to the future and consider the steps necessary to address maximally the needs of children, families, and communities, a handful of key notions coalesce. First, because context matters in both research and practice, and because the contexts in which children and families function are complex, with many mutually influential elements (see Introduction and chap. 1, this volume), we need a more integrative, developmental framework for understanding disasters and their impact. We recommend an ecological perspective as an approach that reflects the realities and mutual influences (i.e., transactions) at play that may have a direct or indirect impact and affect both the pathways children follow in the face of adversity and their environments. For instance, in work to support and facilitate positive adjustment for children following disaster, it is necessary to emphasize the significance of children's environments and the well-being of important adults in their lives. In addition, context and culture can "shape the experience and consequences of disaster exposure" (Norris & Alegria, 2006, p. 323). These notions highlight the salience of also addressing caregivers' needs in efforts aimed at promoting children's adaptation and well-being and of developing contextually and culturally appropriate interventions that are informed by developmental principles and knowledge of and sensitivity to families' beliefs, customs, norms, and history. Our research and applied work need to consider the larger social, cultural, and economic contextual factors that influence children's and families' functioning, both before and after disaster, as well as the core importance of the caregiver–child system and its impact on children's adjustment in the aftermath of disaster.

In that vein, we need to continue to develop and, of crucial importance, evaluate culturally sensitive interventions with direct, proximal effects—that is, those that involve an emphasis on the child, caregiver, caregiver–child dyad, or family system, or a combination thereof (see chaps. 2, 3, and 4, this volume). Such work may include a range of school- or community-based psychosocial or therapeutic interventions (see chaps. 1, 10, and 12, this volume), as well as efforts such as Psychological First Aid (see chaps. 8 and 12, this volume). The schools can be a prime setting for such work (see chaps. 1, 5, and 7, this volume; see also Dean et al., 2008; Gurwitch et al., 2004), and evidence-based approaches have been documented for postdisaster and nonspecific trauma work in the schools, including those noted in chapter 12 and others, such as Cognitive Behavioral Intervention for Trauma in Schools (Dean et al., 2008; Jaycox, 2003; Jaycox, Morse, Tanielian, & Stein, 2006).

Although we advocate firmly for more attention to the caregiver–child dyad (see Introduction, this volume) in disaster research and intervention, it is clear that broader, systems-level change is also necessary. Several authors have advocated for population-based or macrosystems-level interventions and/or public health perspectives in disaster preparation and response (Gurwitch et al., 2004; McGuinness et al., 2008); these recommendations are well founded. Consistent with public health models, we indeed need to ensure coordinated, timely assessment, intervention, and treatment for those at greatest risk, but we also must integrate preventive models to help strengthen those affected and/or modify their environments to reduce vulnerability.

Overall, we need coordinated, collaborative delivery of services and supports to meet the diverse needs of children, families, and communities following a disaster. In fact, when considering system function, it appears that disaster planning and response would benefit from processes and policies adhering to the values and principles that guide the national Systems of Care (SOC) initiatives for children with severe emotional disturbance and their families (Cook & Kilmer, 2004; Hernandez, 2003; Pumariega & Winters, 2003; Stroul & Friedman, 1986).

Although components and configurations of such a system may vary across communities, Stroul and Friedman (1986) underscored that SOCs reflect "a comprehensive spectrum of mental health and other necessary services . . . organized into a coordinated network to meet the multiple and changing needs of children and adolescents . . . and their families" (p. 3). In their view, these systems should be (a) *child centered* and *family focused*, with the needs of the child and the family dictating the nature of the services provided and families as full partners in efforts to plan and implement services; (b) *community based*, such that the locus of services, management, and decision-making responsibility rests at the community level, and networks of services are provided within, or close to, children's communities; and (c) *culturally competent* (see Introduction and chap. 1, this volume). Other key principles in the SOC philosophy include the need for integrated and coordinated services, with professionals across agencies collaborating with one another and nonprofessionals (e.g., family members) to ensure the effective, efficient provision of services (Cook & Kilmer, 2004; Stroul & Friedman, 1986).

The SOC model is most often put into practice via the wraparound approach (e.g., VanDenBerg & Grealish, 1996), characterized by services customized to meet the needs of children and families; active partnerships between professionals and nonprofessionals, including families; and the use of both formal and informal community supports. The wraparound approach involves the mobilization of community resources, including services and supports from multiple agencies and disciplines, working with informal supports to meet family needs, provide flexible services, build on strengths, and empower families (Burns & Goldman, 1999; Cook & Kilmer, 2004; Stroul & Friedman, 1986). These qualities are well suited to postdisaster needs.

Although these qualities may seem to reflect common sense and sound practice, the challenge in disaster work is to lay the appropriate groundwork for the coordination, communication, and collaboration in a system of care before a disaster occurs by modifying the way agencies, government and otherwise, function in a day-to-day manner, such as when they establish disaster preparedness plans. This foundation would need to be well established for the system to function optimally when disaster strikes. All community stakeholders, both professionals and nonprofessionals, would need to play a substantive role in the system's development and implementation; doing so would facilitate "buy in" by participating partners and likely serve to sustain the effort.

The actual implementation of a SOC-like approach would constitute perhaps the most significant challenge—indeed, a substantial literature suggests that implementation issues abound in SOC work (e.g., Cook & Kilmer, 2004; Epstein et al., 2003; Walker & Schutte, 2005). Issues of resource allocation and sharing, responsibility, and jurisdiction would also need to be resolved so that all participants are "on the same page."

Nevertheless, such an approach would translate well to postdisaster contexts. At all levels, government response needs to be well organized and coordinated (and properly funded), but it is also crucial to permit enough flexibility to allow for nongovernmental, informal response, whether via faith-based or other community organizations (see chap. 9, this volume). Services need to be tailored to contexts, settings, and cultures; thus, it is necessary to include local stakeholders in decision making, needs assessment, and response (see Center for Mental Health Services [CMHS], 2007). It is requisite to join with those on the ground in the community being targeted for services; they will bring a deeper understanding of their community and its resources, culture, and context (see chap. 1, this volume; see also, e.g., CMHS, 2007; Dass-Brailsford, 2008). Local stakeholders can also likely assist in the process of ensuring that more resources and services are dedicated appropriately to those who need them most and are most vulnerable, such as families living in poverty (Osofsky, Osofsky, & Harris, 2007). Such efforts toward successful preparation, recovery, and adaptation depend not only on traditional mental health and social services, but also on the identification and use of community resources and strengths. The community at-large and its resources can play an integral role in strategies for promoting healthy adaptation in children and families following disasters (see chaps. 6–12, this volume).

To that end, the field needs to expand its foci to include outcomes that go beyond negative consequences (e.g., posttraumatic stress symptoms) to include outcomes such as resilience or posttraumatic growth (see Introduction). As described by the New Freedom Commission on Mental Health (2003), postdisaster efforts should seek to "focus on increasing consumers' ability to successfully cope with life's challenges, on facilitating recovery and on building resilience, not just on managing symptoms," so that they "are able to live, work, learn and participate fully in their communities" (p. 5). In that vein, providers of services and supports could profitably focus on strengths and methods that empower those with whom they work (CMHS, 2007).

The impact of Katrina was devastating, and many other disasters have had tragic consequences for children, their families, and their communities. In disaster's aftermath, however, we can strive not to limit our responses to those that seek to forestall negative effects or, for that matter, rebuild what has been damaged. Rather, we can seek to go beyond the status quo, to improve and promote. We can work to promote wellness in our children (Cowen, 1994, 2000), resilience in our communities (see chap. 12, this volume), and health and well-being in our families. Paths and processes have been described (e.g., Cowen, 1994, 2000; Norris, Stevens, Pfefferbaum, Wyche, & Pfefferbaum, 2008; Pfefferbaum et al., 2008); therefore, we must not fall back on simply "reconstructing the risk," leaving families and communities "just as exposed to future hazards" by rebuilding communities and their infrastructure as they were before the disaster struck (Cherpitel, 2001, para. 5). Rather, we need to improve overall quality of life (Cutter, 2006).

As Cherpitel (2001) cogently wrote, "There is more to recovery than concrete. Local livelihoods, economies and institutions have to be strengthened and rebuilt. . . . Investment in the social capital of disaster-affected communities is key to building sustainable recovery" (para. 4). As Katrina brought to light, with the disproportionate struggle of the impoverished and historically disenfranchised, natural disasters sometimes serve "to expose the effects of deeper, structural causes—from global warming and unplanned urbanization to trade liberalization and political marginalization. The effects of man's action are often evident—many natural catastrophes are un/natural in their origins" (Cherpitel, 2001, para. 6). We cannot control nature and its forces; we can, however, take initiative and seek to reduce the unnatural (i.e., attributable to humanity) components of disasters.

We can aim to enhance competencies and coping skills in those who have faced adversity, and we can seek their input and give them a voice as a first step toward empowerment; each of these end goals has been identified as a potential path to wellness (Cowen, 1994). Some may view the use of a wellness framework as an unattainable goal in the context of disaster response. However, even if, as is likely the case and as Cowen (2000) acknowledged, a comprehensive wellness enhancement emphasis may "never fully be realized . . . it offers a fruitful, forward-looking framework for guiding conceptual formulations, program development, and research" (p. 497) and can serve as a laudable goal for mobilizing the resources and expertise of psychologists and those in related fields, as well as community stakeholders, in disaster's aftermath. Such work may prove to be more cost-effective, efficacious, and humane in the long term (Cowen, 1994), particularly as we work to address the needs of those most at risk.

REFERENCES

Associated Press. (2008, September 24). *Residents stream into Ike-battered Galveston: 45,000 islanders fled storm's wrath; hotels, shelters open up to residents.* Retrieved January 3, 2009, from http://www.msnbc.msn.com/id/26867313/

Burns, B. J., & Goldman, S. K. (1999). *Systems of care: Promising practices in children's mental health 1998 series: Vol. 4. Promising practices in wraparound for children with serious emotional disturbance and their families.* Washington, DC: Center for Effective Collaboration and Practice, American Institutes for Research.

Canadian Broadcasting Company. (2008, September 11). *"Certain death" for Texans caught in Ike's path, forecaster says.* Retrieved December 23, 2008, from http://www.cbc.ca/world/story/2008/09/11/ike-thurs.html?ref=rss

Casselman, B. (2008, September 12). As waters rise, many decline to leave Galveston Island. *Wall Street Journal.* Retrieved December 23, 2008, from http://online.wsj.com/article/SB122125933796630189.html?mod=googlenews_wsj

Center for Mental Health Services. (2007). *Building bridges: Mental health consumers and representatives of the disaster response community in dialogue* (Publication No. 4250). Rockville, MD: Center for Mental Health Services, Substance Abuse and Mental Health Services Administration. Retrieved December 6, 2008, from http://download.ncadi.samhsa.gov/ken/pdf/SMA07-4250/SMA07-4250.pdf

Cherpitel, D. J. (2001). Introduction: Planning recovery to minimize future risk. In *World disasters report: Focus on recovery.* Geneva, Switzerland: International Federation of Red Cross and Red Crescent Societies. Retrieved December 31, 2008, from http://www.ifrc.org/publicat/wdr2001/intro.asp

Cook, J. R., & Kilmer, R. P. (2004). Evaluating systems of care: Missing links in children's mental health research. *Journal of Community Psychology, 32,* 655–674.

Cowen, E. L. (1994). The enhancement of psychological wellness: Challenges and opportunities. *American Journal of Community Psychology, 22,* 149–179.

Cowen, E. L. (2000). Psychological wellness: Some hopes for the future. In D. Cicchetti, J. Rappaport, I. Sandler, & R. P. Weissberg (Eds.), *The promotion of wellness in children and adolescents* (pp. 477–503). Thousand Oaks, CA: Sage.

Cutter, S. (2006, June 11). The geography of social vulnerability: Race, class, and catastrophe. *Perspectives from the social sciences.* Retrieved December 31, 2008, from http://understandingkatrina.ssrc.org/Cutter/

Dass-Brailsford, P. (2008). After the storm: Recognition, recovery, and reconstruction. *Professional Psychology: Research and Practice, 39,* 24–30.

Dean, K. L., Langley, A. K., Kataoka, S. H., Jaycox, L. H., Wong, M., & Stein, B. D. (2008). School-based disaster mental health services: Clinical, policy, and community challenges. *Professional Psychology: Research and Practice, 39,* 52–57.

Dewan, S. (2008, December 4). Many children lack stability long after storm. *New York Times.* Retrieved January 3, 2009, from http://www.nytimes.com/2008/12/05/us/05trailer.html?_r=3&em

Epstein, M. H., Nordness, P. D., Kutash, K., Duchnowski, A., Schrepf, S., Benner, G., & Nelson, J. R. (2003). Assessing the wraparound process during family planning meetings. *Journal of Behavioral Health Services & Research, 30,* 352–362.

Federal Emergency Management Agency. (2008a). *Hurricane Ike 3 months later: From disaster to recovery.* Retrieved January 2, 2009, from http://www.fema.gov/news/newsrelease.fema?id=47108

Federal Emergency Management Agency. (2008b). *Progress through partnership: Rebuilding communities, reuniting families: Hurricane Katrina facts by sector (Aug. 29, 2005; Aug. 29, 2008).* Retrieved December 27, 2008, from http://www.fema.gov/pdf/hazard/hurricane/2005katrina/facts_sector.pdf

Fernandes, D. (2008, August 28). Three years after Hurricane Katrina, homelessness looms. *Mother Jones.* Retrieved April 13, 2009, from http://www.commondreams.org/view/2008/08/29-1

Gheytanchi, A., Joseph, L., Gierlach, E., Kimpara, S., Housley, J., Franco, Z., et al. (2007). The dirty dozen: Twelve failures of the hurricane Katrina response and how psychology can help. *American Psychologist, 62,* 118–136.

Gray, S. (September, 2008). Hurricane fatigue in New Orleans? *Time.* Retrieved January 3, 2009, from http://www.time.com/time/nation/article/0,8599,1840053,00.html?xid=feed-cnn-topics

Grunwald, M. (2007). Katrina anniversary: The threatening storm. *Time.* Retrieved November 23, 2007, from http://www.time.com/time/specials/2007/article/0,28804,1646611_1646683_1648904-1,00.html

Gurwitch, R. H., Kees, M., Becker, S. M., Schreiber, M., Pfefferbaum, B., & Diamond, D. (2004). When disaster strikes: Responding to the needs of children. *Prehospital and Disaster Medicine, 19,* 21–28.

Hernandez, M. (Ed.). (2003). Special Series: Children's mental health policy. *Journal of Emotional and Behavioral Disorders, 11,* 1–58.

Hurricane Ike: Galveston says 25% ignored evacuation order. (2008, September 12). *USA Today.* Retrieved January 3, 2009, from http://blogs.usatoday.com/ondeadline/2008/09/hurricane-ike-g.html

Jaycox, L. H. (2003). *Cognitive Behavioral Intervention for Trauma in Schools (CBITS).* Longmont, CO: Sopris West Educational Services.

Jaycox, L. H., Morse, L. K., Tanielian, T., & Stein, B. D. (2006). *How schools can help students recover from traumatic experiences: A tool kit for supporting long-term recovery* (Tech. Rep. 413). Santa Monica, CA: RAND Corporation. Retrieved April 3, 2007, from http://www.rand.org/pubs/technical_reports/2006/RAND_TR413.pdf

McGuinness, K. M., Coady, J. A., Perez, J. T., Williams, N. C., McIntyre, D. J., & Schreiber, M. D. (2008). Public mental health: The role of population-based and macrosystems interventions in the wake of Hurricane Katrina. *Professional Psychology: Research and Practice, 39,* 58–65.

"Never again," again. (2008, September 20). *New York Times.* Retrieved January 2, 2009, from http://www.nytimes.com/2008/09/21/opinion/21sun2.html

New Freedom Commission on Mental Health. (2003). *Achieving the promise: Transforming mental health care in America. Final Report* (DHHS Publication No. SMA-03-3832). Rockville, MD: U.S. Department of Health and Human Services.

Norris, F. H., & Alegria, M. (2006). Promoting disaster recovery in ethnic-minority individuals and communities. In E. C. Ritchie, P. J. Watson, & M. J. Friedman

(Eds.), *Interventions following mass violence and disasters: Strategies for mental health practice* (pp. 319–342). New York: Guilford Press.

Norris, F. H., Stevens, S. P., Pfefferbaum, B., Wyche, K. F., & Pfefferbaum, R. L. (2008). Community resilience as a metaphor, theory, set of capacities, and strategy for disaster readiness. *American Journal of Community Psychology, 41,* 127–150.

Osofsky, J. D., Osofsky, H. J., & Harris, W. W. (2007). Katrina's children: Social policy considerations for children in disasters. *Society for Research in Child Development Social Policy Report, 21,* 1–18.

Pfefferbaum, R. L., Reissman, D. B., Pfefferbaum, B., Wyche, K. F., Norris, F. H., & Klomp, R. W. (2008). Factors in the development of community resilience to disasters. In M. Blumenfield & R. J. Ursano (Eds.), *Intervention and resilience after mass trauma* (pp. 49–68). Cambridge, England: Cambridge University Press.

Pumariega, A. J., & Winters, N. C. (Eds.). (2003). *The handbook of child and adolescent systems of care: The new community psychiatry.* San Francisco: Jossey-Bass.

Salmon, J. L., & Hedgpeth, D. (2008, September 4). Gustav evacuees returning to food, power shortages. *Seattle Times.* Retrieved January 2, 2009, from http://seattletimes.nwsource.com/html/nationworld/2008157603_gustav04.html

Scallan, M. M. (2008, September 7). Leaders assess reaction to Gustav. *Sun Herald* [Biloxi, MS]. Retrieved January 3, 2009, from http://www.sunherald.com/220/story/797036.html

Schleifstein, M. (2008, August 28). Louisiana gears up for Gustav as it makes landfall in Haiti. *New Orleans Times-Picayune.* Retrieved December 23, 2008, from http://www.nola.com/news/index.ssf/2008/08/louisiana_gears_up_for_gustav.html

Stroul, B. A., & Friedman, R. M. (1986). *A system of care for children and youth with severe emotional disturbances* (Rev. ed.). Washington, DC: Georgetown University Child Development Center, CASSP Technical Assistance Center.

U.S. Department of Health and Human Services. (1999). *Mental health: A report of the Surgeon General—Executive summary.* Rockville, MD: U.S. Department of Health and Human Services, Substance Abuse and Mental Health Services Administration, Center for Mental Health Services, National Institutes of Health, National Institute of Mental Health.

VanDenBerg, J. E., & Grealish, E. M. (1996). Individualized services and supports through the wraparound process: Philosophy and procedures. *Journal of Child and Family Studies, 5,* 7–21.

Walker, J. S., & Schutte, K. M. (2005). Quality and individualization in wraparound planning. *Journal of Child and Family Studies, 14,* 251–267.

INDEX

and postrecovery environment, 293–294

and preexisting characteristics, 291–293

and psychological resources, 294

Child Routines Questionnaire (CRQ), 80, 84–87

Child-safe areas, 34

Child service needs, 149, 151

Child wellness, 266–268, 273–274

Christian Reformed World Relief Committee, 221

Chronic medical conditions, 146, 153, 156

Churches, 176. *See also* Faith-based organizations

Church life, 229

Church of the Brethren, 221, 228

CISD. *See* Critical incident stress debriefing

Cleaning supplies, 225

Coast Guard, 248

Cognitive Behavioral Intervention for Trauma in Schools, 255

Cognitive–behavioral therapy (CBT), 255, 299, 301, 306

Cohen, D. J., 245

Cohen, E., 185

Collaboration, 155, 259, 283–284

Collective efficacy, 36

Comfort, 155

Commitment, to community, 270

Communal healing, 277–278

Communication. *See also* Media
in communities, 272–273
in families, 99
during planning phase, 206, 207
risk, 283
school, with parents and community, 175–176, 178
during short-term adaptation phase, 199

Community
commitment to, 270
loss of, 31, 304
member investment in, 277
participation in, 270
school communication with, 175–176
sense of, 31, 206, 249, 304

shared sense of loss in, 31
solidarity and cohesion within, 277
supportive, 271–272

Community adaptation, 274

Community assets, 27

Community-based health systems, 317

Community-based interventions, 300

Community-based mental health resources, 41

Community-based services, collaborative, 259

Community-based solutions, 33

Community Emergency Response Teams (CERTs), 278

Community meeting areas, 315

Community partnerships, 155, 206

Community resilience, 269–284
awareness of, 284
communication factor of, 272–273
connectedness, commitment, and shared values as factors in, 269–270
critical reflection and skill building as factors in, 272
defined, 269
disaster planning and management supported by, 282–284
as disaster preparedness strategy, 275–284
disaster prevention, mitigation, preparedness, and response as factors in, 273
and engagement/participation of community, 277–278
growing interest in, 265
and organizational links and networks, 278–279
participation factor of, 270
and recognizing/reducing inequities before disaster, 276–277
resource factor of, 271, 276–277
and social support, 279–281
structure, roles, and responsibilities as factors in, 270–271
support and nurturance as factors in, 271–272
and wellness, 273–274, 281–282

Community resources
disparities in, 276–277
listings of, 155

Displaced families
  frequent moves of, 145–146
  interviews with, 147–151
  social networks of, 202
Displaced students
  number of, 118, 167–168
  transitory nature of, 177
  welcoming, 129
Distortions, correcting, 36
Distrust, of agencies, 205
Diversity, embracing, 270
Domestic violence programs, 230
Donations, 225
"Do no harm," 113
Drug counseling, 150
Dynes, R., 234

Earthquakes, 227, 292, 299
East Baton Rouge Parish (EBRP)
    schools, 168, 172–179
Ecological systems theory, 6–13
  contextual factors in, 8
  correlated constraints in, 8
  cultural competence in, 9–10
  illustration of, 10
  intraindividual factors of adjustment
      in, 7
  predisaster factors in, 11–13
  statement of, 79, 120, 244
Education. *See also* Schools
  community, 259–260
  on disaster reactions, 281
  of general public, 207
  parenting, 150
  of parishioners, 216
  of survivors, 198
Education level, 26, 160, 205
Elderly persons, 224, 230
E-mail, 175
Emergency management, 232–233
Emergency preparedness, 28–30
Emergency support functions (ESFs), 221
Emergent curriculum, 122
Emotional availability, 67, 245, 259
Emotional needs, 227–229
Emotional support, 157–158
Employee assistance programs, 281
Employment
  assistance in finding, 150, 153, 156,
      199, 208

cultural barriers in finding, 154
finding new, 203
in Mississippi and Louisiana, 26
Empowerment, 267, 318
Enabling environment, 39
Engagement, 198
Environment
  enabling, 39
  favorable, 267–268
  physical, 122
  postrecovery, 293–294
  social, 268
Episcopal Church, 228
Episcopalians, 224
ESFs (emergency support functions),
    221
Evacuation, of children with caregivers,
    257–258
Exposure-based CBT, 299
Expression, of traumatic experiences,
    42
Expressive functioning, 99
Extending organizations, 234
Externalizing problems, 86–91

Fairness, 162
Faith-based organizations (FBOs),
    215–235
  arrival of national, 217–218
  and comprehensive emergency man-
      agement cycle, 220–221
  criticism of, 231
  data sources regarding, 220
  defined, 216
  flexibility of, 218–219
  funding provided by, 229–231
  future research on, 233–234
  future role of, 235
  historical significance of, in New
      Orleans, 215–216
  lessons learned from, 231–235
  literature review of, 218–220
  post-Katrina response of, 221–225
  psychological and emotional needs
      addressed by, 227–229
  recommendations for, 231–232
  recovery efforts of, 225–227
  recovery functions of, 216
  response functions of, 216
  structures of, 219

Medical services
    immediate need for, 224
    during impact phase, 196–197
    service-delivery need for, 150, 151,
        153, 156
    during short-term adaptation phase,
        199
Meeting areas, 315
Mennonite Central Committee, 230
Mennonite Disaster Service, 226–227,
    230
Mennonites, 228
Mental health and psychosocial support
    (term), 31
Mental health professionals
    disaster-relief training of, 207
    school, 182–183, 200
    and teacher well-being, 135
Mental health services
    during impact phase, 196–198
    service-delivery need for, 150, 151,
        154, 156–159
    during short-term adaptation phase,
        200–202
    specialized, 32
Metairie Park Country Day, 119
Microloans, 230
Minorities. See also African Americans;
    Hispanics
    disaster research with, 8–9
    and poverty, 8, 9
    social support for, 206
Missing family members, 196, 223
Mississippi
    childhood poverty in, 26
    hurricane-related adversity in, 168
    perceptions of government response
        in, 30
    well-being (ranking) in, 26
Mixed model (of family functioning),
    98, 102, 106–107
Mobile dental units, 224
Mobile medical units, 153, 159
Model teaching strategies, 126
Mood disorders, 245
Morris, P. A., 267
Muslims, 224

Nagin, Ray, 242
Narrative Story Stem Technique
    (NSST), 130

National Center for Posttraumatic
    Stress Disorder (NCPTSD),
    290, 297
National Child Traumatic Stress
    Network (NCTSN), 182, 249,
    290, 297
National Day of Prayer, 229
National Guard, 196, 225
National Organizations on Disability,
    232
National Response Framework, 221,
    222, 233
National Response Plan, 283, 284
National Science Foundation, 123
National Voluntary Organizations
    Active in Disaster (NVOAD),
    221, 227, 232–233
Natural disasters
    cultural beliefs about, 206
    helping children understand, 121
    information about reactions to, 207
    number of people affected by, 289
    PTSD rates after, 56
    scale, scope, and magnitude of, 217
Nazarene Disaster Response, 226
Nazarenes, 226
NCPTSD. See National Center for Post-
    traumatic Stress Disorder
NCTSN. See National Child Traumatic
    Stress Network
Neighborhood associations, 206–207
Neighborhood development, 227
Neighborhood life, 234
New Freedom Commission on Mental
    Health, 171, 318
"New normal," 9–10
New Orleans, Louisiana
    childhood poverty in, 266
    cultural competence for, 247
    inadequate resources in, 271
    job types in, 154
    perceptions of racial discrimination
        in, 29
    politics of, 230–231
    public transportation system in, 153
    as research site, 234
New Orleans Fire Department, 248
New Orleans Franklin Avenue Baptist
    Church, 229
New Orleans Health Department, 248

New Orleans Police Department
(NOPD), 248
New Orleans Public Schools (NOPS),
26, 175, 252
New York City schools, 119–121
No-change model (of family function-
ing), 98
No Child Left Behind Act of 2001, 120
Nongovernmental responses, 318
NOPD (New Orleans Police Depart-
ment), 248
NOPS. *See* New Orleans Public Schools
Normalcy, sense of, 248
Norris, F. H., 181, 274, 276, 283
Northridge earthquake, 292
NSST (Narrative Story Stem Tech-
nique), 130
Nurturing communities, 271–272
NVOAD. *See* National Voluntary Orga-
nizations Active in Disaster

Office of Mental Health (OMH), 242
Okeechobee Hurricane, 204
Oklahoma City bombing, 293
Oklahoma tornadoes (1999), 221
OMH (Office of Mental Health), 242
Operation Blessing, 224–225
Operation Brother's Keeper, 216, 230
Organizational links and networks,
278–279
Organizational patterns, family, 99
Organizational structures, 270–271
Orleans Parish, Louisiana, 118, 145, 202
Orleans Parish School Board, 230–231,
252
Orleans Parish Schools, 118, 253
Osofsky, Howard J., 242, 248, 250
Osofsky, Joy D., 242, 248, 250
Overstreet, S., 29, 79

Page, Timothy, 130
Parental monitoring, 78
Parental psychiatric disorders, 43
Parent–child interventions, 71
Parent gatherings, 180–181
Parenting behavior
after disasters, 12–13
and externalizing behavior, 90–91
positive, 82–83
PTSS effects on, 71

Parenting behavior study, 77–92
discussion of, 88–91
lessons learned from, 92
measures of, 80–81
method of, 79–82
and parent-reported externalizing
problems, 86–88
participants in, 79
procedure used in, 81–82
regression analyses, 83, 85–88
results of, 82–88
strength and limitations of, 91–92
Parenting education, 150
Parent liaison, 175
Parents
emotional availability of, 245
Katrina's impacts on, 38
mental health of, 78
psychosocial training for, 44–45
school communication with,
175–176
Parent University, 44–45, 175
Parr, A., 233
Participation, in community activities,
270
Partnerships
community, 155, 206
interfaith, 227–229
Peer relationships, 35
Perceived threat, 58, 70
PFA. *See* Psychological First Aid
Pfefferbaum, B., 274
Pfefferbaum, R. L., 274, 276, 281
Phillips, Brenda, 222
Physical development, 34–35
Physical environment, curriculum
incorporating, 122
Physical health, 103, 109
Physical security, 34
Picard, Cecil, 250
Planning phase (of hurricane)
child and family considerations in,
194–195
lessons learned from, 206–207
Plaquemines Parish, 247
Playgrounds, 34, 230
Political action, 277
Politics, New Orleans, 230–231
Poor communities, 204, 275, 276
Population-based interventions, 316

Psychological First Aid (PFA), *continued*
   ethical issues with, 304
   LSUHSC provision of, 242
   preparing mental health providers
      with, 257
   as resilience-building strategy, 284
   in school settings, 180, 255
   during short-term adaptation phase,
      200
   survivor engagement and education
      as elements of, 198
Psychological resources of children, 294
Psychological wellness, 266–268
Psychosocial assistance in emergency
     settings
   evolution of, 30–32
   by FBOs, 227–229
   growing interest in, 28
   principles for, 32–37
PTSD. *See* Posttraumatic stress disorder
PTSS. *See* Posttraumatic stress symptoms
PTSS study, 59–72
   associations among key variables in,
      67–68
   design of, 59–60
   discussion of, 69–71
   hypotheses of, 59
   lessons learned from, 71–72
   measures of, 60–63
   method of, 59–63
   plan of analysis for, 63
   regression model in, 69
   results of, 63–69
Public health models, 316
Public responsibility, sense of, 36
Public service messages, 206
Public transportation system, 153

Quarantelli, E. L., 234

Racial discrimination
   perceptions of, 29, 78, 206
   against relocated individuals, 160, 161
   and rescue response times, 205
   in schools, 151
Racial issues, 9
Racism, experience of, 205
RAND Corporation, 182
RAND Gulf Policy Institute, 181
Reading level, 26
Ready America campaign, 297

Realistic control, 11
Recoil phase (of hurricane), 290
Recovery and reconstruction phase (of
     hurricane)
   aid agencies' role in advocating
      during, 39
   defined, 290
   FBOs' efforts during, 225–227, 232
Recovery counseling services, 228–229
Recovery functions, 216
Recovery School District, 118, 231, 252
Red River flood (1997), 119, 120
Reexperiencing, 67
Religion, 235
Relocation, of families, 37–38
Renaissance Village (Baker, Louisiana),
     315
Renters, 151
Representational system, 11–12
Researchers, as volunteers, 112
Research participation, 305
Resilience and resiliency
   of children, 267
   of community. *See* Community
     resilience
   defined, 97, 268–269
   of families. *See* Family resilience and
     resiliency study
   of FBOs, 231–232
   focus on, 318
   individual and community, 268–275
   and sense of normalcy/routines, 248
   supporting, 158
   and wellness, 273–274
Resilience-Building Screen, 296, 304
Resilience-Building Training, 296, 304
Response functions, 216
Reunification services, 223
Risk communication, 283
Risk exposure, 58
Risk factors, 30
Roberts, M. C., 5
Roller coaster model (of family func-
     tioning), 98, 102, 105–106, 109
Routines, establishing, 36, 161, 184,
     248, 258
Ryan, R. M., 185

Safety, 34, 155, 196
St. Bernard Parish, Louisiana, 118, 247,
     248, 250–253, 258

St. Bernard Unified School District, 250–252
St. John Parish, Louisiana, 253
St. Tammany Parish, Louisiana, 99–100, 103
St. Thomas Louisiana State University Health Clinic, 224
St. Vincent de Paul, 227
Salmon, K., 71
Salvage operations, 226
Salvation Army, 196, 225, 227
SAMHSA. *See* Substance Abuse and Mental Health Services Administration
Sanders, Torin, 252
Santayana, George, 289
Saul, J., 277, 278
Save the Children, 175–177
Save the Children Alliance, 31, 33, 42
Schoch-Spana, M., 278
School administrators
    accessibility of, 175
    Katrina's impacts on, 38–39
    psychosocial support for, 44
    role of, 180
    training of, 185
School attendance, 146
School-based interventions, 159, 171–172, 200–201
School-based programs, 42–44, 176–177, 181–182
Schoolchildren
    impact of disaster on, 169–170
    number of displaced, 118, 167–168
    school responses for young, 120–121
    screening of, 119
    transitory nature of displaced, 177
    trauma services for, 250–253
    welcoming displaced, 129
School enrollment
    assistance with, 150
    in East Baton Rouge, 172–173
School mental health professionals, 182–183, 200
School principals, 180–182, 185
School Reactivation Program, 299
Schools, 117–122. *See also* Mayfair Elementary School
    child-safe areas within, 34
    as community centers, 251

context-appropriate practices in, 121–122
disaster preparedness of, 278–279
importance of, in children's lives, 170–171
interventions within, 316
Katrina's impacts on, 38–39
lessons learned about, 39–42
number of hurricane-affected, 117–118
postdisaster issues/challenges with, 171–172
as resilience factor, 269, 270
response of local, 118–122
as safe havens, 252–253
in short-term adaptation phase, 200
trauma services in, 250–253
Schools study, 122–133
    children's hurricane-knowledge interviews in, 130–133
    goal of, 123
    lessons learned from, 133–136
    qualitative survey results from, 127–130
    teacher survey in, 123–127
Screening, of schoolchildren, 119
SCUD missile attack (Israel), 245
Second Harvest, 221, 227
Second Step program, 176–177
Security
    and child development, 33–34
    sense of, 196
Seeger, Pete, 289
Self-care, 260
Self-efficacy, 36, 244, 258
Self-esteem, 36
Senate Committee on Homeland Security and Governmental Affairs, 282
September 11, 2001 terrorist attacks, 119–121, 218, 245, 277, 293
Service delivery, 143–147
    after disasters, 143–145
    collaborative, 316–317
    and environmental context of needs, 146–147
    identifying needs for, 145–146
Service delivery studies, 147–163
    discussion of, 156–157
    of displaced families, 147–151

ABOUT THE EDITORS

Ryan P. Kilmer, PhD, is associate professor of psychology and Bonnie E. Cone Early-Career Professor in Teaching at the University of North Carolina at Charlotte. A child clinical–community psychologist, his research interests center on children and families, particularly risk and resilience; youngsters' adjustment to trauma; and the use of evaluation research to guide system change, program refinement, and service delivery.

Virginia Gil-Rivas, PhD, is associate professor of psychology at the University of North Carolina at Charlotte. A developmental health psychologist, her research interests include the interactive effects of social, cognitive, and emotional factors on adaptation in the aftermath of major life events across the life span and the design, implementation, and evaluation of developmentally and culturally appropriate prevention and treatment efforts.

Richard G. Tedeschi, PhD, is professor of psychology at the University of North Carolina at Charlotte. A licensed psychologist specializing in bereavement and trauma, he has consulted for the American Psychological Association regarding trauma and resilience and recently published the *Handbook of Posttraumatic Growth: Research and Practice* with Lawrence Calhoun. Drs. Tedeschi and

Calhoun have also coauthored *Trauma and Transformation: Growing in the Aftermath of Suffering, Posttraumatic Growth: Positive Changes in the Aftermath of Crisis, Facilitating Posttraumatic Growth: A Clinician's Guide,* and *Helping Bereaved Parents: A Clinician's Guide.*

Lawrence G. Calhoun, PhD, is professor of psychology at the University of North Carolina at Charlotte and a licensed psychologist. His scholarly activities focus on the responses of persons encountering major life crises, particularly posttraumatic growth, and he is the coauthor or coeditor of several books, including *Posttraumatic Growth: Positive Changes in the Aftermath of Crisis, Facilitating Posttraumatic Growth: A Clinician's Guide, Helping Bereaved Parents: A Clinician's Guide,* and the *Handbook of Posttraumatic Growth: Research and Practice.*